International Business

International Business

Edited by Brian Dawes

Stanley Thornes (Publishers) Ltd

The rights of Brian Dawes, David Laughton, Dimitri Ivanov, Nick Foster, Jean Barclay and Wei-Ping Wu to be identified as authors of this work have been asserted by them in accordance with the Copyrights, Designs and Patents Act 1988.

First published in 1995 by:
Stanley Thornes Publishers Ltd
Ellenborough House
Wellington Street
Cheltenham
Glos. GL50 1YW
UK

96 97 98 99 00 / 10 9 8 7 6 5 4 3 2

A catalogue record for this book is available from The British Library.

ISBN 0 7487 1860 5

Typeset by Northern Phototypesetting Co Ltd, Bolton
Printed and bound in Great Britain by
T.J. Press (Padstow) Ltd, Padstow, Cornwall

Contents

Part 2

How to use this book

International Business aims to provide students with an introduction to the theory and practice of international business. While it sets out and analyses the key theory, a major emphasis is placed on how such theory can help individual businesses operate in practice, in contrast to the more macroeconomic bias of some texts. In Part 1 there is a wealth of illustrative case study material to place each theme in context, and this practical emphasis is amplified in the regional case studies in Part 2. Case study exercises at the end of the chapters encourage students to tackle international business issues through the experience of individual firms.

The book is also designed to fit the shift towards modularised courses taught within semesters. While it is organised in a logical structure and can be read as a single text, individual contributors have been encouraged to produce self-sufficient chapters to which a student can be directed for a particular topic or assignment. Each chapter in Parts 1 and 2 includes objectives, a summary, exercises and further reading.

Chapters can also be read in tandem. The book is divided into two parts, the first dealing with techniques for internationalising operations, the second with the markets in which those techniques may be applied. An introductory chapter outlines some key issues in the international economy, as a context for Parts 1 and 2. In Part 1, Chapter 5 provides an overview of the techniques discussed in the previous chapters, as they relate particularly to smaller businesses, and may be read alongside any of those earlier chapters.

Any of the chapters in Part 1 may also be read alongside the individual market case studies in Part 2, to illustrate and amplify how the techniques discussed might be applied in practice. For example, the analysis of market opportunities in Chapter 2 may be compared with the special features of analysing emerging markets in Chapters 7 or 8; and issues of marketing strategy in Chapter 3 may be applied to the special circumstances of the Japanese market discussed in Chapter 10.

Some of these connections are illustrated in the chart on the following page. It is hoped that students will find it easier to reinforce and apply their knowledge of international business in this way.

Wherever possible, we have emphasised the perspective of the Western European firm doing business internationally, and have given a significant emphasis to the experience of small to medium-sized firms, as well as to that of multinational enterprises.

Connections between the chapters

Reasons to internationalise operations	Assess resources	Set objectives	Choose markets	Decide risks of entry	Agree approach	Implement and renew

Reasons to internationalise operations
- *Reactive:* external approach
- *Tactical:* offset domestic downturn
- *Strategic:* establish international base

Assess resources
- *Internal:* physical human financial technological
- *External:* human financial

Set objectives
- *Low note:* occasional sales few markets low share limited investment high margin
- *High note:* high sales range of markets high share high investment lower margin

Choose markets
- *Level of risk v. level of potential:* economic profile political profile import orientation infrastructure culture

Decide risks of entry
- *First-stage:* indirect exporting direct exporting licensing/ franchising
- *Second-stage:* direct sales joint venture foreign direct investment

Agree approach
- Product
- Packaging
- Pricing
- Promotion
- Distribution

Implement and renew

Chapter 1   Chapters 1, 4   Chapter 1   Chapter 2   Chapter 1   Chapter 3

Chapter 5

Chapters 6–10

Introduction:
The firm's global environment

Objectives

By the end of this introductory chapter, you will be able to:

- understand some of the main trends in the world economy.
- understand some of the causes and effects of these trends.
- appreciate the difficulties of forecasting under conditions of rapid, dynamic change.

'You should never make forecasts, especially about the future.'

As we approach the millennium, capitalism seems destined to become the world economic system. Centrally planned economies have not proved successful. Mixed economies are currently in the process of shrinking their public sectors in order to expand the domain of private enterprise and private capital. Cooperatives flourish here and there, but despite their merits they seem quaint and parochial alongside the seemingly unstoppable advance of a world capitalist economic system which even Karl Marx thought superior to anything which has ever existed before. The increasing integration of the world economy is an irreversible trend with an impact on all businesses – including those that are not themselves international. This much seems clear. But what else should we emphasise when describing the international firm's global environment?

Technology and the changing role of government

In the 1960s and 1970s the trend towards increased use of computers led some to predict that the paperless office would exist by 1980. It did not happen. Indeed, in 1995 when nearly every office used a personal computer, there was a shortage of paper. Electronic mail, it seems, merely transfers the responsibility for printing the output from the sender to the recipient of the communication. Perhaps the paperless office is still on its way, but it is not here yet.

In the 1980s the movement towards globalisation was said to be leading to domination of each sector of the world economy by just a few globalised multinationals. Increased globalisation and integration of the world economy is certainly a reality, as is the trend to greater control of all the main sectors by oligopolistic firms. However, the typical firm is still small to medium in size; and even within the multinational sector, only about 25 per cent of firms could be described as global.

The information superhighway has not yet brought about universal access to information, or increased democracy, or a workforce that both works and shops from home – nor indeed any of the other revolutionary outcomes that are often predicted. Most of the information on the Internet is trivial, and the average user shares the same social profile and interests as the readers of *Playboy* magazine. More generally, information technology has not yet, as forecast, reduced the required workforce of the developed world by 90 per cent, with the active 10 per cent producing all the goods and services required. Deregulation, privatisation and increased public shareholding and property owning have not created as much wealth for the bulk of ordinary citizens as some had predicted.

Clearly, in attempting to extrapolate from current trends there is a temptation to exaggerate the speed at which these trends will bring about massive changes in the firm's global environment. On the other hand, it is also easy to underestimate the speed of such changes. In a book called *A Short History of the Future*, Warren A. Wagar depicted the following scenarios:

- The Soviet Union does not disintegrate until 2044 (in the real world it departed the scene in 1991).
- The Communist political system also survives down to 2044, although it adopts a semicapitalist economic policy and then gets thoroughly swept up in the capitalist world economy (in the real world, most of the Communist political system was dumped virtually overnight).

What Wagar and everyone else failed to anticipate (as Wagar himself has admitted[1]) was the extraordinarily rapid pace of events in the real world in 1989 and thereafter – events that changed the geopolitical map of the world fundamentally, and probably permanently.

However, though the timeframes may have been inaccurate, in general the forecasters were not wrong in identifying the main trends: the extension of capitalism to the global level; the escalating technological revolution; and the linking of both these developments to the massively increased role of finance. All three of these trends are increasing the power and flexibility of international, multinational and global firms. To a significant degree, the Third, Second and First Worlds are merging into a One World economy. Furthermore, this is a revolution which is underpinned by liberal/democratic/capitalist philosophy, with its ideological components and values treated as universal norms. According to Robinson[2], 'Multinational business is now international politics.' However, one could equally well turn this around and say, 'Politics is now international and multinational business.'

International firms of all types are finding themselves less constrained by the policies of home and host governments; rather, the role of governments is changing to that of facilitator to private companies. Of course, governments must still impose some restraints; they must raise taxes, and regulate to protect the planet from ecological disaster. They also have to ensure that welfare is provided for the victims of the creative/destructive economic system known as advanced capitalism; in other words, for the victims of market failure. (Traditionally, governments have provided the welfare function themselves, but this may change; indeed, it is already doing so in some European countries such as the UK, where the trend is to privatise these services.)

In the late twentieth century, governments are showing an increased willingness to act as ambassadors for the more important home or host multinationals. In terms of resources, the wealthiest top hundred economic entities in the mid-90s consist of 53 countries and 47 multinational firms. Many multinationals have greater wealth at their disposal than the countries in which they operate, and in this decade doing business by 'operating within' the foreign market has become the rule rather than the exception. For the OECD (Organisation for Economic Co-operation and Development) countries, sales from foreign subsidiaries are far greater than exports, and around one third of total world trade comprises sales between multinational firms. Sales, production, distribution, research and development, the acquisition of materials and components – all these activities tend to be conducted by multinational firms cooperating with other firms in some form of strategic alliance, and often with some support from their home government.

Understandably, some governments are apprehensive about the amount of economic power wielded by foreign firms operating within their boundaries. Japan and the United States tend towards protectionist policies for their domestic economies, while exploiting and advocating free trade for others. In the mid-90s, there seemed to be a real prospect of a trade war between these two countries, arising from disagreements over trade in the car industry. The USA had a debt of some $1 trillion because successive administrations declined to increase taxes, cut public spending and allow standards of living to fall. The Japanese banks had massive amounts of bad loans (anything from $0.5 trillion to $1.2 trillion), and a huge number of Japanese firms were delaying inevitable bankruptcy – ultimately at the expense of the finance sector and the Japanese economy as a whole. America's debt was greater that that of all the less developed countries (LDCs) put together.

The worse their economies perform, the more protectionist the US and Japan are inclined to be towards their domestic industries. The poorer LDCs and the emerging markets are particularly affected by protectionist policies which hurt their exports, and they are no less vulnerable to the volatility and unpredictability of investment flows. The loans that maintain US standards of living and prop up failing Japanese firms could have been made available to the less developed countries.

The LDCs are also often in a weak position when negotiating terms with a multinational enterprise (MNE) considering foreign direct investment (FDI) in their country. After almost fifty years of 'development' many of the world's poorest countries are even poorer in both relative and absolute terms. Multinationals play off the host governments of the poorest countries against each other until they have secured the best deal for their operations. Increasingly the MNEs have the support of their host governments in such negotiations, and can make use of an implicit threat of reductions in trade and aid (most of which is tied to donor country interests anyway).

It is well known that taking all forms of aid and charitable contributions into account, there is a net transfer of funds from the poorest countries to the richest countries as a result of debt crises. LDCs were offered loans from Western commercial banks when interest rates were between 2% and 3%. Rates then floated up to 10%, and debtor countries found that despite having repaid thirty times the sum borrowed, they were still only paying off the interest. This has made the poor countries even more dependent on the resources of foreign multinationals. The worst aspects of those international debt crises are over now, but the crises of US debt and looming Japanese debt still remain.

Information technology and the strategies of firms

Information technology makes the implementation of firms' existing strategies more efficient. But it also enables firms to do *new* things; that is to say, IT can facilitate new strategies, and strategic vision is often necessary to take full advantage of it. In contemporary business, technology is changing the nature of products, and IT is making ancillary services associated with those products a possibility. Take the Korean car manufacture Daewoo, for example. In the UK Daewoo is unique in having dispensed with the 'middle man'; instead of operating through a network of independent dealerships to sell its cars, Daewoo has set up its own sales outlets, and has filled them not with cars but with computers. The customers can view the various models on screen, and then customise the model they choose; only then does Daewoo arrange for an actual vehicle to be adapted to meet the customer's requirements, and made available for a test drive. By dispensing with commission-earning sales staff and large showrooms stocked with vehicles, Daewoo claims to be able to sell its vehicles thousands of pounds more cheaply.

Each new financial services firm sees the possibility of exploiting some aspect of IT to provide a new service, or a traditional service in a new way. In the mid-1980s the Conservative Government's official figures for the failure rate of small UK firms were perceived to be less than the reality. If the failure rate were only 30% or so of the total of new firms, why were there not far more small firms in existence? The answer lay in the new method the Government had introduced for counting bankrupted small firms. As soon as a small firm had registered for Value Added Tax it was added to the list of new start-ups. The novelty came in not counting failures unless the firm had been up and running for two years. As most small firm failures occur within the first two years, this method of counting omitted most of the firms which went bankrupt. Dun and Bradstreet were able to compile and publish figures which showed the total failure rate to be more than double the official figures. Perhaps this is a warning to all governments everywhere, but especially non-democratic ones, of the power and potential of IT.

As well as changing the strategies of firms, IT continues to modify the organisational structure. Big firms can acquire some of the flexibility of operations that small firms enjoy. Routine physical and mental labour can be performed by machines, as can some of the decision-making. Factory floor workers, insurance and bank clerks, middle-managers in all types of organisations are being replaced by the new technologies. For manufacturers, 'lean production' is the name of the game. Within the important globalised industry of car manufacturing Toyota are perhaps a paradigm example of lean production techniques. As the car rolls out of the factory, having taken 15 man-hours to produce, it would be possible to attach the customer's name and address to it if this were necessary. In fact, Toyota might even be *too* lean, as waiting lists have developed for some of their more popular models. (Avtovaz, Russia's largest car maker, could be described as a 'fat' producer; it takes 450 man-hours to produce a Lada, and many have serious mechanical deficiencies including missing parts. See the *Economist*, page 86, 'Modernising the mastodon', June 10th-16th 1995.)

Because of the trend towards globalisation, strategic alliances, and increased concentration in the main manufacturing and service sectors, many have been led to pronounce the death of the small firm. Small may be beautiful, but largeness brings economies of scale which in turn produce the capital required for R&D and innovation. Now that the elephant can dance, the mice are liable to get squashed. These arguments underplay the fact that while global firms are trying to control everything from the acquisition of materials and other supplies to the production and distribution of their products, they are no longer (as in the 1980s) striving to *own* all of these processes. Globalisation may be creating the borderless world, but strategic alliances (or networks) are creating the borderless firm. Big firms cannot internalise all these activities and remain dynamic and free from bureaucracy. There will always be scope for small firms to specialise in some new product or service, and to join one or more of these strategic networks.

International institutions and financial anarchy

The international institutions created at Bretton Woods in 1944 – The World Bank, the International Monetary Fund (IMF) and the General Agreement on Tariffs and Trade (GATT) – have done much to promote free trade, finance trade and alleviate poverty; but developments have outstripped the functions of these institutions. GATT has now been replaced by the newly created World Trade Organisation. The IMF was designed to supervise a system of pegged international exchange rates which ceased to exist twenty-five years ago; and the World Bank, designed to help poor countries, has current loans totalling less than ten per cent of the funds from private investments. These institutions seem inappropriate to the global environment of today.

Less than five per cent of the total finance that ricochets around the world's financial centres is directly connected to the trade in goods and services. The other ninety-five per cent is a mixture of financial products, including those relating to hedging strategies; 'hot money' chasing the highest rates of return; and speculative funds which sometimes deliberately cause currency devaluations to create massive private profit for the individual speculator, at the expense of all those who need to use that specific currency for whatever reason. The problem for the G7 (group of seven richest countries) and others involved in planning reform of the international institutions, and the problem for international firms planning and managing their operations, is that there is no model in finance, economics or international business theory which can adequately explain and predict capital flows of this magnitude – let alone outline satisfactory policies to cope with such flows.

Risk management requires a comprehensive understanding of local and global conditions, combined with a universal approach and a network to ensure prompt action and continuity across operations. However, since such activities often involve firms in switching in and out of specific currencies, many of these risk management activities contribute to the general volatility and instability in financial markets. Asking risk managers if the firm requires more hedging and risk-reduction strategies is like asking a barber if he thinks you need a haircut. And we are talking about very expensive haircuts here. Firms are operating in a world moving towards greater deregulation, and a tendency towards international financial anarchy with significant examples of financial collapse at both company and national level (Baring's Bank, Mexico). As yet, there is no internationally agreed policy to curb these trends.

The world political environment

The collapse of the USSR and the end of the Cold War is the biggest event unfolding at the end of the twentieth century. Gorbachev was the hero of this (counter)revolution. In an effort to retain its status as a military superpower, the Russian-dominated communist bloc bankrupted itself. The centrally planned and controlled economic system had failed and needed to be replaced. It was clear to some political observers from as early as the 1960s that the USSR was a failing economic bloc, and the only question was the timing of its demise. Perhaps the war in Afghanistan was the final straw (just as future historians will probably identify Vietnam and 'Star Wars' as the turning point for the USA).

Although the USSR was faced with no alternative, and although Gorbachev made mistakes, it still required an act of vision and political heroism to change the direction of that region's political and economic development. Gorbachev's original plan was to introduce a radically modified form of socialism involving new political and economic structures (*perestroika*) and a new openness of information (*glasnost*). Socialism cannot contain capitalism by such methods (see the chapter on Emerging Markets for further evidence of this statement). The communist regional bloc, the Council for Mutual Economic Assistance (Comecon), has been replaced by the Commonwealth of Independent States; but the newly created CIS is not likely to survive in its present form, and perhaps not at all.

As with potential regional bloc member countries everywhere (see Chapter 6 for more on regional blocs) a choice has to be made between regional integration and direct international integration. Many of the former communist countries of central and eastern Europe see the European Union as a more attractive proposition. Russia's invasion of Chechnya under the post-Gorbachev administration was a crude attempt to maintain old-style Russian dominance in the region; in the longer term, it is likely to have the opposite effect.

These events provide both threats and opportunities for European firms (see Chapter 8 for more detailed information.) In most respects the central and eastern European economies are in desperate need of technology transfer, consumer goods of all types, investment and foreign exchange. Many firms from Western Europe and elsewhere have successful operations in one or more of these countries, and are expanding their market share while there is little foreign or indigenous competition.

The risks are of two broad types: general political and country-specific risks; and those which can be subsumed under the heading of corruption. The economic and political institutions of the region (including the banks) may have connections with organised crime, and in extreme cases may even be run by criminals. Columbian cocaine and crack has found ready markets in Poland, the Czech Republic, Ukraine, the Baltic states, Belarus and elsewhere. The virtually unregulated financial sector in Moscow, electronically integrated with stock markets in the West, is used to launder drug money. Other countries in the region, notably Poland, have gone into drug production. Protectionist rackets, counterfeiting, prostitution and other Mafia-type criminal activities also flourish throughout the region. In short, it is a interesting and lively place to go for your holidays, but it holds many risks for those firms considering foreign direct investment.

Theoretical models of the world economy

This is easy: there are none – or at any rate, none that work. However, almost all of the traditional theoretical perspectives have interesting and important things to teach students of international business. They include:

- the classical theories of international trade (Smith, Ricardo)
- the more recent theories of international economics and applied economics (international trade, exchange rates, etc.)
- 'theories' of the international firm (Michael Porter's *The Competitive Advantage of Nations*, Macmillan, 1990; and K. Ohmae's *The Borderless World; Power and Strategy in the Interlinked Economy*, Collins, 1990); and
- the central 'theories' of international business (some of which are summarised by J. H. Dunning's 'eclectic theory'[3]).

Generally speaking, the economic theories are complex analytical models which do explain alleged causal connections and predict outcomes. However, these models have numerous variables which interact in complex and unpredictable ways. Economic theory remains a sometimes useful tool for explaining in retrospect why things did not turn out as expected, but it has little practical value for international firms wishing to plan their operations. Most of the other 'theories' are not theories at all in the usual sense. They are mostly analytical frameworks (e.g. the eclectic theory) or paradigms (e.g. Porter's 'Diamond' in the book mentioned above) which have no predictive element.

Other approaches to understanding aspects of international business have been based on concepts such as 'the centre and the periphery'. This suggests that the world comprises a relatively small number of rich countries at the core or 'centre', and a large number of poor countries relatively marginalised at the 'periphery'; the development of the world economy (or lack of development, for the majority of countries) can then be understood essentially as a process of exploitation of the poor by the rich. (See Chapter 7 for some different approaches to explaining 'emerging markets'.)

In short, there are many models, theories, paradigms, analytical frameworks, perspectives etc. which purport to explain specific aspects of international business; but no single, holistic model for the world economy as a whole. Our world, driven by vast quantities of private finance, a technological revolution and the strategies of international firms, has become integrated as never before. This integration, and the main driving forces just mentioned, provide new challenges for the theoreticians. From the chaos theory of contemporary physics, we have learned that the underlying nature of reality is unstable, dynamic, complex, interrelated, always on the verge of collapse but with discernable, underlying patterns. Capitalism appears to share at least some of these characteristics, and for some time to come we can only hope to understand its processes by the judicious use of those limited – but nevertheless essential – theoretical tools available to us.

People

Managers and writers of textbooks are inclined to say that the people within an organisation are its most important resource; but there is very little evidence to suggest that managers actually behave as if this were true. Apart from a number of Swedish multinationals and (to a lesser extent) some of the larger Japanese firms, labour – including junior and middle management – is regarded as a cost to be dispensed with as quickly as possible. Industrial 'relations' have given way to 'human resource management', and the personnel manager is seldom part of the senior management team in an international firm; it is not regarded as an important enough post. 'Flexible employment' translates into 'easy to make redundant' when the market turns down, or when the acquisition of technology enables a firm to 'downsize'.

Advanced capitalist countries are said to be in the 'post-career' phase. The firm's requirements for personnel change fast, and no-one should feel secure about their present job or profession. Advanced capitalism is creating more long-term unemployment, greater disparity between rich and poor within and between nations, insecurity about employment prospects, deteriorating terms of employment, weakening employees' rights, and – in many cases – lower wages and salaries for all but senior managers. This process is probably more advanced in the UK than anywhere else. It was summarised by the British Chancellor of the Exchequer, in a television interview on 16 June 1995, as getting employment restrictions off the back of the employers. Yet it is taking place within the context of a growing awareness by managers of the need to ensure greater commitment from the entire workforce to the goals of total quality, complete customer satisfaction, empowering employees so that they may make a greater contribution, and so on.

Firms that have exploited their new powers, downsizing during a recession and then trying to 'upsize' again when the market for their products improved, have discovered that it is an expensive process. Personnel who are able to get jobs with another company do so. The firm has to retrain a virtually new workforce, many of whom have only accepted a post until they can find another one with a firm enjoying a better reputation. Full-time workers who need to have their wages topped-up to subsistence level by social security payments are not necessarily going to make any extra effort to convince customers that the firm deserves customer loyalty. As we shall see, this position contrasts with attitudes to employment in Japan (see the discussion of culture in Chapter 2).

Even personnel employed by international firms with more enlightened attitudes are likely to find retraining an essential part of their working experience. It is thus more important than ever before that governments provide their people with as good a general education as possible, as a basis for retraining in later life. Firms also need to give training a high priority; if they really do invest in their personnel in this and other ways, they are more likely to win their loyalty and increase their productivity.

Transborder data flows

We have seen that information technology and the strategies of multinationals are accelerating the integration of the global capitalist economy. Also, ability to scan the globe for resources and markets bestows enormous power and control on those who have this facility. In advanced, high-tech economies, knowledge is replacing raw materials as the source of wealth creation. Yet in many respects, knowledge is regarded as an economic externality. The recent business graduate who applies his or her skills and knowledge, and increases the profitability of the firm, is considered very much a part of the productive process; yet the teachers and lecturers who taught those skills and imparted the knowledge are considered as being outside it.

Britain is arguably the most inventive nation on earth; but most of her inventions and scientific discoveries were either consciously made available to the rest of the world for free, or languished for a time because no one could envisage how they might be commercially exploited. Americans patented and commercially exploited many of these British inventions and discoveries, and Britain now buys back the resulting products from the United States. No country would ever consider handing over its raw materials to foreign firms without exacting some payment in return, yet multinationals argue for complete freedom to transfer knowledge from one place to another without restriction or cost.

The information services sector itself is dominated by mainly oligopolistic US firms. Legislation constraining transborder data flows ought to be a topic for the new World Trade Organisation. Countries such as Australia, Austria, Brazil, Canada, Denmark, Finland, France, Germany, Japan, Luxembourg, Norway and Sweden have had such legislation in place for over a decade. Since then at least sixty other countries have passed similar legislation, or are considering it. As Britain discovered to its cost, making knowledge freely available to everyone is only economically viable if everyone else is doing it too.

Questions for discussion _____

1 Protectionism, regulation and restrictions on the movement of goods and resources all limit the ability of international firms to create wealth. Therefore all such restrictions should be abolished. Discuss.

2 International firms and wealthy individuals have utilised the new technologies and deregulated markets to increase their power and efficiency. International institutions such as the World Bank and the IMF have not kept pace with recent developments. Should these international institutions be reformed or abolished?

3 Within the capitalist world economy, management is proving to be internationally mobile but labour is not. Why is this? Do you think that in the international context

labour should move to where the work is, or do you believe that the firms should move to where the labour is located?

4 China wishes to obtain the advantages of capitalism without incurring what it regards as the economic and cultural disadvantages. Identify what you consider China would regard as advantages and disadvantages in this context. China is hoping to remain a communist country linked economically to world capitalism. Is it likely to succeed? (When considering this question, you may wish to refer to the section on Culture in Chapter 2; to Chapter 7 on Emerging Markets; and to Chapter 8 on Eastern and Central Europe.)

Further reading

Most textbooks on international business contain a chapter on the firm's international environment, although this is probably the chapter that dates most quickly (for example, note how many of them discuss the future of GATT, which no longer exists). It is worthwhile to read several of these. For example, Chapter 1 and Chapter 4 of Sonia El Kahal's *Introduction to International Business*, McGraw-Hill, 1994, provide a very useful overview. Chapter 1 in John D. Daniels and Lee H. Radebaugh's *International Business; Environments and Operations* (7th edition), Addison-Wesley, 1995 gives an American perspective.

Many such textbooks provide a speculative chapter on the future of the international business environment – for example, Chapter 21 in Nanshi F. Matsuura's *International Business: A New Era*, HBJ, 1991, and Chapter 22 in Czinkota, Ronkainen and Moffett's *International Business* (3rd edition), Dryden Press, 1994. After looking at some or all of these references, you should be able to determine which aspects of the international environment are the most important or the most interesting; you can then find further information on your selected topics from the following bibliography, as well as other sources mentioned in the chapter itself.

Philip G. Cerny, *Finance & World Politics: Markets, Regimes & States in the Post-Hegemonic Era*, (Studies in International Political Economy), Edward Elgar, 1995.

John L. Daniels and Dr. N. Caroline Daniels, *Global Vision; Building New Models for the Corporation of the Future*, McGraw-Hill, 1993.

J. H. Dunning, *International Production and the Multinational Enterprise*, Allen and Unwin, 1981.

Alain Geledan (ed.), 'The Development of World Economy, 1975-1991', *East European Quarterly*, August 1994.

Richard Gibb and Wieslaw Michalik (eds.), *Continental Trading Blocs: The Growth of Regionalism in the World Economy*, John Wiley & Sons, 1994.

Bennet Harrison, *Lean and Mean: The Changing Landscape of Corporate Power in the Age of Flexibility*, McGraw-Hill, 1995.

Gary Clyde Hufbauer, *The New Europe in the World Economy*, Institute for International Economics, 1994.

Robert A. Isaak, *World Economic Change: International Political Economy* (2nd ed.), Prentice Hall, 1995.

J. Carlos Jarillo, *Strategic Networks: Creating the Borderless Organisation*, Butterworth Heinemann Ltd., 1993.

R. J. Jones, *Globalisation & Interdependence in the World Economy: Rhetoric & Reality*, Pinter Publishers, 1994.

Peter B. Kenen (ed.), *Managing the World Economy: Fifty Years after Bretton Woods*, Institute for International Economics, 1994.

Richard Lamming, *Beyond Partnership: Strategies for Innovation and Lean Supply*, Prentice Hall, 1993.

Michael S. Scott Morton (ed.), *The Corporation of the 1990s: Information Technology and Organisational Transformation*, Oxford University Press, 1991. (In particular see Chapter 3, 'The Past and Present as a Window on the Future', by Joanne Yates and Robert I. Benjamin, in Morton above.)

John Naisbitt, *Global Paradox: The Bigger the World Economy, the More Powerful Its Smallest Players*, Nicholas Brealey Publishing Ltd, 1995.

Gerhard Plenert, *World Class Manager: Olympic Quality Performance in the New Global Economy*, Prima Publishing, 1995.

John C. Pool and Stephen C. Stamos Jr., *Exploring the Global Economy*, Durell Institute of Monetary Science at Shenandoah University, 1994. (Abstract on ABI/INFORM (R) Global CD Database.)

Susan K. Purcell and Francoise Simon (eds.), Foreword by Gonzalo De Las Heras, *Europe and Latin America in the World Economy*, Lynne Rienner Publishers, 1995.

Sally Roberts, 'Changing market will require global view', *Business Insurance*, Vol. 28, Issue 18, 2 May 1994.

Stephen J. Rosow and Naeem Inayatullah (eds.), *The Global Economy As Political Space*, Lynne Rienner Publishers, 1994.

F. M. Scherer, *Common Policies for a Highly Integrated World Economy*, Brookings Institution, 1994. (Abstract on ABI/INFORM (R) Global CD Database.)

Robert Solomon, *Transformation of the World Economy, 1980–93*, Macmillan Press, 1994.

United Nations Centre for Transnational Corporations, *Transnational Corporations and Transborder Data Flows: A Technical Paper*, 1982.

B. V. Yarbrough, and Yarbrough, R. M., *World Economy: Trade & Finance*, HBJ, 1994.

David B. Yoffie (ed.), *Beyond Free Trade; Firms, Governments, and Global Competition*, Harvard Business School, 1993.

Notes

1 Warren A. Wagar, 'A funny thing happened on my way to the future: Or, the hazards of prophecy', *Futurist*, Vol. 28, Issue 3, p. 2125, May/June 1994. (Abstract on ABI/INFORM (R) Global CD Database.)

2 J. Robinson, *Multinationals and Political Control*, Gower, 1983.

3 J. H. Dunning, *International Production and the Multinational Enterprise*, Allen and Unwin, 1981.

1 How firms internationalise their operations

Objectives

By the end of this chapter, you will be able to:

- understand why firms wish to internationalise their operations.
- assess the relative strengths and weaknesses of available options.
- undertake the case studies at the end of the chapter.
- use this chapter to assess the regional case studies in the rest of the book.

Introduction

✎   CASE STUDY

Chris King, managing director of Labelking, a south London printer of adhesive labels, has been working on his plans to break into markets on the Continent since his first meeting with John Drury, an export development adviser from the London Chamber of Commerce.

The owners of the French label printer with which King hopes to establish a joint venture in Spain have visited Labelking's Herne Hill factory and have agreed to carry out joint research of the Spanish and Portuguese markets for adhesive labels.

King is also in touch with some of the 30 French companies which responded to a letter he sent out last year when he first launched his campaign to break into mainland Europe, and he is cultivating these contacts so as not to restrict his options to just one partner.

At his second meeting with King, Drury produces a DTI report on consumer markets in Spain. The two men discuss what information Labelking needs if it is to break into the Continent and into the US, where King sees good prospects. King says he needs a complete list of printers in France, Spain and the US with details of their turnover and the specific products they make. The two men turn to the subject of the US. King has already carried out quite a bit of reconnaissance and has hit upon the south-eastern states as a potentially lucrative market. A population of about 30 million people is served by only five or six printers, none of them big, says King.

> But breaking into the US market will mean Labelking almost certainly having to increase its product liability insurance cover to take account of the more litigous business climate in the US. For example, the company will have to take account of far tougher regulations governing matters such as the contents of adhesives used on food products.
>
> If King's plans for a factory in Spain fall through, Continental markets could at a pinch be served by exports from the UK. But the US is too far away for Labelking to supply from Britain. Label printers have to work closely with their customers and are expected to deliver very quickly. A few years ago customers would be satisfied if they received their labels within two weeks; now many expect delivery within two or three days.
>
> Source: adapted from the *Financial Times*, 23.5.89

The above case study illustrates many of the opportunities, problems and decisions that have to be considered when a firm decides to move into the international arena. Which markets offer the greatest opportunities? How will the firm find out all the relevant information? What are the financial implications of doing business abroad? What choice does the firm have in the ways that it services foreign markets? Should it go it alone or attempt to join with a partner to take advantage of additional resources or expertise? This chapter discusses how firms assess international opportunities and the range of options open to them in developing a successful international strategy: exporting, licensing and franchising, joint ventures, FDI, countertrade and contractual forms of international business. It analyses the advantages and disadvantages of these ways of doing international business in the light of current research and real life case studies.

Why do firms internationalise?

Moving from the confines of a domestic market across national boundaries into one or more international markets can seem a daunting prospect. Indeed, a fairly small proportion of UK companies takes the plunge. It has been noted that less than 1 per cent of American firms, around 2000, account for 70 per cent of US exported manufactured goods and there is a similar pattern in the UK and many other countries[1].

There are a number of reasons why companies internationalise their operations, ranging from the purely reactive and opportunistic to the proactive business decision which sees international markets as a major strategic opportunity.

Many firms that become involved in international business often begin only as a response to an outside enquiry. The resulting business may initially be seen as a sporadic and marginal contribution to a firm's core business, and the emphasis is on minimising risk and investment of time and resources. There is little impulse to grow overseas business.

Companies may move beyond this threshold for a variety of reasons. Sometimes a decision is purely defensive, for example as a reaction to pressures in domestic markets. Overseas demand can help to offset seasonal or cyclical downturns in domestic demand. It can also provide an avenue when a domestic market has become saturated or a product is coming to the end of its domestic life cycle. Cigarette companies facing this situation in the developed world have exploited markets in newly developing countries where demand is on the increase.

At the other end of the spectrum is the firm that sees a wide range of benefits from international business and its domestic market as just one among a range of opportunities within an overall strategy. Beyond the immediate advantages of additional revenue and profit, it may concentrate on the economies of scale that a larger international demand can bring.[2] The Cecchini report on the impact of the single European market argued that failure to expand operations across national boundaries would expose a firm to competition from European-wide producers with lower average costs. Other countries may also offer cheaper production costs. Clothing companies, both in the UK and Germany, for example, have subcontracted some of their operations to the Far East and Eastern Europe because of lower labour costs.

Very few firms can adopt this overall strategic view immediately. The great majority begin cautiously and build from there. Those that are successful can develop comprehensive international business strategies, incurring higher risk and commitment in order to achieve a stronger long-term position. In the pursuit of such objectives many firms are assisted by government programmes – the scope and depth of government help for exporters has been expanding rapidly in recent years[3]. This help ranges from the provision of information on foreign markets to the provision and financing of promotional opportunities and the underwriting of credit. Although internationalising a business raises new problems, the provision of government support has convinced some firms that these problems are outweighed by the new opportunities.

When is a firm ready to do international business?

As we have seen, many firms initially become involved in international business in a fairly unplanned way. Others may be reacting defensively to external pressures. Whether a firm considers itself 'ready' may not be the key factor in getting started, particularly if the method of entry involves relatively low risk. However, if they are to sustain an international venture, firms do need to overcome the common major problems faced by the nascent international business. A report in the UK undertaken by the British Overseas Trade Board suggests the following key difficulties in the export process[4]:

- finance/delays in payment
- export paperwork
- market information
- product suitability.

In the American survey referred to in Note 1, the following major barriers to export activity were identified (in rank order):

- obtaining adequate initial knowledge about exporting
- identifying viable sales opportunities abroad
- understanding business protocols in other countries
- selecting suitable target markets on the basis of available information.

For any specific firm these factors will not be exhaustive – other factors such as limited profitability of a particular export opportunity may also be important – nor will they occupy the same rank order. They suggest that, as well as a varying degree of financial risk, a key issue is management time, commitment and resourcefulness in identifying any international market opportunity. There is an emerging body of evidence which suggests that the role and characteristics of management within a firm are crucial to the decision to move into the export arena. The commitment and enthusiasm of senior managers, the extent of their international orientation, and their ability to lead and develop a consensus on a particular international strategy have surfaced as crucial determinants as to whether a firm will move into exporting or not. Indeed the BOTB report cited above identified the major characteristics of the successful exporter as those of high quality and committed management and the export ethos or culture of the firm.

Cavusgil and Nason[5] argue that those firms which have been through an expansion process at home, for example by increasing their number of suppliers and customers or adapting their products for differing local markets, are more likely to succeed in exporting compared to those that jump from being a local supplier to an international company: 'Some internationalisation ... must take place at home.' Secondly, 'on again, off again' exporting does not appear to be a successful option; rather better results are achieved if exporting is seen in the light of a long-term commitment. Thirdly, passive or reactive exporting is seen to be an approach which is being outmoded due to changes in product/service markets and the integration of the world economy; again active long term commitment is perceived as superior. Finally, a formal, systematic, planned approach to exporting is seen as being preferable to an ad hoc, trial and error approach; the need for business planning is paramount, returning us to the key issues of management vision and skill.

Choosing options

As we have seen, a key issue for many firms is the degree of their commitment to international business as a long-term strategy. This commitment will play a major role in determining their choice of one option over another. A second key issue for firms near to international business is the degree of their ignorance of overseas markets and, thus, the level of risk relative to any investment they make.

Depending on their long-term perspectives, businesses in this position are likely to look, therefore, for an initial strategy that counters their market ignorance and minimises risk while maximising their returns, their degree of control over potential success and their capacity to learn. Such lessons will allow them to move towards a second-stage strategy allowing much fuller involvement and control with the potential of much deeper penetration of the chosen market.

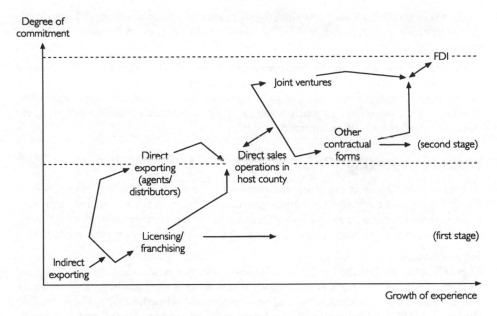

Figure 1.1   Options for international business

There are four basic ways of doing international business:

- exporting
- licensing/franchising
- joint ventures
- foreign direct investment.

These approaches are depicted on the chart above which shows how each approach may be ranked according to the extent of a firm's experience and confidence in international business, and the degree of commitment of resource it wishes to make. This chapter will look at each approach in turn according to the following criteria:

- the degree of resource commitment needed
- the potential balance of risk to return
- the degree of control in maximising success
- the degree of learning it affords.

Firms can, potentially, enter international business at any of these stages and choose to sustain that approach, or move to another option earlier or later in the chain. Most are likely, however, to begin with a first-stage strategy, progressing if they wish to the second stage.

Exporting

Exporting can be defined as selling goods or services from one country to another. It may be contrasted with licensing or franchising which are concerned more with selling the kinds of intellectual property underlying particular goods or services. The relative merits of the two approaches will be discussed in the section on licensing and franchising.

A distinction has been made between indirect and direct exporting. The former involves some sort of intermediary concerned in selling to overseas markets, while the latter implies that the firm deals directly with sales channels overseas. Direct exporting suggests a more proactive approach based on some experience of the markets in question and a higher level of involvement.

Indirect exporting

As we have seen, indirect exporting encompasses the use of intermediaries, generally in the firm's own country and in response to demand from overseas. For the firm with little experience of international business, this is often the starting point from which to move into direct exporting. There are a number of options open for such a business.

Export houses

Export houses are defined by the British Export Houses Association as 'any company or firm, not being a manufacturer, whose main activity is the handling or financing of British trade and/or international trade not connected with the UK'.[6] There are 200 members of the British Export House Association and they are important intermediaries for UK exports dealing with a large proportion of exported goods[7]. UK exporting houses generally prefer to provide a comprehensive exporting service, acting as principal, taking title to the goods and arranging sale and all of the associated administration. This service has obvious benefits for the new exporter, the exporter who wants foreign sales quickly without wishing to commit considerable resources to generating such sales and, in particular, the firm which lacks the management time to operate in this way. The major drawbacks of using an export house are the cost of using such a service and the lack of control the manufacturer will have over the export process, in particular the volume of repeat orders which arises and the way the product is sold abroad, which may not be in line with the firm's overall marketing strategy. This latter point is particularly pertinent if the firm has longer-term objectives in relation to market development. Finally, products which require after-sales service from the manufacturer or require a continuing relationship between supplier and end user would not fit with this form of distribution.

Confirming houses

Confirming houses are another form of passive exporting where the house acts as an agent for a foreign buyer, as an intermediary between two principals. The exporter will register or notify its export possibilities to the confirming house and await contact in the future. The advantage for the exporter is that the confirming house guarantees that the initial order actioned by a foreign importer will be consummated in full and will receive payment from the confirming house, thus reducing one of the major uncertainties in export business. The disadvantages of using this method of exporting are similar to those discussed above for export houses.

Joint marketing

Joint marketing occurs when arrangements are made with other firms to formulate a joint approach to the selling of products in foreign markets. If the firm does not have the relevant 'exportise', the financial ability to approach a particular market, or the time to develop a market strategy on its own in relation to a perceived opportunity, it may consider linking with another firm to achieve such an objective. This approach is sometimes called 'piggy-backing' and could take a number of forms. The firm may forge links with another business which has complementary products/services and a more sophisticated distribution network. Alternatively, the firm may link with a foreign firm in similar vein. This could be a reciprocal arrangement, depending upon the compatibility of products and markets. The advantages of inheriting an established distribution system via such methods are considerable. Speed of market penetration is also an important benefit. The disadvantages are less obvious but would include the difficulty of finding a suitable partner, and the difficulty of maintaining and sustaining this relationship as both organisations evolve and possibly modify their marketing approach.

Direct exporting

From using intermediaries to respond to overseas demand, a business can move more proactively into exploiting foreign markets for itself. In doing so, it can make use of two basic types of intermediary.

Agents
An agent is someone who is legally empowered to act on behalf of a principal; here the principal is a seller. Agents will search out new business and lobby for repeat orders in foreign markets. They may work exclusively for the exporter or for a number of exporters, taking under their wing one product or a range of products which may either compete with each other or not, as the terms of their contractual relationship dictate. It has been estimated that over half of world trade by value was handled by agents in 1987.[8] The main advantages of using agents are that they have detailed knowledge of local markets, have often built up a network of contacts, which may be particularly useful if tendering for government contracts for example, and are paid on a commission only basis, so where there are no sales there are no fees payable. The exporter will have a better chance of receiving market information when using agents (as opposed to an export house or confirming house) and hence possibly influencing the strategy in any given market. The disadvantages of using agents relate to the extent to which a firm's products will be given prominence within the activities of the agent, and the facts that agents are not usually responsible for marketing and promoting a product and that it may be difficult and costly to terminate agency agreements if the international strategy of the firm changes. Furthermore, using an agent may not be the most appropriate way of exporting if such things as after-sales service are deemed to be important.

Distributors
A distributor is someone who agrees to take title to the exports of a firm before attempting to sell them in the distributor's (foreign) market. The exporting firm may have to come to a more detailed agreement covering such issues as the geographical size of the distributorship and the sale of competing goods. The relationship between exporter and distributor is symbiotic, with both parties, in theory, benefiting from the successful activities of the other. For the exporter, this method of distribution allows more scope for controlling the main components of the marketing strategy: place, promotion and price, and provides the kind of physical presence in the market which makes such things as customer service and maintenance arrangements a genuine possibility.

Distributors can also provide detailed and up-to-date knowledge of trends in the market that a firm can use to adapt its product or marketing approach.

The disadvantages of using a distributor include the possibility that the exporting firm's product will be one of several/numerous products which will constitute the distributor's product range. The degree of effort put into selling any one product may therefore vary. Additionally, changing or moving away from a distributor could be difficult and costly because of contractual arrangements. Notwithstanding, using distributors appears to be the most important way in which UK exports are sold[9].

CASE STUDY

Technic group is a UK company established in 1987 which manufactures retreaded tyres and sells most of its products abroad. Technic developed its overseas business by signing exclusive distribution agreements in each country for the two brands it produced, Technic and Eurospeed. Distributors are able to build their own national markets avoiding direct competition. The company believes that dealing with a small number of customers gives it an advantage over other companies. Distributors are visited at least three times a year and visits are organised to the UK factory at Burton. This relationship helps the company to keep up with new developments in tread patterns and tyre sizes and to assess levels of demand for existing tyre types.

Source: adapted from the *Financial Times*, 29.6.93

The most radical form of direct exporting is, of course, selling directly to foreign retailers or industrial and commercial users. This could involve making contact and dealing with the functional departments of the customer to negotiate orders, transportation, delivery times, finance and so on. Alternatively the exporter could appoint sales people or even establish a sales office within the export region. Such moves would indicate a fundamental commitment to an export strategy and would carry with them direct costs and fixed overheads which would need to be recoverable within the parameters of the marketing plan. Also, there might well need to be time for such an approach to bear fruit as the sales representatives/office would need to build a client base and a web of contacts as a basis for stimulating export orders. As the sales force became part of the company's organisational structure this would present an additional management task as issues of accountability and control had to be addressed. However, this method of distribution would allow for greater direction and co-ordination of the marketing strategy abroad and so could provide important long-term benefits compared to other methods of exporting. The case study opposite illustrates the shift from distribution to this more direct control over exporting.

✎ CASE STUDY
Exporting: the case of Flymo

Flymo is a medium-sized British company employing 450 people which makes lawnmowers. In the late 1980s Flymo believed it would be difficult to establish itself in the European marketplace due to perceived lack of demand for 'hover' mowers with which the company had made its name in the UK. As a consequence, it developed a wheel rotary mower especially for continental markets, which it launched in 1989. However, the performance of the new product was disappointing, but, surprisingly for the company, after improving the design of its hover mowers, sales of these began to accelerate, particularly in France, Denmark and Norway. Such was the turnaround in export fortune that management predicted a quadrupling of export sales in the next four years.

Underpinning these sales projections was a major change in distribution strategy. The company's products were previously distributed and sold by a number of continental sales companies belonging to Flymo's parent group, Electrolux. These companies tended to sell to wholesalers with disastrous results. The mark-up from sales company to wholesaler to retailer effectively doubled the equivalent UK price. In Scandinavia, for example, the final selling price was more than four times the factory cost compared with less than two and a half times the factory cost in Britain.

Flymo first persuaded the companies to sell directly to retailers, cutting overheads and thus selling prices. They also argued for adding mass distribution outlets (for example hypermarkets) to the network of specialist retailers. To reinforce this shift, Flymo proposed a fundamental two-stage change in control. Firstly, staff from the sales companies would cease to report to Electrolux: they would instead be integrated into Flymo itself via a central organisation run from the UK. Its managing director would be responsible for all Flymo sales, including export sales. Key managers would be appointed in major markets and staff there made directly accountable.

The second stage would be to replace the current structure of four European regions with a pan-European distribution structure serviced by a single UK warehouse guaranteeing three-day delivery. From Autumn 1993, local sales staff in France were brought into Flymo and linked directly to the UK computer network with shipping, though not invoicing, undertaken directly from the UK. The intention was to transfer this structure eventually to other European markets.

Source: adapted from the *Financial Times*, 25.5.93

The Flymo and Technic case studies illustrate the opportunities and the risks involved in distribution arrangements. Such arrangements do not automatically involve major commitment of resource, but they do allow a degree of control and learning on which to build a sustained export programme. However, a major risk, as Flymo discovered, is the capacity of the distributor to adapt to the needs of the product market niche. The wrong choice can tie a business into an unsuccessful partnership from which it would be difficult to withdraw. In Flymo's case, the business found it necessary to become more directly involved, shifting from a distribution to more direct control and the integration of the distributor into its own sales network. This shift underlines the key point of a firm's export success relying on its willingness to think long term and to take ultimate responsibility for its own export success.

Licensing

Licensing occurs where one business agent (the licensor) allows another (the licensee) to utilise or sell intellectual property, in return for compensation, usually financial. Intellectual property can take several forms including for example, technology, products, brand names, trademarks, designs or any combination of these. Once the decision is made to share this knowledge, there is a risk that it will 'leak' to competitors, even if protected by appropriate contractual terms.

Contractor has undertaken work to synthesise current research on the advantages of licensing[10]. At the level of the firm, licensing may be appropriate to the small firm, especially one involved in significant research activity. It cuts out the additional production, promotion and distribution costs of exporting. If the rate of technological turnover is high, it can allow a rapid, low-risk entry into an export market, allowing a firm to maximise returns before competitors or further technological advances catch up. As speed and timeliness become ever more important in a firm's competitive armoury, licensing is likely to gain further in importance in the future. At the country level, its low cost may be appropriate where there is significant political or competitor risk, or where tariff barriers are high. Some governments favour licensing arrangements as a means of importing technological know-how, and it may be easier to repatriate royalties than profits or dividends.

One Australian study of 43 firms looked beyond the immediate to the longer-term benefits of licensing[11]. These included, in ascending order, the export of equipment to the licensee, the acquisition of overseas market knowledge and skills, and the return flow of technology and other information from the licensee. Licensing can, therefore, score highly as a means of building expertise in overseas business.

✎   CASE STUDY
         Creating a worldwide yen for Japanese beer
Japanese brewers are trying to cultivate overseas drinkers' taste for their beers by stressing they, rather than western brands, go best with sushi and sukiyaki.

Although the high yen, expensive transport costs and low profit margins have curbed Japanese brewers' overseas expansion, stagnation in domestic sales due to market saturation is forcing the companies to turn to international expansion. High overseas demand for Japanese beer, due to the increasing popularity of Japanese cuisine and rising numbers of Japanese expatriates, has also motivated Japanese brewers to look abroad for markets.

Kirin brewery, the world's fourth biggest and Japan's largest brewer, recently announced a licensing agreement with Charles Wells brewery of Bedford, England. Wells will start producing Kirin lager next year. Kirin has had a licensing deal with Molson, the Canadian brewer, since 1987, as well as a contract with the Hong Kong arm of Philippine brewer San Miguel.

Kirin has opted for overseas production rather than exports. It believes that freshness is the most important factor for beers, adding that tariff barriers can be avoided through overseas production.

For the big four brewers, Kirin, Asahi, Sapporo and Suntory, the US is their largest overseas market, consuming over 70 per cent of foreign sales. They add that Asian markets have the greatest potential since beer is a relatively new drink and Japanese brands are popular.

The beer companies admit they are cautious about rapid overseas expansion, and their foreign sales are still only about 1 per cent of turnover. But the companies believe that the industry has become a world leader in brewing technology. They also say that the taste of Japanese beer is gaining international acceptance as a compromise between overly light American beers and heavy European beers.

Source: adapted from the *Financial Times*, 7.10.94

A major potential drawback in any licensing arrangement is whether or not the licensor is equipping a partner with the technology and know-how which enables it to become a powerful competitor when the agreement comes to an end. It is not always possible for all aspects of intellectual property to be relinquished or returned.

Licensing also involves the same risk as the use of a distributor or other intermediary in exporting: that the latter will not prove effective in maximising sales potential. Despite technical and quality specifications, it can also be difficult to guarantee equipment and product quality in practice by the licensee. Indeed, the hidden 'policing' costs of licensing have contributed to its relatively low profitability in the past. Similarly there may be limited control over how a product may be redeveloped and remarketed by a licensee. In 1969, the French magazine *Elle* granted a licence for a Japanese edition to a local firm, Mag House. The Japanese version evolved beyond the initial concept and the contract was cancelled in 1988.[12] With this kind of experience in mind, the Australian study mentioned earlier identified and grouped the costs of licensing as follows:

- the learning process of licensing
- the location and assessment of suitable licensees
- the enactment and finalisation of the negotiation.

Flexibility and initial cost-saving have to be balanced against the greater problems of control in relation to alternative approaches such as an agency or distribution arrangement.

CASE STUDY

How Caterpillar China coped with key obstacles in major licensing deal

Caterpillar started selling equipment to China in 1975. By 1980 the company had put together a strategy which included sales, product support and technology transfer. The aim was to make a long-term commitment to building a leading position ahead of competitors.

In the past the company had used licensing mainly to overcome entry barriers to particular markets emanating from local competition or government activity. Caterpillar used licensing now in China because it believed this method offered greater freedom and control, and a greater certainty of securing hard currency income, than a joint venture approach.

In 1984 Caterpillar signed its first technical licence in China for power-shift transmissions with two government bodies and two factories in Sichuan. In 1985 the company was asked to bid for a programme covering 10 factories to produce components and complete machinery. Caterpillar was competing with Komatsu for these contracts. Its ultimate success was put down to factors other than price:

● in response to China's chronic foreign exchange shortage Caterpillar offered a countertrade programme through the Hong Kong office of Caterpillar World Trade (countertrade is discussed later in this chapter). CWT was to purchase manufactured goods from factories under the auspices of the State Commission of Machinery Industry and return the foreign exchange from overseas sales over to the factories in order to pay for Caterpillar semi-knock down kits, components and equipment.

● the company targeted officials in the factories rather than those in Beijing and persuaded them to back the Caterpillar bid, eventually in total, which ended up as being crucial support for the Caterpillar proposals.

The deal was completed by 1987 and included five technology transfer contracts, a countertrade agreement and a used-equipment sales agreement. The technical knowledge and countertrade agreement was to run for eight years. Any improvements implemented in other Caterpillar plants around the world would be automatically transferred to the Chinese licensees and vice versa. The agreement included training for Chinese workers in the US and on-site assistance from Caterpillar engineers.

Compensation was to take the form of an initial fee and royalties paid throughout the duration of the eight years. It was speculated that the deal would be worth more than $5 million to Caterpillar. Unusually, royalties were to be based on unit of output rather than on net sales or net values added. This was a tactic used by Caterpillar to avoid the complexities and uncertainties of using China's pricing system.

In an attempt to avoid the unplanned and unwanted diffusion of Caterpillar intellectual property, the company's designs, factory production and management techniques were protected by confidentiality clauses for the term of the contract. Although such a position could not be assured completely, the company had a relaxed attitude to this potential problem given that at the time when the deal was concluded the best Chinese factories were estimated to be about ten years behind most Western manufacturers in these respects. A more difficult issue was the possibility that the Chinese factories might attempt to export equipment based on Caterpillar designs, introducing a new competitive element in other foreign markets. No agreement appeared to be reached on this issue.

Adapted from article with above title, appearing in *Business Week International*, Vol 34, No. 28, July 13, 1987, reprinted in *International Marketing Strategy*, H. Thorelli and S. Tamer Cavusgil (eds).

Franchising

Franchising is a form of licensing which allows the franchisee the right to undertake business activity in a prescribed manner, over a certain period of time, in a specified place, generally in return for royalties or fees and, often, an initial payment[13]. Franchising provides a package which can include all of the following:

- use of a registered trademark, copyright, design or patent
- training, management support and the transfer of know-how
- control by the franchisor over the practices and procedures of the franchisee's business through stipulation and review, and over the quality of the final product.

The franchisee is a separate business entity from the franchisor and bears the commercial risk like any other independent commercial concern. Franchising takes various forms in the UK[14]:

- the manufacturer-retailer franchise, where the manufacturer is the franchisor and the franchisee sells directly to the public. Major examples of this form are car and truck dealership and petrol service stations
- the manufacturer-wholesaler relationship, a form which is common in the soft drinks industry and used extensively by companies such as Coca-Cola and Pepsi when they franchise their product to independent bottlers who then serve retail outlets
- the wholesaler-retailer franchise, familiar in the UK grocery sector where the wholesaler, acting as franchisor, will supply retailers on a voluntary franchise basis. Examples include Spar and Mace
- the trademark, tradename, licensor-retailer franchise, more often referred to as business format franchising, exists where the franchisor allows its product or service to be marketed under a common tradename in identifiable and usually standardised outlets and premises.

The growth of franchising has been described as phenomenal. It has been estimated that in the US 533 000 franchised locations were expected to produce sales of $716.7 billion in the early 1990s, employ 7.7 million people and produce a level of sales which would account for 34 per cent of all retail sales in the US[15]. Similar growth has been experienced in the UK. In 1984 the number of franchised outlets was estimated at around 80 000. A more recent survey which restricted its focus to business format franchising estimated that there were around 250 franchises with 15 000 outlets, employing 145 000 people and having a turnover in the region of £3.1 billion[16]. Franchising accounts for 10 per cent of retail sales in Great Britain, and is expected to increase its share to 25–30 per cent in the next few years[17].

Falbe and Danridge[18] suggest a number of factors which have contributed to the growing importance of franchising as a business form. Franchising is especially suited to the growing service sector of the developed economies. Together with the fact that they have escaped competition and restrictive practice legislation in the US and EU, franchises have thus far proved less likely to fail in their first five years than other forms of business, and have consequently attracted funding support from banks, reinforcing their success.

Like licensing in general, franchising allows a quick penetration of foreign markets with a minimum of capital outlay. As an example, Benetton was able to grow from 0 to 650 shops in the US in five years[19]. In return for agreed payments and systems of control, franchisors can offer franchisees the marketing benefit of a well known trademark, the provision of product know-how and training, and potentially easier finance on the back of the franchisor's reputation, making franchising attractive for both parties.

As with licensing, many of the problems are those of effective quality control in practice, however stringent contractual arrangements might be. An early study of US firms summarised the following problems in order of priority:

- government/legal regulations
- difficulty in recruiting qualified franchisees
- insufficient local funding
- control of franchisees
- adapting a franchise package for local markets
- trademark/copyright obstacles.

As an example of these sorts of selection and control problems, the Swedish furniture manufacturer IKEA was forced to reassess its three-year old franchising operation in the North American market in 1979 when it discovered poor supply as a result of low inventories in underfinanced stores[20]. In the early 1990s both Nissan and Toyota UK took steps to take control of their franchised distribution network so that they could achieve a more coherent sales and marketing strategy, shift the relative emphasis between retail and fleet sales and control the selection, training and co-ordination of the dealer network more effectively[21]. However, such an attempt to alter or revoke a franchise can be very costly, as McDonald's found when it had to withdraw the licence of its largest franchisee in France for failure to operate 14 outlets according to the company's standards. Finally, franchising may not provide the potential level of return of joint ventures or FDI, once franchisee income is taken into account.

As we have seen with exporting, the balance of resource commitment and risk has to be set off against the level of control a business may feel necessary to maximise its return, particularly as its familiarity with an export market grows. It will be at this point that businesses such as Flymo or Toyota may wish to move to a second-stage strategy involving a new level of direct commitment/risk, control and potential return. The second half of this chapter will analyse such second-stage strategies as joint ventures and foreign direct investment.

Joint ventures

There has been considerable growth of and interest in joint venture activity in the post-war period. A joint venture is one form of strategic alliance which can be defined as 'a commercial collaboration between two or more unrelated parties whereby they pool, exchange, or integrate certain of their respective resources'.[22] Such alliances therefore represent a move from direct competition between firms to an element of co-operation as they attempt to engineer and take advantage of market opportunities.

Joint ventures can be characterised either as equity/operating joint ventures, or contractual joint ventures. The former has been defined as 'partnerships by which two or more firms create an entity, a "child", to carry out a productive economic activity. Each partner takes an active role in decision making, if not also in the child's operations.'[23] The essential characteristic of an equity joint venture is this separate legal personality – they are usually seen, at least initially, as long term commitments; indeed an agreed 'life' may be stated in the initial agreement. The General Motors–Toyota joint venture NUMMI, which operates in the US, specified a life of twelve years in the original agreement[24].

A contractual joint venture is a business venture with a partner or partners where no separate body with a legal personality is formed. Firms will co-operate and share the risks and rewards of the co-operation in clearly specified and pre-determined ways. In this form it is usual to see the rights and duties of both parties contained in a set of agreements which might cover such things as the utilisation of technology, research and development, distribution arrangements and so on. On the surface, such joint ventures appear more formal, with a clearer specification of responsibilities and perhaps a more focused task in comparison with equity joint ventures.

The emerging importance of joint ventures as a form of international business has been traced back to the 1960s. The rise of joint venture activity at this time has been associated with government policy in developing countries, for example restriction of foreign equity participation in host country enterprises, import substitution policies and associated quota restrictions on imports aimed at defending infant industries. Recent empirical work is tentative in its suggestion of increasing joint venture activity, although the popular view is clearly that such alliances are increasing. However, three trends do command broad agreement:

- there has been a diversification of activity in joint ventures towards Asia, particularly SE Asia, where much Japanese investment takes this form;
- there has been a diversification in the sectoral activity of joint ventures where the service sector, for example financial services, has been increasingly important;
- 'while joint ventures in the past were used mainly by multinational firms as vehicles for market entry, mostly in developing countries, recent international coalition agreements are more strategy-, technology- and market-oriented.'[25]

Work by Glaister[26], focusing more specifically on western firms, suggests a predominance of equity joint ventures concentrating mainly on manufacturing, usually involving only two partners and in which UK partners were most likely to have a junior stake.

As has been noted, one historical advantage of joint ventures has been as a means of overcoming restrictions on foreign investment or imports. The shift from labour to capital-intensive industrial processes has also pushed firms towards sharing costs, as has the rate of technological change which has encouraged the pooling of resources to share both cost and risk. A shared approach also permits economies of scale and a greater potential speed to market. In November 1993, British Aerospace and Taiwan Aerospace agreed to establish a joint venture for the production of a regional jet aircraft. BAe was able to transfer some of its final asembly work to Taiwan where labour costs were lower[27]. The pooling of technological skills can also be seen in the announcement in February 1993 that Tioxide Group, a subsidiary of ICI, was to take a 50 per cent stake in a chloride titanium pigment plant in the US, giving it access to a technology in which Tioxide had little previous experience[28].

Joint ventures can be invaluable in gaining knowledge of particular markets or access to a partner's distribution channels, as the following case study illustrates.

CASE STUDY
Elle goes European: the internationalisation of *Elle* magazine

The women's weekly magazine *Elle* was first launched in France in 1945. In 1983 its publisher, Hachette, decided to sell a monthly edition of *Elle* in the US in a joint venture with the Murdoch group. In this 50–50 partnership Hachette provided the concept and News Group Publications of the Murdoch Group provided the logistics for launching the magazine and the use of its distribution network. In 1988 *Elle* US made a profit of $16 million.

After this experience joint venture arrangements provided the means for Hachette to offer *Elle* in a variety of international markets. In 1985 a British version of the magazine was published, again in partnership with the Murdoch Group. In 1986 *Elle* was offered for sale in Spain in alliance with the group Cambio 16. In 1987 *Elle* ventured into the Italian market as the product of an arrangement with RCS Rizzoli.

This approach was also used to sell the magazine in Hong Kong, Sweden, Brazil, Japan, Netherlands, Australia, Turkey, Germany, Portugal, Greece, Canada and China.

Source: *Elle goes European: the internationalisation of Elle magazine*, B. Cova, F. Rad-Serecht, M. C. Weil, in *European Marketing, Readings and Cases*, C. Halliburton and R. Hunerberg, 1993

A joint venture can be used as part of a global strategy when other approaches may not be appropriate. In 1989 Lucas Industries placed part of its car wiring systems business in a joint venture with Sumitomo of Japan. The former had a 70 per cent stake and the latter a 30 per cent stake. The aim was to enable Lucas to win more business from Rover and Honda and other Japanese car manufacturers setting up in the UK. The venture was also intended to reduce the likelihood that Sumitomo or other Japanese manufacturers might consider setting up their own wiring harness operations in competition with Lucas on green field sites in the UK[29].

Set against these advantages, one of the salient features of joint venture arrangements, confirmed by empirical evidence, is their essentially short-term life. 'Estimated failure rates range from 30–61 per cent depending on region, with joint ventures in developing nations suffering from greater instability than those in developed countries'[30]. This instability is sometimes deliberate. Some joint ventures may be seen as part of a strategy whose ultimate aim is an FDI presence; the joint venture is therefore a stepping stone on the way to this objective and will be terminated when appropriate. In addition, most studies do not compare the life cycle of joint ventures with other market entry arrangements, for example FDI. Choudhury in one such study concluded: 'If the entry modes (international joint venture and wholly owned subsidiary) are judged either by exit rate or duration of active life (longevity) the IJV's performance appears to be relatively better than WOSs (wholly owned subsidiaries), a surprising finding given that WOSs are thought to be superior to IJVs in this regard.'[31] However, it is apparent that there are numerous areas of potential conflict between the partners which could be cause for the termination of the co-operation agreement. These would include:

- disagreements over the strategic direction of the venture
- operational/managerial disagreements
- the fact that one partner may take a more active role with the other perceived as free riding
- disagreement over use and appropriation of profits
- cultural differences between managers which may make it difficult for them to form effective working relationships
- inadequate initial assessments of market and/or technology potential undermining the *raison d'etre* of the joint venture.

The issue of a common approach has been well summarised by one senior manager. 'Compatibility can be readily measured,' notes Richard Dulude, President Telecommunications at Corning Glass Works. 'Joint ventures work if one partner has the technology and the other management and marketing expertise,' he explains. 'Also, the parents must have similar values and corporate cultures. Because Corning is technology based, we look for a partner that shares our perception of the purpose of technology: to make something useful and worthwhile. The prospective partner's outlook is more important to us than whether it has the same technology, since the very concept of a joint venture implies a long-term relationship. We further believe good ventures are grounded in joint decision making and we therefore want a partner that is compatible with sharing authority.'[32]

✎   CASE STUDY

In the late 1980s Marley Automotive Components Limited of the UK entered a joint venture with Davidson Instrumental Panel–Textron of the US. Marley is a leading manufacturer of building materials and a supplier of quality components to the European motor industry. Davidson Instrument Panel, a division of Textron, is a component supplier to the automotive original equipment manufacturers. The firms engaged in a 50/50 joint venture, located in Born in The Netherlands, selected for its proximity to its major customer, Ford. The venture was promoted by Ford Europe which asked Marley to supply components for its 'world car' to be produced at its Genk plant. Ford wanted world-wide sourcing which made a joint arrangement with Davidson Instrument Panel sensible.

Critical issues which surround the success and failure of joint ventures, specifically conflict, goals, management styles and degrees of commitment, were addressed in this joint venture in the following ways.

The venture has a board of directors with two members from each parent. All major decisions were to be decided by this board. To ensure production and development deadlines were not compromised before production actually began, Ford requested that Marley retained one less voting share on major issues until the commencement of production in 1993. Both the general manager and human resource manager were appointed after a joint selection exercise by the two partners. A clear delineation of roles was specified in the arrangement whereby Marley supplied the local market knowledge and was to negotiate with local suppliers, and Davidson supplied the technology and financial systems.

Both parents transferred experienced employees to the joint venture. The general manager who was appointed was a Dutch national, a recognition of the importance in adjusting to the employment practices of the host country.

Marley established a sales and marketing group in The Netherlands with the aim of looking for new contracts. Both parent firms were to offer training programmes and support for key employees. These and other start-up costs were to be shared among the partners.

The general manager and human resource manager were given freedom to select, appraise, train and compensate the 250–300 workers who were to be hired by August, 1992. However the strategy for recruitment, training and compensation was developed jointly by senior human resource executives at Davidson and Marley and agreed upon by the Davidson Marley board.

The general manager and key members of staff are employed by Davidson-Marley BV. As such they are not on secondment from their parent organisations, and have their future careers rooted within the joint ventures rather than within the parent organisations.

Source: adapted from R. Schuler, P. Dowling and H. D. Cieri, *The formation of an international joint venture: Marley Automotive Components* in the *European Management Journal*, Vol. 10, No. 3, September 1992

Other contractual forms of international business

Management contracts

The essence of management contracts is the transfer of managerial skills and capabilities in the operation of a business in return for remuneration. More formally a management contract has been defined as 'an arrangement under which operational control of an enterprise, which would otherwise be exercised by the directors of managers appointed or elected by its owners, is vested by contract in a separate enterprise which performs the necessary managerial functions for a fee.'[33] There is no reliable information on the extent of this form of market servicing, but it is recognised as being important in industrial/service industries, public utilities, tourism and agriculture. Indeed the management contract is the most important operational approach used by international hotel groups.

Canada's Four Seasons Hotels will become the world's largest operator of luxury hotels under an agreement with the Japanese parent of the Regent International chain. EIE International, the financially-troubled Japanese developer, will transfer management of five Regent hotels, including those in New York and Milan, to Four Seasons. Regent manages ten hotels, expects to negotiate contracts for five others, and has several projects under development. Four Seasons said it would provide advisory services for various properties still managed by the Japanese group.

Source: adapted from the *Financial Times*, 18.3.92

Management contracts not only allow firms to benefit directly from the sale of their knowledge and expertise, but can also provide opportunities for earning revenues in related activities. For example, the contractor may generate additional business in the form of technical and marketing fees, associated sales of equipment and technology; the contract may also be associated with the licensing of a product or process, where the aggregate transaction is a bundle of intellectual property rights which the firm has at its disposal. In addition management contracts could be used in a more strategic way, for example as a way of gathering vital overseas experience which can then either be transferred to other markets or used as a way of gaining knowledge and ideas which can be transferred to what the firm considers to be its core markets. Management contracts have been used to maintain a presence in foreign markets in the face of protectionism and political expropriation, and as a way of penetrating otherwise closed markets.

Perhaps unsurprisingly, one of the problems associated with this form of international business activity is the maintenance of a working relationship which is amenable to both the contracting parties. As the contract evolves the host nation firm will need to take more control of operations which may conflict with the priorities of the contractor. Similarly the priorities of the parties may change over time and eventually a differing emphasis may be apparent. Contract length may not be specified but where it is, a time scale of between five and seven years is not unusual, suggesting that the project life cycle will evolve through different stages, possibly creating some of the problems mentioned above.

Turnkey operations

Turnkey operations are a form of international business involving a contract which includes the design, construction and establishment of a facility or business operation, on behalf of a client, in return for a fee. The size of such contracts is a differentiating factor from other forms of international business, running into hundreds of millions of pounds. This field of activity is therefore dominated by large rather than small and medium-sized firms, particularly in the field of industrial equipment and construction. Turnkey operations were given a major boost during the period of rapid increases in the price of oil as OPEC states began to recycle petro-dollars by spending and investing in large scale projects.

Companies may tender for turnkey projects themselves or form into consortiums in an attempt to strengthen a particular bid. National governments are often the clients in this area, and so to be successful the tendering company(ies) will have to possess well developed political and negotiating skills as well as more obvious attributes such as commercial experience and reputation, and a competitive price. Indeed, all other things being equal, these 'process' skills and abilities may well be crucial.

An example of a turnkey project was the 3576 feet suspension bridge, offered for tender by the government of Turkey, to be built over The Bosphorus. The successful bidders, a Japanese consortium, were helped by the Japanese government which offered subsidised low-cost financing in response to a stipulation that the contractor had to arrange overall financing for the project[34].

The protracted nature of the tendering/negotiating process is only one of the potential problems associated with turnkey projects. To be successful, the contractor may well have to have a network of political contacts and support which needs time and resources to develop. Turnkey projects may take several years to complete, which means financing and exchange rate risks have to be taken into account. A final payment may only be made after satisfactory completion of the project. What this actually means in practice will have to be carefully worked out and agreed in order to anticipate any wrangling at the end of the contract. However, contractors may find that they are still involved in the project after completion, for example by providing technical support and training on an ongoing basis. The full benefits from such a venture may not therefore be fully realised at the outset.

Contract manufacturing

Contract manufacturing occurs when a company places an order for the manufacture or partial sub-assembly of components with another firm, often in the developing world or in Central and Eastern Europe. The products are then exported back to the initiating firm for marketing. This process is based on the technical division of labour, where the contractor attempts to take advantage of the attributes of a foreign manufacturer, for example low labour costs, specialised skills, access to raw materials and other inputs. The clothing and textiles industries in Europe, particularly in the UK and Germany, are examples of sectors which have used contract manufacturing to secure competitive advantage.

Contract manufacturing in this form has been encouraged by the growth of export processing zones around the world, for example the Special Economic Zones in China, and favourable import regimes in the US and Europe for the re-entry of such products.

Contract manufacturing is also relevant to more technologically intensive processes, for example weapons manufacture where a number of firms may contract to develop individual elements or components under the auspices of a lead firm.

There are a number of variations to contract manufacturing activity, although the basic characteristic remains the same: a mutually beneficial relationship with both parties gaining from the capabilities of the other firm which are not available or feasible in house.

Countertrade

Before looking at the most radical second-stage strategy available to an internationally minded business, foreign direct investment, we need to look briefly at an emerging medium of exchange between businesses: countertrade, which has been described as the most important new trend in international business.

Countertrade involves agreement between two parties to pay in goods and services. In recent times, countertrade has been associated with developing countries struggling with depressed commodity prices and national indebtedness, and with new markets in China and the former Eastern bloc, for example. Estimates of the scale of countertrading vary[35], but it has grown sufficiently to spawn a global countertrade service industry providing trade, finance and information services. This service, based mainly in North America, Europe and the UK, covers such products as industrial goods, agricultural commodities, chemical products, consumer goods, service, aerospace and defence products in such regions as Asia–Pacific, Eastern Europe, the Middle East and S. America[36]. The US Trade Commission suggests five types of countertrade[37].

- **Barter**, the direct exchange of goods, is, perhaps, the least important in business.
- **Clearing agreements** provide a framework setting out the terms and timetable of exchange: goods are delivered at agreed intervals and any deficit made up with hard currency.
- Among the most significant types in the Far East, particularly in China and Japan, is **compensation**, sometimes known as buy-back. Here payment for plant, equipment or technology is made in output from the materials originally sold, often over a period of 5–20 years. As an example, Hewlett-Packard concluded a compensation agreement in China in 1985 in which it set up a joint venture operation. Hard currency from this operation's exports was then used to finance imports from Hewlett-Packard[38].
- The popularity of compensation in the Far East is followed closely by **offset**, especially in the defence and commercial aircraft industries. Here the seller is required by the buyer government to help market goods from the buyer country or to use local producers in its manufacturing operations.
- Finally, in the US the main form of countertrade is **counterpurchase** when an exporter agrees to buy products unrelated to the original exchange. As an example, Beijing Capital Iron and Steel imported equipment from Northern Telecom, Canada for a telephone switchboard system (valued at US$ 12 million), in exchange for which Northern Telecom counterpurchased US$8 million in steel products[39].

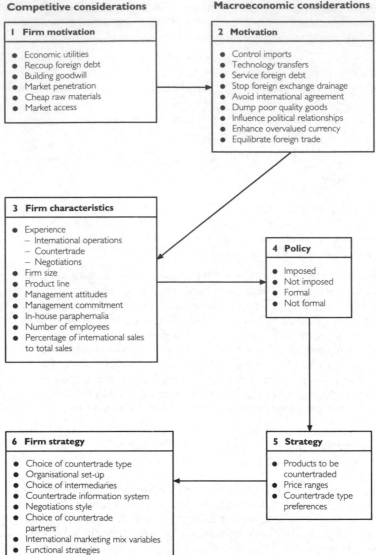

Competitive considerations   Macroeconomic considerations

1 Firm motivation

- Economic utilities
- Recoup foreign debt
- Building goodwill
- Market penetration
- Cheap raw materials
- Market access

2 Motivation

- Control imports
- Technology transfers
- Service foreign debt
- Stop foreign exchange drainage
- Avoid international agreement
- Dump poor quality goods
- Influence political relationships
- Enhance overvalued currency
- Equilibrate foreign trade

3 Firm characteristics

- Experience
  - International operations
  - Countertrade
  - Negotiations
- Firm size
- Product line
- Management attitudes
- Management commitment
- In-house paraphernalia
- Number of employees
- Percentage of international sales to total sales

4 Policy

- Imposed
- Not imposed
- Formal
- Not formal

6 Firm strategy

- Choice of countertrade type
- Organisational set-up
- Choice of intermediaries
- Countertrade information system
- Negotiations style
- Choice of countertrade partners
- International marketing mix variables
- Functional strategies

5 Strategy

- Products to be countertraded
- Price ranges
- Countertrade type preferences

Figure 1.2   Implementing International countertrade: a step by step approach. Source: S. Okoroafo, 'Implementing International Countertrade: A Dyadic Approach', Industrial Marketing Management, 23, 1994

As the earlier example of Caterpillar in China illustrated, countertrade can open up trade where a country faces a shortage of hard currency or imposes strict exchange controls. For the exporter it can provide cheap raw materials, components or semi-finished goods without the risk of exchange fluctuations. This is also where its problems lie – in finding a mutually acceptable rate of exchange and in coping with protracted and complex negotiations, particularly if governments are involved. Okoroafo[40] suggests that firms need to adopt a step-by-step approach, blending microeconomic analysis of a firm's requirements with macroeconomic country-specific analysis, as the diagram opposite illustrates.

Governments, particularly in developed countries, and international institutions have been less than openly supportive of the rise of countertrade. However, it is likely to grow as a way of expanding overall world trade for both firms and governments, especially in emerging economies.

Foreign Direct Investment

FDI has been variously defined, but perhaps most helpfully as 'the establishment or acquisition of income-generating assets in a foreign country, over which the investing firm has control.'[41] It may be contrasted with other forms of foreign investments, usually grouped under the heading of portfolio investment. These forms, for example foreign bonds, are purely financial, with no control over assets. FDI usually involves either taking control of an established business in an overseas market or developing a 'green field' site there, creating a tailor-made business operation.

As has been mentioned FDI demands the greatest commitment from a firm, not only in capital and management resources, but in long-term commitment to a particular market. Such a degree of resource commitment (and, therefore, risk) means that most FDI emanates from the larger multinational firm.

One obvious reason for considering FDI is defensive: to circumvent tariff quota or exchange control restrictions by governments which undermine direct exporting. As an example, Japanese FDI in the European Union has increased substantially, both as a means of circumventing EU barriers and maximising opportunities within the Single Market.

✎   Case study

Toshiba opened the first Japanese-owned factory to produce air-conditioning units in the UK in February 1992. When full production levels were reached in 1993, the plant was intended to produce 25 000 units of various sizes worth £30–£40 million, with half of these for export. The company wanted to secure its position ahead of the European Single Market reforms. The EC imposed tariffs on imported Japanese air-conditioners of about 5 per cent, and the company wished to act in anticipation of any future increases. Europe is an attractive site for Japanese producers who have identified a long-term growth potential. The use of air-conditioning in the UK commercial sector is seen to be much lower than in Japan.

Source: adapted from the *Financial Times*, 17.2.92

Beyond a defensive reaction, FDI can be a means of making most effective use of indigenous production resources within an overseas market, given the right balance of skill, flexibility and cheapness in the labour force, or the availability of cheap raw materials without the disadvantages of high transport costs. This cheaper production base can be enhanced by host government incentives for inward investment.

✎   **CASE STUDY**

In 1989 Bosch of (then) West Germany decided to invest £100 million on a production facility in Miskin, north west Cardiff, with the aim of producing car components, chiefly high technology alternators. The company had taken nearly a year to make a decision on the relative merits of the Miskin site and one in Spain. One of the key considerations when making the final choice was the availability of a Welsh labour force which had already demonstrated its energy, flexibility and willingness to adapt at Japanese transplants in the region. In addition, the company's figures demonstrated a situation of lower labour costs compared to those in Germany: in 1987 its average employment cost for a German worker was DM33 an hour compared to DM18 for a British counterpart. The overall effect of this on company planning was that Bosch expected to produce alternators for 15–20 per cent less than the comparable cost in Germany.

Source: adapted from the *Financial Times*, 18.4.89

Allied to these advantages is the strategic goal to which many companies may be working, the maximum closeness to and penetration of an overseas market. FDI allows the most speedy and sensitive response to local demand.

✎   **CASE STUDY**

In 1992 Levi Strauss began work on a new production plant on the outskirts of Plotsk, north of Warsaw, Poland. Although the jeans produced by the plant would cost consumers a third of the country's average monthly salary, there appeared to be no shortage of demand. Indeed Levi's Warsaw store at that time had the biggest sales for its size of any of the company's outlets in Europe. Although its products were difficult to get hold of under communism, the brand had long been one of the best known in Europe. According to the general manager of Levi Poland, 'The one thing we were sure of was that we had a willing customer.'

Production was predicted to be in the order of 3 million pairs within three years, with over half of these to be exported to the EU.

Source: adapted from the *Financial Times*, 6.7.92

Some of these motives for FDI can be seen in the choice of location. In 1993 Plant Location International, part of the Price Waterhouse Group, undertook a survey of 300 international companies to establish their priorities in choosing a particular location on a rating of 0 to 10.[42] The results were:

Availability and quality of phone, fax and data lines	8.48
A stable political situation	7.91
Reasonable level of labour costs	7.68
Reliability of power supply	7.54
Market proximity	7.23
Healthy economic situation	7.15
A stable social climate	7.15
Availability of skilled workers	7.04

Interestingly, investment incentives do not appear in the above list. Dr Wilfried Vossen, managing director of Plant Location International, believes that these may play an important role, but that they will probably enter the decision making process after other considerations have been examined.

The work of Buckley, Mirza and Sparkes[43] on 24 European firms with a manufacturing base in Japan emphasised both the size, regional importance and growth of the Japanese market plus the difficulty of penetrating the market by less direct means. FDI was seen as a long-term commitment to build customer loyalty and market presence as well as a means to 'exchange threat' with Japanese producers in Europe. Finally, gaining feedback from the Japanese market from customers and in terms of technical information was also seen to be important.

These impulses towards FDI are counterbalanced by the level of risk. The Plant Location International survey emphasised the importance of political and economic stability. Ketelhohn[44] identifies three main concerns in this respect:

- the security of fixed and liquid investments
- the business unit's economic feasibility
- its ability to move hard currency freely in and out of the host country.

Alongside these macroeconomic considerations are the degree of autonomy given to a subsidiary and whether or not to use expatriate managers – often a high-risk strategy.

Despite these limitations, FDI appears to have grown significantly during the 1980s. The nations which had the largest stock of outward FDI are as follows (figures are for 1991)[45]:

US	$385 billion
UK	$226 billion
Japan	$158 billion
Germany	$91 billion
France	$69 billion.

In terms of outflows the US was overtaken by both the UK and Japan for the first time in 1988. With respect to inflows, the US had long been the most important destination of FDI. However, the UK overtook the US in this respect in 1990. During the second half of the 1980s the EC attracted an increasing volume of FDI, with inward flows rising from $12.2 billion in 1985 to $72.2 billion in 1990.

The US is the largest outside investor into the EU, with the UK being the largest recipient of this investment, but with Germany and the Netherlands also important. One half of US FDI in the EU is in manufacturing, with another quarter in banking, finance and insurance. The remaining investment is mainly in the petroleum and commerce sectors[46].

Japanese investment is increasing in the EU, though presently accounts for no more than 7 per cent of the total for individual union members. The stock of Japanese investment in the EU, however, increased four times in the years 1986–90, and there are no reasons to suggest that this trend will alter. The main target for these inflows is the UK, with 38 per cent of the total, and the Netherlands with 25 per cent. The addition of Luxembourg to these two countries accounts for over 75 per cent of Japanese investment in the EU. The finance sector accounts for most of this investment, followed by the manufacturing then commerce sectors[47].

The growth in FDI is partly a general reflection of the recovery of economic activity in the 1980s, backed by a greater ease of investment and the opportunities created in particular by the liberalisation and privatisation of service sectors[48]. Part of the growth has also been attributed to the response of Japanese firms to foreign trade barriers and the rise in the value of the yen and the counter-response of firms to earlier waves of FDI generally. Beyond these impulses Thorensen[49] concluded that the desire to be closer to chosen markets was more significant than factor-based motives concerned with the greatest degree of production advantage in one location.

Summary

This chapter has outlined the range of options open to a business looking to internationalise its operations in the light of the degree of commitment and risk involved, set against the level of control and closeness to market each option affords. The possible relationship between these options is shown in Figure 1.3, opposite. There are, of course, many other permutations, and a firm may begin at any of these points. In this chapter, some of the advantages and disadvantages of each option have been discussed in relation to the needs and strengths of differing types of firm. There is no one simple answer in each case. As some of the case studies, for instance that of Flymo, illustrate, a firm may start with one option and then, by experience, move towards another.

To test your knowledge of the choices a particular firm might consider, look first at the case study for Labelking at the beginning of the chapter. Chris King has asked you to write a report for him dealing with the following questions:

1 What are the potential advantages and disadvantages of a joint venture with the French label printer King has been in discussion with?
2 What options would you recommend for entry into the US market? What problems might Labelking face?

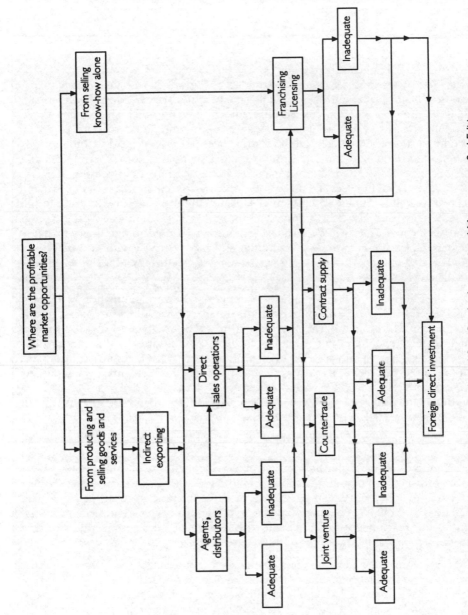

Figure 1.3   Choosing options in international business. Source: adapted from Brooke, International Management, 2nd Edition

As an alternative, try the two case studies, Highland Attractions and Danlan Corporation, which follow.

✎   CASE STUDY
            Highland Attractions

Highland Attractions is a food processing company which specialises in the preparation of high quality and luxury foods taken from its native Scottish hinterland, including smoked salmon, cooked pheasant, grouse and other game, patés, cured products, preserves and pickles steeped in spirits and liqueurs. The company employs just over 50 workers and had a turnover last year of nearly £3 million. At the head of the organisation structure is the managing director/owner. A sales and finance manager and a production manager are responsible for organising the work of supervisory staff in sales and the various food preparation processes. The company has well established contacts with several large restaurants, particularly in Edinburgh and London, and also sells its products through a large number of catering and tourist-oriented centres in Scotland. The company is used to working with fairly demanding customers who require prompt and speedy service without variation in quality, and within an environment where demand fluctuates and is sometimes difficult to predict.

The distribution of finished products is undertaken by a combination of its own small fleet of vans, some of which are refrigerated, and when the firm's own fleet is fully occupied, through outside transport firms. The company prides itself on its high-quality reputation and its ability to develop innovative and appealing new product lines; it currently has the largest product range it has had since its inception. At present 95 per cent of its turnover comes from its UK base. Some overseas orders have been received in the past and presently the firm has orders from France and Germany, mainly from restaurants. The company does not have any links with wholesalers or retailers in these countries.

The managing director of Highland Attractions has been pleased with the small number of export orders; although they were, and are presently, seen as a sideline in relation to the firm's major business clients, the profitability of these orders was far greater than those which are generated from the UK sales base, and the company was prepared to accept a delay in payment until after the products had been delivered and used. Although the organisation of export sales has been fairly time-consuming, this again was not seen as a problem, with one of the sales administrators taking overall responsibility for dealing with the orders in a very enthusiastic way.

A French firm is seeking a business relationship; it has suggested a plan whereby it would actively target high quality restaurants in major French cities and encourage them to use Highland Attraction's products. It would then pass these orders on to the firm in Scotland. In addition the French firm wishes to produce some of the product lines and recipes itself in its home market, while still selling them under the Highland Attractions label. The French firm has suggested that they build on this co-operation by eventually moving their joint operations into a third European Union country, although this is seen very much as a long-term aim.

Questions for discussion

1 Identify the firm's strengths and weaknesses as it decides whether or not to internationalise its operations.

2 Outline the potential advantages and disadvantages of the arrangement put forward by the French firm.

3 What changes to Highland Attractions' operations and practices would you suggest should occur if the firm decided to go it alone with an export growth strategy?

✎   CASE STUDY
       Danlan Corporation

Danlan Corporation is a South Korean multinational enterprise, which has subsidiaries, mainly in South East Asia. Its core business can be described as the manufacture and processing of chemicals, which are used to produce a wide range of products, but mainly man-made fibres for the textile and clothing industries, animal feed stock for the agricultural sector and paints and dyes for industrial and commercial users. It is both a cash rich and ambitious MNE; its latest strategic plan involves further geographical diversification in Europe to increase the proportion of sales generated from this region, where market research suggests significant growth opportunities up to the year 2000.

Using the UK as the base for investment, Danlan's aim is to establish a plant to produce man-made fibres. How this plant is to be established has not yet been determined. One possibility is to buy an existing plant from a UK firm which already serves the market. The chemical sector in the UK is currently undergoing a period of rationalisation, and a number of firms are involved in reducing capacity and changing their firms. Danlan feels it could be worth opening discussions with one of the established UK producers with the aim of buying production capacity as a going concern.

Another possibility is to open discussions with an established UK producer which has a clear strategic intention to stay in this particular line of business. The aim here would be to form an agreement to build a joint operation for the production of man-made fibres. Danlan Corporation has experience of negotiating such alliances in the Far East and has enjoyed particular success with joint ventures in Indonesia.

The final possibility open to the Corporation is to go it alone and build a new plant which would be a wholly owned subsidiary of the parent company. Discussions with UK government officials have indicated general support for this form of investment, and several local authorities have been asked to produce reports on the desirability of their locations in relation to the intended investment.

A decision on which option to choose will be reached at a meeting of the Corporation's steering group in a week's time.

Questions for discussion

I As a member of a working group established to investigate the above options, you have been asked to produce a report which addresses the following issues:

   a) the potential advantages and disadvantages of each option

   b) who should manage the new plant, with reasons for your choice

   c) which options you would recommend, giving reasons for your choice which include why the other options were rejected.

Further reading

The following are particularly recommended:

S. Young, J. Hamill, C. Wheeler and R Davies, *International Market Entry and Development*, Harvester Wheatsheaf, 1989.

M. Z. Brooke and P.J. Buckley (eds.), *Handbook of International Trade*, Macmillan, 1988.

F. Bradley, *International Marketing Strategy*, Prentice Hall International, 1991.

Other useful books and articles:

R. Axtell, *The Do's and Taboos of International Trade*, John Wiley and Sons, 1994.

M. Z. Brooke, 'International Management Contracts : Servicing Foreign Markets and Selling Expertise Abroad', *Journal of General Management*, 11(1), 1985.

M.Z. Brooke, *Selling Management Services Contracts in International Business*, Holt, Rinhart and Wilson, London, 1985.

F. J. Contractor, *Licensing in International Strategy: A Guide For Planning and Negotiations*, Quorum Books, 1985.

F. J. Contractor and P. Lorange (eds.), *Co-operative Strategies in International Business*, Lexington Books, 1988.

J. W. Dudley, *Exporting*, Pitman Publishing, 1991.

J. Dunning, *Multinational Enterprises and the Global Economy*, Addison Wesley, 1995.

C. Falbe and T. Dandridge, 'Franchising as a Strategic Partnership: Issues of Cooperation and Conflict in a Global Marketplace', *International Small Business Journal*, Vol. 10 No. 3. 1993.

S. Goldenburg, *International Joint Ventures in Action*, Hutchinson, 1988.

E. P. Hibbert, *Marketing Strategy in International Business*, McGraw-Hill, 1989.

'The Internationalisation of Business: Theory and Evidence', *International Marketing Review*, Vol. 7 No. 4, 1990.

L. K. Mytelka (ed.), *Strategic Partnerships and the World Economy*, Pinter Publishers, 1991.

P. Nicolaides, 'F.D.I.: Its Causes, Contribution and some of its Consequences', *Business Strategy Review*, Vol. 13 No. 2, 1992.

A. Palia, 'Worldwide Network of Countertrade Services', *Industrial Marketing Management*, Vol. 19, 1990.

H. B. Thorelli and S. Tamer Cavusgil (eds.), *International Marketing Strategy*, Pergamon Press, 1990.

S. Thorensen, 'Integration Through Globalisation', *National Westminster Quarterly Review*, February 1992.

Notes

1 R. Axtell, *The Do's and Taboos of International Trade*, page 10, John Wiley and Sons, 1994.

2 For a discussion of the importance and extent of economies of scale in various industries, see C. Pratten, *Economies of Scale in Manufacturing Industry*, and F. M. Scherer, *The Economics of Multiplant Operation*.

3 See the case study in the introduction to this chapter for one example of the kind of help available at the micro level to British exporters.

4 *Into Active Exporting*, Small Business Research Trust Survey, B.O.T.B., 1987.

5 S. Tamer Cavusgil and R.W. Nason, 'Assessment of Company Readiness to Export' – in H. B. Thorelli and S. Tamer Cavusgil (eds.), *International Marketing Strategy*, Pergamon Press, 1990.

6 E. P. Hibbert, *Marketing Strategy in International Business*, page 123, McGraw-Hill, 1989.

7 According to Young et al., this is 20% of U.K. exports – S. Young, J. Hamill, C. Wheeler and R. Davies, *International Market Entry and Development*, page 82, Harvester Wheatsheaf, 1989.

8 Hibbert (see 6 above), page 117.

9 J. W. Dudley, *Exporting*, page 67, Pitman Publishing, 1991.

10 F. J. Contractor, *Licensing in International Strategy: A Guide for Planning and Negotiations*, Quorum Books, 1985 – summarised in Young et al. (see 7 above), page 123.

11 L. Welch, 'Outward Foreign Licensing by Australian Companies' – in P. Buckley and P. Ghauri (eds.), *The Internationalisation of the Firm*, Academic Press, 1993.

12 B. Gova, F. Rad-Serecht and M-C. Weil, 'Elle goes European' – in C. Halliburton and R. Hunerberg (eds.), *European Marketing: Readings and Cases*, Addison Wesley, 1993.

13 F. Bradley, *International Marketing Strategy*, page 328, Prentice Hall International, 1991.

14 P. Stern and J. Stanworth, 'The Development of Franchising in Britain', *National Westminster Quarterly Review*, May 1988.

15 C. Falbe and T. Dandridge, 'Franchising as a Strategic Partnership: Issues of Co-operation and Conflict in a Global Marketplace', page 40, *International Small Business Journal*, Vol. 10 No. 3, 1993.

16 Stern and Stanworth (see 14 above), pages 39–40.

17 Falbe and Dandridge (see 15 above), page 40.

18 As 17 above.

19 Bradley (see 13 above).

20 J. Steed, 'Selling Swedish Style' – in H. B. Thorelli and S. Tamer Cavusgil (see 5 above).

21 *Financial Times*, 30.1.92.

22 *Corporate Finance*, May 1992, special supplement, page 5.

23 K. Harrigan, 'Joint Ventures and Global Strategies' – in Buckley and Ghauri (see 11 above), page 138.

24 E. P. Hibbert, ' The Growth of International Coalitions in Product and Market Strategy', page 86, *Journal Of European Business Education*, Vol. 11 No. 2, 1992.

25 Hibbert *ibid*, page 64.

26 K. Glaister, 'U.K. Joint Venture Formation in Western Europe', *European Business and Economic Development Review*, Vol. 2 Part 3, 1993.

27 *Financial Times*, 20.11.93.

28 *Financial Times*, 2.2.93.

29 *Financial Times*, 6.7.89.

30 Young et al. (see 7 above), page 228.

31 Choudhury, 'Performance of International Joint Ventures and Wholly Owned Subsidiaries: a Comparative Perspective', *Management International Review*, Vol. 32, 1992.

32 S. Goldenburg, *International Joint Ventures in Action*, page 30, Hutchinson, 1988.

33 D. D. Sharma, 'Management Contracts and International Marketing in Industrial Goods' – quoted in Hibbert (see 6 above), page 151.

34 'How Japan Won a Contract to Build Turkey a Bridge', *Wall Street Journal*, 29.5.85 – quoted in Thorelli and Cavusgil (see 5 above).

35 15–29% of total world trade, according to Young et al. (see 7 above), page 200; 20–25%, according to page 506 of C. Czinkota, I. A. Ronkainen and M. H. Moffett, *International Business*, Dryden Press, 1993; 20-40 %, according to Axtell (see 1 above).

36 A. Palia, 'Worldwide Network of Countertrade Services', page 69, *Industrial Marketing Management*, 19, 1990.

37 'Analysis of Recent Trends in US Countertrade', 1982 quoted in A. Palia and O. Shenkar, 'Countertrading Practices in China', page 58, *Industrial Marketing Management*, 20, 1991.

38   Palia and Shenkar (see 37 above).

39   Palia and Shenkar (see 37 above).

40   S. Okoroafo, 'Implementing International Countertrade: a Dyadic Approach', *Industrial Marketing Management*, 23, 1994.

41   *Panorama of European Industry*, EC, 1991.

42   *Financial Times*, 11.10.93.

43   'Direct Investment in Japan as a Means of Market Entry' – in Buckley and Ghauri (see 11 above).

44   W. Ketelhohn, *International Business Strategy*, Butterworth Heinemann, 1993.

45   P. Nicolaides, 'F.D.I.: its Causes, Contribution and Some of its Consequences', *Business Strategy Review*, Vol. 13 No. 2, 1992.

46   *Panorama of European Industry*, EC, 1991.

47   As 46 above.

48   Nicolaides (see 45 above).

49   S. Thorensen, 'Integration Through Globalisation', *National Westminster Quarterly Review*, February 1992.

2 Identifying market opportunities

Objectives

By the end of this chapter, you will be able to:

- appreciate the differing ways of classifying markets.
- assess some key economic indicators for a potential market.
- understand the importance of a market's political profile and import orientation.
- describe the key issues in considering a market's infrastructure and the problems raised by cultural distance.
- answer the case study exercises at the end of the chapter.

Introduction

CASE STUDY

Lager Tout: Kronenbourg's search for new markets

The French lager manufacturer, Brasseries Kronenbourg, part of the BSN Group, has pursued an active policy of expansion into selected European markets. Given the relatively high costs of transportation, logistics and marketing, Kronenbourg initially concentrated on premium beers with a sufficiently high margin to offset costs. However, this strategy could not lead to high volume, and volume sales required a significant position in a foreign market, a broader range of products, including lower-priced beers, and therefore higher costs of distribution and marketing.

To gain such a position, broaden its product range, acquire an established brand position and distribution network, Brasseries Kroenbourg believed that the best approach was to take over the local number one or number two brewery in a targeted market. As the owners of the target firms were not always ready to sell, another more indirect method was to take a minority share and then to increase it. This type of solution was implemented in Italy, Belgium, Spain and Greece.

Several criteria were considered in selecting the priority countries for international development:

- A permeable upmarket segment of beer drinkers receptive to Kronenbourg's premium beers.
- Growing demand for beer.
- Signs that the competitive structure of the industry might be beginning to con-

centrate, allowing Kronenbourg to acquire one of the growing players before it became a major competitor and use it to build a dominant market position as concentration increased.

The Mediterranean countries typically were in this situation in the 1980s, and it was regarded as vital to establish a position in these countries before other international competitors did so. In Spain, for example, beer consumption had regularly increased by 3-4% a year in the 1980s, a trend expected to continue in the 1990s. From 72 litres per person per year in 1989, experts forecast an increase in consumption to 100 litres per person per year by the end of the century.

To take advantage of this market, Kronenbourg acquired a 33% stake in Mahou, the number three in the market, investing in new plant to build Mahou's position so as to give Kronenbourg a strong position in the Spanish market.

Source: adapted from G Johnson and K Scholes, *Exploring Corporate Strategy (3rd edition)*, 1993, pp. 490-2

This chapter discusses the ways companies select markets. How carefully do they need to choose, what criteria should they apply, and how do they find out about potential markets? In the last chapter, we related attitudes to doing international business, and choosing an appropriate way of internationalising operations, to a firm's sense of the importance of overseas markets and the degree of learning and resource allocation it might be prepared to commit to them. This motivation is also crucial to how a company goes about selecting potential overseas markets.

A company which sees overseas trade as an occasional, low margin contribution to its core activities is unlikely to want to invest time and effort in researching markets. It is more likely simply to react to overtures from potential importers, and to leave market analysis to them. With minimal levels of risk and investment, research for new markets and channels of distribution may well be relatively sporadic and superficial. Research suggests that many SMES in particular do little or no market research, and as many as 60% begin by reacting to an outside approach.[1] However, longer-term success is increasingly seen to depend on a more proactive approach in locating new markets and building a position in them.[2] This need has been strengthened by the increasingly competitive international climate outlined in the introduction. Work by Pawar and Driva on British computing firms in the German market has stressed that, while companies only undertake limited market research, success is dependent on the ability to target the right markets for a product or service and the key market segments within them.[3] Research effort needs to be balanced by the number of markets an exporter may wish to target at any one time. Some companies may, for example, adopt a 'scatter gun' approach, attempting to access a wide range of markets quickly, perhaps via agency or distributor agreements. At present there is no consensus on whether it is better to target a few or many markets.[4] However, even with a diversification strategy, some element of market selection and research is needed.

For most firms, research will be influenced by two elements: the research initiatives they set in motion themselves, and the chance contacts (perhaps through an unsolicited approach) which unlock potential export opportunities. Each should be used to complement the other. If it is low risk, a company may well wish to exploit a chance contact, either building on it or developing other channels as its own market expertise develops.

The firm that recognises this need for focus, and sees overseas trade as essential to its success – perhaps as the key way to extend the life-cycle of its core product range, maximise its economies of scale to secure a lower cost base, and offset the impact of downswings in domestic demand – will want to be sure it is targeting the right markets in the right way. This need will be especially acute for a company that is considering a significant level of commitment to a market, whether through setting up its own sales operations, establishing a joint venture, or taking direct control through FDI as Kronenbourg set out to do in the initial case study.

For these firms, it is crucial to undertake detailed analysis of a country's market potential, set against the level of investment risk it presents, and their research is likely to be rigorous and detailed. They will use the full range of methods discussed in this chapter. Those firms which stop short of this level of involvement, perhaps because their scale of operations or degree of export experience pushes the level of risk too high, will not require quite the same degree of research. However, they will want to be able to select the best markets, and to assess their potential and the key issues in reaching consumers. This understanding may well be invaluable in, for example, the choice of an agent, distributor or licensee, and the way his or her export performance will be assessed, and in setting targets for export sales.

If such investment in understanding overseas markets is to pay off, it needs to take shape from a company's sense of its strategic purpose, and especially from an understanding of its competitive advantage. How a business achieves competitive advantage in its domestic market will be an essential starting point in analysing potential export markets. As an example, a business which sees cost leadership and price competitiveness as its key source of competitive advantage domestically will need to be sure that price is the key issue in an overseas market; and if so, that such an advantage can be sustained in the face of the cost of exporting, or competition from local producers and rival exporters. It may find that in a market less familiar with the product, premium pricing to enable a higher level of service support may be more appropriate in meeting customer needs. Similarly, a firm which has built competitive advantage on meeting the needs of a particular market segment must be able to identify a similar segment in an overseas market – and to be sure of accessing it, and meeting its needs, as precisely as it does in the domestic market.

The great majority of small to medium-scale businesses, in particular, will begin with an existing product range and a competitive position in their chosen domestic market segment. Their first step will be to investigate replicating that product success by identifying similar segments in overseas markets, and trying to reproduce their competitive advantage. From this often tentative start, the firm may move into some modification of its current competitive mix to fit new conditions, and even into new initiatives appropriate to those conditions. This approach will be characteristic of firms with significant export experience and reliance on export sales.

Once a company has a clear sense of its priorities, it can begin to consider selecting appropriate markets and researching ways of finding out about them. We have already noted that many companies do not initially undertake detailed research, and often lack the resources or expertise to do so. They will be reliant on external advice. However, they will need to be able to make some intial choices on the kinds of market to investigate and to know enough to assess the advice they are given. The following sections provide a starting point for such an analysis. They focus on some of the basic issues involved as a context for some of the more detailed analysis we will encounter, for example, in chapter 7 and 8 on emerging markets and Central/Eastern Europe. They will also consider some of the channels available for locating customers and potential partners within those markets. For most businesses, the process of market selection will focus first on individual countries and potential target segments within those countries, whether defined nationally by customer type or locally by region, for example. However, this choice may well be influenced by the existence of regional trading blocs, discussed in Chapter 6. Gaining access to one country may provide a stepping stone to others within the bloc, as part of a longer-term international strategy.

Numerous ways have been developed for classifying overseas markets. Some methods appropriate for particular types – for example, emerging markets – will be discussed in Chapter 7. However, most classifications cover the following key themes:

- economic profile
- political profile
- import orientation
- infrastructure
- culture.

Once they have decided on a particular classification, some commercially-available reports then seek to weight these categories according to their relative contribution to the level of investment risk, and score countries according to the relative balance of risk to revenue potential. Countries can then be grouped into a range of investment types according to a mix of potential, level of risk and investment/experience required. These reports can be a helpful starting point for more detailed analysis, isolating potential target countries and issues to consider, but they are rarely satisfactory on their own.

There is inevitably a degree of subjectivity in how such data is interpreted, and in the ranking and scoring process. Such a process may not reflect the priorities of a particular individual company. Translating national or regional figures into what is truly representative of any particular group of consumers is also fraught with difficulty. Most firms are concerned with particular market segments appropriate to them; and trends in the size, income and behaviour of these groups may be obscured by a broader perspective directed to the needs of potential investors.

Economic profile

Few businesses are able to look in detail at a country's economic profile, but they can make a provisional assessment by looking at some of the basic measures available. An obvious starting point in assessing a country's economic profile is its gross domestic product (GDP).[5] This is a measure of the overall level of economic activity and, like other measures, is best assessed over time, from which an overall trend can be extrapolated. An immediate problem is comparability of individual sets of nationally-collected figures. Differing countries have differing criteria for the way they collect and arrange data, and their reliability may vary widely.[6] Comparisons are therefore likely to provide only an approximate picture. Since GDP comparisons require a common currency base, exchange rate fluctuations and differing levels of inflation can also distort the position when comparing trends between individual countries.[7] Most measures of GDP make some allowance for these distortions in measuring 'real' GDP.

Once you have at least roughly comparative figures for GDP, an obvious first adjustment is to divide GDP by population to get a picture of average GDP per head, providing a broad first indicator of individual wealth. This figure needs to be adjusted again to allow for differences in prices between countries, using such measures as purchasing power parity.[8] An example of the impact of such adjustment to arrive at a more realistic assessment of purchasing power is shown in Figure 2.1.

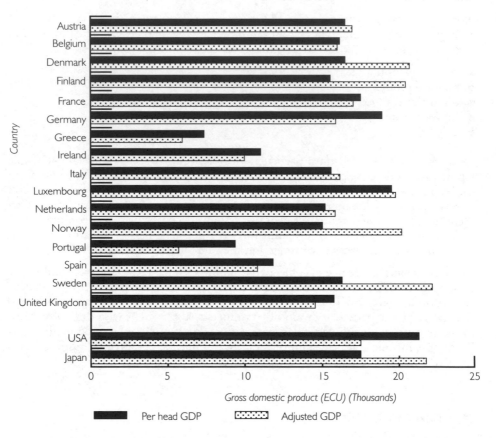

Figure 2.1   GDP per head and GDP per head adjusted for purchasing power, 1991 (Source: Eurostat)

This measurement of comparative potential consumer spending power is a helpful starting point, though it only provides a rough and potentially misleading national average. Behind that average is a much more complex picture of income distribution across differing social groups. As an example, adjusted GDP/head for a country like Egypt or India may suggest they are relatively unattractive markets, but there are nevertheless significant trade opportunities within the right segment. We will look at ways of segmenting the market later in the chapter.

The economic potential of a market is not, of course, a static phenomenon. Greater market potential will lie, on the whole, in those economies which are expanding. Measuring past GDP growth and likely trends will, again, suggest the most dynamic economies on which to concentrate attention. Figure 2.2 below illustrates average percentage growth rates in GDP over a five year period for selected EU and other countries. This may be compared with the GDP growth of 'emerging' markets shown in Chapter 7, pp. 172–3.

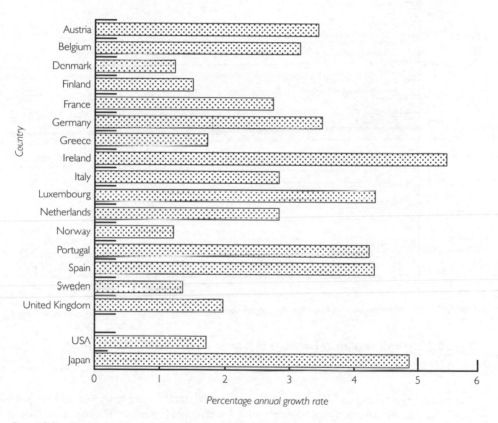

Figure 2.2   Economic growth across Europe, 1986–91 (Source: Eurostat)

A growing economy may not, of course, be a stable one. One measure of stability is a country's rate of inflation. A sustained high rate of inflation is a potential warning sign of economic instability, with a significant impact on consumer spending power and confidence, as well as on exchange rates. An overall rate lower than in the UK will tend to put pressure on a UK firm's price competitiveness, as its costs increase faster than those of its overseas market; whilst a higher rate may allow a firm some flexibility in relation to local competitors. Comparative inflation rates for selected counties are shown in Figure 2.3. As we will see in chapter 7, inflation is seen as one of the major problems in exporting to some Asian markets.

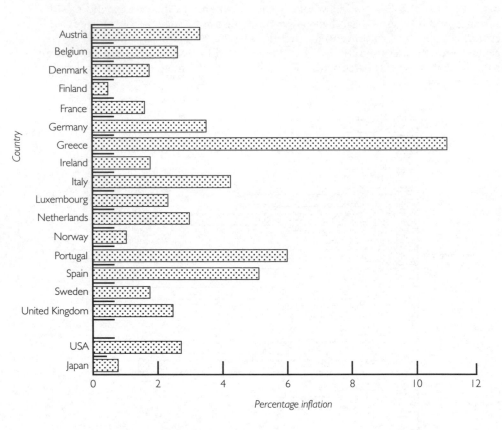

Figure 2.3   Inflation rates across Europe, 1994 (Source: The European, 13.5.94)

This trend needs also to be balanced against other trends – for instance, in exchange rates over time. An exchange rate moving in favour of sterling reduces purchasing power in a target market; one moving against sterling makes UK goods cheaper to import. Longer-term shifts in the exchange rate, and the degree of short-term volatility, may therefore have a major impact on price competitiveness. Companies whose competitive advantage does not lie in price leadership may be able to weather some instability, but most prefer reasonable stability in both these measures so that they can plan coherently in the longer term. More sophisticated analytical models will take a range of these and other measures into account in market assessment. They may look, for example, at such indices as the level of external debt and the scale of foreign currency reserves in assesing how far a country may be able to sustain import growth. Analysis of such micro-economic indicators as the balance of payments, and levels of savings and investment, also provide evidence of the degree of economic stability and potential for growth. These analyses will also look at how effectively governments are acting to control problems in the economy. More detailed models of this kind are discussed in chapter 7 on emerging markets.

Trends in unemployment may also provide a broad indication of levels of consumer spending and confidence, as Figure 2.4 shows. These trends may be compared with others such as changes in consumer prices. Unemployment may also be a useful indicator for a business looking to move production operations to a lower cost country, especially if combined with a relatively low GDP suggesting lower overall expectations and greater labour availability. This assessment will need to be balanced by the costs of employment imposed by government in working out overall labour costs. Vietnam and China, for example, are emerging as attractive sites for low-cost production with the added benefit of access to the Pacific Rim. In Mexico, labour costs are currently around a tenth of those in the States. Combined with Mexico's membership of NAFTA, this makes Mexico a potentially attractive base for developing wider export activity in the Americas.

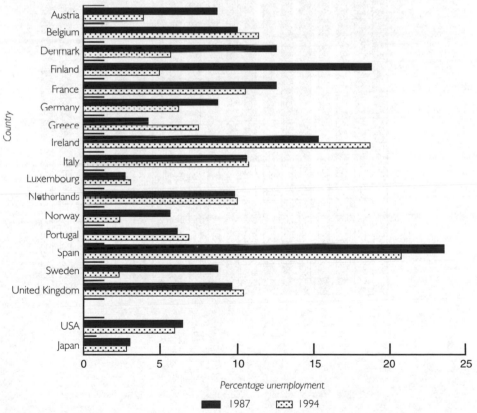

Figure 2.4   Unemployment in Europe, 1987 and 1994 (Source: Eurostat and The European, 13.5.94)

Once a firm has made an assesment of potential market attractiveness from broad indicators of this kind, it may try to pin down the potential of a specific market segment for its products or services. Many countries, for example, produce statistics on social classification which allow a business to begin to match its UK customer profile to those in overseas markets. In Poland, for example, European firms have recognised a generally weak market for consumer durables with often high levels of ownership and low incomes, but a rapidly-growing market for the right kind of western non-durables filling a vacuum of traditionally poor product choice. Ways of segmenting the American market are discussed in Chapter 9, for example. Other ways of segmenting markets include broad division by sector (whether primary, secondary or tertiary), or by particular industry.

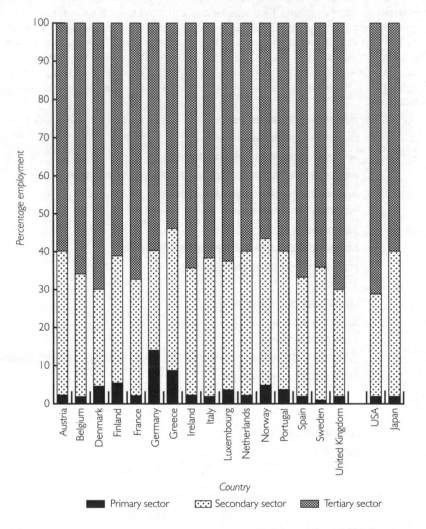

Figure 2.5   Economic structure in Europe by contribution to GDP (percentage) 1991 (Source: Eurostat)

A mature economy with a declining primary sector (agriculture, mining and other industries extracting raw materials), an increasingly specialised and diversified manufacturing (secondary) sector, and most growth in tertiary sectors such as retailing and services, will have very different needs from an economy still reliant on agriculture or 'heavy' industry. The size, structure and distribution of particular industries will provide some indicators both of potential market sizes for firms supplying goods and services for that sector, and of the possible level of competitive intensity for those in the same business.

Political profile and import orientation

Economic activity can only flourish in stable political conditions, so an assessment of the political situation is crucial. An obvious first problem is the threat of political instability, which may disrupt the operation of the market and threaten investment, especially for firms considering direct operations. It is not surprising that a 1993 survey by Price Waterhouse identified a stable political situation as a prerequisite for FDI. A recent example is Mexico where the revolt in one of its southern states in 1994 played a significant role in damaging confidence and in the resulting currency collapse at the end of 1994. Countries may be ranked according to various measures of the continuity of the political system and the degree of group opposition. In most cases firms may prefer to avoid the more extreme situations, unless they have considerable experience in that kind of market and can balance the level of risk against potential attractiveness of return.

A second political issue is the overall level of political involvement in economic activity and its impact on business opportunities. This involvement may include the overall scale of government apparatus and the tax burden it imposes on consumers; the amount of public ownership of industry and overall direction of economic activity; the extent of the State's social protection for its population (and its resulting impact on labour costs, for example); and how interventionist it is in regulating such commercially-significant areas as consumer safety, advertising, technical standards or environmental issues. Argentina, for example, still has complex labour hours and a protected labour market, complicating FDI. Exporters to Mexico traditionally faced a host of product standard regulations, rationalised in 1993 legislation. The significance of changing levels of government intervention for business in Britain, for instance, can be seen in a survey of UK small businesses between 1984 and 1991; this showed the level of taxation and government regulation and paperwork as accounting for 28% of the problems identified by managers in 1984, compared to just over 9% in 1991.[9]

As the Introduction indicated, governments have increasingly reduced the level of their intervention in their economics, for example by privatisation of state-run industries. This shift has generated significant export opportunities. In China, for example, liberalisation of the agricultural sector and increased independence for state enterprise combined with a lack of technical know-how and a backward infrastructure has resulted in a number of opportunities for European businesses in contributing to major capital projects.

A third political issue is a country's attitude to potential importers, whether hostile or welcoming. For 'emerging' markets in particular, the involvement of Western business in their country's economy is a highly sensitive issue, especially (though not exclusively) in those countries with a colonial heritage. There may be conflicting pressures on a government – on the one hand, to encourage the influx of capital, technology and expertise to boost the local economy, but on the other, to restrict foreign control over local enterprise, or perceived exploitation of the local workforce, or the transfer of profits out of the country. These pressures may have significant implications for a firm's choice between FDI and joint venture. In India and Brazil, for example, foreign investors have at various times been expected to form a joint venture with a local firm in which the latter must be the major equity-holding partner. Firms such as IBM have felt it necessary to alter their operations there as a result. In other countries, there are legal stipulations on the percentage of local labour that must be employed, and on local access to R and D activity.

Countries such as Canada and Australia, for example, have formal procedures for the official examination of all proposed inward foreign direct investment. These procedures require the investing firm to demonstrate in some considerable detail how its proposed operations will benefit the host economy. Even if the foreign firm is successful at this stage, it may face penalties when, after a few years, its proposals and forecasts are measured against actual performance. If it is considered to be exploiting the host nation without adequate compensatory contributions, then ultimately it can even be required to withdraw.

Even if some key economic indicators are favourable and the overall political situation stable, a potential export market may be undermined by various kinds of protectionism, whether tariffs or quotas, or by restrictions on income flows out of the country. Until recently, countries like Mexico and Brazil were typified by a vast array of restrictions and regulations. There were import vetos, tariffs and quotas, problems in obtaining import licences, an array of custom fees and taxes, restrictions on foreign investment and ownership, controlled exchange rates and a substantial amount of state intervention within business. As chapter six indicates, many of these barriers are now clustering around regional blocs with companies seeking to set up operations within those blocs to circumvent such barriers.

A firm will also need to be aware of the less visible potential barriers to trade – for example, the complexity and speed (or otherwise) of customs and other procedures and documentation – in assessing how quickly and easily it will be able to do business there. A 1987 BOTB survey identified delays in export documentation as a key problem in doing business orders. In Canada, for example, importers face not only federal duties and regulations but provincial government taxes and measures protecting local industry and consumer interests. Paperwork costs can be saved by using the facilities of the Simplification of International Trade Procedures Board (SITPRO), which has estimated that the saving may be as much as 50 per cent of such costs. Many of the problems of documentation and transport can be delegated to a specialist firm of freight forwarders. (This may be especially suitable for markets that are not likely to expand. Where growth is expected, the company often prefers to see the skills developed among its own staff.)

As discussed in the Introduction, many governments now see their role as facil rather than inhibitors of foreign investment. As an example, Korean companies such Daewoo have been attracted to set up operations in France and the UK partly in response to EU, national and regional incentives and help. They have also seen such investment as a way of circumventing EU tariffs to access a major regional market characterised by relatively high purchasing power and growth potential, and have been attracted by competitive labour costs and levels of skill.

Infrastructure

Even if there are no official barriers to import activity, a business may find its options severely limited by the institutions and networks which underpin economic activity. An obvious example is the quality and reliability of a market's transport network, or how developed or complex its retail distribution system is in getting goods to a particular target group of customers at the right time and cost, and in a way which will attract them. The Mexican market, for example, has traditionally been complicated by the small size of many retail outlets, requiring frequent and costly restocking of small quantities. While Japanese tariffs are lower than in the US or EU, exports have often been frustrated by the notorious complexity and cost of the Japanese distribution system, with its different levels of wholesaler, discussed in more detail in Chapter 10. In general, the quality of a country's communications infrastructure will be crucial to the speed and flexibility of setting up and running an export operation. As we saw in Chapter 1, communication issues are especially important in more complex kinds of operation such as FDI. A 1993 Price Waterhouse survey identified availability of telephone, fax and data lines as the single most important issue in planning FDI operations. Business in countries such as Argentina, Brazil or India is complicated by limitation in the communications network, though these very limitations themselves generate potential export opportunities for business in the transportation and communications sectors.

These issues are linked to such factors as population concentration and geography – whether consumers are grouped together in densely-populated urban centres, or scattered in small communities – and may have a profound impact on the feasibility, cost and speed of distribution. A difficult terrain, or physical barriers such as mountain ranges, may effectively segment one market into several. As an example, Canada may be divided into at least 5 regional markets, defined by geography, language, industrial structure, demographic profile, history and provincial legislation and policy.

Other key infrastructural issues include the sophistication of mechanisms for international banking transactions, and an appropriate legal structure to underpin contractual agreements with the appropriate bodies to enforce it. This latter issue is especially relevant in sensitive areas such as licensing or franchising. In Eastern Europe, for example, a 1993 EBRD survey identified infrastructural issues as the main element of risk for Western business, ranging from an efficient and regulated stock market, supported by an appropriately trained investment analyst and accounting profession able to value local business, to a properly-regulated framework for protecting investors.[10] Infrastructural issues are discussed in detail in Chapter 7 on emerging markets.

One essential, if less tangible, infrastructural requirement will be the willingness and

in a potential market to think and act commercially. An obvious
...usiness in Central and Eastern Europe, where societies are in deep
...ollectivist mentality, focused around the Communist Party and cen-
...wards an entrepreneurial, individualistic culture. Characteristics of
...re include a particular management concern with protecting the indi-
...n within the system; passing responsibility on in the chain of command;
...f elaborate 'old boy' networks behind the official system, focused around
fam..., ...contacts and patronage; and a widespread acceptance of corruption as part
of doing business. This is an issue which the chapters on emerging and Eastern European markets discuss in more detail.

Culture

Perhaps the most intangible element in assessing a potential market is its culture. However, it has been defined by some analysts as 'the single greatest barrier to business success',[11] and we will therefore consider it in particular depth here. The term itself is
difficult to define. It can, perhaps, be best understood as the shared beliefs of a group.
One of the most important pioneers of research in the area of management and
national culture, Geert Hofstede, defines culture as 'collective mental programming: it
is that part of our conditioning that we share with other members of our nation, region
or group, but not with other nations, regions or groups'.[12]

As this definition suggests, culture both operates on a multitude of levels and is defined
exclusively – it is concerned with values and beliefs unique to a group. Many people
think of culture first and foremost in terms of a *national* culture. The shared language,
political structures, historical memories and other features which may help to generate
a sense of national identity provide a powerful cultural force. However, cutting across
these kinds of cultural identity are others operating at the level of region, class, religion,
ethnicity, age or sex, or even at a supra-national level, generating a sense of (for example) European, Western, African or Muslim cultural identity. In some cultures, an
established sense of national identity may be in conflict with a growing awareness of
the need to think and act internationally, paradoxically encouraging an even stronger
nationalism within those resisting such a new identity. In others a sense of national culture may still be struggling to emerge from the culture of family, tribe or region.

The challenge for a company is to identify the range of cultures at work in its chosen
markets; to assess which may be most influential; and to identify points of intersection
with, and difference from, the cultures in which it is accustomed to operate. The
dilemma is that many aspects of culture are unstated and unconscious assumptions
within a group. Since they are by definition unique to that group, identifying them
becomes especially difficult. The picture is complicated further by mutual stereotyping
between differing groups, especially at national level. We all carry around images of
other nationalities which distort our reading of their behaviour, and vice versa. Unfamiliar behaviour tends to reinforce these stereotypes. One of the first things we need to
do is to recognise this process, and seek to analyse cultural difference more objectively.

The need for firms to understand cultural differences is threefold:

- An appreciation of the cultures at work within a potential market segment enables a company to assess customer expectations and aspirations more fully against the proposition it is offering to the market.
- Such an understanding allows the company to frame its message to a chosen market segment much more appropriately and effectively.
- Finally, a knowledge of the cultures at work will provide an insight into the issues and problems of operating in that market, and will provide a greater opportunity for a successful collaboration with potential partners.

Not all these elements will be of equal importance. A firm seeking to export a pioneering piece of labour-saving machinery to overseas manufacturers may need to concentrate mostly on the last element, though it would still be well advised to pay attention to the first two in raising the speed and scale of its market penetration. One which is exporting consumer goods in a highly competitive market will need to concentrate on all three to maximise its chances of success.

The scale of the challenge will also be related to the cultural 'distance' of the market. For a European firm such distance will be measured, for example, by how much the target market may draw from and identify with a European or Western cultural tradition. Later in this section, we will look at a range of models for assessing cultural distance. However, even those cultures which seem close, for instance American or Canadian, repay careful analysis to pick up the potential range of customer and supplier responses to a firm's products and the way they are presented. A misreading of those responses led, for example, to the setting up – and subsequent failure to perform – of a range of Marks and Spencer stores in the North American market (see Chapter 9).

In deciding how they approach cultural issues, firms may be divided into various types. They can try to treat the world as a homogeneous market place, decline to adapt their products or strategies for foreign markets, and operate and sell in just the same way as at home. Such firms are called 'ethnocentric', and can be successful in some circumstances: companies such as Coca Cola, Pepsi, McDonald's and American Express have generated powerful international brands that deliberately transcend national boundaries. At the other extreme, firms can adapt to foreign markets to such an extent that they lose any discernible national bias. Between these 'geocentric' firms and the 'ethnocentric' approach lie the majority of 'polycentric' firms, which retain a core cultural identity, but seek to adapt it to other cultures.

Cultural models

Most businesses, even those able to exploit an 'ethnocentric' approach as a powerful marketing tool, are well advised to be aware of the cultural dynamics of overseas markets if they are to avoid potential marketing disasters or compromising effective business operations in that market. Analysts of culture have developed a range of models to isolate distinctive cultural types. The pioneering work of Geert Hofstede suggested four key determinants of culture:

- Individualism versus collectivism
- Large versus small power distance
- Strong versus weak uncertainty avoidance

● Masculinity versus femininity.

In the first, Hofstede contrasted national cultures in countries such as Australia, the USA or the UK, where a premium is placed on individual self-expression and initiative, with those such as Japan, Pakistan or Ecuador where group identity and loyalty are seen to be more important.[13] 'Power distance' seeks to measure the degree of inequality and hierarchy in a society, whilst 'uncertainty avoidance' suggests the level of tolerance for uncertainty and lack of control over events, suggesting a more relaxed, fatalistic approach to life. Plotting power distance against uncertainty avoidance reveals that Latin and Mediterranean countries score high over countries like Great Britain, Denmark or Sweden, with the USA and Norway in the middle.

The final dimension measures the relative status and division of labour between the sexes, and the consequent emphasis on masculine or feminine values within a culture. Masculine societies are seen as more aggressive, and more concerned with establishing and protecting power and status. Of the 50 countries he considered, Hofstede classified Japan, Australia and Latin American countries as most masculine, while the Scandinavian countries were amongst the most feminine.

Hofstede's work may be compared with more recent research, such as that by Hampden-Turner and Trompenaars in their *The Seven Cultures of Capitalism*.[14] They identify seven 'fundamental' valuing processes crucial to wealth creation, each with a set of contrasting directions. Managers need to choose between these contrasting paths in the way they set about business – choices influenced by the broader culture in which they operate. These valuing processes and the 'dilemmas' they create are summarised below.

Valuing process	Dilemma
Making rules and discovering exceptions	Universalism v. particularism
Constructing and deconstructing	Analysing v. integration
Managing communities of individuals	Individualism v. communitarianism
Internalising the outside world	Inner-directed v. outer-directed orientation
Synchronising fast processes	Time as sequence v. time as synchronisation (speed v. co-ordination)
Achieved status v. ascribed status	Choosing amongst achievers
Sponsoring equal opportunities to excel	Equality v. hierarchy

This model was used to create a questionnaire testing managers on which direction they would take, given any of these dilemmas; it was then tested on managers in seven differing countries to see whether different national cultures influenced management styles. The model mirrors some of the key issues identified by Hofstede, most obviously in the dilemma of individualism versus group loyalty, and questions of hierarchy and status. It also picks up and develops Hofstede's emphasis on tensions between a rule-bound culture concerned with certainty and integration, and one more concerned with uncertainty, adaptability and coping with the exceptional.

> ✎   CASE STUDY
> Culture clash at CMB Packaging
>
> CMB Packaging was formed in 1989 as an Anglo-French merger of the old Metal Box Company and Carnaud. On the surface there were good reasons to be optimistic about the merger, which was worth about £800m. The packaging industry was fragmented and facing increased concentration in its major buyer industries of consumer goods and food. Mergers had already occurred in packaging and appeared to be relatively successful. The two companies' activities seemed fairly complementary. Carnaud was strong in France, Germany, Italy and Spain, while Metal Box was the leader of the UK market with some Italian activities.
>
> In the event the real world interfered with the vision and highlighted differences in management philosophy. Although this is a common problem even with mergers in the same country, many of the problems could be traced back to cross-country differences. At the top level the president, Jean-Marie Descarpentries, was described as 'flamboyant, a showman, an archetypal Frenchman full of French management school ideas, like the inverted pyramid with customers at the top and management at the bottom'. By contrast, the old Metal Box group operated with a typical British, top-down, centralised management approach. This clash of cultures at the top led to indecision about the company's strategy and organisation. This in turn led to declining performance.
>
> The conclusion drawn by many people was that perhaps this friendly type of merger is the most dangerous form of cross-European co-operation – particularly if there are significant differences in management style. Unfortunately, management styles are different throughout Europe and present a challenge to European corporate integration. They vary from the authoritarian Italian *padrone* to Germany's consensus approach. If cultures clash, perhaps the best way forward is either through outright takeover – where one culture triumphs over another – or, if this is impractical, through a looser and simpler form of co-operation.
>
> Source: *The Times*, 12.9.91

The work of anthropologists and sociologists like Hofstede, Hampden-Turner and Trompenaars may be criticised on various grounds. Their models can only go so far in pinning down the complex mix of cultural forces, of which national culture is only one, which influence any one individual manager or market segment. As we have suggested, a national culture is itself often a hotly contested area, differently constructed, subscribed to and interpreted by cultural sub-groups, making generalisation and prediction very difficult. Hampden-Turner and Trompenaars, for example, have been criticised for failing to match their model satisfactorily to the actual responses of managers and basing some of their conclusions on differing, more subjective assumptions and observations. The principal value of their model is in providing a framework for identifying potential points of cultural difference, and suggesting some of the attitudes which may underlie them. Whilst such models have significant empirical limitations, they are an invaluable starting point.

Applying cultural analysis in business – the case of Japan

As we have seen, a key issue for any company considering overseas markets is an assessment of the potential degree of cultural 'distance' in a target market, and its implications for doing business successfully, especially in countries where such a distance is clearly considerable. Perhaps the most obvious examples are such Asian cultures as Japan or China. How can we use cultural models to measure and assess such distance?

One clearly relevant dichotomy is that between individualism and group loyalty. Western culture has traditionally placed a premium on individual self-expression and achievement. In business, this has found its expression in such phenomena as a pioneering entrepreneurial tradition with a high proportion of new product development centred in countries like the US or the UK; and in a relatively high level of mobility between and within companies. In contrast, a high premium is placed on the group in many Asian societies. In Japan, for example, an individual's identity and social status is determined as much by a sense of belonging to (and the standing of) the group of which he or she is a member, as by his or her individual performance and achievement. Companies themselves are a major focus for such identity and status.

As a result, Japanese businesses are characterised by such features as continuity of employment and a high degree of group co-operation, both within the company and between business partners. Teamwork is driven by the desire to improve the standing of the group, whether it be a quality circle on the shopfloor or the company as a whole. Group loyalty also points to a concern with consensus and harmony, rather more than with conflict and individuality, with an accompanying premium on politeness and with thorough preparation and reflection by the group as a whole, more than with speed and adaptability. This group loyalty is also associated with other cultural factors. As a traditionally 'masculine' society, the Japanese place a considerable emphasis on achieving and maintaining status, and confer respect on age and seniority. 'Face', with its connotations of standing, reputation, authority and honour, is a particularly important and complex concept in the East.

In their classic analysis of these two types of cultures, Ouchi and Jaeger contrast in the table below some of the characteristics of these models:

Type A (for American)	Type J (for Japanese)
Short-term employment	Lifetime employment
Individual decision-making	Consensual decision-making
Individual responsibility	Collective responsibility
Rapid evaluation and promotion	Slow evaluation and promotion
Explicit, formalised control	Implicit, informal control
Specialised career path	Non-specialised career path
Segmented concern	Holistic concern

If we try to distinguish the three main values which divide these cultural models, they are the following:

Type A (for American)	Type J (for Japanese)
Be independent	Be dependent
Truth has a value	Truth destroys harmony
Take responsibility	Do not take responsibility

Reading from these models helps one to understand better the rules for successful business dealings with the Japanese. Some of these have been summarised as follows:

- Never put a Japanese in a position where he can be embarrassed or helpless.
- Lean towards modesty and humility about your product or your service; let your advertising literature present your virtues.
- Understand the concept of 'face', and don't be afraid to use it to your advantage in negotiations when it is true and warranted.
- Respect seniority and age.
- Harmony is a key word. The concept of *wa* is one of the most important things in the Japanese cultural understanding of social relationships. *Wa* means calmness; a reconciling of conflict.
- Have patience. It is said that Americans think in terms of days, weeks and months, and the Japanese think in terms of years and decades.
- Gift-giving is a must and has its own rules, including special rules concerning the value of the gift, and the colour and the way of packaging.
- Entertainment with the Japanese is a part of their way of doing business. The main purpose is to bond friendships.
- 'Yes' does not necessarily mean 'yes'.
- Don't be disturbed by periods of silence or by lack of direct eye contact.
- Proper behaviour – from dress, to dining, to decision making – is the cardinal rule in all relationships.
- Avoid fixed schedules. The Japanese may use this as a negotiating weapon against you. It is far better to be flexible and open to change.

Japanese attitudes to such issues as employment and decision-making in business, and Japanese aspirations as consumers, are discussed in more detail in Chapter 10, which focuses on doing business in Japan. Later in this chapter, and in subsequent chapters, we will look in more detail at ways of applying these models in other contexts, as part of a business export strategy. In Chapter 5, for example, we will see that companies exporting to Germany were careful to make cultural analysis an important element of their marketing strategy, recognising the relative formality, consensus and punctuality of German business culture and the importance of deferring to national sensibilities by using German despite the prevalence of English speakers (a theme we discuss in the next section).

Language and communication

As the brief summary of some of the rules for doing business in Japan indicates, communication involves far more than language. In a meeting between two people, age, sex, appearance, ethnicity, body language, punctuality, surroundings, the exchange of presents, even certain colours or accents, all communicate messages which may alter, and even swamp, verbal communication.

However, language remains a key characteristic of a culture. It provides a structure through which the world can be described, and the nature of that structure both reflects and shapes the concerns of a group speaking a particular language. Indeed, as a form of cultural expression, it can be a sensitive political issue. Speaking English to a member of the Canadian French community, where there is strong pressure for independence from Canada, for example, or French to a member of the Flemish community in Belgium, may undermine one's credibility from the start.

Non-verbal communication: the cultural significance of colour

- In the Orient, yellow is considered an imperial colour, suggesting grandeur and mystery
- White is right for brides in Europe and in the US, but not in India, where red or yellow is used. White is the colour of funerals in Japan.
- Green has been the nationalist colour of Egypt, and should not be used in that country for packaging. The French, Dutch and Swedes associate green with cosmetics and toiletries. In Malaysia, consumers complained about a green product because it was associated with the jungle and disease.
- Purple is an aristocratic colour in the West and Japan, for example, but a colour for funerals in Burma.

Learning a language is not, therefore, merely a way of speeding up communication by dispensing with the need for an interpreter. It is both an act of respect for a culture and a means of entry to it. It allows broader access to the local population, and opportunity to pick up the nuances which define cultural difference and articulate the differing models on which they are based. The failure to do so not only potentially reduces one's access to, and acceptance by, a different cultural grouping; it can, at the simplest level, lead to some classic translation blunders as the following examples illustrate.

- Ford experienced slow sales when it introduced a car in Mexico under the name of Cholent. Only later did Ford discover that *cholent* is slang for 'streetwalker' in Mexico; the name was changed to Comet.
- An American hosiery company tried to tell a Spanish audience that anyone who didn't wear its brand of hosiery just 'wouldn't have a leg to stand on'. When translated, the copy said the wearer would 'only have one leg'.
- An American company marketing tomato paste tried to market it in the Middle East – only to learn that in Arabic, the term 'tomato paste' translates into 'tomato glue'.
- The Sunbeam Corporation used the English words for its 'Mist-Stick' mist-producing hair-curling iron when it entered the German market, only to discover after an expensive advertising campaign that *mist* means 'excrement' in German.
- When promoting a car in Belgium, General Motors intended the advertisement to state that the car had a 'body by Fisher' (Fisher is GM's auto-body pressing operation). Instead, the phrase was translated into Flemish as 'corpse by Fisher'.

Although the most widely spoken language in the business world remains English, the significance of learning other languages is increasingly being recognised by British business. Whilst Chinese remains the mother tongue of the largest number of the world's people, followed by English, Hindi and Russian, the most significant languages for business are French, Spanish and Chinese.

Managing cultural communication

It is likely that many companies new to international business may be wary of markets with an obvious cultural distance, of which language may be a part. However, there is a range of ways of off-setting the obstacles.

The first and most important is an awareness of their existence, and the potential issues involved. It is here that models of cultural difference have a valuable role to play. The second is the use of intermediaries with experience of the market to help plan and support any initial contact. As we shall see in the next section, there are many people – from other companies with experience in the field to local Chambers of Commerce, agents and Embassy staff – able to offer advice and support in achieving this initial step. Careful research and preparation of the first move is likely to be critical in laying the foundations for a future relationship.

For firms with a long-term commitment to an overseas market, one source of such support is the joint venture. Whether as a main strategy, or a prelude to takeover, joint ventures allow direct access to local expertise and contacts in managing cultural adaptation and acceptance. On the other hand, the relationship of the two joint-venture partners may itself fall victim to the tensions of cultural distance. This may be a factor in the higher than average failure rate of Japanese joint ventures with American companies.

Once a business has established itself overseas, it faces the potential problem of the ongoing management of its foreign operations. If this requires particularly regular supervision, the question then arises of whether the manager should be from the home country, or from the market in which the business is operating. Either choice has advantages and disadvantages. Transferring a manager from a unit in the home country should mean that the overseas operation is being steered by someone who is very familiar with the company and its culture.

Conversely, the host country manager will be familiar with the business culture within which the 'foreign' unit must operate. However, the empirical evidence suggests that the newly recruited host country manager tends, initially, to be more loyal to his or her country than to the company. International firms need to consider what potentially sensitive roles and information they offer these managers during the period before they become corporate personnel, and to monitor their performance carefully to ensure it remains focused on company objectives. The evidence suggests that it takes about two years before locally recruited managers switch their main allegiance from the host country/government to the company.

Most international firms find it desirable to move their own nationals from one country to another at some stage in their careers, so that they can acquire greater experience of the firm's operations. Some people are better at adapting to foreign cultures than others, and firms must strive to make correct decisions on who they send where, for mistakes can be very expensive. Copeland and Griggs have estimated that the direct costs to US firms of failed expatriate assignments is over $2 billion a year[15]. Unsuccessful managers overseas can ruin the reputation of the company in that country in a way that is not easily retrievable. The managers themselves may suffer loss of confidence due to an inappropriate overseas posting, and might not regain their previous level of competence even after some years back in familiar surroundings.

Cross-cultural adjustment has been studied for at least the last thirty years. Many studies have either directly or indirectly tried to identify the personality characteristics that appear to be associated with successful adaptation to a foreign culture. What follows is a synthesis of the main personality characteristics for successful adaptation, as identified by numerous research projects:

- outlook geocentric, rather than ethnocentric
- tolerance of ambiguity and failure
- self-effacement
- flexibility in approach and in choice of objectives
- an open-minded, non-judgmental view of life
- empathy
- good communication skills (ideally including a facility with foreign languages – although, interestingly, this facility is not as important as many of the other characteristics)
- self-reliance
- sense of humour.

One thing is clear: this is not the typical profile of the successful, entrepreneurial, target-achieving executive. Our successful adapter to foreign cultures is much more relaxed, philosophical and socially orientated. If someone like this already exists in the firm, he or she is likely to be in the personnel department, rather than head of production or marketing. Mr or Ms Adapter may well integrate quickly and establish good personal relationships with business colleagues and officials in the foreign environment, but will they achieve the company's desired sales targets? Even if they are already employed at some level within the company, can you send them to represent the company abroad? In Europe (and Japan) it is thought necessary to send your most able personnel to the foreign location, and they must be more able than the local managers if they are to gain acceptance.

IBM strive to resolve this paradox by sending two managers abroad where previously they sent one. They send both Mr or Ms Adapter *and* a more traditional executive. The former makes all the contacts and consults with the foreign counterparts, while the latter's functions are to see that IBM's targets are met for that subsidiary. Most firms would find this too bureaucratic; an alternative approach would be to try and select from suitably experienced and qualified personnel, and then provide training to increase the likelihood of successful adaptation.

Clearly, one of the main objectives of a training course would be to eliminate, or at least reduce, the risk of culture shock by preparing the subject for the specific nature of the overseas experience. Other objectives of the training course are likely to include development of:

- a capacity to adapt to local conditions quickly, and integrate with the local community
- a sympathetic appreciation of the host culture and characteristics of the indigenous population.
- a good knowledge of the local business culture
- a good knowledge of the specifics of the post, and improved potential to fulfil the responsibilities effectively.

The amount of time that needs to be spent on training will vary with the circumstances, including the previous experience of the individual and the duration of the overseas contract. Most contracts for foreign posts are between three and five years. It is hard to imagine that much would be achieved in a course lasting less than one week, and such a pre-departure course should be reinforced with in-country training/briefing sessions.

Research into cross-cultural postings and training tends to support the view that the typical experience takes the form of a 'U' curve. That is to say, expatriates' morale is at a high point on arrival, as they are stimulated by the prospects of a new job in a different environment. After six months or so, morale plummets to rock bottom (the bottom of the 'U' curve) as they realise that they are unable to achieve everything they set out to achieve, and that the amount of adaptation required from them is greater than they at first realised. Once they have reached this realisation, morale improves, and they are once more stimulated by the challenges involved, but with a more realistic sense of what they can achieve and the methods that must be adopted in order to succeed.

There is some evidence to suggest that when the expatriate manager is married, the 'other half' also experiences a 'U' curve in morale, but the cycle of highs and lows is out of phase with their partner's. It is important, where there are families to consider, that they too receive training and have realistic expectations. American multinationals are said to provide the least attention to the selection and training of personnel for foreign appointments. They have the highest failure rate, and in some 70% of cases the cause for early termination of a foreign posting is the unhappiness of the partner, rather than the firm's employee.

Taking the first step

There is a range of sources and bodies to which firms can turn in exploring potential overseas markets. It is possible to distinguish three types of information source. The first is information a business can gather itself in constructing a profile of a potential target market. The second is sources of advice on locating and interpreting that information. Finally, there are contacts with experience of the practical issues involved in doing business in a particular market; these can help the business plan its first step, link it up to potential distributors or clients, for example, and provide support services such as legal help in drawing up agreements or assistance with export documentation.

Initial information on potential markets may be gleaned from the press. Newspapers like the *Financial Times* and magazines such as *The Economist* or *European Business* often carry profiles of particular countries. They also issue more detailed reports which are available via the local library, TEC or Chamber of Commerce, for example.

If your initial focus is on market opportunities in the EU, you can consult the EU's own statistical service, Eurostat. Eurostat publications will be available in larger public libraries or Chambers of Commerce, for example, and include summaries such as *Basic Statistics of the Community* and *Europe in Figures*, together with more detailed surveys such as *Portrait of Regions* in three volumes. The EU also has much of its information on database: for example, *Tenders Electronic Daily* which advertises large public sector contracts. A firm's research into Europe using these and other sources can also be assisted by the 22 European Information Centres (EICs) sponsored by the EU in the UK, often located within the local TECs or Chambers of Commerce. Their staff have access to a wide range of material, and can provide advice on an appropriate research strategy.

EICs provide information on EU grants for small business activity. They are also likely to have access to, and to be able to advise the company on, the wealth of commercially-produced material available for markets within and beyond Europe. One of the most useful for Europe as a whole (including the EU) is *Euromonitor*, which records annual consumption and spending levels for many different types of product, together with an assessment of past and future market trends. Centres usually also have access to the range of business directories available, including the Kompass series which provides directories for each country, giving details on types of products and the companies which manufacture them. They can provide helpful information on potential competitors, suppliers or joint-venture partners.

Chambers of Commerce also have access to networks such as BC-NET (Business Co-operation Network), a computerised business 'dating agency' which links businesses seeking potential suppliers, distributors or partners. In assessing such information beyond Europe, firms can make use of Export Development Advisors within Chambers of Commerce, who work with individual clients in focusing on key issues and undertaking some of the research. In the Labelking case study in Chapter 1, we saw how an Export Development Advisor from the London Chamber of Commerce was able to assist the company in ideas and information for developing an export strategy for the French, Spanish and American markets. Many Chambers of Commerce and TECs undertake their own export initiatives, including sponsorship of overseas trade missions. The British Overseas Trade Board has Area Advisory Groups made up of business people with experience in individual countries.

The DTI has a wealth of material for use by business, including its own database, Spearhead, and guides to individual countries and regions and to other sources of information a business can access. These support materials are provided by its Export Market Information Centre, the Single Market Unit (for the EU), and individual country desks in London; and also through its regional officers and support for similar centres in TECs. The DTI backs up this information by offering a free business review to companies on a possible export strategy, and can subsidise strategy development costs. It also sponsors opportunities to link companies with potential partners and customers through trade fairs, seminars and inward missions bringing foreign buyers together with potential UK suppliers.

✎   CASE STUDY
'A target for first-time exporters'
In February 1995, *Overseas Trade* reported that the DTI's Business in Europe branch had launched a campaign entitled 'Begin in BENELUX'. Primarily aimed at first-time exporters, it would encourage more experienced firms to look again at Britain's third largest market. The campaign, which would continue into 1996, would begin with 20 events – mostly briefings – held throughout the UK between March and June.

In September, the campaign would move into the BENELUX markets, staging at least 20 on-the-spot events, running through to summer 1996. 'Old and new hands alike can count on the help and advice of the two Export Promoters who have been seconded from industry to help firms with presentation of products and services and how to make a successful approach to the market. They are available to answer questions, visit companies and follow through.

Emphasis on the 'Begin in BENELUX' campaign, said *Overseas Trade*, would be on the practicalities of doing business there. All the briefings would be chaired by Mike Rose, Chairman of the DTI's BENELUX country group, who had 30 years experience in exporting to BENELUX countries.

At each briefing, both Export Promoters would speak on how to do business in their respective markets, and there would be case studies showing how a local company broke into each market. Seminars would also feature an 'all you need to get started' section with questions from delegates.

Source: *Overseas Trade*, February 1995

If the DTI can help get a business started, the commercial section of relevant British Embassies can take it further into a specific market. Such services as the Overseas Status Report Service and the Export Representative Service help to profile markets and locate potential distributors; and commercial sections can also assist in promoting new products.

It is not surprising that material from embassies of potential target countries should be treated with some caution – their interest is likely to be in attracting the right kind of investment, rather than encouraging competition with their indigenous businesses. However, if you are considering a possible joint venture or form of FDI, embassies and foreign ministries may be a useful source of information on grants and other forms of incentive.

Apart from official bodies of this kind, many UK and overseas banks now provide a good deal of free information and support, especially for smaller businesses. As an example, NatWest produces a monthly 'lonely hearts' *International Trade Bulletin* where exporters and importers from all over the world advertise their requirements. It also operates its own database, Pharos, which allows a company to assess the European law relevant to its operations. The larger management consultancies and accountants can provide similar assistance, ranging from market intelligence to handling some of the administration in export dealings. Trade Associations can also provide specific information on product opportunities in particular industries. Some of these sources are summarised in figure 2.6 overleaf.

There are also a number of commercial organisations that now specialise in providing firms with a range of support services to help them capitalise on export opportunities. They provide expertise in spotting opportunities, establishing potential contracts and undertaking some of the administration. One firm providing support for the Chinese market is discussed below.

CASE STUDY
Magpie Trading Company
For smaller firms seeking new markets, China is simultaneously hugely inviting – and terribly intimidating. Its fast-growing economy and vast population should be full of opportunities for ambitious British firms, but a lack of understanding about

the country and how it works daunts many trying to sell there.

Terry Tsakok has the inside story, and he is building it into a thriving business. His Magpie Trading Company started off by selling Chinese goods in Britain, but now he has reversed the process and is helping UK companies to sell to China. His customers range from small private companies to giants such as Scottish & Newcastle and Inver House Distillers.

Terry began to move into consultancy in 1991. China's new private enterprises wanted to buy UK goods for the flourishing domestic market. A number of UK companies wanted to do business in China, but they needed advice and help which Magpie could provide. Terry hired consultants in Beijing, Hong Kong, Chengdu (the capital of Sichuan province) and Shenzhen to provide a skilled marketing network. The first orders for the UK were for office lifts, followed by back-up batteries for telecommunications equipment. These were made by Chloride, which then negotiated a deal to sell battery-making equipment.

Magpie began actively to seek out British companies whose products were needed in China, charging a 5% commission. Success fees reached £50,000 on one occasion. In 1992 it succeeded in arranging the distribution of Inver House whisky and gin under the Embassy Club label, and around 500,000 bottles have been sold so far. This was followed by a straight import deal with Scottish & Newcastle. The brewer was looking for a Chinese distributor to organise the marketing of its brown ale in China, and Magpie arranged for the beer to be sold at Western Hotels and top restaurants. Negotiations are currently under way between S&N and Peking Brewery to brew the beer locally.

But not all the companies seeking business are blue-chip groups. Magpie helped the medium-sized Ormerod Diesels company to sell reconditioned diesel generators to Chinese companies.

In the financial year to August 1994, Magpie made fees of about £150,000 and profits of around £30,000, compared with break-even on fees of £55,000 in 1993. Fee income was expected to top £200,000 in 1995. In early 1995 the company had five staff in the UK and eight in China, including two part-timers, and projects were getting bigger; the firm was involved in plans to raise £50 million to finance construction of a Hilton hotel.

Terry believes there are plenty of opportunities for smaller firms to benefit from China's growth. His tips are:

- Invest in up-to-date information.
- Products must be correctly priced and meet local safety standards.
- Examine all marketing and distribution options.
- Use an agent. The majority operate from Hong Kong, and it is best to negotiate a success fee rather than pay a daily rate.
- Trade missions can be effective.

Source: *Financial Mail on Sunday*, 5.2.95

Finally, agents, franchisees/licensees and FDI partners can be an invaluable source of market information and contacts. A key issue is the correct choice of such a partner, and it is here that some prior knowledge of a market and the key issues involved in selling there is essential. In China, for example, the right contacts within relevant central and provincial government departments may be crucial to exploiting official contracts. In Mexico, regional differences are very strong, and a business may require more than one agent. It will need to satisfy itself that an agent can deal with the complexities of the distribution system in the Mexican market, for example.

Stage	Need	Facility/Scheme	Source
1. Preparation for export	Market research	➤ Export Marketing Research Scheme ➤ Export Data Services ➤ Market Information Enquiry Service ➤ Country desks	DTI
	Assessment of whether company is capable of exporting, e.g. is production capacity or cashflow sufficient?	➤ Free business review Subsidised consultancy 5–15 days if <500 employees ➤ Export Development Advisors ➤ Cash flow advice	DTI Chambers of Commerce Banks
	Information about licences, regulations and standards, etc.	➤ Technical help to exporters ➤ Information	DTI Chambers of Commerce Industry organisations
2. Finding and serving customers	Finding customers directly a. Public relations	➤ New Products From Britain	DTI and British Embassies
	b. Meeting potential customers	➤ Inward Trade Missions ➤ Outward Trade Missions (not DTI) ➤ Trade Fairs (financial help, free advice) ➤ Shop window for UK products ➤ Seminar support	DTI TECs Employer/ Industry organisations Chambers of Commerce Banks
	Finding an agent	➤ Export Representative Service ➤ Overseas Status Report Service	DTI and British Embassies
	Teaming up with local companies in a target market	➤ European Economic Interest Grouping ➤ Exporter/importer matching	EU e.g. NatWest and London Chamber of Commerce
	Translation	➤ Finding a translator	Chambers of Commerce
	Organising direct mail operation	➤ Help and advice with selling by direct mail methods	Royal Mail International
3. Administration and finance	Credit insurance	➤ Insurance against not getting paid	Export Credit Guarantee Department
	Transport	➤ Delivery and clearance through customs	Freight forwarders

Financial services	➤ Currency transactions/transfers	Banks
Meeting different VAT rules for EU transactions	➤ Information and advice	Customs and Excise
Documentation	➤ Ensuring goods do not get held up at borders because of incorrectly filled in forms	Simplification of Trade Procedures Board (SITPRO)
	➤ Free telephone advice	DTI

Figure 2.6   Summary of support services in planning an export strategy

Summary

As the Introduction suggested, the international economic climate is becoming ever more demanding for business. These pressures mean that a more planned, proactive approach to doing international business is becoming more important in achieving export success. Business will find it increasingly unsatisfactory to abdicate responsibility and wait for an outside approach or to expect an outside agency to do all the work for them.

The more dynamic business will, therefore, use the range of skills and sources of help outlined in this chapter to build an export strategy of its own. As an example, let's take the example of the Chinese market mentioned in the preceding case study. Some key economic indicators are outlined in Chapter 7 on emerging markets (pp. 184–90). These suggest a recent slowing down in GDP growth, a significant rise in inflation and a currency under some pressure. Combining this with other factors, such as a shortage of hard currency, high unemployment, a relatively poor infrastructure and weak copyright legislation, suggests a difficult consumer market, despite a population of 1.3 billion. On the other hand, continuing investment in the infrastructure and a deregulated agricultural sector, for example, has created opportunities for involvement in capital projects in this and other sectors, and it is here that a business might begin.

Now, try out your skills in identifying market opportunities, and test your understanding of possible cultural problems, by reading the following case studies and answering the questions that follow them.

✎   CASE STUDY

Looking overseas

Hetherington's is a Yorkshire-based company which has built a successful UK business in prefabricated farm buildings, from grain stores to milking parlours. Traditionally, it has catered for small to middle-sized farms, emphasising cost, speed of delivery and construction, and the ability to customise. The firm is now looking for the first time at overseas markets. Given its current competitive mix and transportation costs, the managing director feels that a joint venture or even a small subsidiary could be worth exploring, providing labour and raw material costs are right. At various times the French, German and Spanish markets have been mentioned as possibilities.

The managing director has asked you to provide an initial assessment of those markets. She has also mentioned two possible candidates for setting up any initial arrangements: Jim Morrison, the deputy production manager; and Jane Harris, the young, newly-appointed marketing manager. Jim, married with two grown-up children, is described as aimable and thorough, but not very dynamic. Jane, who has just bought a house with her partner, has a reputation for being very adaptable, forceful and decisive.

Questions for discussion

1 Using the information in this chapter, provide an initial assessment of the three markets the managing director has mentioned. What others might be suitable? In considering your options, look at the analysis of individual countries in Chapter 7 on emerging markets. Which of these might Hetherington's consider?

2 Describe the limitations of your assessment, and other information you may require.

3 Outline a possible research strategy for acquiring the information you need, including finding the names of potential partners.

4 Assess the problems either Jane or Jim might face in any secondment overseas, and how they might cope with them.

CASE STUDY
An Asian in Texas

Wu Ping Wong, a Korean national, had recently arrived in Dallas, Texas on a six-month secondment to the head office of a large US multinational corporation, Texas Wings, by whom he was employed in Korea. He had now completed two months of his secondment and was confiding his work problems to a colleague, Sun Ye Tsing.

Wu explained that his problems started during his first week of employment in Dallas, when several American colleagues had separately suggested that they should meet up at the weekend. Wu had accepted the first offer and reluctantly refused the other proposals. This he had done with great difficulty, and wherever possible tried to avoid meeting these colleagues during the rest of the week to avoid their embarrassment. He had then waited in his hotel room all weekend awaiting a phone call. Alas, none came; and then on the Monday he discovered that the American colleague for whom he waited had been out of town on a long-standing appointment. This made Wu feel even more insecure with his other colleagues whose invitations he had refused. Although he had been advised that Americans were informal, he had not been prepared for this snub.

During the following week he was asked to make a presentation on the sales prospects for the company's major product line in Korea. He had therefore spent several days working until the early hours of the morning, collecting information, analysing sales statistics, researching competitors and producing a report. At the presentation, he was initially questioned about why there had been no documentation circulated beforehand; and then constantly interrupted by all the employees present, whatever their position in the company, about the accuracy of his statistics, the extent of his knowledge and the basis of his analysis. He felt that this detracted from his presentation. He was also concerned that no one was willing to remain behind after the meeting to continue the discussion of the points that he had been unable to elaborate fully.

Feeling very dejected, he returned to his hotel room determined to announce the following day that he intended to return to Korea. He was therefore greatly surprised the following day to be complemented upon the thoroughness of his presentation, and to be told that the managers were hoping to put some of his proposals into action!

The latest difficulty for Wu had arisen only the previous week. Two weeks earlier his superior, Tex Peterson, had asked him to undertake some market research on the estimated demand for a new product range in the Pacific Rim countries. Wu believed that the potential demand for this product was small, but was determined to produce a well-researched report to back his views. Such a report, Wu believed, would normally require four weeks to complete. When asked by Tex when he could produce the report, Wu was naturally reluctant to give a date, and instead asked Tex when he would need to have it. Feeling most frustrated, Tex demanded the report for the following week, a date Wu felt unable to refuse.

Wu once again spent long hours researching and writing the report, but failed to complete the analysis of one item in the product range. This was commented on in a sarcastic manner by Tex when reviewing the report; he also asked Wu why he didn't tell him that he needed a few extra days to finish it. Wu could not understand why Tex Peterson had not initially known that the report would require more than two weeks to complete, and why he insisted upon humiliating him in front of his colleagues in the office. After all, he felt, Tex Peterson must have known that he had spent every spare minute working on the report!

Questions for discussion

1 What kinds of behaviour caused Wu problems, and why?

2 What kind of preparation could Wu have had to make his secondment easier?

3 What kind of briefing might Wu's American colleagues have had, which could have helped Wu to feel more welcome?

Further reading

Issues of market selection are discussed in a range of texts, including the following:

John D. Daniles and Lee H. Radebaugh, *International Business: environments and operations* (7th edition), Addison-Wesley, 1994.

Charles W.L. Hill, *International Business: competing in the global market place*, Irwin, 1994.

Richard M. Hodgetts and Fred Luthans, *International Management*, McGraw-Hill, 1991.

Sonia el Kahal, *Introduction to International Business*, Magraw-Hill, 1994.

Henry Mintzberg and James Brian Quinn, *The Strategy Process: concepts, contexts, cases* (3rd edition), Prentice Hall, 1995.

Kenichi Ohmae, *The Borderless World: power and strategy in the interlinked economy*, Fontana, 1991.

Stanley Paliwoda, *International Marketing* (2nd edition), Butterworth-Heinemann, 1994.

S. Young, J. Hamill, C. Wheeler and R. Davies, *International Market Entry and Development*, Harvester Wheatsheaf, 1989.

Two good introductions to the cultural dimension of international business are:

Jean-Claude G. Usunier, *International Marketing: a cultural approach*, Prentice-Hall, 1993.

V. Terpestra and K. David, *The Cultural Environment of International Business* (3rd edition), South Western, 1990.

Other useful books and articles on international business culture include:

Roger E. Axtell, *The Do's and Taboos of International Trade*, John Wiley, 1991.

J.S. Black, 'The Relationship of Personal Characteristics with the Adjustment of Japanese Expatriate Managers', *Management International Review*, Vol. 30, 1990/2.

J.S. Black and H.B. Gregerson, 'Serving Two Masters: Managing the Dual Allegiance of Expatriate Employees', *Sloan Management Review*, Summer 1992.

J.S. Black, M. Mendenhall and G. Oddou, 'Toward a Comprehensive Model of International Adjustment: An Integration of Multiple Theoretical Perspectives', *Academy of Management Review*, Vol. 16 No. 2, 1991.

J.S. Black and M. Mendenhall, 'The U-Curve Adjustment Hypothesis Revisited: A Review and Theoretical Framework', *Journal of International Business Studies* , Vol. 22 No. 2, 1991.

M.R. Callahan, 'Preparing the New Global Manager', *Training and Development Journal*, March 1989.

Edward T. Hall and Mildred Reed Hall, *Understanding Cultural Differences*, Intercultural Press, 1990.

Charles Hampden-Turner and Fons Trompenaars, *The Seven Cultures of Capitalism*, Piatkus, 1994.

Geert Hofstede, *Culture's Consequences: International Differences in Work-Related Values*, Sage Publications, 1980.

B. Kogut and Harbir Singh, 'The Effect of National Culture on the Choice of Entry Mode', *Journal of International Business Studies*, Fall 1988.

Klaus Krippendorff, 'Major Metaphors of Communication and some Constructivist Reflections on their Use', *Cybernetics and Human Knowing*, Vol. 2 No. 1, 1993.

Nanshi F. Matsuura, *International Business: A New Era*, Harcourt Brace Jovanovich, 1991.

M. Mendenhall and G. Oddou, 'Acculturation Profiles of Expatriate Managers: Implications for Cross-Cultural Training Programs', *Columbia Journal of World Business*, Winter 1986.

Michael J. Reddy, 'The Conduit Metaphor – A Case of Frame Conflict in Our Language about Language' – pp. 284-324 in Alan M. Andrew Rugman and Richard M. Hodgetts, *International Business: A Strategic Approach*, McGraw-Hill, 1995.

Richard S. Savich and W. Rodgers, 'Assignment Overseas: Easing the Transition Before and After', *Personnel*, August 1988.

J.B. Shaw, 'A Cognitive Categorisation Model for the Study of Intercultural Management', *Academy of Management Review*, Vol. 15 No. 4, 1990.

Notes

1 M. Powell 'Exporting by German SMEs: small company perspectives', *European Business and Economic Development*, vol 1 Part 4, January 1993 pp. 27–88; H. Olsen, F. Wiedersham-Paul and L. Welch, 'Pre-export activity: the first step is internationalism', *Journal of International Business Studies*, vol. 9 no. 1, 1978; pp. 47–58; M. Z. Brooke and P. J. Buckley, *Handbook of International Trade*. Macmillan, 1988, p118.

2 S. Beamish, N. Craig and D. McLellan, 'The Performance Characteristics of Candian versus UK Exports in small and medium-sized firms', *Management International Review*, vol. 7 no. 4; S. Aksoy and E. Karnack, 'Expert Behaviour of Fresh Produce Marketers: towards a Co-ordination with a good theory of exporting', *International Marketing Review*, vol 11 no. 2, 1994.

3 K. Power and H. Driva, 'An Investigation of British Computing Service firms exporting to Germany'. *European Business Review*, no. 4, 1992.

4 The issue of concentration versus diversification is discussed in C.S. Lee and Y.S. Yang, 'Impact of export market expansion strategy on export performance', *International Marketing Review*, Vol. 7 No. 4.

5 GDP may be defined as a measure of the value of goods and services produced in a country in a given period of time. It does not include the income of firms and house-

holds from the property they own abroad, which is measured by gross national product or GNP. Though the difference between GNP and GDP in most industrialised countries is small, countries whose domestic companies have a large number of branches or subsidiaries overseas, which repatriate their profits, can have a larger GNP than GDP. Kuwait, which invests a substantial proportion of its oil revenue abroad, had a GNP 35% higher than its GDP in 1989.

6 Italy's GDP was revised upward dramatically in 1987, when government statisticians realised that the official statistics were seriously underestimating it. After additional surveys of small businesses and consumer spending on home repairs, meals out and rent from holiday homes, all fertile fields for the black economy, the estimate of Italy's GDP for the year was raised by 18%. The revision raised Italy's GDP well above that of the UK, and just above that of France.

7 Comparisons of GDP between industrialised and 'emerging' economies based on actual exchange rates can be very misleading. At the market exchange rate, China's GDP was estimated to be US$370 per head in 1992. Recent estimates of GDP per head for the same year, using more direct comparisons of living standards, have been at US$2,460 per head – more than six and a half times higher.

8 To provide more realistic comparisons of living standards, a purchasing power parity (PPP) index, which reflects differences in the level of prices between countries, is estimated by international organisations such as the OECD and the World Bank.

9 SRBT Quarterly Survey of Small Business in Britain, vol. 7 no. 1, 1991.

10 *Private Investment in Central and Eastern Europe: survey results*, Working Paper No. 7, ERBD, London 1993.

11 Edward T. Hall, in *Understanding Cultural Differences*, Intercultural Press, 1990, p. 5

12 'The Cultural Relativity of Organisational Practices and Theories', *Journal of International Business*, Fall 1983, p. 75.

13 Geert Hofstede, *Culture's Consequences: International Differences in Work-Related Values*, Sage Publications, 1980.

14 Charles Hampden-Turner and Fons Trompenaars, *The Seven Cultures of Capitalism*, Piatkus, 1994.

15 Lennie Copeland and Lewis Griggs, *Going International: How to Make Friends and Deal Effectively in the Global Marketplace*, Random House, 1985.

3 International marketing strategies

Objectives

By the end of this chapter, you will be able to:

- assess the impact of international operations on each component of the marketing mix.
- understand the choice between approaches dictated by a national strategy, a common international approach, or one tailored to individual markets.
- understand the distribution issues facing international business.
- undertake the case studies at the end of the chapter.

Introduction

✎ CASE STUDY
Relaunching Lobkov

In May 1995, *Marketing Week* reported that Lobkov lager was about to be relaunched on to the UK market in a venture backed by the former Kevin Morley Marketing Director, Stephen Smith. Smith was a director of 1466, a company run from KMM's London offices, which acted as an importer for the Czech lager; and he intended to expand the business into other alcoholic and soft drinks.

Lobkov was launched in the UK in early 1994, but the venture ended in disaster. The first shipments to the UK were of poor quality, and the UK business developed cash flow problems.

1466 took over Lobkov at the end of 1994, and was expected to relaunch it in mid-1995. According to *Marketing Week*, Smith said that the main weakness in the past was an over-emphasis on marketing rather than distribution. He added that contracts with pubs, off-licences and wholesalers were imminent. The company intended to continue with the premium-pricing strategy adopted by the previous owner. However, the design of the Lobkov glass and bottle would change.

Smith claimed the relaunch would be successful because '(This time) it is better co-ordinated, better financed and has better people.'

Source: *Marketing Week*, 5.5.95

As this case illustrates, marketing a product in an overseas market relies on the classic marketing blend of product, price, promotion and place, which is familiar in marketing it domestically. International marketing introduces a key new dimension of choice in this blend: at what point to switch from an existing national to an international approach, and whether to develop a single international marketing strategy, or one tailored to each national market segment. This new layer of choice is illustrated in Figure 3.1.

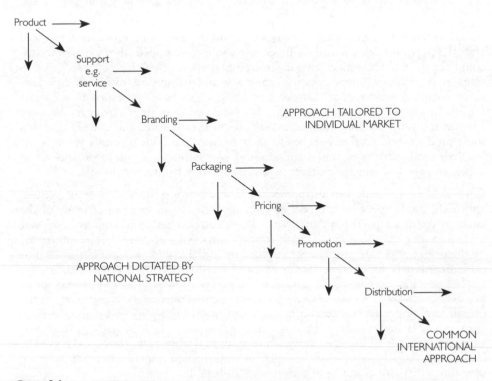

Figure 3.1

In this chapter we will look in turn at each element in the mix, to determine the kinds of choice that need to be made. As was suggested in the first chapter, much depends on the degree of the firm's commitment to exporting. Those businesses that see exporting as a marginal activity will attempt to retain as much of their original national approach as they can, to minimise cost and resource commitment; whilst those that place exporting at the heart of their operations will commit most to tailoring their approach to individual target segments. Amongst the latter group will be those that – because of a mix of the perceived advantages of a consistent approach, and the pressures of cost control given the scale of international marketing – opt to evolve a unitary international marketing strategy for all markets, national and overseas.

Product

Many firms, especially those new to exporting, begin with what Chapter 2 described as an 'ethnocentric' approach. They see international business as a means of selling more of an existing product developed for the core home market. Export sales are seen only as a helpful bonus, and the emphasis is on minimal modification to reap immediate returns from what may initially be seen as marginal or secondary sales. As research into the exporting activities of smaller and medium-sized German business indicates, this approach is especially characteristic of smaller businesses, and can have significant success.

Some firms see export sales as a means of extending the product life-cycle beyond what would be feasible for their core markets. In extending an existing production run well after the initial investment and set-up costs have been recouped, they are able to discount the price of these older lines in 'emerging' markets where for example, expectations of the latest developments in technology and fashion are different, especially when balanced against price. Citroen and Volkswagen have continued to sell older models in this way long after they have been deleted from their ranges for Western Europe. It is generally only when export sales become established and more central that some product modification may begin, with the aim of producing either variants tailored to local markets or (more ambitiously) an international model engineered to appeal to as wide a range of markets as possible, national and international.

General Motors has adopted an approach mid-way between this and an 'ethnocentric' approach, producing a basic model of some of their ranges stripped of many of the ancillary features expected by American or European purchasers, and offered at a lower price to markets with more utilitarian requirements. This decision will be influenced by the degree of pressure for change imposed by individual markets. Differing technical standards may, for example, dictate a host of variants of a single core model, or push the business into developing what is, in key respects, a new product or products for its key export markets. In making these decisions, a company may be constrained by the overall level of production costs it faces. A significant burden of set-up and development costs, or high ongoing running costs, may make it insufficiently profitable to adapt a product at additional expense, in relation to likely returns from export sales. It is not surprising, therefore, that the degree of modification is smaller in manufacturing operations than, for example, in consumer non-durables.

The logistical pressures of operating internationally place particular pressures on the service aspects of a product. A company needs to be sure it can honour any international guarantee, or that the distributors representing it are in a position to do so satisfactorily. An added complication is the differing legal contexts in which a warranty may exist, and the corresponding degree of exposure if service arrangements fail. Service expectations and needs may well differ significantly from market to market, with some requiring much fuller support for less familiar technologies where technical know-how and infrastructure are lacking. In these cases, enhancing customer service may prove to be a significant weapon of competitive advantage. Where it is not possible to provide a full level of customer support, selective investment may still pay dividends. Providing well translated and appropriately tailored instructional manuals is an obvious, if often neglected, example of low-cost but effective international customer service.

Branding and packaging

For many businesses, the key to their international marketing operations lies less in core product differentiation than in the way the core product is presented. Appropriate packaging and a brand name tailored to a particular market can transform a product from market to market. Such an option may well be relatively low-cost compared to product redevelopment – though there may still be pressures to achieve economies of scale in international marketing costs by a consistent approach. With large-scale international operations in particular, there is often a tension between imposing a uniform international image and offering a range of distinct brand images adapted for individual markets, which reflects a debate about the relative merits of the two within the field of marketing generally. Some companies see benefit in generating a single global image recognised in any market. The growth and success of franchising mentioned in Chapter 1, which depends on brand strength, suggests some evidence in favour of this view. As the following case illustrates, many international businesses are moving further in this direction, though not without potential risk in particular markets.

✎   CASE STUDY
            Andrex

In May 1995, *Marketing Week* reported that the imminent disappearance of Andrex from supermarket shelves was causing dismay among some of its local marketers and joy among rivals. As the seventh biggest grocery brand in the UK, it had been one of the most established names around. But now it was to be a casualty of a global realignment of brands at its parent Scott Paper.

Details of the move were still being discussed, but it was understood that the first step would be to endorse Andrex with the name Scottex – under which it was already marketed in most of Europe – and then gradually to increase the emphasis on Scottex, while withdrawing Andrex. A spokesman at the US company's Philadelphia headquarters said the strategy was a 'revolution for Scott. Our overall strategy is to capitalise on the Scott name globally.'

The famous Andrex puppy advertising – by 1995 in its 23rd year – would continue. It was being rolled out to promote Scott toilet tissue worldwide, targetting the European and Asian markets, with the puppy concept also being used in US advertisements. JWT Europe Accounts Manager, Carrie Dodo, was reported by *Marketing Week* as urging caution: 'A name change in the UK is under discussion. But we have to consider what Andrex stands for. It is exceptionally well known.'

Marketers at Kleenex, owned by rivals Kimberly-Clark, saw the confusion in the Andrex camp as an opportunity to do what would have been unthinkable just a few years earlier: overtake Andrex. In mid-1995 Andrex was still the dominant force in the market, though in recent years its market share had plummeted – it had suffered because of the rise of price-fighting brands, aggressive own-label expansion and a more concerted marketing effort by Kleenex. 'We hope to overtake them this year,' said a source close to Kleenex. 'They would be nuts to lose the Andrex name.'

Source: *Marketing Week*, 19.5.95

The ability to convey a single image is challenged by the range of barriers that individual cultures and markets erect, from the obvious barrier of language to the varying cultural meanings given to a particular set of images or words and the range of legal and technical specifications for labelling within individual countries.

Even that most successful of international brands, Coca Cola, has had to change its brand name for the Chinese market. One solution adopted by companies like Kelloggs has been to produce identical breakfast cereal boxes with the required multinational details on content in nine different languages and encompassing the range of legal requirements imposed by each country. An even more flexible solution has been adopted in the case below.

✎   CASE STUDY
       Oil of Ulay

The makers of Oil of Ulay cosmetics products, Proctor and Gamble, decided to update the packaging of this brand so that it was recognisably the same all over Europe and Scandinavia. It was positioned at the upper end of the market with an appeal to all ages. A difference that was retained was the alternative brand name of Olaz used in some countries, but this was used with the new uniform design, shape, typeface, colours and packaging, so the product was still recognisable. The six-sided black shape that is the well-known trademark of the product was retained but reduced in size.

Allowance had to be made for some individual country requirements so that, for example, in Belgium, Flemish is used on one side and French on the other, while in Scandinavia, the typeface was reduced so that three languages could be used.

More and more companies are making this decision to present a uniform image of their products across the Single Market.

Pricing

In Chapter 1, we encountered the case of Flymo and some of the special problems of international pricing that it faced. In some respects, pricing decisions in international business are influenced by factors common to any market. On the one hand, a business faces the pressures of its cost base and the need to maximise its return; on the other, it faces the constraint of the market's perceived value of its offering, and the degree to which it is swayed by competing products or services. For many businesses, assessing the appropriate balance in the international sphere is complicated by relative distance from, and inexperience of, potential overseas markets. The pricing decision can also be made more demanding by the degree to which a business can sustain a differentiation or focus strategy over simple cost leadership in its competitive advantage in an overseas market. (A differentiation strategy might involve offering an exceptional level of service with a product; while a focus strategy, for example, concentrates on meeting the specific needs of a particular market segment.) With a product originally developed for domestic competitive advantage, or as a relatively standard international product, such strategies may be difficult to sustain, placing additional pressure on the pricing decision.

This pressure will be increased if exporting is seen as a relatively marginal activity. In this case, a business is likely to take one of the more short-term pricing strategies available: either cost-based or market-skimming pricing. In cost-based pricing, a company simply aggregates all its production, distribution and agency costs per unit produced, and prices so as to cover them plus an additional mark-up to provide a level of return over costs. As we shall see, the relative complexity of the distribution chain in international business can lead cumulatively to a significantly inflated price which pre-empts any real penetration of the target market.

✎   CASE STUDY
        Courier sector competition: cost leadership versus differentiation
The impact of technological change may be clearly seen in the courier industry. Until recently the major form of competition in this industry was either price competition or reliability. Companies believed that the key items customers required of the service that they offered were a low price and an assurance that the goods would arrive rapidly at their destination. Recognising the limits of price competition, courier industry companies turned towards improvements in the service they offered their customers as a new way of obtaining a competitive edge. These were achieved through more integrated networks and a stronger customer focus within the organisation.

A key element in achieving this objective was the use of information technology. Both FedEx and UPS have introduced unique tagging identities on their parcels that make it possible to locate the parcels' position throughout the journey. Moreover, customers are given reference numbers which enable them to call up the home page of the companies on the Internet; on quoting the reference number of their parcel, they can themselves discover its location. Not surprisingly, this has given greater emphasis once again to speed and reliability, and both FedEx and UPS have announced the introduction of some same-day services within Mexico, Canada and the United States.

A conservative approach to pricing may alternatively lead to a market-skimming strategy, which aims at a premium price and maximum return, even at the expense of any significant market penetration. This approach can be successful where market need and purchasing power are high, focus or differentiation is high, and competitive intensity low. Producers in specialised sectors such as luxury goods, pharmaceuticals or high-tech industries may have both the freedom and the incentive to capitalise on an initial period of market leadership before competitors catch up. An international sphere of operations allows a business of this kind to maximise its returns during the initial period of relative dominance. The use of patents and the legal protection of trademarks and brands is of major importance in underwriting the price differential; it follows that lack of an appropriate legal infrastructure, with a resulting threat of piracy, can be disastrous to this kind of strategy.

If branding can be developed to create the right image, some companies can succeed in capitalising on their products' more exotic and exclusive feel in an overseas market. In their home markets of Belgium and France respectively, Stella Artois and Kronenbourg are sold as relatively cheap, lower-price drinks. In the UK, they are promoted as being relatively exclusive, and premium-priced accordingly.

Relatively few companies have the kind of sustained influence over a market which allows them to price this way with impunity. In the case of the two lagers mentioned above, the removal of customs barriers and easier, cheaper access to the Continent may well undermine this differential pricing, as consumers buy in another country for consumption back home. Significantly, inflated international pricing also runs the danger of parallel exporting, where unauthorised distributors buy at the cheaper domestic price and export themselves at a lower price than the originating firm is offering.

Where these kinds of pressures apply, firms are pushed into alternative pricing strategies. Many are likely to adopt a competitor-orientated strategy, pricing to ensure equivalence with their main existing competitors in the target market. Their aim will be to follow the market price set by other players, and thus effectively to neutralise price as an issue in the purchase decision. The customer selects the products on other criteria: a different brand image, a more appropriate mix of features, easier availability, etc. Depending on how aggressively competitors price, this strategy can offer an acceptable balance between pricing as a potential weapon of competitive advantage and the pressure to cover costs.

Where businesses are new to export markets, this can be a safe first strategy to adopt. It may be contrasted with, perhaps, the most aggressive of pricing strategies: market penetration pricing. In these circumstances, companies deliberately seek to undercut competitors in an attempt to win market share. The focus on market share is generally long term – the company accepts a lower rate of profit, or even losses, as the price to be paid for achieving market dominance. Once a product is sufficiently strongly established, the corresponding economies of scale may help to offset the lower price, and there may be flexibility in gradually increasing prices to parity with the competition, customer loyalty having already been gained.

CASE STUDY

Watching your prices

Marketing Week reported in April 1995 that the Lowe Group had picked up the first pan-European product launch by an Indian multinational – worth an estimated $10m (£6.4m). The watch manufacturer Titan Industries planned to roll out a range of watches into ten European countries later in the year, with a particular concentration on the UK, Germany, France and Italy. The company had already taken 60 per cent of the Indian quartz analogue watch market since its formation in 1987. Television was not being ruled out, though the bulk of advertising would use the press.

Titan is part of Tata, India's $7bn (£4.46bn) steel-to-hotels conglomerate. The watches are made in Bangalore, but designed in France, and are based on Japanese technology. The company claimed customers who usually bought Japanese brands would be attracted by 'the medium price coupled with quality on a par with Swiss watch-making'.

Source: *Marketing Week,* 28.4.95

As a means of building a market position quickly from a position of weakness, market penetration pricing can be a very effective way of breaking into an overseas market. Such a strategy has been favoured by Japanese companies, for example. It has also sometimes been employed defensively by companies faced with surplus stocks or capacity, especially capital-intensive 'heavy' industries where there is considerable pressure to sustain production to cope with the burden of operating costs. This kind of 'dumping' has traditionally been outlawed by many governments anxious to protect the profitability of their domestic industry from unfair competition. The issue has become more important with the general reduction of trade barriers following successful GATT negotiations, together with the growth of regional trading blocs such as NAFTA, and governments are likely to become more vigilant in this area.

This kind of pricing strategy is the antithesis of cost-based pricing in the dialogue within a business between recouping costs and achieving market penetration. It is high-risk in that it places price at the heart of competitive advantage, provoking a potentially protracted price war. Without the resources or long-term perspective to withstand the resulting pressure, most firms – especially smaller to medium-sized companies – are likely to avoid such a strategy, especially as their distribution costs in particular will be higher than local businesses.

As we have seen, a major pressure for any company in its pricing decision is its cost base. This is particularly acute for a firm doing international business, where distribution and agency costs may be a significant extra burden. The extent of this burden may be illustrated in the fictitious case shown in Figure 3.2.

SAMPLE EXPORT DISTRIBUTION COSTS FOR A FIRM

	£
Factory price (including 15% markup)	100.00
Export administration costs	8.00
Domestic transport	10.00
Shipping and insurance costs	18.00
Import duties (10%)	13.60
Importer markup (15%)	22.40
Agent/distributor fee/markup (20%)	34.40
Retail markup (50%)	103.20
Final price	309.60

Figure 3.2

Most businesses face this pressure of incremental costs, generated by the length and complexity of the export distribution chain. In the above case, the final price, if a business is to cover all its costs, is three times the factory gate price. This kind of pressure makes market penetration pricing very difficult, and puts pressure on the company to seek competitive advantage through a strategy involving differentiation or focus, rather than cost leadership. It also puts pressure on firms to simplify the distribution chain by substitution – that is, cutting out intermediaries and the mark-up they impose. It was precisely this pressure that pushed Flymo, as discussed in Chapter 1, from its reliance on third-party distribution to more direct control and the elimination of wholesalers from the distribution chain.

Substitution requires a business to take more responsibility for controlling pricing and distribution itself. Whether a firm is prepared to assume this responsibility – with its demands on time and resources – depends, as has been reiterated at key points in the text, on how highly it values international business as a part of its overall operations.

The issue of control in enabling a firm to price as it wishes for its target market, rather than losing that control in transferring risk and responsibility earlier on in the distribution chain, also affects the terms of trade which the firm is prepared to offer to distributors. The seven most common terms of sale (for price quotations) are shown in Figure 3.3, and are referred to as INCOTERMS. The difference between them relates primarily to the point at which the responsibility for the carriage of the goods is transferred from the seller to the purchaser.

TERMS OF SALE

Incoterms	Transfer of risk to purchaser
EXW (ex works)	Factory gate
FCA (free carrier, named point)	FOB at a named inland point
FAS (free alongside ship)	Quay
FOB (free on board)	'Over the ship's rail'
CFA (cost and freight)	Purchaser's port
CIF (cost, insurance and freight)	As CFA
DDP (delivered duty paid)	FOB at importer's choice of delivery point

Figure 3.3

Should the terms of sale for the price quotation be EXW, this would imply that the buyer is responsible for transport and all associated costs from the place of manufacture of the goods, whereas at the other extreme DDP would require the exporter or seller to bear the costs and associated risks of transporting the goods to the final delivery point.

In practice, the two most commonly used terms are FOB and CIF, requiring delivery respectively either on board the ship (or plane, etc.) or to the buyer's choice of port. In the former case, the seller is responsible for the costs of unloading, wharfage and loading the goods on board the ship, with the buyer responsible for onward transportation and insurance. In the latter case, the buyer is only responsible for carriage, etc. from the port of delivery of their choice.

Each represents a differing and more advanced stage to which the originating firm retains control over the cost and mode of delivery within the distribution chain, giving it greater influence over the final price charged to the consumer (accepting in return, of course, more of the risks of shipment). At its furthest, such control may be almost equivalent to a business operating its own export operation or dealing with markets through joint venture or FDI.

A final critical element in the issue of price control is the currency in which a business decides to quote. Again, the choice is closely linked to the transfer of risk from the seller to the buyer; but in this case it is a matter not of transportation risk but of foreign exchange risk. In any transaction, a period of time elapses between the initial quotation, the subsequent agreement to purchase by the buyer, and receipt of the payment by the seller. With exports this period will be longer than in domestic transactions, and could typically last several months. During the period the exchange rate between the buyer's and exporter's currencies (assuming they are not in a fixed relationship) may vary, causing the price of the goods in the other currency also to vary. This can be demonstrated by the simple example in Figure 3.4.

IMPACT OF EXCHANGE RATE VARIATIONS

UK price	Exchange rate	US price
£10.00	1:2	$20
£10.00	1:1.5	$15
£10.00	1:2.5	$25

Figure 3.4

If the exporter gives the quotation in its own currency, in this case sterling, then it will always be protected from exchange rate variations, and it will always receive the full amount expected (£10 per unit). The US buyer, however, will be faced with a variable final price.

If, on the other hand, a quotation is given in the buyer's currency – in this case, let us say US$20 – then only if the exchange rate between the two currencies remains constant at 1:2 will the seller receive £10 per unit. If the exchange rate were to change to, say, 1:1.5, then the final payment the exporter would receive would be substantially more than £10 per unit; no problem there! However, if it were to move in the opposite direction – to, say, 1:2.5 – then the exporter would receive less than the desired minimum of £10 per unit.

In most foreign exchange transactions, it would be normal for the party exposed to the foreign exchange loss or gain to seek some form of financial protection in the financial markets. This would usually involve a foreign exchange contract with their bank. With this protection, the currency of the price quotation has now become a competitive factor used by companies to gain advantage in the market place, with a greater willingness of companies to offer foreign currency price quotations. Evidence from Department of Trade and Industry publications would suggest that (with the exclusion of products such as oil, which are priced solely in dollars) companies operating in the more competitive sectors are more likely to offer foreign currency quotations as a way of controlling the final price to the customer.

Research by Samuels, Greenfield and Herrick on British SMEs[1] confirms this picture. They balance it by noting that most firms are reluctant, once an agreement on a particular rate of exchange has been reached, to make any further alteration. When asked if they would change sterling prices if sterling rose against the local currency, and looked likely to remain at the stronger level, only 12% of those responding said they would lower their sterling price to keep the local price competitive. 88% of respondents said they would not change the sterling price even if this meant an increase in the local price. Correspondingly, firms were found to be unwilling to change the sterling price when the value of the pound fell against a local currency. 50% of companies said they normally only reviewed their export prices once every year.

Ways in which banks can help protect firms in transacting foreign business are discussed in more detail in Chapter 4. The question of currency quotation underlines the point that sustained export success requires a business to be able to control as many of the key aspects of its international strategy as it can, to ensure that it presents the most persuasive proposition to the customer.

A final issue in any consideration of pricing issues in international business is differential pricing between and within markets. Such an approach within markets may be more appropriate for the services industry, where the service cannot be resold between customers, e.g. healthcare or education. It may also apply to goods for which there are distinctive and separate market segments. Within the consumer goods sector, a separate market has been created for retailers, which is separate from that of the individual customers and enables the retailers to be charged a lower price. Geographical separation could also offer an opportunity for differential pricing, with higher prices for goods being charged in capital cities or in tourist areas, compared to those charged in the more rural areas. Many companies also automatically offer a discount to customers who are willing to purchase large quantities of their product, and have special rates for associated companies. In certain countries (e.g. the United States), some of these practices are deemed to be anti-competitive and are therefore illegal. In Canada, differential pricing can result from differing taxes and duties imposed by provincial governments.

Promotion

Promotion of any kind involves two key processes: the framing of a message, and the means by which it is communicated. International business complicates both processes. The range of markets, the more limited experience of their dynamics, the barrier of language, and the impact of cultural distance – all these both multiply the potential number of messages and make judging and framing the right ones more difficult. The same issues, together with the more complex and costly logistics of international business, also constrain the means of communication and increase the danger of the message being distorted in transmission from sender to receiver. A classic example of the kind of problem a company can encounter is described on the next page.

> ✎   CASE STUDY
> Esso's 'Put a tiger in your tank' campaign
>
> Esso established a strong brand image with a campaign associating its petrol with the powerful image of the tiger. The campaign was both graphic and verbal, depicting a tiger's tail emerging from the petrol tank of a car with the accompanying slogan 'put a tiger in your tank'. This campaign was translated into a wide range of languages. What the advertisers failed to grasp was that it would be difficult to recreate the message in other languages and cultures with the same nuances as the original version. The result was a literal interpretation that simply baffled some foreign audiences, including France. In India the campaign was further undermined by the reverence in which the tiger was held as a religious and national symbol.

Communicating a promotional message from sender to receiver involves a series of steps, moving from creating awareness to generating an understanding of the proposition and, finally, to persuasion/conviction and action. The constraints of cultural distance put pressure on each of these steps. The disruption of the process of understanding in the Esso case put in jeopardy the links in the communication chain which should have followed.

Framing the message

These problems of distortion in both the message and its transmission throw particular emphasis on researching the range of target audiences. The problems in business to business promotion – where a decision is more likely to revolve around such issues as suitability for a precisely defined business need, technical specification, price and delivery – will be less acute than those in consumer promotion, where choice is likely to be more personal and subjective. However, even in the former case, a message tailored more closely to the wants and aspirations of its audience is far more likely to succeed in a market place of competing messages jostling for the attention of the customer. This kind of research requires the use of suitably qualified intermediaries with experience of the market.

Other businesses with a track record of successful exporting to the market in question; export development advisers; agents or retailers and advertising agencies with experience of promoting to the same target groups in the countries in question – all these may be able to offer invaluable advice on the message and how it ought to be framed. They may, for instance, help the company to draw on the wealth of consumer research available for selected markets. As an example, official statistics tell you that Denmark has the fourth largest per capita GDP in Europe; but an attitude survey by Gallup found that many Danes feel they have difficulty managing on their income despite a narrow gap between rich and poor. An advertising message stressing value for money may, therefore, be more appropriate. Similarly, the use of the cultural analysis outlined in the last chapter to explore the more 'feminine' qualities of Scandinavian culture may lead to a message stressing co-operative, family-orientated elements rather than more competitive, materialistic values.

The choice of an agency to frame the right message is not simple, and will depend not only upon costs (although agencies often receive their income predominantly from the advertising medium rather than their client), but also the market coverage of the agency, whether national or international, and the quality of service offered. The final decision will be largely company-specific. This view is reinforced by the evidence obtained from recent surveys, which show that international companies vary considerably with respect to agency choice, with some (e.g. Levi Strauss) choosing one agency for all their activity, whereas other companies (e.g. Texas Instruments) choose specific agencies for their operations within individual markets, and therefore utilise several simultaneously. Naturally, the ability to undertake standardised advertising is reduced by multiple agency use. On the other hand, the advantages of using multiple agencies stem from the increased country-specific knowledge of each – especially for those markets perceived as difficult to penetrate, e.g. Japan.

Market-specific or global promotion?

For an increasing number of companies, a key issue in international promotion is whether to tailor separate messages and campaigns for individual markets, or to develop a global international image designed to appeal to a broad range of markets. As was mentioned in the discussion of branding, this is a growing development – particularly in larger companies where, amongst other things, the costs associated with a major international advertising campaign can be more effectively controlled.

Such campaigns often rely on a heavily visual approach to overcome the obvious barriers of language. The cultural reach of certain Western values, together with the widespread use of English, has made it possible for particularly influential brands such as Coca Cola to frame campaigns around simple easily recognised slogans in English, such as 'Coca Cola Is It'. Benetton's use of incongruous and often controversial images, combined with an unchanging slogan, 'United Colors of Benetton', to advertise its range of fashionwear is a classic piece of international brand promotion.

CASE STUDY
Century-old legislation bans advertisements

The *European* reported in July 1995 that a Benetton advertising campaign had hit the headlines yet again. However, this time the controversy had done more than create free publicity for the Italian clothing company. A ban on some Benetton press advertisements by a German federal court had also highlighted a wide-ranging century-old law which restricts advertising. The federal court of justice upheld an earlier lower court decision in Frankfurt against Benetton and Grüner and Jahr, publishers of the magazine *Stern*, banning three advertisements in 1992. These showed South American child labour, a duck trapped in an oil slick, and a human body stamped with the words 'HIV positive'. Benetton was now considering an appeal.

The law which led to the banning of the Benetton ads was the 95-year-old *Gesetz gegen den unlauteren Wettbewerb* (law against unfair competition). Two main clauses in the law apply to advertising, banning publicity which is considered misleading or which offends *gute Sitten* (good manners). Dr Peter Schotthöfer, a Munich-based lawyer, said: 'We have had many, many cases.' He explained that the concept of 'good manners' is all-embracing, so any form of advertising seen to transgress can be banned. He added, 'In Germany, it is more or less forbidden to use comparative advertising. It is both against "good manners" and it is also misleading.'

Major brands have tended not to fall foul of the law in Germany because their experienced advertising agencies are well aware of the long-established laws. Any attempt to bypass them can be swiftly dealt with. According to Schotthöfer, 'A complainant can go to court and have an advertisement stopped in two hours.' A worldwide Pepsi Cola campaign starring Hollywood star Cindy Crawford, which relied heavily on comparative advertising to the extent of showing the rival Coca Cola can, did not run in Germany.

Source: adapted from *The European*, 14-20.7.95

However, as the Esso example illustrates, there are significant risks associated with such a strategy. A uniform international promotion strategy faces the risk of fitting no one market effectively and even falling foul of cultural expectations in those markets. Such expectations are often reflected in the regulations governing promotion in the country concerned. As we have seen, Benetton ran into difficulties in some markets with a highly visual approach.

One reflection of this kind of risk is seen in the widely differing regulations governing advertising in particular countries. Alcoholic beverages, underwear and condoms are examples of products that have both formal and informal restrictions applied to their public display. In the Middle East, all three of these products have severe restrictions placed on their promotion, whereas in France, a more liberal attitude is adopted and few restrictions apply.

The most heavily-regulated product of all is tobacco, for which different restrictions apply throughout the world. In the UK the restrictions cover where and when the advertisements may be shown, whereas in Finland such advertising is banned altogether. Restrictions are also placed on the message that the advertisement conveys (e.g. requiring the inclusion of government health warnings), or on its content (e.g. a requirement that the advertisement should not display success).

CASE STUDY
The European newspaper competition
The European is available on news stands throughout the EU and beyond. In July 1994 it ran a competition with a limited edition Lotus Elan car as prize, but anticipated problems in awarding the prize if the winner came from certain countries.

In Germany, high-value prizes are illegal, as they are seen as an undue inducement to the consumer to buy the product (in this case the newspaper). In Italy, permission for awarding the prize would have to be sought from the Finance Ministry, and entries are supposed to be sent to an Italian address. In the Netherlands, the value of the car exceeded the legal limit for prizes there.

This illustrates the difficulty of operating a pan-European promotion. As it turned out, the winner lived in the UK and so there was no problem.

A similar range of restrictions applies to the use of incentives, such as free gifts, as Figure 3.5 and the previous case study both illustrate. These regulations often reflect deeper differences in cultural values which advertisers must be aware of. As an example, attitudes to dress codes and the depiction of relationships between men and women vary enormously. The use of women in advertising may be a highly sensitive issue in Muslim countries. In countries with a more 'masculine' cultural profile, the image of a speeding car may convey power and influence, whilst in other cultural traditions it may be seen as reckless or wasteful.

	UK	Irish Republic	Spain	Germany	France	Denmark	Belgium	Netherlands	Portugal	Italy	Greece	Luxembourg	Austria	Finland	Norway	Sweden	Switzerland
On-pack price reductions	✔	✔	✔	✔	✔	✔	✔	✔	✔	✔	✔	✔	✔	✔	✔	✔	✔
Banded offers	✔	✔	✔	?	✔	?	?	✔	✔	✔	✗	?	?	?	?	?	✗
In-pack premiums	✔	✔	✔	?	?	?	?	?	✔	✔	✔	✗	?	✔	?	?	✗
Multiple-purchase offers	✔	✔	✔	?	✔	?	?	✔	✔	✔	✔	✗	?	?	?	?	✗
Extra-product	✔	✔	✔	?	✔	✔	?	?	✔	✔	✔	✔	?	✔	✔	?	?
Free product	✔	✔	✔	✔	✔	✔	?	✔	✔	✔	✔	✔	✔	✔	✔	✔	✔
Reusable/alternative use pack	✔	✔	✔	✔	✔	✔	✔	✔	✔	✔	✔	✔	?	✔	✔	✔	✔
Free mail-ins	✔	✔	✔	✗	✔	?	?	✔	✔	✔	✔	?	✗	✔	?	✗	✗
With-purchase premiums	✔	✔	✔	?	✔	?	?	?	✔	✔	✔	✗	?	✔	?	?	✗
Cross-product offers	✔	✔	✔	✗	✔	?	✗	?	✔	✔	✔	✗	?	?	?	?	✗
Collector devices	✔	✔	✔	✗	?	?	?	?	✔	✔	✔	✗	✗	?	✗	✗	✗
Competitions	✔	✔	✔	?	?	?	✔	?	✔	✔	✔	?	?	✔	✔	✔	✔
Self-liquidating premiums	✔	✔	✔	✔	✔	✔	✔	?	✔	✔	✔	✗	✔	✔	✗	✔	✗
Free draws	✔	✔	✔	✗	✔	✗	✗	✗	✔	✔	✔	✗	✗	✔	✗	✗	✗
Share-outs	✔	✔	✔	✗	?	✗	✗	✗	✔	?	✔	✗	✗	?	?	✗	✗
Sweepstake/lottery	?	?	?	?	?	✗	?	?	?	?	?	✗	?	✔	✗	✗	✗
Money-off vouchers	✔	✔	✔	✗	✔	?	✔	✔	✔	?	✔	?	?	?	✗	?	✗
Money-off next purchase	✔	✔	✔	✗	✔	✗	✔	✔	✔	?	✔	✗	✗	?	✗	✗	✗
Cash backs	✔	✔	✔	?	✔	✔	✔	✔	✔	✗	✔	✗	?	?	?	✔	✗
In-store demos	✔	✔	✔	✔	✔	✔	✔	✔	✔	✔	✔	✔	✔	✔	✔	✔	✔

Table reproduced by kind permission of IMP.   ✔ Permitted   ✗ Not permitted   ? May be permitted

Figure 3.5   Source: Marketing Without Frontiers – The RMI Guide to International Direct Marketing, *Royal Mail International, 1991*

Communicating the message

As was mentioned at the beginning of this section, international business also complicates the process of communicating a message. The scale and level of operational overhead involved puts particular pressure on the use of an international sales team, for example. The use of third-party representation as an alternative in the third-party American market is discussed in Chapter 9. If this is to be used effectively, a sales force needs to be carefully briefed to cultivate and follow up the most likely prospects and to focus on significant orders. In addition, in some cases its use will be constrained by cultural and other factors. Female reps, for example, might find it difficult to operate effectively in the more 'masculine' cultures. In addition to travel costs and added support in sustaining and controlling international sales operations, it is important to consider the necessary training costs involved in coping with unfamiliar systems and cultures, training reps from local cultures and negotiating the legal and tax issues involved.

Targeting sales time and expertise effectively means relying on other mechanisms to canvass initial interest. The choice of other promotion channels will depend on their appropriateness in conveying the message and reaching the target audience, and in sustaining the chosen volume, range and frequency of communication; on their availability and appropriateness to the target market; and on their level of cost. It is this combination of elements that has encouraged the growing use of direct mail activity in international business, backed up by the increasing sophistication of database technology, including the growing number of available databases and the emergence of geographical information systems.

In a market like Canada, discussed in Chapter 9, the poor quality of customer databases places an emphasis on a mix of other promotion channels, including inserts in magazines and couponing. It is these other channels we will discuss next. They include the following:

- films and slide shows
- trade fairs and exhibitions
- couponing
- company brochures and catalogues
- free gifts and samples
- point of purchase displays and materials
- company magazines.

The most widely used of these categories is the company brochure or catalogue, which is often considered the standard sales aid. Typically, the company catalogue will list or illustrate the range of products that the company is offering for purchase, together with appropriate details that the consumer will require to make the purchase decision. Brochures may be limited to one item from the company range, or cover a series of related items or the full range of products. Consequently, a producer of sports equipment may have various catalogues targeted towards different consumer segments – e.g. individuals, educational purchasers and sports clubs. The design of such catalogues is of great importance, since it has to achieve the dual goals of imparting information and creating a desire to purchase. Further, the catalogue may need to be used in different ways, with individuals using the catalogue to view the range of products and to make a direct purchase from the catalogue, while retailers wish to use it as a sales aid. It therefore needs to be designed and structured so as to be attractive, to create initial interest and to give the maximum publicity to the premium items.

Of more limited use is the company magazine, which is targeted primarily towards company employees, offering them a broad insight into the scope of activities undertaken by the company. Some companies also send their magazine to existing customers, with the aim of making them feel part of the company 'team'. This approach is used by most motor manufacturers, who target existing purchasers of their marque in order to gain further sales when the customers change their vehicle. In both of the above cases, the language (and, where appropriate, translation) of the brochure, catalogue or magazine is an important consideration.

Trade fairs and exhibitions play an important role in certain industrial sectors, with the most noticeable examples being in transportation or fashion, where annual motor and aviation exhibitions or fashion shows enable the manufacturers to display their latest models and product developments. Other sectors where trade fairs or exhibitions are important are those involving industrial goods. For manufacturers of these products, such shows are an important element within their marketing strategy, allowing their customers to view their products and compare them directly with those of their competitors. In the consumer goods sectors, such exhibitions are more limited in their operation, and often admit trade customers only (e.g. the annual UK toy fair).

As we saw earlier, the use of free gifts and samples is constrained by legal restrictions in some countries, and is therefore not used internationally as widely as it is within the UK. Examples of such promotions vary from gifts included with the purchase of another product possibly manufactured by the same company (as commonly observed in breakfast cereal packages), to samples distributed through the post to targeted consumers (Oil of Ulay has been distributed throughout the world in this way), to gifts offered in competitions. In all of these circumstances legal restrictions often apply, and may relate either to the value of the gift or to the product itself.

CASE STUDY
Frequent flier miles

The advent of increased competition between the world's airlines, both in domestic markets and international markets, has led to a series of marketing actions. The initial price competition seen in the domestic US markets has given way to a more varied series of policies. This was made more obviously necessary by the bankruptcy of some of the low-pricing airlines, such as People's Express. Recent years have seen improvements in quality, better service, and alliances between airlines in order to improve their competitive position.

Possibly one of the most successful moves has been the introduction of Frequent Flier programmes. In these schemes the airlines offer passengers flier miles that relate to the mileage flown on their particular airline. Frequent fliers can then exchange miles for free tickets or upgrades. The success of these programmes may be seen by their rapid spread throughout the world's airlines – British Airways, British Midland, American Airlines, USAir and so on. The expectation is, of course, that frequent fliers will use the particular airline wherever possible in order to increase their flier mile account.

As their usage grew within the airline industry the form of the competition changed, and airlines extended the schemes, allowing members to gain credit by using the services of a partner in the travel sector, such as car hire companies or hotels. The ability to accrue miles has also been extended to credit card usage. Airlines have discovered, however, that this form of competition also has costs, with large credits being built up by their programmes' members which should be shown as a debit on their accounts. This has resulted in the introduction of limits to the life of their flier miles.

Other airlines such as Southwest have chosen a low pricing strategy, with few 'frills' during the flight. The large airlines such as United, Delta, American and USAir must now decide on which marketing strategy to adopt in their various markets.

A related promotional technique is that of couponing, where consumers are given coupons that enable them to obtain a reduction in the selling price if they purchase a certain product. This too is constrained by legal restrictions. Coupons are typically distributed by mail to selected customers, or through newspapers; and are accepted by the retailer when the item is purchased. Recently coupons have increasingly been made available in the retail store itself, as an alternative to price reductions. In all such promotions the cooperation of the retailer is essential, and this is not always possible because of the additional costs that it imposes upon them. Many supermarkets do not check that specific items are purchased when accepting coupons, limiting their effectiveness. Couponing also has cultural associations, with greater use in certain countries (e.g. the United States) and by certain customers.

Point of purchase displays and offers are most often associated with displays in retail department stores and supermarkets; but in practice they are operated by a very wide range of companies, including the service industries (e.g. banks, housing agents and travel agencies). The display may be a simple advertising board, or involve a salesperson who offers demonstrations of the product or free samples. Examples of this type of promotional activity may also involve the use of video, film or slide shows. Again, these can be used either in conjunction with specialised sales staff, or as stand-alone exhibitions. An example of combined usage is that of the sale of time share properties, where a combination of films, free prizes and personal selling is used to achieve a sale.

Public relations

A further element of communication policy is public relations activity, which is normally considered to be an adjunct to other forms of promotion. The greatest advantage of public relations is that it is normally free, or at least costs little. Consequently, companies may be able to achieve some of their marketing objectives in a more cost-effective manner than is possible through other channels of promotion. An article in a popular newspaper or magazine that praises a company policy (e.g. the environmentally friendly nature of a particular company or product), or mentions it in a positive manner, may reach a larger audience and have a more favourable impact than a series of expensive advertisements. Similarly, awareness of a product is an important objective that can be achieved through public relations.

Many companies either employ public relations staff or use the services of specialist companies to aid and control their activities in this area. This is especially important if managers have had little experience of briefing reporters etc., and are unable to gain maximum advantage from this channel. Public relations experience is also necessary to avoid or limit the impact of bad publicity – many company managers do not believe the adage that all publicity is good publicity. This may be observed when disasters occur, with companies wishing to avoid any linkage between a failure, however caused, and their product or company. In the case of the ferry disaster at Zeebrugge, the company changed the name of its shipping division.

Choice of media

The final decision related to advertising is the choice of which media to utilise. Once again this will be partially product-determined, but within this classification there exist numerous variations that need to be considered. It would be inappropriate to advertise machine parts in a lifestyle magazine; while although the advertising of leisure clothing in such a magazine would be acceptable, the choice of *which* magazine still has to be made.

Before consideration is given to the choice of media, the advertiser needs to set the framework for that choice. The four most important considerations underlying media choice, besides that of the nature of the product, are:

- objectives
- frequency
- reach
- continuity.

Advertising can have three broad **objectives**, although there is overlap between the categories:

- *informative advertising*, where your target audience is made aware of the product. This may then be followed by:
- *persuasive advertising*, in which a desire to purchase the product is created; and finally:
- *reminder advertising*, which aims to maintain the product in the mind of the consumer and counter competitors' advertising.

The **reach** of the advertisement is simply the choice of the number of people who will be exposed to it at least once.

The **frequency** of the advertisement relates to the number of times the audience is exposed to it.

Finally, the **continuity** of the advertisement relates to the length of time the advertising campaign should operate, and the pattern of that campaign.

The above framework, together with associated cost considerations, will in practice limit the media choice available for international advertising. The full range of media is now considered below, but it is important to be aware that the choice and use of the media will vary from country to country, and expert advice is normally sought.

Newspapers. These are the most commonly used medium, although they vary considerably in coverage and pattern. Newspapers can be aimed at an international audience (the *International Herald Tribune*), a national audience (*USA Today*), or a regional audience (the *San Francisco Gazette*). Furthermore, they can have different publishing patterns – a daily (normally interpreted as six days per week) or weekly pattern being the two most commonly chosen. Some newspapers, however, attempt to bridge these geographical and publishing patterns; for instance, in Germany national papers may contain a regional supplement (the *Frankfurter Allgemeiner Zeitung*); and there may be weekly editions comprising excerpts from the daily editions (the *Guardian Weekly*). Newspapers are also often directed towards specific segments of the market that are advantageous for the prospective advertiser. The advantage of newspaper advertising is the relative low cost compared to that of other media offering a similarly large reach – although this will include many readers who have little or no interest in the product. The greatest disadvantage is the continuity element, since the life of the newspaper is very short.

Magazines and periodicals. These may offer a more targeted market. As in the case of newspapers, the circulation statistics are fairly accessible and enable an informed choice to be made. Information is often also available on the readers of individual magazines, as a result of regular surveys. Consequently, although the circulation of a specialist magazine like *Cyclist World* may be lower than that of a regional newspaper, it offers the advantage that a large percentage of the readership is likely to constitute potential customers for a cycle manufacturer. Additionally, the life of magazines – typically several weeks – tends to be longer than that of most other forms of media. Indeed, some periodicals may have a life of over a year, as exemplified by the numerous specialist yearbooks available. This could cause slight difficulties, however, if the product range were to change.

Outdoor and transportation sites offer a huge range and variety of potential advertising locations. Transportation sites are those located either within or on transport services. Throughout the world, hoardings and billboards are used to advertise a full range of goods and services. They are of particular importance in those countries where there is a lack of other media choice, and are widely used in the Third World. One disadvantage of this form of advertising is the legal restrictions that are applied to both the location and content of the hoardings. Moreover, many of these advertisements will be seen only for short periods at any one time, limiting the message to a short slogan.

Radio is an effective and widely used communication medium in many parts of the world, and is especially useful for advertisers in areas of high illiteracy. It is used primarily for the advertisement of either services or consumer goods, is relatively cheap compared to television advertising, and is an especially popular medium in Latin America. The number of radio stations within any area is often regulated, but where a wide choice is allowed it is possible to target consumers, either by their geographical area or by their listening choice. Besides national and local radio stations there are a limited number of international stations, though many of these (e.g. the BBC World Service) do not accept advertising as such. The number of advertisements allowed within a certain period of time is sometimes restricted by law – for example, to ten minutes of advertising per hour of broadcasting; it also has an effect upon the number of listeners, who may prefer stations with fewer advertisements. Recently there has been a growth in the number of sponsored programmes in order to avoid these limitations.

Television is possibly one of the most advanced communications media for advertising, although its importance varies considerably for different companies and products because of the relatively high costs. The actual costs will be related to the timing and positioning of the advertisement; advertising spots in the peak viewing hours are sold at a much higher cost than those on the less popular channels in the late evening. Legal restrictions also apply to television advertising. As with radio advertising, some of the limitations of the medium may be avoided by the sponsorship of programmes, or by 'televerts' – programmes that are essentially advertisements and which often feature a prominent personality. The imposition of national restrictions is in fact becoming more difficult as a consequence of the growth of international television broadcasting using cable networks or satellite receivers, which offer advertisers an alternative choice. With the growth in consumer choice within television, the ability to target audiences becomes more feasible; indeed, during the most recent period channels devoted completely to selling consumer products have begun to be broadcast, with viewers being encouraged to phone and purchase the items as they are displayed. (An example is QVC.)

More specialised advertising media exist, although these account for a relatively small percentage of the total expenditure. Examples of these are the use of advertising in cinema (for instance in countries like India where it can be used to achieve mass coverage), advertising on packaging of other products (e.g. books of matches and theatre tickets), or advertising on the electronic 'super-highway', with electronic catalogues allowing home sales for households with appropriate equipment. Several retail stores in the United States (e.g. Sears) already produce an electronic version of their catalogue. Linked to this development is the existence of electronic stores from which consumers can order via their telephone or computer modem, paying by credit or charge card.

The impact and importance of the various media in practice may be observed from statistics published in Terpstra and Sarathy,[2] which were themselves extracted from material published by Euromonitor Publications[3] and in the *International Journal of Advertising*.[4] In the 1980s the advertising media expenditure on television varied from zero in Indonesia to 64% in Venezuela. Similarly, spending on radio ranged from 20% in Thailand to zero in Sweden; and that on outdoor media from 2% in Brazil to 22% in Japan (where expenditure on printed materials was 36%, compared to 96% in Sweden and 81% in the then West Germany). This clearly demonstrates the need to choose advertising media on the basis of informed choice, and to recognise that the optimum choice may be very different from one country to another.

Distribution in international marketing

The final core element affecting international marketing decisions is the distribution of the product into overseas markets. This consists of two aspects, namely

- the mode of entry
- the physical distribution system.

The first of these is considered in detail in Chapter 1; here we will therefore focus solely on the second of the choices, involving the physical distribution or logistics system. This may be considered in two parts, the first relating to the transportation of the goods to the overseas customer, and the second relating to the storage or warehousing of the goods.

There are several alternative choices for the transportation of products overseas, which may be used either independently or in conjunction with one another. Each of these modes includes several alternatives. The available modes are:

- road freight
- rail freight
- shipping
- air transport
- the postal service.

For many products, or overseas markets, the choice is strictly limited; whereas for other items there is a range of choice. The export of large industrial products would normally be undertaken by road freight and shipping, whereas a replacement part for an essential piece of equipment would probably be air-freighted to the overseas customer. The actual arrangements for the transportation of the product, together with the documentation, are normally undertaken either by a specialist intermediary, the freight forwarder, or in large companies by the company's own logistics section. The choice of transport mode depends upon several factors; the cost, the nature of the goods and the transit time are the most important of these.

The postal service offers one of the most reliable methods of delivery overseas at a cost which depends upon the specific option chosen – i.e. transit time, and collection and delivery points. The postal authorities impose limitations on the physical nature of products that can be sent overseas by this mode; for example, hazardous or bulky items are not allowed.

The other modes of transport are more flexible about the nature of the goods (i.e. size, weight, fragility and value), but vary considerably in terms of transit time and cost. The most costly mode, air freight, also offers a very reliable and speedy service; for this reason, it is growing in popularity amongst exporters, and has gained supremacy in the transport of certain categories of product – particularly items of high value such as gold bars.

Shipping remains the dominant transport mode over long distances; and a large number of different categories of vessel, both general cargo and specialist, have been developed to cope with the range of products needing to be transported. Growing competition amongst shipping lines and challenges to some of the shipping conference cartels, where routes were shared between companies, has resulted in lower costs in recent years.

Similarly, the growth of air freight companies has also produced cost savings, and this has offered a very competitive alternative to ocean shipping for some manufacturers. Both modes offer regular and bookable services throughout the world.

Transport over shorter distances is dominated by road freight where, as in the case of shipping, a large number of specialist trucks have been developed to carry general cargo, containers, liquids or bulk items. The greatest limitations on road freight relate either to the nature of the product, with weight restrictions applied to truck axles when loaded; or to transit times, with regulations limiting the driving time permitted for drivers, and also the movement of trucks on certain days (e.g. Germany and Austria both restrict truck movements at weekends).

Although often competitive with road freight, rail transport has less flexibility, since most companies are required to transport the goods to rail depots and arrange collection from depots overseas. Both of these modes are often used in conjunction with shipping.

The second logistics decision is that of the storage or warehousing of the goods. This is linked with the broader policy of inventory management for both the supplier and the customer. An international warehousing policy may enable companies to reduce their transport costs, and to improve their competitiveness by offering a faster and more responsive service to their customers. This is possible if the company maintains warehouses for its products in its overseas markets. From these they can quickly service their customers; but at the same time, by adequate inventory control, they can utilise slower but less costly forms of transportation. Furthermore, the linkage of the international logistics system is backward as well as forward: companies should also consider their internal production processes, and how these may be integrated into a complete physical distribution system that offers the company a competitive edge.

Summary

This chapter has concentrated on the range of choices faced by the potential exporter in promoting and distributing a product or service. For most SMEs in particular, development of new product or significant product modification specifically for international markets may not, at least initially, be cost-effective. This places pressure on other aspects of the marketing mix. As we have seen, a major theme is the degree of control an exporter wishes to exert over the marketing and distribution process, and the consequent level of risk, in ensuring a successful export operation. The prime example is greater control over pricing through appropriate terms and quotation in a foreign currency. Together with this issue of control is the question of how far to tailor a marketing strategy to individual markets or to adopt a global approach. For many companies, both large and small, a major factor is cost. In the case of Bonas Machine Company, discussed in chapter 5 (p.139), one SME used a range of marketing techniques, including catalogues and videos translated into a number of languages, to build a market position. Initial success allowed it to capitalise on its position, moving from the use of agents to establishing its own sales and service centres in key markets. In this way it made a successful transition to direct control over marketing geared closely to the needs of individual countries.

With these issues in mind, look at the following case study and answer the questions which follow.

✎   CASE STUDY
        Country Gardens
Country Gardens is a small Cotswold-based manufacturer of toiletries, with a mid-price range of soaps and perfumes which is pitched below the more exclusive names, and targeted at a largely middle-aged, middle-income audience attracted by its clas-

sically English brand image and distinctive floral packaging. Initial research suggests potential market demand in the USA, Germany, Italy and Japan. Since an extended production run would reduce unit costs for the range, and would help margins on the core UK product while taking up spare capacity, there is some flexibility on costs. The managing director is keen to keep export prices under control, having suffered in past export ventures from the range being effectively priced out of its target markets.

Questions for discussion

The managing director has asked you to provide a report on the following issues:

a) In what ways could Country Gardens control pricing in export markets? The managing director is considering the alternatives of using an agent or researching direct approaches to retailers – what impact might each of these approaches have on pricing?

b) What promotion channels could Country Gardens use in reaching its target audience in its various export markets?

c) Country Gardens has had some success with prize draw promotions. What problems might there be in arranging such promotions in the Italian or German markets, for example? What alternatives might it consider?

d) What issues might Country Gardens consider in choosing a promotion agency?

Further reading

There are many books on international marketing, and 'international business' texts also often incorporate sections or chapters on international marketing. The list below contains four titles which are both readable and thorough in their coverage.

G. Albaum, L. Dowd, E. Duerr and J. Strandskov, *International Marketing and Export Management* (2nd. edition), Addison Wesley, 1994.

H. Chee and R. Harris, *Marketing: A Global Perspective*, Pitman Publishers, 1993.

S. Paliwoda, *International Marketing* (2nd. edition), Butterworth Heinemann, 1993.

V. Terpstra and R. Sarathy, *International Marketing* (5th. edition), Dryden Press, 1991.

Notes

1 J. Samuels, S. Greenfield and H. Mpuku, 'Exporting and the Smaller Firm', *International Small Business Journal*, Vol. 10 No. 2, 1991/2.

2 V. Terpstra and R. Sarathy, *International Marketing* (5th edition), Dryden Press, 1991.

3 *International Marketing Data and Statistics*, Euromonitor page 401, Euromonitor 1988.

4 'Advertising Statistics', *International Journal of Advertising*, 1988, pages 17–93.

4 Financing international operations

Objectives

By the end of this chapter, you will be able to:

- identify the main features of the financial instruments available to international firms, to finance foreign investment.
- identify the financial markets available for the supply of these financial instruments.
- analyse the financial risks that international firms face, and understand the main means by which such risks may be reduced.
- understand the workings of the foreign exchange markets, and their importance for international firms.
- evaluate the role of the international banking sector in servicing the activities of international firms.

Introduction

> ✎   CASE STUDY
>   Amway sparks interest in global Japanese issues
> The *Financial Times* reported in July 1994 that the previous month's global offering by Amway Japan, the Japanese arm of the US home care products group, had attracted a wide range of international buyers. A well-known name, a stable profits record and extensive presentations to investors were regarded as the ingredients for the deal's success.
>
> Many Japanese companies, the *Financial Times* said, have now begun to look to overseas equity markets for funds. Earlier the same month Nippon Telegraph and Telephone, the country's partially privatised telecommunications operator, had announced it was applying to list on the London and New York stock exchanges to enhance its profile among the global financial community. In Japan the domestic market remained tightly regulated by the ministry of finance. Foreign investment houses were pointing out the difficulty in selling shares in bulk due to restrictions which limit the number an investor can acquire in a public offering.
>
> Japanese companies have long raised capital on overseas bond markets as a result of the tightly regulated domestic market. It might not be long, said the *Financial Times*, before a similar trend developed within global equity markets.
>
> Source: adapted from the *Financial Times*, 11.5.94

The international firm has to interact with a financial world both more complex and more diverse than that which faces firms operating in just one country. It has to transact business in different currencies, deal with new financial systems, and become familiar with the operation of international financial markets and institutions. This chapter is concerned with the risks and opportunities arising from these activities, and looks at how firms take them into account in the management of the financial side of international operations.

Financing the international investment

International firms use three main financial instruments to finance foreign investment: loans, bonds and equity. Loans and bonds taken together are known as debt financing. These three instruments are available through various financial markets including the domestic markets of the firm's own country, the local debt and equity markets of the other countries within which it operates, and the international financial markets.

Loan markets

In general, most international firms tend to use local and domestic loan markets to raise at least part of their working capital, and often for longer term finance. Borrowing from local markets can be less expensive than borrowing from domestic markets in the international firm's home country, especially where local loans are subsidised by the foreign country government as part of its strategy toward inward foreign investment.[1] However, for larger companies, the most important loan market is the international money market, more usually known as the eurocurrency market.

Eurocurrency is the name given to any currency, deposited in a bank outside its country of issue, that banks are willing to accept as a eurocurrency deposit. When pounds are deposited in banks in Britain, the transaction takes place in the domestic market; but if they are deposited in a bank in France, for example, or in banks in the US, Hong Kong or indeed any country other than Britain, they become europounds (or eurosterling) and the transaction is a eurocurrency transaction in the eurocurrency market. This is the case for all participating currencies. Francs become eurofrancs when deposited in banks outside France, yen become euroyen when deposited in banks outside Japan, dollars become eurodollars, and so on.

Eurocurrency markets started in the late 1950s,[2] when large amounts of dollars were being held outside the US as bank deposits in Europe and elsewhere. The dollar was the currency most frequently used in international trade transactions, and it was more convenient for business purposes that dollars paid and received by international companies were kept in international banks rather than domestically in banks in the US. In addition, some countries preferred to keep their international trading dollars outside the US for political reasons. Since then, the eurocurrency market has expanded and now includes all the world's major currencies.

The eurocurrency market is not in fact one market, but a set of markets, each of which is located in a major world financial centre. The London eurocurrency market is the largest in the world, accounting for nearly twenty per cent of all transactions by value.[3]

Only banks have direct access to the markets, and companies borrowing from the eurocurrency market do so indirectly by acquiring loans from participating banks. Eurocurrency markets deal in short term loans and deposits with a maturity of one year or less. (It is possible to borrow for longer than this, but such longer loans are known as 'eurocredit'.)

The greatest demand for loans comes from banks for interbank transactions, followed by demand from governments; only about twenty per cent of the market is taken up by loans to companies. The loans are funded by deposits made by banks, companies, governments and individuals.[4]

Interest rates are generally lower for borrowers, and higher for depositors, in eurocurrency markets than in domestic markets. This is as a result of specific structural features unique to these markets. First, eurocurrencies are not counted as part of domestic money supply, because they are held outside their country of issue. They are therefore not subject to domestic monetary or interest rate policies; this means that interest rates on eurocurrency loans and deposits reflect only the supply and demand situation for loans and deposits in particular eurocurrencies, in the markets where the transactions take place.

Second, eurocurrency markets deal only in large scale wholesale transactions which have to be of a minimum acceptable size. In eurodollar markets, for example, this is rarely less than $1 million.[5] Because transactions are large, costs per unit of currency transacted are reduced, lowering the cost of loans to borrowers.

Lastly, eurocurrency markets are unregulated. In domestic loan markets, banks are required to hold reserves equal to a certain minimum percentage of the deposits they take, to ensure coverage of withdrawals on demand. These reserves are held in cash, which does not pay interest, and in highly liquid assets with very low interest rates. In eurocurrency markets deposit takers do not have to hold reserves, which means that lower interest rates can be offered to borrowers and higher rates to depositors.

The interest rates charged are based on the interbank interest rate of the country where the transaction takes place. In London the interbank borrowing rate rate is called the LIBOR (London Inter Bank Offer Rate), and the interbank deposit rate is the LIBID (London Interbank Bid Rate). Loans to companies are made at a small percentage above the LIBOR, depending on the creditworthiness of the company.

Bonds

International investment can also be financed by issuing bonds. Bonds are long term securities, usually with a maturity of between four and ten years. Interest is paid on them for their period of issue, and their ownership can be traded through the secondary bond markets. There are various types of bonds, the main ones being fixed rate bonds, floating bonds and equity option bonds.

The fixed rate bond, which is sometimes called a straight bond, is the most common type; it gives a fixed rate of interest which is usually paid annually. The floating rate bond gives variable interest, with the interest rate usually being adjusted on an annual or six-monthly basis. Equity option bonds also pay interest, but include an equity option which allows bondholders to convert the bond into a shareholding in the company at a later date, should they wish to do so.

For issuing purposes, bonds are further differentiated into domestic bonds and international bonds, with international bonds being of two kinds, foreign bonds and eurobonds. Domestic bonds are issued through domestic bond markets by residents of that country.

Foreign bonds

Foreign bonds are issued by international companies because they give access to potential investors in another country, increasing the amount of money that can be raised; many companies operating internationally issue foreign bonds in addition to domestic bond issues. Foreign bonds are those issued in a particular bond market by foreign borrowers, rather than by borrowers resident in that country; they are subject to the same conditions of issue as domestic bonds in that market. They are denominated in the currency of the country in which they are placed, and underwritten and sold by national underwriting syndicates in the lending country.

Eurobonds

A eurobond is an international bond underwritten by an international syndicate and sold in countries other than that of the currency in which the bond is denominated (Buckley, 1992). The eurobond market grew particularly rapidly in the 1960s and 1970s because of restrictions on the use of markets in the USA; these were imposed first on foreign firms, and later on US MNEs too, as part of a US government policy of reducing balance of payments deficits.[6] Even though these restrictions are no longer in force, the eurobond market has continued to grow and is now an important source of long term funding, particularly for MNEs. Eurobonds are sold simultaneously in several countries, rather than just in one at a time as is the case with foreign bonds; this enables larger sums of money to be raised. Since 1989, a variant of the eurobond, which has beome known as the global bond, has been issued in international capital markets. These are very large issues, which are sold simultaneously in the world's major capital markets in Europe, the USA and Asia.[7]

✎   CASE STUDY
        Grandmet launches further $200m issue

In August 1994, the *Financial Times* reported: 'The traditional August lull, exaggerated by a national holiday in Switzerland, started yesterday, with only a few new issues launched in a generally subdued way.

'Grand Metropolitan, the UK food and drinks group, added a $200m tranche to its $400m offering of five year bonds launched in May. The proceeds of the new issue will be used to repay existing long term debt. "We wanted to strengthen our balance sheet by further pushing out the maturity profile of our debt," according to a Grandmet treasury official.

'The $400m deal launched in May, the company's debut in the eurodollar bond market, was also designed to improve the group's name recognition among European bond investors.'

Source: adapted from the *Financial Times*, 2.8.94

Equity financing

Equity financing involves the issue of shares through a stock exchange. This is usually done through the stock exchange of the home country of the international firm, but where domestic markets are too small to meet substantial demands, companies may seek to obtain a listing on a foreign stock exchange. Such listings give the company a higher profile internationally, and diversify sources of finance. The International Stock Exchange (ISE) based in London has the highest number of foreign listings, but the New York and Tokyo exchanges have larger turnover in foreign equity. About sixty per cent of all share trading outside home countries is completed via London.[8]

CASE STUDY
'Nokia to raise more than FM 2bn in global issue'

In May 1994 the *Financial Times* reported that Nokia, the Finnish telecommunications group, had just announced plans to raise more than FM 2bn ($370m) of new equity in the biggest international share issue ever made by a Finnish company.

Up to 6 million new preferred shares would be offered, increasing total outstanding shares to 74.9 million. At the previous day's closing price of FM 410, the issue would raise more than FM 2.4bn. The offer could take foreign ownership in the group above 50 per cent. An estimated 46 per cent of the company's capital was already held by foreigners compared with 20 per cent a year earlier. Around 90 per cent of the shares would be targeted at non-Finnish institutions, with the balance being offered on the domestic market. Most of the international offer would be directed at the US, where the company planned to seek a listing on the New York stock exchange. Mr Jorma Ollila, Nokia's president, said the funds would be used to finance the group's rapidly growing telecommunications and mobile phone businesses and to strengthen its balance sheet.

The company, the world's second biggest supplier of mobile phones after Motorola of the US, had seen huge growth in sales of mobile and fixed telephone equipment. Its share price had risen five-fold between the beginning of 1993 and May 1994. Nokia intended to launch the issue during the summer, but was first seeking shareholder approval at an extraordinary general meeting.

Source: adapted from the *Financial Times*, 26.5.94

Euroequity

Euroequities are shares traded on a stock exchange outside the home country of the firm. Borrowing by means of euroequity is different from obtaining a listing on a foreign stock exchange, in that it involves the simultaneous sale of a firm's shares in several different countries with or without listing the shares on exchanges in these countries.

The venture capital market

This market is used by firms seeking finance for activities which are considered to be of too high a risk to fund through other financial markets. Such activities may include the opening up of a new market or developing a new product; most venture capital financing is associated with the development of high technology products by smaller firms which are unable to attract finance from other sources.

The providers of venture capital may be independently owned organisations set up solely to provide capital for such high risk investment, or banks, insurance companies and insurance funds. International companies such as 3i, as well as international banks, provide this form of finance. The UK has the largest venture capital base in Europe, followed by that of France.

Although there is such a wide variety of financial markets, for many international firms the local and domestic markets meet their needs for finance, whether in the form of bank loans, equity or bonds. Only the largest international firms have access to all the international markets. However, all international firms are subject to risks from foreign currency fluctuations, and it is to this aspect of international financial management that we now turn.

Financial risk

An international firm faces more financial risk than a purely domestic firm, because it has to transact business in foreign currencies. The additional risks arise from exchange rate fluctuations among different currencies, and international firms have to adopt appropriate strategies to minimise their impact. The term 'exposure' is often used in this context, and means that the home currency value of assets, cash flows and profits changes as exchange rates change.

International firms face three types of exposure to foreign exchange risk: translation exposure, transaction exposure and economic exposure.

Translation exposure
This comes about because accounts have to be prepared to cover the whole of the international firm's activities. For MNEs this means amalgamating the accounts of foreign subsidiaries and other companies into group accounts, and translating the accounts into the home reporting currency. The question that translation exposure poses is which exchange rate to use in the translation. Companies have three main choices: the historic rate, which is the rate that applied when the transaction was recorded; the current rate, the rate in force when the translation was made; or some variant of the two, such as a weighted average of exchange rates over the period between the times when the transaction was made and the translation prepared. For volatile currencies, the translated accounts may differ considerably according to which rate is used.

Transaction exposure
Transaction exposure arises because the value of transaction carried out in another currency may vary because of changes in exchange rates. This risk affects all cash flows denominated in foreign currency, including receipts and payments, and loans and bank deposits in foreign currencies.

Economic exposure
Economic exposure has similarities to transaction exposure, but refers to the exposure of *future*, as distinct from current, cash flows and assets denominated in foreign cur-

rency; it arises from changes in the wider economic environment within which foreign operations take place.

Managing translation exposure

Translation exposure is different from transaction and economic exposure in that it does not change the value of the firm's cash flows, assets and profits, but just restates them in another currency. This means that the exposure itself changes according to the method used for the translation.

As a risk, translation exposure is no longer seen as a major problem for international companies; most countries have a set of rules for reporting group accounts to shareholders, and a standardised set of accounting principles and procedures to ensure comparability.

CASE STUDY
US accounting cuts Fiat losses

In July 1994 the *Financial Times* reported that the US accounts of Fiat, the Italian automotive and industrial group, showed a 1993 net loss almost L1,000bn ($662m) lower than the loss shown by the group's European results. The disparity was the result of accounting differences.

In May 1994, Fiat announced a record consolidated loss of L1,783bn for 1993, after minority interests, extraordinary items and tax. In the US accounts, deposited with the US authorities at the end of June 1994, the net loss is L794bn. (The comparative profits in 1992 were L551bn in the European accounts, and L375bn in the US equivalent.) At the same time, shareholders' equity was slightly higher in Fiat's US accounts for 1993: L18,725bn, compared with L17,427bn in the European accounts.

Mr Carlo Gatto, a senior vice president in Fiat's administration and audit division, explained that the difference in the net results was particularly marked in the 1993 accounts because the group implemented changes to US rules on accounting for deferred tax liabilities and assets. When the cumulative effect of the changed accounting principles was included, Fiat's US profit and loss account was adjusted upwards by L1,308bn, although this figure was offset by other negative items. The adjustment to shareholder's equity was mainly due to differences in accounting for goodwill in acquisitions.

Fiat had indicated at its shareholder meeting at the end of June 1994 that it would return to net profit for 1994.

Source: adapted from the *Financial Times*, 14.7.94

Managing transaction exposure

Transaction exposure is usually managed by some form of hedging. A hedge is an asset or some other financial instrument whose value moves in the opposite direction to the exposure and offsets it; although the exposure still exists, it has effectively been neutralised. The international firm has a wide choice of hedging techniques, which may be categorised as those which can be incorporated into the firm's internal operating procedures, and those which involve external transactions in financial markets.

Internal techniques

Risk shifting. This can be undertaken in different ways, but in all cases it involves shifting the risk to someone else through the currency used in the invoicing for foreign transactions. One method is to invoice only in the home currency; the risk is then passed on to the customers, who have to exchange their local currency for the home currency to pay for their purchases. This method can only be used where there is little or no competition, or where competitors adopt the same procedure – otherwise there is a danger of losing customers to firms who do not use this method of invoicing. Alternatively, invoice prices may be directly linked to exchange rates; invoices are issued in the currency of the customer, who then pays a surcharge – or receives a repayment – based on movements in the exchange rate between the time the invoice is sent out and the payment date.

Risk sharing. This is a technique which has been used for some considerable time. It is widely used for long term and high value contracts, and where companies have a long history of trading together. The price remains fixed, provided exchange rates remain within a limited range. If they go outside this range, the buyer and seller negotiate some mutually acceptable means of sharing the resulting gain or loss.

Leading and lagging. These techniques are used for intergroup transactions between foreign subsidiaries, and between subsidiaries and the parent company, when it is anticipated that exchange rates will rise or fall significantly. They either speed up or delay payments in foreign currency. Leading involves collecting foreign currency accounts owed before the due date for payment, when the foreign currency is expected to weaken; and paying foreign currency accounts before they are due when the foreign currency is expected to strengthen. Lagging delays receiving foreign currency accounts if that currency is expected to strengthen, and delays paying foreign currency accounts when the currency is expected to weaken. These strategies of leading and lagging reduce the transaction exposure risk for the whole group of companies.

Netting. This can be used by associated companies in different countries which trade with each other. Such companies will have various cash flows in foreign currency going between them at any one time. Netting involves calculating the net cash flow in the currencies passing between them, with the debtor company paying the balance.

Matching. Here a company receiving foreign currency uses it to pay accounts due in that currency, so that there is no need to convert the foreign currency into home currency when received, and then back again to pay accounts in the same foreign currency.

However, not all these techniques are available at all times. Netting, matching and leading and lagging are illegal business practice in some countries, and their use is heavily restricted in some others.[9]

External techniques

External techniques involve the use of external markets, and include forward contracts, foreign currency lending and borrowing, and the use of currency swaps, futures and options.

Forward contracts. These involve using forward foreign exchange markets. The company contracts to buy foreign currency at an agreed price for delivery at a future date – which may be in thirty days, three months, six months, a year or longer. Only the most commonly used and stable currencies can be contracted for. Using forward contracts means that the price of foreign currency is known in advance. However, risk is not eliminated altogether. There is no guarantee that the forward rate will be cheaper than the prevailing rate at the time of delivery; if it proves not to be, then the currency is actually more expensive under a forward contract.

Borrowing. A company which has a guaranteed succession of payments coming in a particular currency may arrange a loan in that currency, using the incoming payments to pay off the loan, so that the company does not have to convert the foreign currency received into home currency at all. For this method to be viable, interest payments on the loan have to be less than the costs of converting the foreign currency into home currency, allowing also for any changes in the exchange rate in the firm's favour over the life of the loan.

Currency swaps. These involve two firms in different countries. Each company borrows its own currency in its own home market. Then, working through a swap dealer, the two companies swap their currency at an agreed rate, with each company paying the interest on the other's loan.

Futures. A futures contract is an agreement to buy or sell a standard quantity of a specific currency at a future date, and at a price agreed, through an organised futures exchange, such as the London International Financial Futures Exchange (LIFFE), the International Monetary Market (IMM) in Chicago, or the Philadelphia Stock Exchange (PSE). Such contracts are similar to the forward contract in that a price is agreed in advance. However, for international companies financial futures contracts are not necessarily better than forward contracts for covering foreign exchange risk. There are only four delivery dates a year, whereas forward contracts can be arranged for dates convenient for the company; and only a small number of currencies are dealt in. In addition, futures contracts are for amounts which cannot be varied; if, for example, dollars were available in blocks of $100,000, this would mean that $100,000 could be contracted for, or $200,000, but not $150,000. Thus a company cannot necessarily contract for the amount it wishes, as in a forward contract; it may have to accept an amount smaller or larger than it requires. Because of this, these markets tend to be used mainly by currency traders and speculators, with only a small number of contracts taken out by international companies seeking to cover foreign exchange risk.

Options. Currency options enable companies to benefit from favourable movements in exchange rates, whilst not committing them to buying or selling currencies when movements are unfavourable. Only the major world currencies are traded in the currency options markets. When a company takes out a currency option, it pays a premium for the right (but not the obligation) to buy or sell a specific currency at an agreed price, at any time up to an agreed date. If it decides not to exercise its option, only the premium is lost, plus any fees paid.

CASE STUDY
Down to earth treasurer

The *Financial Times* of 2 June 1994 quoted Richard Desmond, group treasurer of the tobacco and insurance group BAT Industries, as saying that at BAT (with sales of £13bn in 1993) 'the size of the organisation is large in relation to the size of foreign exchange risks'.

The treasury department is centred in the UK, and Mr Desmond's team both deals and devises the foreign exchange strategies. The group reports to shareholders in sterling but it is a worldwide operation, with costs and revenues in many different currencies. Exposures across the group are netted so that a subsidiary which has, for example, dollar costs can obtain dollars from the head office at a budget rate. As the BAT treasurer pointed out, there are four potential elements of a company's foreign exchange risk: the third party transactions of operating groups; non-remitted profits of subsidiaries; dividends and other financial flows to the core; and foreign currency assets.

On third party transactions Mr Desmond said that 'every subsidiary should be managing its foreign exchange exposure', although he pointed out that most subsidiaries' exposures should not be large, since they had local cost factors. The subsidiaries were not without guidance on how they should handle their foreign exchange dealings. BAT ran a course in which all financial staff were trained in the style of the group. The head office also had a range of policies to cover what the subsidiaries could do, and substantial transactions had to be approved at the sub-operating group level.

Non-remitted profits which were being retained by subsidiaries for future growth were not hedged. They were recorded by the parent company after having been translated at the average exchange rates for the year.

Dividends and other financial flows were managed actively but conservatively, according to Mr Desmond. 'When volatility goes up, our strategy gets more conservative; when it goes down we become slightly more active. If volatility goes down a bit we use an option strategy. The cost is lower if the volatility is lower.'

For much of the time, BAT made straightforward transactions in the spot and forward markets, or using stop-loss strategies with the target of achieving the average exchange rate for the year.

When it comes to dealing with the exchange risk created by foreign currency assets, Mr Desmond said there were three possibilities. The first was to make it abundantly clear to shareholders that the group has foreign currency assets, which are not hedged, and let them assess the attractiveness of the shares on that basis. This approach would mean that all the company's borrowings would be denominated in sterling, the currency in which the results are reported. The second strategy was to match the debt exactly with the assets in currency terms so that when foreign exchange markets bob up and down, the value of the group's reserves stays the same.

Mr Desmond said BAT used a third approach. 'We are a little more sophisticated. We look at the currency ratio of the future cash flows as well as the assets.' He explained that this meant that when 'currencies move our debt/equity ratio and interest cover ratio will tend to be stable.'

Source: adapted from the *Financial Times*, 2.6.94

In addition to these methods of managing transactions exposure, most countries have government agencies which provide insurance against foreign exchange risk on import and export transactions for their own home-country firms. For example, in Britain this facility is available from the government-funded Export Credit and Guarantee Department (ECGD), in France from COFACE, and in the US from the Eximbank. In return for a fee, agencies such as these take on the cost of adverse movements in exchange rates, and receive the profit from favourable movements.

Managing economic exposure

Techniques for the management of economic exposure are less clear cut than those for the management of translation and transactions exposures. There are two main strategies which companies may opt to use. First, they can hedge by ensuring that debt is denominated in various currencies, in the hope that a change in the exchange rate of any one of these currencies may be offset by a change in the exchange rate in at least one of the others. The second option is to move production to a country where exchange rates are considered to be more stable, or to change sourcing to another country. In general, however, decisions as central to the firm's operations as these are usually based on wider considerations than just economic exposure.[10]

Foreign exchange markets

Foreign exchange market is the term used to encompass all the locations where currencies are bought and sold. Most transactions take place through the interbank market, which is an informal arrangement of large commercial banks and a number of foreign exchange brokers engaged in buying and selling currencies. The commercial banks act as foreign exchange traders, buying and selling currencies, and brokers try to link buyers and sellers in one transaction. Commercial banks are the primary source from which individuals and companies obtain foreign currency for business and travel purposes, with the banks buying and selling foreign currencies on their behalf.

The banks and the brokers are linked together by a worldwide computer and communications network known as SWIFT (the Society for Worldwide International Financial Telecommunications).[11] Central banks are also involved in the markets, buying and selling home and foreign currencies to ensure that the exchange rate of their home currency moves in line with policies established by their governments.

Speculation

Although speculators are often considered to be a separate group of participants in foreign exchange markets, in actual fact banks, companies, governments and indeed individuals can also speculate in foreign currencies. Speculation involves buying foreign currency without at the same time contracting to sell it, and holding it until exchange rates move in such a way that the currency can be sold at a profit. Alternatively, foreign currency may be sold at a profit before it has been paid for.

Arbitrage

The exchange rate for any particular currency varies between locations, because of different patterns in buying and selling. In general, however, differences in the prices at which currencies are bought and sold in the various markets throughout the world are very small because of foreign exchange arbitrage. Arbitrage involves simultaneously contracting in two or more foreign exchange markets to buy and sell foreign currency, profiting from different rates being offered in different markets. Arbitrageurs are usually large commercial banks, or institutions or individuals who engage in such large transactions that worthwhile advantage can be taken of very small differences between exchange rates in different currency markets.

Foreign exchange transactions

Exchange rates also vary according to the type of foreign exchange transaction involved. There are four main types of foreign exchange transaction: spot and forward transactions, futures and currency options. (The last two of these were considered earlier in this chapter.) Of these, spot and forward transactions make up the bulk of foreign exchange market business (58 per cent and 39 per cent respectively, in 1992) with a much lower proportion of futures and options – 0.5 per cent and 2.5 per cent respectively (*Euromoney*, June 1994).

Spot markets

A spot transaction is defined as an exchange of currencies completed in one day – although in practice this is extended to within two business days of the agreed exchange. Rates are quoted by currency dealers in the form of two prices: the bid price, which is the price at which they will buy the currency; and the offer price, the price at which they will sell the currency. The difference between the two prices is known as the 'spread', and is the margin on which profit is earned.

The rates can be quoted either directly or indirectly. A direct quote refers to the amount of home currency necessary to buy one unit of foreign currency; while the indirect quote is the reverse – in other words, it indicates how much foreign currency can be bought with one unit of home currency.

Another term used in spot markets is the cross rate, which is an exchange rate calculated from two other rates. Currencies are quoted through the dollar. The cross rate for the Swiss franc and the Spanish peseta, for example, is calculated by converting Swiss francs into dollars using the Swiss franc/dollar spot rate, and then converting these dollars into Spanish pesetas using the dollar/peseta spot rate. All currencies have cross rates except the dollar.

Forward markets

The forward rate is quoted by foreign exchange traders for the exchange of a specified amount of currency at a fixed future time. As in the spot market, traders quote both offer and bid rates. The most important determinants of the forward rate are the spot rate, and the direction in which it is expected to move over the forward period. If the forward rate is less than the spot rate it is said to be at a discount; if it is more than the spot rate, it is said to be at a premium.

Governments and exchange rates

Governments intervene in foreign exchange markets in an attempt to influence their home currency's exchange rate against other currencies. The amount and degree of intervention is directly an outcome of the foreign exchange system the country is operating. There are two basic types of exchange rate system, fixed and floating. In fixed systems the currency is given a parity or fixed rate, usually against another currency, and governments intervene by buying and selling the home currency to maintain this parity within pre-agreed limits. Under a floating exchange rate system, the currency's value against others is intended to be determined solely by the forces of demand and supply in the foreign exchange markets. (In practice, however, governments usually intervene to manage the value of the currency to some extent.)

Under the Bretton Woods system which operated from after the second World War until the beginning of the 1970s, participating currencies were given a parity against the US dollar, whose value was linked to gold. Currencies could move within pre-agreed limits (usually one and a quarter per cent) either side of parity. When the value of a currency moved outside this band, however, the issuing government was committed to intervening in foreign exchange markets, buying or selling the currency to restore its value to within the agreed limits. If a currency had persistent difficulty staying within these limits, the parity value could be renegotiated through the International Monetary Fund (IMF); the currency would be revalued or devalued, giving a new parity against the dollar from that time on.

Since the breakdown of the Bretton Woods system in 1973 major currencies have operated under floating rate systems, with the majority of developing countries' currencies being pegged to particular currencies such as the dollar or franc, or a weighted average of major currencies. Although the major currencies are floating, it is 'managed' floating, with governments intervening extensively to maintain or influence the value of home currency in line with their own economic policies.

The European Monetary System (EMS)

The EMS was created in 1979 with the intention of creating exchange rate stability within the then European Community, and to encourage closer monetary co-operation between the member states. The two main elements which have a direct effect on exchange rates are the European Currency Unit (ECU) and the Exchange Rate Mechanism (ERM).

The ECU
This is a monetary unit made up of a 'basket' of all member states' currencies, weighted in accordance with the size of each country's GNP and the volume of intra-European Union trade it transacts. The composition is reviewed on a regular basis every five years, but review also takes place when the weighting factors of any one currency change by 25%.

Composition of the ECU (September 1989)

Currency	Weighting
Deutschemark	30.4
Dutch guilder	9.6
Belgian/Luxembourg franc	8.1*
Danish krone	2.5
French franc	19.3
Irish punt	1.1
Italian lira	9.7
Pound sterling	12.6
Greek drachma	0.7
Spanish peseta	5.2
Portuguese escudo	0.8

*The exchange rate between the Belgian franc and the Luxembourg franc is fixed with no margin of fluctuation.

Source: *Economic Briefing No. 1*, December 1990

Figure 4.1

Within the countries of the European Union, the ECU is the means of settlement between central banks and the unit of account for official EU business. It is also a currency quoted on foreign exchange markets and in international money markets. More recently ECU bonds have been issued on international markets, and there is also trading in ECU futures and ECU options.

The ERM

While all members' currencies are included in the ECU, members of the EU are not automatically members of the ERM; they have a choice as to whether or not to join. Britain was only a member between 1990 and 1992, for example, and Greece has never joined. The ERM was designed to provide exchange rate stability between member currencies. Participating currencies are assigned a central rate, expressed as units of currency per ECU. From these central rates a parity grid or set of cross rates can be derived, showing the bilateral rates between any pair of currencies.

The central banks of participating currencies are committed to intervening when currencies move close to specified outside margins around the bilateral rate with another currency. Until August 1993 this margin was plus or minus 2.25% (or 6% in the case of both the pound and the peseta). This meant that if a currency fell to its floor of 2.25% against another, then that country's central bank was committed to selling the stronger currency, and the central bank of the stronger currency would buy the threatened currency. In this way stability of member states' currencies against each other was guaranteed within certain known limits. If a currency had persistent difficulties staying within these margins, it could be realigned within the Mechanism and given a different central parity against the ECU.

In September 1992 the ERM system was disrupted by heavy speculative selling of many of its participating currencies on foreign exchange markets. Severe pressure was placed first on the pound and then on the lira. This was followed by problems caused by large scale selling of the peseta, the escudo, the punt and the French franc, which resulted in Britain and Italy suspending their membership of the ERM and returning to managed floating. Continuing pressure on the peseta, the escudo, and the punt led first to the peseta being devalued within the ERM, and then the introduction of exchange controls by Spain, Portugal and Ireland in order to control currency movements in and out of their countries. After seven realignments of currencies, it was finally decided in August 1993 to widen the intervention limits to plus or minus 15%.[12]

Forecasting exchange rates

Exchange rate forecasting has to take into account the courses of action the participants in foreign exchange markets are likely to take under different circumstances. This has led to various competing explanations of the causes of exchange rate movements. The main theories of exchange rate change are concerned with the current account of the balance of payments; with interest rates; and with inflation rates.

Current account. The current account of the balance of payments records the value of imports and exports of both goods and services. When import values exceed export values there is a deficit on current account, and demand for foreign currency to pay for imports exceeds demand for home currency to pay for exports; the value of the home currency should then fall. When exports exceed imports, demand for home currency is greater than for foreign currency, and the exchange rate should then rise.

Interest rates. The main theory which tries to explain exchange rate movements by movements in interest rates is that of the international 'Fisher effect'. This forecasts future spot rates by comparing the difference in interest rates in different countries. According to the theory, if interest rates go up in one of a pair of countries, then that country's exchange rate should depreciate against the other country's currency by an amount equal to the difference in interest rates.

Inflation rates. The theory of Purchasing Power Parity (PPP) states that exchange rates change in such a way as to eradicate differences in the inflation rate between countries. When one country has an inflation rate higher than another, its exports are likely to be more expensive relative to those of the other country. Demand for these exports should therefore fall, leading to deficits on the balance of payments and a resulting fall in the value of the currency. This situation is only corrected when inflation rates become equalised between the two countries.

Although no one of these explanations alone explains all movements in exchange rates, taken together they do identify some of the major economic influences – often called 'fundamentals' – which may affect exchange rates in general. Even so, rates are difficult to predict, and they can also be affected by unexpected political, economic or other events which can result in fluctuations in both spot and forward markets.

✐   CASE STUDY
        Cabinet row hits lira
Philip Gawith reported in the *Financial Times* of 19 July 1994 that fall-out from a Cabinet squabble in Italy had dominated foreign exchanges the previous day, as the lira fell to a low for the year. The first serious schism within Italy's two month old government had driven the currency to a new low against the D-Mark, before recovering to finish firmer in London. Traders were concerned whether what appeared to be Mr Berlusconi's first serious policy error might not spill over into problems in management of the economy.

The D-Mark was stronger on the back of political uncertainty in both Italy and France, where the communications minister had resigned over the weekend. Sterling had an uneventful day, with the market ignoring the June public sector borrowing figures which were below expectations.

Source: adapted from the *Financial Times*, 19.7.94

Companies rarely engage directly in exchange rate forecasting. Some larger companies employ the services of specialist technical analysts or 'chartists', who attempt to predict future exchange rate movements by extrapolating past exchange rate trends into the future. In general, however, most companies tend to rely on trends and forecasts published by the major financial and other institutions.

This service, along with many others, is provided by international banks which have been an essential element in the expansion of international business.

International banking

Banks, of course, are international businesses in their own right with networks of different kinds of banking operation on a worldwide basis, involved in all aspects of international finance. They operate through a variety of different forms of organisation, including correspondent banking, branch banks, subsidiary and affiliate banks, consortium banking and representative offices and agencies.[13]

Correspondent and branch banking

Most major banks have correspondent banking relationships with local banks in other countries, providing a variety of services for each other and facilitating transactions for each other's clients. These services usually include providing letters of credit and dealing in bills of exchange, collecting payments and providing information.

A foreign branch bank is wholly owned by the parent bank. Branch banks are usually set up abroad to gain access to local clients, and are often used to replace correspondent banking operations.

Subsidiary and affiliate banks

Subsidiary banks have a separate legal identity from the parent bank, and are mainly concerned with investment services. Affiliate banks are similar to subsidiary banks, but are usually a joint venture involving the parent bank and other foreign banks or local banks.

Consortium banking

Consortium banks are formed by banks from several countries, each contributing to the formation of another bank to operate internationally. These specially-formed banks are able to deal in larger loans for longer periods, and usually participate in eurocurrency markets. Consortium banks are often involved in the underwriting of large international bond issues, and in the organisation of international mergers and acquisitions.

Representative offices and agencies

A representative office is the legal representive of the parent bank in a foreign country. Much of the work of a representative office involves gathering information, and although it can give advice it cannot accept deposits or provide other banking services. Representative offices are usually set up in countries where foreign banking activities are limited. Agencies are banking offices owned by a parent bank. They can make loans, issue letters of credit and trade in bills of exchange; but they cannot take deposits.

All banks operating abroad are subject to local regulation and licensing; this limits the type of operation that can be undertaken and, to some extent, protects the home market against foreign competition. Within the European Union, the Single Banking License provision of the Single European Act allows banks to operate in all member states without separate licensing for each country. This effectively turns foreign banks into domestic banks within the EU; they can undertake all the banking operations allowed by their own home-country licence in all the other member states.[14]

✎ CASE STUDY
   Full branch in Beirut for ING
The *Financial Times* reported in July 1994 that Internationale Nederlanden Bank (ING), based in Amsterdam, had won authorisation from Lebanon's central bank to establish a full branch in Beirut — the first such approval granted in 25 years, and a sign of Lebanon's desire to revive the country's lost role as a banking and financial centre. ING, said the *FT*, promised to be only the first of several new arrivals in Beirut, with a number of French and British groups also pursuing licences to open either representative offices or branches in Lebanon.

Foreign banks had previously been told they must buy a local institution to participate fully in the domestic market. But in a drive to attract new foreign institutions,
the central bank was now permitting banks to open a branch in the country, provided they met a capital requirement of $5m and reinvested 30 per cent of locally-
collected deposits domestically. Foreign newcomers would be restricted to a single
branch, but otherwise would have no conditions on their operations.

ING Bank would join 15 or so foreign banks long established in Beirut including
Citibank, American Express Bank and Chase Manhattan Bank. A spokesman for
ING in Amsterdam said he expected the branch to begin operations within a couple
of months. It would become ING's sole Middle East branch and would concentrate
on international payment transfers, corporate banking and trade finance, the
spokesman said.

The same week, Lebanon's central bank had also authorised UBAF, the London-
based group owned by Arab and French banks, to set up a representative office in
Beirut. Robert Fleming. the British investment bank, was also applying for a licence
to open a Beirut representative office.

Source: adapted from the *Financial Times*, 18.7.94

International banking services

International banks provide a wide range of services for international companies,
including loans, export financing, foreign exchange trading, and advice and information. We have already considered the foreign exchange aspect; here we will look briefly
at loans and at the advice and information the banks offer, and then (in more detail) at
export financing.

Loans

Banks are the major source of lending for companies, and are involved in debt financing of all kinds, ranging from loans for working capital and medium and long term
financing to borrowing in the eurocurrency markets. For very large loans international
banks may come together to form a syndicate, sharing the loan between them and
spreading the risk.

There are usually three types of bank involved in syndicated loans: lead banks, managing banks and participating banks, often from different countries. The lead banks are
those which organise the loan on the borrower's behalf. Other banks (the managing
banks) agree to provide the whole of the loan if necessary. Portions of the loan are then
taken on by another group of banks, the participating banks.[15]

> ✎   CASE STUDY
> Banks chase new business
>
> The rapid evolution of the international bond markets in recent years has encour-
> aged more and more borrowers to tap the capital markets directly for their core
> financing, forsaking the syndicated loans market. However, after a decline in the
> volume of conventional syndicated credits over a period of years, by the mid-1990s
> there were some signs that this decline was being reversed.
>
> In 1993, international syndicated loans volume reached some $130bn, according to
> the Organisation for Economic Co-operation and Development's *Financial Market
> Trends* – about $12bn higher than the previous year. However, more than $60bn of
> that total consisted of refinancing of existing debt, particularly by US companies, so
> the total volume of new loans was $70bn, the lowest since 1986.
>
> But the international bond markets place certain demands on borrowers: they must
> generally have a relatively high credit rating, they cannot repay the debt as and when
> they want to, and they must rely on the receptiveness of the market at a given time.
> For these and other reasons, direct bank lending, syndicated or otherwise, still per-
> forms a number of vital functions.
>
> Source: adapted from the *Financial Times*, 26.5.94

Advice and information

International banks provide a range of specialist information and advice for their
clients. Utilising their networks of bank branches, subsidiaries, representative offices
and other overseas operations, they can provide economic and political risk analysis
reports on particular countries, as well as information on legislation, import restrictions, exchange controls, and other factors that may affect their clients' transactions.
They will usually also prepare reports on the creditworthiness of particular companies,
and provide documents needed for international trade.[16]

Export financing

Financial services specifically for exporters include (in addition to loans) letters of
credit; bills of exchange, or drafts; factoring; and forfaiting.

Letters of credit
Letters of credit are issued by banks, which promise to pay the exporter a specified
amount on a specific date, on behalf of the importer. For example, if a British company
is exporting goods to Germany it can ask the German company to request its bank to
issue a letter of credit. The cost of arranging this is normally borne by the importer, and
the level of costs may be negotiable to some extent.[17] The letter of credit guarantees payment at a specified time; this may be as soon as any required extra items such as invoices
or insurance documents are available, or at a later date – after (say) 30, 60 or 90 days.

The letter of credit is sent to the exporter's bank in Britain, along with any necessary
documents. Once it is received, the goods are dispatched to Germany. The exporter

draws a draft on the German bank against the importer's bank account, according to the details of the letter of credit, and takes this to its own bank in Britain for payment. The British bank pays the exporter, and then sends the draft and the documents back to the importer's bank in Germany. The German bank then pays the British bank, drawing on funds from the importer's account.

When letters of credit are described as irrevocable, none of the terms laid down in the agreement can be changed without the consent of both interested parties.

Bills of exchange, or drafts

Both the above terms are widely used. The exporter asks its bank to prepare the draft, which orders the importer or the importer's bank to pay a specific amount by a specific day. There are different types of draft. Trade drafts are addressed to the importer, while bank drafts are addressed to the importer's bank. A sight draft is a trade draft or a bank draft that must be paid upon presentation. A time draft gives the importer a specified time to pay – usually 30, 60 or 90 days after the date on the draft.

Time drafts addressed to, and accepted by, the importer are known as trade acceptances; while those addressed to, and accepted by, the importer's bank are known as banker's acceptances. As banker's acceptances are guaranteed by the importer's bank, these are less risky than trade acceptances in terms of credit risk; they can also be sold in money markets at a discount before the date specified on the draft. Once the draft has been accepted, title to the goods can then be taken by the importer, although the latter will usually also need to be in possession of other documentation such as bills of lading, a commercial invoice, and a packing list.

Factoring

Factoring is undertaken by specialised factoring houses as well as banks. Exporters can sell accounts they are owed to a factor at a discount, and the factor then receives the payment from the importer. The rate of discount depends primarily on the amount involved, and the time period before the payment is due. Factoring is often used when there is a possibility of credit risk, or where there is some political risk involved in the transaction.

There are other advantages too, especially for smaller firms. The exporter has smoother cash flow, because the factoring house will pay it up to 85% of the total payment amount immediately the goods are delivered. The balance, less the factor's fee or discount, is paid when the customer pays or goes out of business.[18] As well as relieving cash flow problems, the services provided by factoring houses can simplify export administration, and allow a company to obtain client and market information which could help with strategic planning. The fee or discount range for this service is between 1% and 3% of the invoice value, and the service is only applicable where dealings are on open account (see p. 124) and in markets seen as reliable.[19]

✎   CASE STUDY
Dunford Wood Designs
Overseas Trade reported in December 1992 that factoring had proved to be the key to financial stability and the launch pad for continued success for Warwickshire-based Dunford Wood Designs. The company produced some of the finest hand-painted silk garments in the world. It was in 1990, when bank after bank rejected a

new business plan on the basis that it was 'not a viable proposition', that the company had first turned to factoring as a means of increasing cash flow to keep up with customer demand.

'While we export to many countries,' a spokesman was reported as saying, 'our biggest overseas market is Italy. Though this is a great compliment to the quality of our designs, it also presented problems as Italians are reputed to be bad payers. We employed Alex Lawrie, firstly to manage these slow-paying customers, and most importantly to carry out credit checks on potential customers abroad ... By using Alex Lawrie, 70% of the value of export sales invoices is available within 48 hours.'

Source: *Overseas Trade*, December 1992

Forfaiting

Forfaiting is a method of financing the export of goods (especially large capital items) where the importers are allowed to stage payments, thus not completely paying for the imported items until some agreed time in the future. The originating exporter arranges a series of bills of exchange, each with a different time to maturity. If these bills are accepted by the importer, the exporter can discount them all at a relevant bank in exchange for cash, in this way acquiring immediate finance for the export order and transferring the risk of non-payment to the bank.

Forfaiting is usually undertaken when the transaction is subject to a high degree of political risk, or there is uncertainty about the creditworthiness of the importer. It is similar to factoring in that the exporter in effect sells the export account at a discount to the bank, which then collects payment of the account from the importer. In the case of forfaiting, the bank also negotiates an 'aval' or guarantee of payment from a government bank in the importing country. Forfaiting charges are usually quite expensive for the exporter, because the high risk of non-payment is reflected in both the fees and the discount charged by the forfaiting bank.

Forfaiting has been most extensively used for transactions with Eastern European countries, but is now increasingly being used for exports to emerging markets in other parts of the world. It is especially popular for transactions of between two and five years' duration.[20]

CASE STUDY
Forfaiting on the increase
The *Financial Times* reported in January 1994 that forfaiting might well provide an increasing source of support for exporters during that year. Forfaiters, usually operating from a separate unit within a bank, could provide non-recourse finance (essentially funds which are only repayable if the exporter fails to supply the goods) to exporters seeking to boost and secure foreign cash flow. Now the range of export markets for which they were prepared to provide this service was expanding.

This essentially reflected forfaiters' perceptions of improved political and commercial risk in a number of key markets – principally in Latin America, the Asia-Pacific region, and Eastern Europe. Funding for deals in Brazil, China and Slovakia had all featured in forfaiters' books in recent months. Moreover, forfaiting was also providing a way into markets as difficult and diverse as Romania, Vietnam and Peru.

Brazil was emerging as an increasingly acceptable risk, with some fundings extending for up to five years. Forfaiters were encouraged by the country's rate of growth, growing foreign reserves and positive current account flows. According to a leading Zurich-based forfaiter, 'The markets have totally opened up for Latin America.' Among Far Eastern risks, China was a growing attraction. Providing transactions carried the guarantee of a leading state bank, forfaiters were happy to help fund the country's vast imports of capital goods.

The Czech Republic, Hungary and Poland were key eastern European markets where forfaiters were now more likely to provide funding.

Source: adapted from the *Financial Times*, 27.1.94

Payment for exports – other options

Apart from letters of credit and drafts, several other options are available for receiving payment for exports.

Advance payment. It is obviously an advantage for the selling firm if the buyer is prepared to pay for the goods in advance, before they are shipped. From the importing perspective, however, this puts pressure on cash flow, and is unlikely to be a desired option. Although such terms may be desirable from an exporter's viewpoint, it may therefore not be possible to insist on them, given the nature of international competition.

Open account. Here a firm is paid for exports only after the goods have actually been received by a foreign customer. The importer is allowed time to re-sell the merchandise and then pay the exporting firm – e.g. after 30, 60, or 120 days. This approach is perhaps best used after a business relationship has evolved to include a degree of trust, since there is clearly some risk of non-payment for the exporter. It may not be the most appropriate strategy when dealing with new customers.

Consignment. Under a consignment arrangement, the exporter sends goods to a foreign customer but retains ownership of those goods until they have actually been resold in a foreign market, at which point payment is made. From an exporter's perspective this is possibly the most unpopular form of trade finance, since there is a significant risk of non-payment, and logistical and accounting difficulties often arise.

Export insurance

As well as choosing the appropriate means of payment, firms may well feel it important to take out insurance against the risk of non-payment. The nature of this risk may take a number of forms:[21]

- The foreign customer may become bankrupt.
- The customer may delay payment.
- The customer may fail to accept the goods once they have been despatched.
- A consignment may be diverted from its original route, incurring greater transport costs than envisaged which the foreign customer may not be prepared to cover.

The risks of non-payment tend to vary with changes in the general political and economic environment. However, they can be significant, even in the EU; one report on this subject stated that in the year from September 1992 to September 1993 '... one in 11 UK companies experienced a loss as a result of non-payment by buyers in France, one in 12 in Italy, one in 13 in Spain, and one in 20 in Germany.'[22]

The largest organisations offering insurance for the international trading activities of UK companies are:

- **NCM Credit Insurance**. This firm took over the business of short term insurance, through competitive tender, from the Government's Export Credit Guarantee Department (ECGD) in 1991. It has more than 70% of the short term market (the bulk of UK exports are insured on a short term basis), and provides cover in 220 countries.
- **The ECGD**. This – the agency providing government-funded support for export insurance – is now active mainly in the medium term (two to five years) and long term markets. The three basic services it offers are guarantees of payment to banks providing export finance; insurance for non-payment on export contracts; and export finance at fixed (often relatively low) rates of interest.
- **Trade Indemnity**. This is the second largest short term insurer after NCM. Although the rationale for undertaking insurance may be a sound one, Trade Indemnity suggests that the number of companies who currently take out export insurance represents no more than 15% of the total potential market.[23]

Summary

International firms have to interact with the international financial environment. They may have to raise finance in new ways, and deal with new forms of financial instruments. They will have to conduct business using foreign currencies; and to adopt strategies to minimise the risks from foreign exchange exposure, and from inexperience in unfamiliar and sometimes unpredictable markets. In all these activities international banks are important to their operations, and successful international companies make full use of the range of services available to them.

> ✎   CASE STUDY
>   The financing of Eurotunnel
> In April 1995, according to the *Financial Times*, Eurotunnel had 722,000 shareholders and was involved with 225 lending banks. In a refinancing operation in May 1994, it had raised £816m of new equity and arranged a £693m debt facility. It subsequently faced operating postponements which delayed operating revenues by some months. Revenues in 1994 were £30.6m, well below the £137m predicted the year before.

Cash flows rose above operating expenses for the first time only in March 1995. A second problem it had to face was that of funding. In April 1995 Eurotunnel was paying just under 9% interest on its £8bn of bank debt. This did not include the £693m facility, which the *FT* believed it was likely to start drawing in the middle of 1995. Funding costs would rise £50m per year for every 1% rise in short term interest rates. It was paying 2.5% above the LIBOR on the £693m facility. A big problem was the continuing rise in short-term interest rates in Europe. Some 54% of Eurotunnel's debt was variable-rate, and it had not swapped into longer term maturities in 1994 because that would have added about £100m to funding costs.

Eurotunnel was now facing the decision whether to reduce its funding costs in talks with banks, or to boost cash flows. (However, even if cash flows were boosted there was likely still to be a need to reduce funding costs as well.) According to the *FT*, there were a number of options. First, Eurotunnel could opt for a rights issue and raise more money from shareholders. Second, the banks could reduce the level of interest on the debt, or waive interest payments. They would be unlikely to do so without being compensated, for example by a debt for equity swap.

Third, Eurotunnel could refinance its bank debt either on international capital markets or through a debt replacement. Up to that point it had been unable to tap bond markets without an operating cash flow. However, it had already talked to US investment banks about the possibility of a debt refinancing. According to the *FT*, directors believed the most attractive possibility would be a convertible bond issue.

Source: adapted from the *Financial Times*, 11.4.95

Questions for discussion

1 What are the main financial instruments available to international firms to finance investment?

2 As at April 1995, Eurotunnel was financed by a mixture of equity and debt. What problems do international companies face from each of these methods of raising finance for investment?

3 What impact do changes in European interest rates have on the finances of Eurotunnel?

4 What are the advantages and disadvantages of debt financing from a US investment bank?

5 How far would you agree that a convertible bond issue would be the most attractive option available to Eurotunnel, in the circumstances quoted by the Financial Times?

Further reading

The following are particularly recommended:

Robert Z. Aliber, *The International Money Game* (5th edition), Macmillan, 1988.

Adrian Buckley, *Multinational Finance* (2nd edition), Prentice Hall, 1992.

Istemi Demirag and Scott Goddard, *Financial Management for International Business*, McGraw Hill, 1994.

David K. Eiteman and Arthur I. Stonehill, *Multinational Business Finance* (6th edition), Addison-Wesley, 1992.

Alan C. Shapiro: *Multinational Financial Management* (4th edition), Allyn and Bacon, 1992.

Notes

1 R. Grosse and D. Kujawa, *International Business,* (2nd edition), Irwin, 1992, page 187.
2 See Adrian Buckley, *Multinational Finance*, (2nd edition), Prentice Hall, 1992, pages 309–11 for discussion of the development of eurocurrency markets.
3 J.D. Daniels and L.H. Radebaugh, *International Business: Environments and operations* (7th edition), Addison-Wesley, 1995, page 717.
4 Ibid, page 717.
5 Buckley, *op cit*, page 311.
6 *Ibid*, page 326.
7 See *Financial Market Trends*, OECD, June 1994, pages 56–8 for discussion of evolution of the global bond market.
8 *Stock Exchange Fact File*, 1994.
9 See M.R. Czinkota, I.A. Ronkainen and M.H. Moffett, *International Business*, (3rd edition), The Dryden Press, 1994, page 538.
10 See *Ibid*, page 549.
11 Buckley, *op cit*, page 65.
12 For discussion of these and subsequent events, see *European Economy*, Annual Economic Report for 1994, No. 56, 1994, European Commission.
13 Nanshi F. Matsuura, *International Business, A New Era*, HBJ, 1991, pages 287–9.
14 Richard Brown, *Managing in the Single European Market*, Butterworth-Heinemann, 1993, page 164.
15 Buckley, *op cit*, pages 312–13.
16 Jill Preston (ed.), *International Business: Text and Cases*, Pitman Publishing, 1993, pages 89–92.
17 R. Axtell, *The Do's and Taboos of International Trade*, John Wiley and Sons, 1994, page 161.
18 *Overseas Trade*, December 1992, page 18.
19 *Overseas Trade*, December 1993, page 20.
20 R. Bennett, *Selling to Europe*, Kogan Page, 1991.
21 *Ibid*, page 107.
22 *Overseas Trade*, February 1994, page 24.
23 *Overseas Trade*, October 1994, page 20.

5 The small firm and international business

Objectives

By the end of this chapter, you will be able to:

- describe the characteristics of the 'pre-international' behaviour of a firm, and their impact on the decision whether or not to engage in international business.
- describe the key components of export success for a small firm.
- construct a market development plan relevant to a specified small firm.

Introduction

CASE STUDY
Tony Stone Images
The following report appeared in the May 1994 issue of *Overseas Trade*:

'Millions of negatives are held by the London photographic stock library Tony Stone Images. They are used by advertisers, designers and publishers to reflect just about every aspect of society and the human condition. Also, they are an economic alternative to specially commissioned photography.

'The company's success, particularly in the US, has led to it being one of few creative services to gain the Queen's Award. The US is the world's largest market for stock photography and home of most of Stone's major international competitors.'

Overseas Trade said the company had established offices in Los Angeles, New York, Chicago and Seattle, and others in Toronto, Paris and Munich. There were also exclusive licensing arrangements in a further 11 countries, from Belgium to New Zealand.

Started on a modest scale in 1969, the company was anticipating a worldwide 1994 turnover in excess of £20 million. Three quarters of this would come from outside the UK. 115 people were employed in London and another 145 at its other offices.

The company was among the first to apply digital technology to photography. It had invested more than £500,000 in equipment for the electronic scanning, manipulating and enhancing of images.

Source: *Overseas Trade*, May 1994

In the previous chapters we have looked at the ways companies select markets, choose a means of entry, develop a marketing strategy, and finance that strategy. In this chapter we will see how some of these approaches have been applied in practice, and how they relate specifically to the problems faced by small firms.

Although there are different ways of defining the term 'small firm', these differing definitions do not alter the fact that most firms in Europe are small; and such firms make a significant contribution to the economic health of the European Union and its member states. However, although they are a driving force in the economies of the EU, small firms are in general less likely to become involved in international business than larger ones. There are many reasons for this, but all of them are related to the resources that small firms have at their disposal (finance, management time, information etc.), and the primary motivations and objectives of senior managers in the firm, which often have a domestic orientation.

As trade barriers around the world are reduced, and information and trade finance opportunities increase, international business is becoming a more realistic possibility for many small firms. In addition, both the European Commission and the national governments of member states are currently extremely interested in supporting the activities of small firms, in recognition of their important contributions to general economic health. International business activities are therefore becoming more common in the small firms sector, as this sector reacts positively to such developments.

Although research suggests significant variation in the approach that small firms adopt towards their international activities, this chapter will investigate the 'pre-international' behaviour of firms, and survey the issues involved in constructing a strategy for exporting or licensing, the two major approaches to foreign market entry for small firms. Factors which influence success in international markets will then be considered, and this will be followed by an examination of the key problems experienced by small firms in this context – especially trade finance and market development – and possible responses to these problems.

The small firm defined

In the UK the Committee of Inquiry on Small Firms chaired by J. E. Bolton submitted its report in 1971 (supplemented by the recent reassessment *Bolton – 20 years on*). This report contained a wealth of data on small firm activities and characteristics, and has formed the basis for much of the subsequent research in this area. The report defined a small firm as one with a relatively small market share, managed by its owners in a personalised way, and independent i.e. free from outside control in decision-making. In addition, it was acknowledged that a more robust definition was needed as a basis for surveying the small business sector, and so a second, statistical, definition was offered in the report. As Figure 5.1 shows, this definition varied by industrial sector, since the committee recognised that, for example, the characteristics of a small firm in the retailing sector would be different from those in construction.

Industry	Statistical definition of small firms adopted by the committee
Manufacturing	200 employees or less
Retailing	Turnover £50,000 p.a. or less
Wholesale trades	Turnover £200,000 p.a. or less
Construction	25 employees or less
Mining/quarrying	25 employees or less
Motor trades	Turnover £100,000 p.a. or less
Miscellaneous services	Turnover £50,000 p.a. or less
Road transport	5 vehicles or less
Catering	All firms except multiples and brewery-managed public houses

Source: Bolton Report, page 3

Figure 5.1

The report also highlighted a set of common characteristics which, the committee believed, arose mainly from the following factors: the legal status, ownership, management and organisation of the small firm; its financial structure; its role as an employer; the motivations and origins of the owners; and its role in the community.

According to Bolton, small firms tend to be unincorporated, and are either partnerships or sole traders. The firms are almost exclusively controlled by their proprietors, and a large proportion of them are family businesses. 'There is rarely a formal management structure; firms are simply run by their owners.'[1] Most of the chief executives of small firms do not have any formal post-school management qualifications – a situation significantly different from that in large firms. Merger and acquisition activity was seen as significant in the sector, and most firms believed they had a large number of competitors.

In relation to financial structure, the survey sample revealed that the average small firm generated a slightly smaller proportion of its finance from external borrowing than the average large firm; bank credit was the most significant source of external finance. The committee also reported, after acknowledging measurement problems in this area, that the average small firm in the survey had a higher profit ratio than the average publicly quoted firm. The small firm tended not to be unionised, was disrupted little by strikes and, compared with large firms, tended to pay 'lower wages for similar jobs'[2]. The motivation of small firm managers focused on the delivery of a personal service and 'the need to attain and preserve independence'[3].

Some writers have criticised the economic and statistical definitions used in the Bolton report. Storey has commented[4], for example, that 'the Bolton criterion that a small business is "managed by its owners or part owners in a personalised way and not through the medium of a formal management structure" is almost certainly incompatible with its "statistical definition" of small manufacturing firms which could have up to 200 employees'. Indeed, alternative economic perspectives have been developed. Wynarczyk et al. (1993)[5] suggest three central aspects in the difference between small and large firms: uncertainty (e.g. due to a limited customer and product base); innovation (e.g. the niche role adopted by many small firms); and evolution through a number of stages, which impact on the structure and organisation of the firm as it increases in size.

The lack of a single definition of smallness presents technical difficulties of comparison, as do the different upper limits placed on turnover and employees for the different sectors. The European Commission subsequently took a lead on this issue by using the phrase 'small and medium enterprises' (SMEs), defined in terms of employment levels. SMEs are distinguished at three levels:

- micro-enterprises, employing between 0 and 9 employees;
- small enterprises, employing between 10 and 99 employees;
- medium enterprises, employing between 100 and 200–250 employees (recently revised downwards from 499).

Storey believes that this approach is less flawed than the definitional approach of Bolton; for example, it reflects the shift to 'marked formality' which occurs in firms around the ten to twenty employee level. However, even this definition cannot capture the diversity of small firm activity in the EU. But while there is no satisfactory single definition, it is clear that there is a range of key issues clustered around smaller-scale operations: low and potentially vulnerable market share, a no-nonsense hands-on management style, pressures of finance, and a focus strategy meeting the needs of a niche market. All these characteristics affect the approach of small businesses to international markets.

Small firms, the UK and the EU

Measurement problems abound in charting the contribution of small businesses to employment and economic activity in the UK over the last thirty years. Methods and details in the collection of data have changed, making direct comparisons between the present day and earlier periods difficult. However, since 1979 VAT statistics have enabled a more sophisticated analysis of these issues. One study based on this data showed that between 1979 and 1986 in the UK, the total number of businesses rose from 1.791 million to 2.471 million. Of the 1986 total, 12,000 had 200 or more employees; and only 4,000 had 500 or more. 'The share of enterprises with fewer than 500 employees increased from 57.3 to 71.3% of total private sector employment between 1979 and 1986.'[6]

Large enterprises with over 500 employees were, however, responsible for 29.4% of the aggregate turnover of all enterprises in 1986; and enterprises which had 100 or more employees were credited with 53.7% of aggregate turnover, demonstrating their disproportionate role in the UK economy. Virtually all sectors of the UK economy played a part in the increase in employment and the number of businesses from 1979 – the two exceptions being agriculture and retail distribution. This increase in activity was located in all regions of the UK, although the distribution was not even.

In the European Union the number of enterprises and employment by size classification (%) in 1986 was as shown in Figure 5.2.

Size	% of total enterprises	Share of employment (%)
Micro	91.4	26.9
Small and medium	8.5	45.0
Large	0.1	28.1

Source: Commission of the European Communities, 1990[7].

Figure 5.2

The larger countries in the EU (apart from Italy) show a pattern similar to that in the UK, in which large firms dominate sales. 'In the Community SMEs have 50% of manufacturing sales, 67% of services and 90% of construction and trade sectors'[8]. The very smallest firms tend to sell predominantly to the final consumer in niche and segmented markets, whereas small and medium sized firms are involved in the sale of intermediate goods and services; the larger the firm, the more likely it is to export.

Problems experienced by small firms

The Small Business Research Trust has surveyed small firms since 1984, and asked firms to indicate the major problems they experience. The results over a period of time are shown in Figure 5.3. This demonstrates that financial issues have come to dominate in the 1990s, in the context of the tougher business conditions identified by 23% of respondents in 1991.

When access to finance and cashflow are added to concern over interest rates, 42% of those responding indicated concern in these three areas. Some problems appear more cyclical than others – for example, lack of skilled employees became a significant concern at the end of the 1980s, but subsided in the early 1990s with the advent of the UK recession. Interestingly, the majority of problems identified could be considered external in nature. Indeed, since 'internal difficulties' have been added to the questionnaire, only 0.7 to 2.2 % of firms have seen these as their most pressing source of difficulty[9]. The key issue has been the vulnerability of small business to downturns in trade, and the knock-on effect this has on sustaining cash flow and managing credit. These problems are then compounded by the need for an overstretched management to devote time to such issues, rather than generating new business proactively.

The small firm and international business

Given that 99% of all businesses are small[10], and that small firms are seen to have certain characteristics and problems, the implications for the small firm operating in an

	Access to finance	Interest rates	Total tax burden	Competition from big business	Lack of skilled employees	Low turnover or lack of business	Cash flow payments	Govt regulations and paper-work	Shortage of material/ supplies	High rates of pay	Premiums rents and rates	Inflation	Other	No response	Number of replies analysed
1984/4		17.1	15.9	12.0	5.4	15.3		12.6	1.1	4.2		3.5	10.9	1.4	3,056
1985/1		19.4	15.9	10.0	4.4	14.5		15.7	1.3	3.4		3.8	9.5	1.5	1,795
1985/2		22.1	16.1	10.8	4.3	14.3		12.5	1.3	2.4		5.0	9.1	1.5	1,181
1985/3		23.6	12.8	1.2	4.9	13.3		13.1	1.9	3.7		2.0	8.6	3.8	1,090
1985/4		24.0	16.6	1.1	5.6	15.7		10.2	0.9	2.0		2.2	9.2	2.0	1,072
1986/1		21.4	17.1	1.7	7.2	14.4		9.6	1.8	2.0		3.0	9.9	1.3	1,326
1986/2		29.9	16.3	9.1	7.3	12.6		9.9	1.2	2.2		1.7	9.4	0.6	1,052
1986/3		21.3	16.6	11.5	7.3	17.0		7.3	0.9	1.4		0.9	13.7	2.0	1,285
1986/4		25.0	17.7	11.8	7.2	14.7		6.8	1.3	1.3		1.1	10.0	3.1	1,435
1987/1		26.4	16.0	12.0	8.0	13.0		7.4	1.3	1.6		0.9	9.1	4.2	1,166
1987/2		23.7	17.7	10.7	9.6	12.0		7.6	1.5	2.6		1.0	10.3	3.3	1,746
1987/3		20.3	17.9	11.5	11.8	12.9		6.6	2.2	1.9		1.1	10.5	3.5	1,113
1987/4		18.0	21.3	12.5	1.1	13.0		6.3	1.3	1.3		1.1	9.6	4.5	977
1988/1		21.6	20.1	11.4	1.1	9.6		6.1	1.9	2.3		0.7	14.9	0.3	1,042
1988/2		19.4	15.5	14.4	12.7	10.2		8.0	2.3	1.8		1.0	13.7	1.4	933
1988/3		17.6	13.7	11.4	17.7	11.3		8.3	2.7	2.4		0.9	11.4	2.4	983
1988/4		25.5	12.5	10.4	16.9	8.7		6.0	3.3	1.3		2.8	10.6	1.9	950
1989/1*		25.1	11.2	1.2	13.2	7.2		8.4	0.4	5.9		5.5	17.4	4.7	1,523
1989/2		26.1	13.0	6.0	13.4	8.0		6.7	0.8	0.6		5.4	14.4	4.7	947
1989/3		33.5	6.0	7.0	12.9	12.2		6.2	0.5	1.6		6.5	12.2	1.5	2,236
1989/4		38.1	5.2	5.3	9.4	13.8		5.5	0.4	1.2		7.1	12.3	1.2	792
1990/1	3.0	27.5	4.2	—	5.8	15.4	13.5	6.2	0.6	3.0	9.7	3.7	4.6	2.0	1,064
1990/2	3.9	25.8	2.5	—	5.4	14.0	12.4	6.5	0.4	1.4	7.6	6.9	8.6	1.3	1,344
1990/3	3.3	28.9	4.3	3.0	5.9	15.3	15.5	3.5	0.0	2.1	4.6	4.6	5.0	1.8	1,027
1990/4	1.9	25.4	5.2	4.6	4.9	17.5	8.9	6.7	0.3	0.2	4.6	8.0	8.7	2.3	1,250
1991/1	4.0	28.6	3.5	2.7	2.9	22.2	10.7	6.1	0.5	0.9	3.5	6.6	5.0	1.3	1,239
1991/2	4.5	20.7	4.3	3.1	2.8	23.2	16.8	5.1	0.2	0.4	8.1	3.5	5.9	0.9	984

*From Survey 18 (1989/1), all figures shown in this table have been weighted to the 1988 VAT sectoral distribution.
Source: SBRT Quarterly Survey of Small Business in Britain, Vol. 7 No. 1, 1991.

Figure 5.3 Problems experienced by small firms, 1984-91   Source: J. Stanmouth and C. Gray (eds), Bolton 20 years on: The Small Firm in the 1990s, page 42.

international context can now be usefully discussed. An examination of the nature of the UK's foreign sales shows the pattern illustrated in Figure 5.4.

	%
Exports as a % of total foreign sales	59.5
Licensed sales as a % of total foreign sales	7.0
Foreign production of UK companies as % of total foreign sales	33.5
	100.0

Source: M.Z. Brooke and P.J. Buckley (eds.), *Handbook of International Trade*, 1988, page 8.

Figure 5.4   The pattern of UK foreign sales

Given the nature of the commitment that needs to be made when developing foreign production facilities, discussed previously in Chapter 1, it is clear that the international activity of small firms will tend to be concentrated in the areas of exporting and licensing (including franchising). As relatively low risk, low resource intensive activities, these particular forms of international trading are best suited to the capabilities of the small firm, and can be undertaken at a level described by some writers as 'passive', as well as in a more active way. The rest of this chapter will therefore focus on issues and concerns which relate predominantly to these two forms of trading.

Parnell[11] offers an interesting insight into the level of formality in the export operations of German SMEs (the *Mittelstand*), which are generally recognised for their export success. Parnell investigated the exporting activity of small German companies which sold to the USA. The research was based on questionnaires and surveys from 79 companies – across a wide range of industries, but predominantly in the metal trades business – which had a significant exporting track record.

'An initial finding appeared to establish that special products were not developed purely for export markets, nor were major modifications of existing products undertaken for such markets. The overwhelming majority of companies exported products which were identical to those produced for the domestic home market.'[12] The most often quoted difficulties in selling to the US market were fluctuating exchange rates, and the appreciation of the D-Mark against the dollar, although one third of the companies surveyed did not report *any* problems in exporting to the USA. Nearly three quarters of the companies did not have specific and detailed strategies for developing their target markets; and two thirds of them did not supply an essential service with their product.

Parnell draws the following conclusion: 'If the success of German small company exporters to the USA is generally representative of SME export success, then it appears, on the basis of the evidence provided by this research, not to be based on a dynamic, professional approach to marketing their products.'[13]

Parnell's research is interesting, because it tends to contradict much contemporary marketing thinking, which emphasises a package approach to competitive strategy and customer satisfaction alongside a detailed and targeted marketing plan. This is not to say that such an approach has any less merit; rather, it shows that, for small firms, it is the evolution and development of a highly specific competitive advantage which will have implications for their operations in the international business field. As was noted in Chapter 1, other research suggests that merely passive exporting is becoming less viable in an increasingly competitive international climate.

The pre-export behaviour of small firms

As we discussed in Chapter 1, it is usual for a new exporter already to have had a range of experience in the home market – experience which has enabled it to develop a capability to engage in international business. The home market experience may help the firm develop confidence in a growth strategy; develop the skills and expertise needed to service markets from long distances; and expand the number and range of business contacts the firm deals with. Olson and Wiedersheim-Paul identify two further factors as being crucial to the decision to internationalise: the role and characteristics of important decision makers in the organisation, and the impact of internal or external stimuli on the firm[14].

Internal pressures and influences include the development of a new product; the existence of excess capacity in the firm, and business objectives involving growth and expansion. External stimuli include such things as inquiries and unforeseen orders; possibilities suggested by other local firms or business sources (e.g. Chambers of Commerce), and difficult domestic market conditions. These forces place decision makers in a position of choice: whether to begin exporting and make the necessary preparations; or to ignore the opportunity, or at least defer action. So-called 'passive' firms may, of course, become active exporters in the future, if subjected to further internal or external stimuli.

Caughey and Chetty applied the methodology of Olson et al. to a sample of manufacturing firms in New Zealand[15]. Overall, their study confirms the crucially important part played by decision makers in the pre-export context discussed in Chapter 1. However, they suggest a number of additions to this model. Firstly, they believe it relevant to insert a feedback loop from the decision not to export, back to the characteristics of the firm. Secondly, the link between the characteristics of the firm and export stimuli is seen to be a two-way process, as is the relationship between decision-maker characteristics and perceived internal and external stimuli. This introduces a dynamic element to the model, allowing a more realistic analysis of the development of an export approach over time.

In addition, Caughey and Chetty introduce five more variables which are seen to be important – size of firm, education, internal change agents, external change agents, and export barriers. Their amended Olson et al diagram is displayed on page 136 as Figure 5.5.

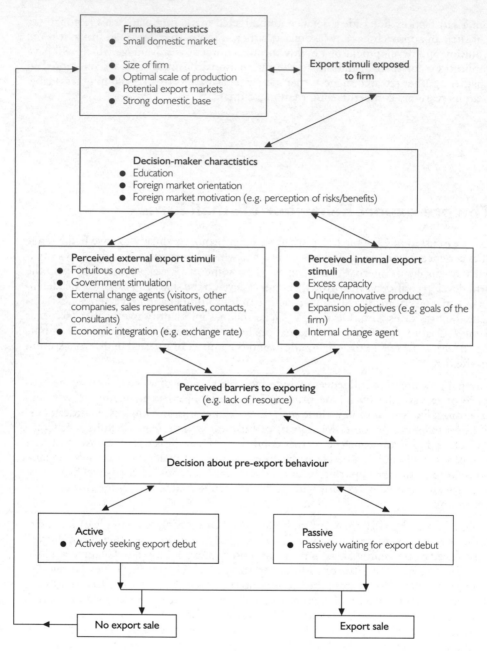

Figure 5.5   Source: M. Caughey and S. Chetty, 'Pre-export Behaviour of Small Manufacturing firms in New Zealand', *International Small Business Journal*, Vol. 12 No. 3, April/June 1994

> ✎   CASE STUDY
>   What to wear at the gates of hell
> Although Edward MacBean has been in existence for nearly 120 years, in the last few
> years it has established itself as a market leader in the industrial and public utility
> foul weatherwear market in the UK and Europe. The *Financial Times* reported in
> January 1995 that its sales, which were £1.1 million in 1987, had reached nearly £7
> million in 1994, on which it made pre-tax profits of £550,000. Some £2.25 million
> of that turnover was exported, making MacBean a substantial exporter for its size.
>
> In 1982 Tootal, which had acquired MacBean in 1970, sold it to a London-based
> investment company, Peter Deal Associates, which headhunted James Hunter as
> Sales Director. Mr Hunter found a rundown plant, 22 employees and an order book
> which would just about last seven days. For three years he struggled to bring order
> to MacBean's sales effort, expanding the customer base, and gaining the relevant
> accreditations with key customers such as the Ministry of Defence. At the start of
> 1986 he was made Chairman and Managing Director; 18 months later he negoti-
> ated a mangagement buy out from Deal. The recent expansion of MacBean followed
> a decision, taken in 1988, to enter Europe. It began in Holland, where it formed a
> partnership with Mauritz, a Dutch clothing company which is now its base for sales
> in Benelux countries. Macbean also established a partnership in Switzerland, which
> also handles Austria, and later set up MacBean Deutschland, serving Germany and
> a base for expansion into Scandanavia, Finland and France.
>
> Source: adapted from the *Financial Times*, 31.1.95.

As far as external stimuli are concerned, it appears for the most part that exporting
occurs with little prior investigation, and mainly as a reaction to an unforeseen inquiry:
according to Brooke and Buckley, 'Studies in various countries indicated that the proportion of companies beginning to export in this way is relatively high – as many as
50–60 % in some samples.'[16] Moreover, many firms never move on from the passive to
the active exporting phase, and the risk of failure is greater in the early period of exporting than at any other time in a firm's international development[17]. Aksoy and Kaynak[18],
after surveying a number of recent studies on this issue, summarised the factors which
determine the export behaviour of firms; these are shown in Figure 5.6 below.

Characteristics	Exporters	Non-exporters
Managements perceptions of:		
costs and risks in exporting	lower	higher
exporting barriers	no difference	
necessity for external assistance	lower	higher
export profitability	no difference	
Management's qualities and attitudes:		
awareness of government export promotion programmes	lower	low
activity in seeking market opportunities	higher	lower
attention to R and D	higher	lower
attention to customer preferences	higher	lower
dynamic and change oriented behaviour	more	less

Characteristics	Exporters	Non-exporters
Firm characteristics:		
firm size	larger	smaller
number of years in business	no difference	
foreign equity participation in the firm	higher	lower

Figure 5.6

Having surveyed the characteristics of – and differences between – exporting and non-exporting firms, and the pre-export behaviour of firms, we should now examine the factors which influence export success.

Factors determining export success

All firms are interested in being 'successful', but a definition of success in this context is less than straightforward. In particular, a perception of success will depend on the objectives that have been set. However, studies which have attempted to develop quantitative measures of success have tended to focus on export level (export sales as a proportion of total sales), export growth and export profitability[19]. More difficult indicators to measure, but possibly of at least equal importance, would be such things as the reputation of the exporter and brand awareness amongst consumers and retailers; the extent of overseas organisational structure; and the extent of product differentiation and innovation[20].

Furthermore, it must be borne in mind that the major determinants of export success will vary between countries, with their different business cultures and environments.

Katsikeas[21] proposes a classification scheme, based on a number of studies, which highlights three main areas: firm-specific factors (e.g. efficiency, technology, product innovation); marketing policy elements (e.g. pricing, promotional activities, customer service); and external factors (e.g. cost of raw materials, access to finance, the proximity of the export market). In this sense, success is based on familiar business fundamentals, with organisational strengths and capabilities being matched to environmental opportunities.

An interesting study by Beamish, Craig and McLellan[22], which looked at Canadian and UK firms, found positive relationships between the number of markets served and the level of sales; between the commitment of the firm to exporting and export success; and between export profitability and the maintainance of ongoing distribution arrangements in the export market. Linkages were also made between the setting of marketing objectives and export sales levels, and between the firm's attention to customer service and export success. Differences were identified in the product characteristics of Canadian and UK firms in the study, with the former possessing competitive product characteristics, and the latter more willing to compete on a non-unique product basis in markets where close subsitutes were available. A positive relationship between a wide product range and export success was also discovered.

To a certain extent, these findings may appear to contradict those on German SMEs discussed earlier. What they in fact suggest is that, while smaller firms may begin by responding to an external stimulus and focusing solely on exporting their domestic product, lasting success depends on building systematically on that foundation from a clear understanding of domestic competitive advantage, and setting targets at which to aim. Given the relatively limited resources of SMEs, it appears to be advantageous to have a clear understanding of what they are trying to achieve, and how they are to achieve it.

✎   CASE STUDY
Bonas Machine Company

By the mid-1990s Bonas Machine Company, a Gateshead firm, had a whole cabinet of Queen's Awards – a total of seven, including four for export – despite being in one of Britain's hardest-hit industries, textiles machinery. In the mid-1980s it identified an opportunity for textile production to be revolutionised through computer technology. It developed a world-beating electronic jacquard, which monitors looms and 'tells' them what fabrics, designs and quantities to weave, giving labour-saving flexibility and productivity. Seven major machine manufacturers incorporated the jacquard into their equipment, and it was also sold as a separate add-on unit.

By 1994 the company had its own sales and service centres in Hong Kong, India, Germany, Italy and the USA, plus a network of 50 agents. Literature was printed in nine languages, includinging Japanese and Korean. There was also a corporate video, dubbed in ten languages.

The company's attention to putting its message across fluently to its markets has won it DTI language awards. Continuous research and development also helps keep the company ahead of its competitors; a large purpose-built facility for R and D was established next to its factory in 1992. As a result, in 1994 95% of Bonas Machine's output was going to export, and turnover had risen by 60% between 1990 and 1993.

Source: *Overseas Trade*, May 1994

An organising framework for the international involvement of the small firm

As the firm moves into international business it will have to consider such things as:

- **its objectives** – and whether these have short term or long term dimensions;
- **its product or service strategies** – e.g. modification or promotion of existing products;
- **its organisation** – e.g. whether it will need to establish a separate export or international section; what new procedures or administrative requirements will be necessary; and
- **aspects of a marketing approach** – e.g. advertising, packaging and labelling, and pricing.

These deliberations will take place against the background of resource availability.

Figure 5.7, which is similar to the chart included earlier in 'How to Use This Book', attempts to place such considerations within an overall framework for the export planning process. The process described is an iterative one, with each activity following on from a previous and necessary stage, although the feedback loop introduces a dynamic and strategic element to the cycle. The adoption of such an approach will not guarantee success, of course, but it can be used to analyse any deviation from an intended or anticipated outcome, thus allowing for more informed management information and control.

✎   CASE STUDY
British computing services firms and the German market

In the early 1990s, Pawar and Driva surveyed several SMEs in the Midlands which were involved in the German market. From the evidence gathered, they were able to make observations about the German market, and the approach adopted by UK firms in their attempts to penetrate it. The market was perceived as being a high-growth one, underpinned by significant spending power. However, penetration was not seen as easy; it required an ability to demonstrate high quality, and a well-developed after-sales service capability. Business protocol was classed as formal, and advertising in the German language was seen as essential. Respondents had found that bills were settled promptly.

Firms had contacted three departments within the UK's Department for Trade and Industry for information on the German market (the Single Market Unit, the Export Department, and the DTI German Desk), and had also used trade associations and management consultants in this context. Interestingly, none of the firms surveyed undertook significant market research before entering the German market – two entered through contacts, several others after a small amount of research. All the firms felt that barriers to trade would still exist after the 1992 programme of the EU came into effect.

After distilling the results of their research, the authors were able to suggest a number of general points relating to exporting to the German market, under three headings:

Business manner – use a formal approach; produce all documentation in German; German buyers tend not to be interested in one-off deals; advertising tends to be regional rather than national.

Selling your product – trade fairs are heavily used; develop or adapt the product to find market niches; quote all prices in Deutschmarks; ensure delivery dates are met; attempt to make regular visits to customers.

Knowing the market – the total market is very large, therefore target key groups and potential customers; choose agents or distributors carefully, given the unwritten and informal customers and aspects of the German retail market; plan financing on the basis that there will be a delay (possibly up to two years) before operations begin to make a profit.

Source: K. Pawar and H. Driva, 'An investigation of British computing services firms exporting to

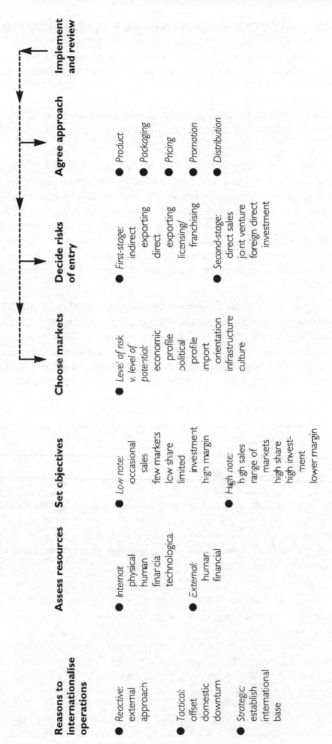

A FRAMEWORK FOR EXPORT PLANNING

Reasons to internationalise operations	Assess resources	Set objectives	Choose markets	Decide risks of entry	Agree approach	Implement and review

Reasons to internationalise operations
- *Reactive:*
  external approach
- *Tactical:*
  offset domestic downturn
- *Strategic:*
  establish international base

Assess resources
- *Internal:*
  physical
  human
  financial
  technological
- *External:*
  human
  financial

Set objectives
- *Low note:*
  occasional sales
  few markers
  low share
  limited investment
  high margin
- *High note:*
  high sales
  range of markets
  high share
  high investment
  lower margin

Choose markets
- *Level of risk v. level of potential:*
  economic profile
  political profile
  import orientation
  infrastructure
  culture

Decide risks of entry
- *First-stage:*
  indirect exporting
  direct exporting
  licensing/ franchising
- *Second-stage:*
  direct sales
  joint venture
  foreign direct investment

Agree approach
- Product
- Packaging
- Pricing
- Promotion
- Distribution

Implement and review

Figure 5.7

Market focus – diversification versus specialisation

As a firm establishes its international operations, one strategic decision which will need to be made concerns the extent of market diversification that it feels appropriate. Studies which have examined the behaviour of exporters have identified the choice as being between market concentration (i.e. where efforts and resources are focused on a relatively small number of markets, defined geographically[23]) and market diversification (i.e. where a firm would accept what might be a small market share in a relatively large number of markets).

The arguments in favour of concentration include the increased ability of the firm to resource marketing and servicing initiatives appropriately; the opportunity to develop deeper and more informed relationships with agents and organisations in the foreign market; and the possibility of less complex administrative and organisational procedures for servicing the export market. The disadvantages of such an approach revolve around a possible overdependence on markets which may eventually offer lower growth and business prospects compared to others which may be seen to offer these opportunities; and the question of whether the firm is capable of selecting the appropriate markets in the first instance.

The alternative strategy of diversification may increase the possibility of making profits and extending sales in emerging and fast-growing markets; and it may, for example, be a more appropriate option for a firm which has developed a niche product or service, and does not wish to rely on a volume strategy. The potential downside to this approach could be an inability to penetrate any particular market in depth – in particular through resource constraints – thus perhaps missing out on opportunities which presented themselves.

CASE STUDY
'Softly, softly catchee foreign market'

In January 1995, the *Financial Times* reported that specific targeting of markets, rather than a 'scattergun' approach, lay behind the export success of IMI Airconditioning, part of the big publicly-quoted IMI engineering group. In 1990 the company had 'set out its stall' for exporting into Europe. The need for this move was heightened by the slump in the UK market because of the recession. Since then, export turnover had grown fast, from £2.9 million in 1992 to £3.6 million in 1993 and about £4.3 million in 1994.

The key to success had been the decision to look at one market at a time, not necessarily treating it in the same way as the UK market, or assuming that an identical approach would work in the next country it looked at. 'We look closely at what the local competition are doing, but we do not necessarily do the same.' Instead the company aimed to find an 'angle' which would differentiate it from the competition. Specific markets were first targeted through desk research, and then field research was undertaken by overseas sales agents or design engineers. To aid growth overseas, a data base of countries and relevant market conditions had been set up.

Source: adapted from the *Financial Times*, 31.1.95

Empirical studies have attempted to define an optimal strategy for improving export performance. However, after reviewing a number of recent studies on this issue, Lee and Yang[24] concluded: 'There has been no consensus among researchers with regard to which strategy, market concentration or market diversification, is expected to lead exporting firms to better export performance.' (Lee and Yang's own research suggested that those who opted for diversification did best.)

The lack of agreement among different studies can partly be attributed to the differing methodologies they used – for example, the measurement of export performance is not always the same. However, it has also been argued that the optimal strategy will depend upon 'situational factors' such as product, company and marketing considerations, so that variation in that strategy is to be expected.[25] For example, where markets are perceived as being unstable, this may contribute to a decision to go for diversification rather than concentration.

Overcoming SMEs' major problems in the international arena

Earlier in this chapter we looked at feedback from UK small firms on the major problems they experienced. Two key areas of difficulty were identified as finance (cost of finance, access to finance, and cash flow), and low turnover or lack of business. These two sets of issues become even more difficult to deal with in an international setting, in view of communication difficulties, time delays, and the extra commitment and resources required to sort such problems out.

The financing of international trade

New, or additional, orders from abroad will increase the demands made upon the financial resources of the firm. Immediate expenses will be incurred in responding to the order, but the receipt of payment for goods and services produced and provided may not be synchronised with their actual provision. In addition the risk of delayed payment, or indeed non-payment, may well be higher than in the domestic environment of the firm. These factors will have to be borne in mind when negotiating payment for goods and services with foreign importers. If you have not already read Chapter 4, Financing International Operations, it would be useful to do so at this point.

Here, we will look briefly at a study which focused specifically on SMEs. Samuels, Greenfield and Mpuku[26] studied questionnaire responses from randomly selected SME members of the Birmingham and West Midlands Chamber of Commerce. The aim of the research was to investigate the pricing behaviour, and attitudes towards risk, of small firms operating in the international marketplace. These are some of their main findings.

Export credit practices. For the most part transactions were based on one form of credit or another; in only 8% of cases were firms able to ask for advance payment. In 97.7% of cases the time lag between sending the goods and receiving payment was between one and six months. Net settlement and other credit terms were used widely in the (then) EEC, North America and other developed countries. 'In general,' said Samuels et al., 'developing countries do not receive very favourable credit terms, being required very often to open letters of credit or make advance payments on their transactions.'

Currency of invoicing. The study found that invoicing was mainly in the exporter's currency, reinforcing the findings of previous empirical studies on this issue.

Exchange risk hedging. Of those companies that were exposed to some form of exchange risk, 51% carried their own exchange risk – i.e. did not hedge. These tended to be the smaller companies in the sample. Companies which minimised their exchange risk mainly used the forward exchange market. Matching exposure in a currency by linking purchases in that currency with money to be received was the second most popular option. Only two companies used money market hedges.

Price changes in response to exchange rate movements. As noted in Chapter 3, 88% of respondents said they would not change the sterling price if sterling rose against the local currency, even if this meant an increase in the local price. Correspondingly, firms were unwilling to change the sterling price when the value of the pound fell against a local currency. 50% of companies said they normally only reviewed their export prices once every year.

Use of ECGD facilities. Only 17 exporting firms said that any of their exports were covered by ECGD guarantees (note that this was at a time when the ECGD still handled most export insurance, even in the short term market). Of the firms which did not use the ECGD's services, 30 of them stressed issues of expense, uncompetitiveness, and inappropriate structure of policies.

UK and EU help for SMEs' international activities

Given the importance of trading performance for national economic health, it is not surprising to find a wide range of measures aimed at supporting the international trading activities of firms in both the UK and the EU. Two areas of support stand out: the provision of information, and financial support.

The UK perspective. Financial support for UK exporters comes mainly in the form of providing export insurance; this was discussed in Chapter 4. Information and networking support has been a recent priority of the government in the UK, as it attempts to halt the relative decline in the country's share of international trade. The overall strategy is made up of many small measures and initiatives, which are discussed in Chapter 2.

The European perspective. Mulhern[27] has identified a number of strands in European Union support for the international activitites of SMEs:

- Intensification of competitive markets, most recently through the Single Market programme, thus creating further opportunities for international business.
- Provision of information – the European Commission funds over 200 Euro-information centres which distribute information on EU policy, with the aim of helping firms reduce their information costs.
- Encouragement of trade and export.
- Alleviation of financial constraints on small firms – e.g. the Commission has issued

directives on legal limits for late payments to SMEs by governments. Some financial support schemes are specifically targeted at SMEs.

- Public procurement and subcontracting now open to international tender (such contracts being equivalent to 15% of European GDP).
- Emphasis on promotion of new technologies, co-operation between firms, and training (e.g. the Brite and Esprit programmes).

The EU's general approach is one of making markets work more efficiently, rather than attempting significant interventionist measures aimed at replacing the operation of the market mechanism. The overall impact is to extend the range of opportunities available to the SME sector in Europe.

Summary

This chapter has reviewed the opportunities presented by international business from the perspective of small firms, alongside some of the problems, strategies and experiences of small firms which have engaged in this form of business activity. Having read and understood the material in this chapter, you should now be in a position to identify the characteristics of the small firm that begins to engage in international business; the main categories of an international business plan for a firm embracing export activities for the first time; and the approaches and strategies available as a response to the two major problems that small firms experience in this area: trade finance and the generation of repeat orders. Finally, you will now be able to appreciate the importance of the international activities of small firms – an importance recognised in the policies of EU member states and the European Commission.

CASE STUDY
F.M.U. Engineering

F.M.U. is a small engineering firm based in the West Midlands. It makes valve systems and compression units which are used mainly in the construction industry, in heating systems for buildings. It also designs and manufactures hydraulic systems which are used in the capital goods industry. It has served the UK market and Eire using a range of distribution techniques: agents, three distributors in the UK, and three sales representatives employed by the firm.

An agent based in the United Arab Emirates has proposed that a business arrangement be formulated which will allow F.M.U. to sell its products in parts of the Middle East – in particular, the United Arab Emirates, Oman and Saudi Arabia. The aim would be to target government departments and contractors responsible for construction work in these countries. The senior management of F.M.U. have been very enthusiastic about this idea, and in the last few months they have had several meetings with the agent to discuss possibilities further.

In the last week the agent has been in touch to say that three contractors in the targeted region are interested in meeting F.M.U., with a view to entering into negotiations on supply arrangements with the company. This has been hailed as a major breakthrough by the senior management of F.M.U., who have recently decided upon their negotiating team

As a senior officer in the accounts department, you have been asked by your superior to undertake some research; the findings from this will form a background for discussions with the contractors which are due to take place in the UAE in the near future. The objective of F.M.U. in these discussions is to conclude as long a supply arrangement as possible, with the firm exporting its UK-made products to the Middle East.

Questions for discussion

1 Describe the nature of the financial risk that F.M.U. would face if the deal was negotiated as the company intended.
2 What practical recommendations would you make to the senior managers of the company, given the objective of minimising the financial risks associated with such an international business arrangement?
3 How do fluctuations in exchange rates complicate things for F.M.U.? What could the company do to minimise exchange rate risks?

✎   CASE STUDY
              Fabulous Fruits
The soft drinks market in Europe is dominated by large multinational companies such as Coca Cola and Cadbury Schweppes. A major component of the strategies of such firms has been an emphasis on segmentation of the market, with a focus on the differing life styles of potential consumers. This has proved to be an extremely successful approach, with marketing campaigns as well as products tailored to the consumer profile in different parts of Europe.

Although this approach has allowed large companies to grow and prosper, the fragmentation of mass markets has produced opportunities for smaller firms when these large firms have found it potentially unprofitable to exploit some of the smaller market segments.

Fabulous Fruits plc is a UK-based SME which produces pure and blended fruit juices targeted at higher income groups in the market for soft drinks and beverages. It has had recent success with several of its products – most notably a blend of kiwi fruit, apricot and mango juices which it has attempted to brand using its own name, and sell as a 'start the day' breakfast drink. However, it has also packaged this drink in smaller containers, aimed particularly at people who eat and drink fairly informally during their working day.

In the past three years it has had some success selling its products in France, and has a number of stable, long term contracts with various wholesalers in that region. Recently it has attended several trade fairs in Europe, sponsored by the DTI, in Belgium, Germany and Holland. After evaluating the experiences from these fairs, it now believes there is real potential in diversifying further into the Dutch and Belgian market. It has also identified some possibilities in the German market; however, these are relatively less promising at present, and the company has therefore decided not to focus its efforts on that country.

The company has involved itself in negotiations with distributors in Holland and Belgium, and is committed to a significant marketing drive in each of those countries.

Questions for discussion

1 What details do you feel would be relevant when the firm began to assess its resource capability in relation to the market opportunities identified above?

2 What objectives do you think would be appropriate in this context, during the first six months of its market development strategy? Give reasons.

3 What are the advantages and disadvantages of developing each of the identified markets in turn, as opposed to simultaneously?

Further reading

The following are particularly recommended:

J. Stanworth and C. Gray (eds), *Bolton 20 Years On: the Small Firm in the 1990s*, Paul Chapman Publishing, 1991.

D.J. Storey, *Understanding the Small Business Sector*, Routledge, 1994.

J. Wilson, *The Barclays Guide to International Trade for the Small Business*, Blackwell, 1990.

A.H. Kuriloff, J.M. Hemphill and D. Cloud, *Starting and Managing the Small Business*, McGraw-Hill, 1993.

Other useful titles:

G. Bannock and H. Albach, *Small Business Policy in Europe: Britain, Germany and the European Commission*, Anglo German Foundation, London, 1991

P.W. Beamish, R. Craig and K. McLellan, 'The Performance Characteristics of Canadian Versus U.K. Exporters in Small and Medium Sized Firms', *Management International Review*, Vol. 33 No. 2, 1993.

Department of Employment, *Small Firms in Britain 1991*, H.M.S.O., 1991.

M. Hay and K. Kamshad, 'Small Firm Growth: Intentions, Implementation and Impediments', *Business Strategy Review*, Vol. 5 No. 3, 1994.

C.S. Lee and S.Y. Yang , 'Impact of Export Market Expansion Strategy on Export Performance', *International Marketing Review*, Vol. 7 No. 4, 1990.

A. Mulhern, 'The European SME Sector: Definitional Problems and the Policies of the European Union', *Journal of European Business Education*, Vol. 4 No. 1, 1994.

H. Olson, F. Wiedersheim-Paul and L. Welch, 'Pre-Export Behaviour: the First Step in Internationalisation', *Journal of International Business Studies*, Vol. 9 No. 1, 1978.

M. Parnell, 'Exporting by German SMEs: Small Company Perspectives', *European Business and Economic Development*, Vol. 1 Part 4, 1993.

K. Pawar and H. Driva, 'An Investigation of British Computing Services Firms Exporting to Germany', *European Business Review* No. 4, 1994.

N. Piercy, *Export Strategy: Markets and Competition*, Allen and Unwin, 1982.

J. Samuels, S. Greenfield and H. Mpuku, 'Exporting and the Smaller Firm', *International Small Business Journal*, Vol. 10 No. 2, 1991/2.

STRATOS, *Strategic Orientations of Small European Businesses*, Avebury, 1990.

J. Sweeney, 'A Small Company Enters the European Market', *Harvard Business Review*, Sept–Oct 1970.

Notes

1. Report of the Committee of Inquiry on Small Firms, chaired by J.E. Bolton, 1971, page 6.

2. As 1 above, page 21.

3. As 1 above, page 23.

4. D.J. Storey, *Understanding the Small Business Sector*, page 10, Routledge, 1994.

5. Discussed in Storey (see 5 above).

6. J. Stanworth and C. Gray (eds.), *The Small Firm in the 1990s*, Paul Chapman Publishing, 1991.

7. Quoted in A.D. Koning and J. Snijders, 'Policy on Small and Medium Sized Enterprises in the Countries of the European Community', *International Small Business Journal*, Vol. 10 No. 3, 1991/2.

8. A. Mulhern, 'The European SME Sector: Definitional Problems and the Policies of the European Commission', *Journal of European Business Education*, Vol. 4 No. 1, December 1994.

9. Stanworth and Gray (see 6 above), page 48.

10 Stanworth and Gray (see 6 above), page 7.

11 M. Parnell, 'Exporting by German SMEs: Small Company Perspectives', *European Business and Economic Development*, Vol. 1 Part 4, January 1993.

12 Parnell (see 11 above), page 27.

13 Parnell (see 11 above), page 28.

14 H. Olson and F. Wiedersheim-Paul, 'Factors Affecting the Pre-export Behaviour of Non-exporting Firms' – in M. Ghertman and J. Leontiades (eds.), *European Research in International Business*, pages 283–305. Also H. Olson, F. Wiedersheim-Paul and L.Welch, 'Pre-export Activity: The First Step in Internationalisation', pages 47–58, *Journal of International Business Studies*, Vol. 9 No. 1, 1978.

15 M. Caughey and S. Chetty, 'Pre-export Behaviour of Small Manufacturing Firms in New Zealand', *International Small Business Journal*, Vol. 12 No. 3, April/June 1994.

16 M.Z. Brooke and P.J. Buckley, *Handbook of International Trade*, page 118, Macmillan, 1988.

17 Brooke and Buckley (see 16 above), page 118.

18 S. Aksoy and E. Kaynak, 'Export Behaviour of Fresh Produce Marketers: Towards a Co-ordination with General Theory of Exporting', pages 16–32, *International Marketing Review*, Vol. 11 No. 2, 1994.

19 See, for example, C.S. Lee and Y.S. Yang, 'Impact of Export Market Expansion Strategy on Export Performance', *International Marketing Review*, Vol. 7 No. 4.

20 Aksoy and Kaynak (see 18 above).

21 C. Katskeas, 'Export Competitive Advantages: The Relevance of Firm Characteristics', *International Marketing Review*, Vol. 11 No. 3, 1994.

22 'The Performance Characteristics of Canadian versus UK Exporters in Small and Medium Sized Firms', *Management International Review*, Vol. 33 No. 2, 1993.

23 A report by the Betro Trust Committee, *Concentration on Key Markets*, Royal Society of Arts, London, 1976, suggested a market concentration yardstick of between 5 and 10 – quoted in S. Young, J. Hamill, C. Wheeler and R. Davies, *International Market Entry and Development*, page 82, Harvester Wheatsheaf, 1989.

24 Lee and Yang (see 19 above), page 41.

25 See, for example, I. Ayal and J. Zif, 'Market Expansion Strategies in Multinational Marketing', pages 84–94, *Journal of Marketing*, Spring 1979; and N. Piercy, *Export Strategy: Markets and Competition*, Allen and Unwin, 1982.

26 'Exporting and the smaller firm', *International Small Business Journal*, Vol. 10 No. 2, 1991/2.

27 See note 8 above.

PART 2

6 Regional blocs

Objectives

By the end of this chapter, you will be able to:

- demonstrate the trend towards increasing regional integration in the world economy.
- identify the main forms that such integration may take.
- analyse the major static and dynamic effects of integration, and their effects on international firms.
- understand the structure and characteristics of the major regional blocs – the EU, NAFTA, MERCOSUR and ASEAN – and their importance for international business.

Introduction

CASE STUDY

Europe and the South Koreans

Following on from the Japanese in the 1980s, the 1990s have seen a rapid growth in South Korean foreign direct investment in Europe. This investment is part of South Korea's plans for global expansion. The moves have been led by Samsung which is one of the largest conglomerates or *chaebol* in South Korea. Such *chaebol* dominate the economy of South Korea. Over the period from autumn 1994 to spring 1995 Samsung announced plans for a £450m consumer electronics complex in North East England and a deal with NEC, a leading Japanese electronics company, to make computer memory chips in Europe.

According to the *Financial Times* of 10 February 1995 other *chaebol*, including Daewoo, Hyundai and LG, also had plans to invest in Europe. Daewoo had committed itself to projects that would raise its European investments from $300m to $1.3bn, with the probability of more to follow. Samsung had announced its intention to buy or build a large European chip factory, and Daewoo was considering a car assembly plant in Britain. The London advisory office of one large international consultancy firm which had no Korean clients two years earlier was quoted as saying that it was now advising more than 40 on plans to set up in Europe.

A mixture of motives lies behind these moves. Although in some respects they are following Japan, they also have motives of their own. Like Japanese firms, Korean companies face growing pressure to globalise their business by shifting part of their export effort into offshore production. High labour and land costs at home are eroding the competitiveness of some industries. Historically Europe has not been important to Korea, accounting for less than 10% of its annual exports. In the 1990s, however, European governments have stepped up efforts to win a bigger share, encouraging inward investment with trade missions and offers of generous financial assistance. The European Commission has also been involved.

Many Korean companies have been attracted to Europe by opportunities to obtain industrial know-how. Another stimulus was a succession of anti-dumping cases brought by European manufacturers, claiming they were being injured by Korean exports sold at artificially low prices. Korean manufacturers have therefore chosen to set up plants in Europe before Brussels opened formal anti-dumping proceedings. For example, according to the *FT*, a complaint by European excavator manufacturers triggered such moves by Samsung and Hyundai.

Experience of Japanese operations has helped to reduce opposition to Asian inward investment into the EU; many countries are now very keen to encourage it, and this enthusiasm is matched by South Korean companies. Daewoo Electronics has four French plants deliberated sited in areas of high unemployment. According to the February 1995 article, up to that point Germany had proved the most popular EU location for Korean direct investment, attracting 20% of the total. Britain accounted for 16% and France for 14%.

However, the Koreans may still have hurdles to overcome. It has been said that the *chaebol* did little research on Europe before investing there, relying on their experience in the USA. It is possible also that the speed and scale of the *chaebol*'s global expansion could lead to political tensions. Brussels officials were quoted by the *FT* article as saying that unless Korean companies' strides into the EU were matched by equal access for European businesses in Korea, Seoul would face mounting pressure to lower its barriers to imports and foreign investment.

Source: adapted from the *Financial Times*, 10.2.95

The formation and development of regional blocs is becoming an increasingly significant feature of the international business environment. Such blocs are formed by groups of countries aiming to increase the benefits from trade by eliminating or reducing barriers to the free flow of goods and services across their national borders. The rationale for regional blocs arises from experience in the 1930s; at that time world trade decreased by about a third, as more and more countries restricted imports and raised tariffs and other barriers to trade, in their attempts to overcome the unemployment caused by economic depression. These measures led to a downward spiral of retaliation and increasing protectionism which further depressed world economic activity. After World War Two, countries were anxious not to repeat this experience; the prevailing view was that co-operation between countries was needed both to stimulate world trade and to achieve longer-term economic growth and stability.[1]

Since the 1950s there has been a growing momentum towards greater regional economic integration, in the form of regional trading blocs which are now to be found in all areas of the world. It has been suggested by some observers that the regional developments of the 1980s and 1990s may be only the beginning – that we may see more and more regional arrangements, eventually leading to a fully integrated world economy.[2] Developments have included the completion of the Single European Market within the European Union (EU), as well as its further enlargement; the coming into force of the North American Free Trade Agreement (NAFTA) between the USA, Canada and Mexico, and the possibility of extending this agreement to include other countries in the region; new moves towards increasing regional integration in Latin America, such as the formation of MERCOSUR; and developments in the countries of the Pacific Rim concerned with increasing regional economic co-operation by various means.

This chapter is concerned with the structure and characteristics of regional blocs, and with the risks and opportunities such blocs present to international firms. It starts by identifying the various forms regional blocs may take, and the most important issues raised for international firms. It then considers the main features of the major regional blocs, and finally examines the impact such blocs may have on the decisions and actions of international firms doing business within them.

International firms and regional blocs

Regional economic integration has many effects on international firms. It affects decisions on where to locate production and which markets to serve, the choice of entry strategy, and the approach adopted to deal with competition. Many international firms have developed regional strategies to deal with these new regional markets; they often see it as important to have a base within a regional bloc to serve its markets, or to develop specific strategies for doing business in participating countries. In this way, regional blocs have acted as an impetus for foreign direct investment by international firms outside the bloc; they have also led to increased merger and acquisition activity, joint ventures and strategic alliances – both by companies already located within participating countries, and as a means of entry to these markets (and to the internal benefits of the bloc) for firms located outside it.

The nature and extent of the effects on international firms depends on the form of integration chosen by the countries participating in a regional bloc. In general, the greater the degree of integration, the greater the effects are likely to be.

Forms of economic integration

In order of increasing integration, regional economic arrangements may take the following forms: a free trade area, a customs union, a common market and an economic union. (The next stage beyond economic union would be political union, where countries finally merge to form an entirely new country.)

Free trade area

When countries form a free trade area they dismantle tariffs, quotas and other barriers to trade between them; but each participating country retains autonomy in its trading arrangements with countries outside the free trade group, and is free to impose or reduce restrictions on trade with such countries independently. The free trade area is the loosest form of regional economic integration, as it applies only to trade in goods and services; indeed, it may only apply to certain categories of goods or services, with others being exempt from the agreement. Until relatively recently the best known free trade area was the European Free Trade Area (EFTA); however, most of its members have now either joined the EU or made bridging arrangements with it, and currently the major example of a free trade area is NAFTA.

Customs union

A customs union goes one stage further than a free trade area in terms of economic integration; in this case there is a common external tariff (CET), whereby member countries adopt common trade policies with respect to non-member countries. In other words, customs union members no longer have independent trading arrangements with non-members, and identical tariffs, quotas and other restrictions are set for goods and services entering participant countries from outside the customs union. For companies located in countries outside the bloc, this means that all restrictions are therefore the same, no matter which country in the participating group they are trading with.

In addition, customs unions operate as a bloc in trade negotiations – not as individual countries, as the members of a free trade area would do. (Thus the EU, which has a common external tariff, negotiates as a bloc in international trade discussions whereas the EFTA countries negotiated separately.)

Common market

A common market is a customs union with the addition of freedom to transfer resources, such as people and capital, across the borders of member countries. The intention is that these resources will then be employed in the most efficient way within the bloc, thereby increasing the prosperity of member countries as a whole. The aim of the Single European Act was to establish a full common market within the EU by the end of 1992.

Economic union

Economic union takes the common market one stage further, by requiring the integration or harmonisation of economic policies throughout member countries, in addition to the free movement of goods, services and resources. This means that participating countries pursue identical or harmonised policies in core economic areas – particularly with respect to fiscal and monetary management, tax rates and interest rates, as well as policies affecting competition and industry. Full economic union requires a common currency, as well as supranational economic policy-making bodies whose authority supercedes that of national bodies. Steps towards economic union were the focus of the Maastricht Treaty signed in 1991, and since then have been under active discussion in the EU.

The process of integration

The process of integration is often difficult, and such difficulty increases with the degree of integration aimed at by participating countries. As more economic activities are drawn into the integrative process, more control over economic decisions is exercised by central rather than national authorities, and this can lead to friction particularly over issues of national sovereignty.[3] Countries wishing to form regional economic groupings may choose to stop at the free trade level of integration, as going beyond this level may prove too difficult to sustain.

Effects of regional economic integration

The expected effects of increased economic integration are usually divided into two types: static and dynamic. The static effects are those which have an impact on the use of resources within the bloc; while the dynamic effects are concerned with changes in the economic structure of participating countries and of the bloc as a whole.

Static effects

The major static effects are categorised as trade creation, trade diversion, and changes in the productivity of resources within participating countries.[4] Let us look briefly at each of these.

Trade creation
Trade creation is usually defined as the substitution of lower cost sources of supply for higher cost sources. When tariffs are eliminated, companies and consumers have an opportunity to buy goods and services from lower cost producers in the bloc – whereas, before the formation of the bloc, such producers' prices would have been higher than those of domestic producers because of protective tariffs or other restrictions. In this way, efficiency is encouraged and trade flows are expected to increase within the bloc, having previously been prevented by restrictive barriers.

Trade diversion
Regional economic integration may also lead to trade diversion. This is the opposite of trade creation, and is defined as the substitution of higher cost sources of supply for lower cost sources. Barriers are removed only for trade among the group of countries participating in the bloc; a common external tariff or other barriers are applied to imports from non-participating countries. Such barriers may now increase the relative cost of goods from producers outside the bloc, because their price has the CET added to it, whereas otherwise higher-cost producers within the bloc are more competitive because of the removal of tariffs. Thus tariffs may prevent the most efficient producers selling their products within a regional bloc, and producers within the bloc are artifi-

cially protected from such competition. It is these aspects of trade creation which cause concern that new forms of protectionism may arise from the growth in regional economic integration. When the EU decided to complete its common market, fears were expressed that trade diversion would increase, with producers in non-member countries no longer able to compete in the EU market with companies located within it. The phrase 'Fortress Europe' was often used to express these fears.

Increased resource productivity
The formation of a common market enables resources to be transferred freely across national borders. This means that resources can potentially flow to those areas where they are used most productively, and so will be used in the most efficient way possible by companies within the bloc – thereby increasing productivity.

Dynamic effects

The main dynamic effects are expected to be economies of scale, both internal and external; increased competition; and effects on the terms of trade.[5]

Economies of scale
Internal economies of scale – those aspects of increasing size which lead to a lowering of unit costs for individual firms – are expected to arise from regional economic integration, because firms have access to a larger tariff-free market. This induces individual firms to grow in size, expanding production to meet the demands of the newly available market and achieving scale economies in the process. More firms should also be able to achieve their minimum efficient scale more quickly. Such benefits are particularly marked where the individual countries of a bloc have small domestic markets; without the larger market the bloc provides, such countries cannot support the size of plant necessary to make economies of scale and thus achieve low cost production. Various regional integration efforts in Latin America, where many countries have relatively small populations, have had this as their aim.[6]

External economies of scale refer to cost savings that a particular firm may achieve through the expansion of the industry or economy of which it is part. External economies can arise in a number of ways, including access to improved technology, the emergence of new suppliers, and improvements in economic infrastructure such as transport networks and communications.[7]

Competitive benefits
Regional economic integration may also affect the economic structure of participating economies more directly, by altering the nature of the competitive environment for both home-based and international companies.[8] It is usually expected that regional economic integration will intensify competition, both by opening previously protected markets to competitors from other member countries, and by fostering the establishment of new firms in various industries – again bringing down costs and encouraging the efficient use of resources in production as a competitive weapon.

Terms of trade
The terms of trade are the rate at which goods and services are exchanged for those of other countries. A common measure of the terms of trade is the ratio of movements in

a country's export and import prices. Any trade diversion that occurs from the formation of a customs union may alter the terms of trade between participating and non-member countries, to the advantage of participating countries. It is possible, on the other hand, that this will prove only a short term phenomenon. The beneficial economic effects which participating countries achieve through integration – such as economies of scale in production, and increased productivity and economic efficiency – may increase growth and thereby disposable income, creating increased demand for imports from countries outside the bloc.[9]

The impact of static and dynamic effects

Although the static and dynamic effects of regional economic integration may bring increased economic activity and prosperity to the region as a whole, there is no accompanying expectation that it will be spread evenly among participating countries; while all are likely to benefit to some extent, some will gain more than others. The greatest benefits are likely to be experienced by those which take the fullest advantage of the potential offered by the new preferential access to the markets of the group, and the increased investment opportunities.

For international firms, the major competitive advantage of operating within a regional bloc is that of servicing a larger regional market, with economies of scale to be gained particularly from production and distribution activities. These advantages are likely to vary in scale and scope, depending on the nature of the regional bloc; and we now turn to consider the main features of the current major regional groupings.

The European Union

The European Union has developed from initial attempts to rebuild the economy of Europe after the devastation of World War II. Along with other initiatives, a plan was put forward in 1950 for France and Germany to pool their coal and steel production; this resulted in the signing of the Treaty of Paris in 1951, establishing the European Coal and Steel Community (ECSC). Leading on from the success of this co-operation, further discussions were held to consider how further integration could be developed within Europe, primarily to generate access to wider markets. This led to the signing of the Treaty of Rome in 1957, creating two additional communities: the European Economic Community (EEC) and the European Atomic Energy Community (EURATOM), which became operational on 1 January 1958. The founding states of the three communities were France, Germany, Italy and the BENELUX countries – Belgium, the Netherlands and Luxembourg.

The first of several enlargements took place in 1973 when Denmark, Ireland and the UK became members. In 1976 it was decided to amalgamate the three communities, which then became known as the European Community (EC). Greece became a member in 1981, and Spain and Portugal in 1986. The area which was formerly the German Democratic Republic (East Germany) automatically became part of the Community on reunification with West Germany in 1990. With the coming into force of the Single European Act on 1 January 1993, the EC was renamed the European Union (EU); this reflected the new aims inherent in the Act, and also the wider moves towards greater economic union contained in the Maastricht Treaty, signed in 1991 and ratified in 1993.

Further enlargement took place on 1 January 1995 when Austria, Sweden and Finland became members. It is anticipated that the EU will continue to grow over the next decade, with countries from Eastern Europe such as Hungary, Poland and the Czech Republic being admitted as full members.

The aims of the EU

The primary aim of the steps taken in the generation of the European Union has been to promote economic, social and political cohesion between its members, in order that Europe may be strong enough to influence world affairs and constitute a major world economic power. This aim was to be achieved in five ways. First, establishment of a customs union in which no tariffs were imposed on members, and a common external tariff to be imposed by members against non-members. Second, establishment of a common market, so that resources such as labour and capital would be free to move between countries. Third, adoption of a Common Agricultural Policy (CAP) which aimed at higher productivity, a fair income for farmers, stable markets, security of supply and reasonable prices for consumers. Fourth, achievement of economic union, through common transport and trading policies and the co-ordination of member states' own financial and commercial policies to encourage competition. Fifth, closer political cohesion with common foreign policies and policies on security and defence.

The organisation of the European Union

There are four main institutions responsible for achieving the aims of the EU. These are the Council of Ministers, the Commission, the European Parliament and the Court of Justice.

The Council of Ministers

This is the principal decision-making body of the EU. Each country has a seat on the Council. The term Council of Ministers is in fact a little misleading, as there is no one Council – rather, a set of specialist Councils dealing with specific aspects of EU policy such as agriculture, transport, the internal market and so on. Councils are attended by the relevant ministers from the member states, and by the President of the Commission.

The Council becomes known as the European Council when Heads of State meet to determine long term policy objectives for the EU. This Council meets twice a year, and is accountable to the European Parliament.

The Commission

The Commission is the 'guardian of the treaties' which set up the EU, and it is therefore responsible for ensuring their implementation by member states and for the general administration of the Union. The Commission proposes policy, but does not finally decide it – that is the responsibility of the Council of Ministers. The members of the Commission are chosen from the member states after consultation with, and with the agreement of, their governments. Commissioners do not represent the interest of their home country, but are required to act in the interest of the European Union as a whole. Each Commissioner is appointed for four years, and can be removed from office by a vote of censure from the European Parliament.

The Commissioners are involved in policy formulation through the Directorates General (DGs), each of which is responsible for a designated aspect or area of EU policy – industry, foreign affairs, transport and so on. There are 23 DGs, and the Commissioners are responsible for leading their work. Regular discussions are held between the Commissioner's Directorate and interested parties, lobby groups and special interest groups. As a result of these discussions draft proposals are formulated, and are then discussed by all the Commissioners, who decide on the nature of the final proposals for presentation to the Council of Ministers.

The European Parliament

The European Parliament is directly elected by the people of the European Union. It is not a Parliament in the national sense, but fulfils a different role within the EU. This role is to advise the Council of Ministers on Commission proposals, and together with the Council of Ministers to decide the budget. Under the EU Treaties, the Parliament has to deliver a formal opinion on most proposals before they can be adopted by the Council. It has the power to dismiss the Commission by a two-thirds majority vote, and is also empowered to reject the Council's proposals for the Budget. As the EU has no powers to raise finance other than through the Budget, the European Parliament thus has ultimate control over budgetary matters.

The European Court of Justice

The European Court of Justice, again, is not a Court in the national sense. Its role is to rule on the interpretation of the EU treaties and laws. Its decisions are binding on all member states. There is also an additional Court – the Court of First Instance – which was set up in 1989 to speed up decisions; this is able to consider certain types of cases, subject to a right of appeal to the Court of Justice.[10] These Courts make judgments on matters raised by companies, governments, institutions and individuals; they also interpret the competition and merger rules laid down by EU law.

EU law

There are various categories of law within the EU, which differ primarily in terms of the *degree* to which they must be carried out by member states. The EU Treaties give the Council of Ministers and the Commission the authority to make regulations, issue directives, take decisions, make recommendations or deliver opinions. Regulations have general application; they are directly binding in their entirety in all member states, and specify the method of implementation. Directives are binding on member states; although the method of implementation is delegated to the governments of member states, the required outcome is specified, together with a time limit for achieving it. Regulations and directives override national law.

Decisions refer to specific individual cases, and are usually made by the Court of Justice. They are binding in their entirety on those to whom they are addressed, whether they be member states, companies or individuals. Recommendations and opinions have no binding force, but merely state views on matters raised.[11]

The Single European Market

The customs union was achieved in 1968, with no customs duties between member states, and with a common external tariff for non-member countries, administered by the Commission (Barclays Briefing, No. 76, April 1988). However, movement beyond this was slow and the drive towards a common market appeared to have lost momentum. This was a major area of discussion at the European Council in 1985, and member states committed themselves at that time to the establishment of a genuine Single European Market (SEM), which would complete the formation of the EU common market. The Commission was asked to draw up a detailed plan showing how this might be achieved.[12] Although there had been no customs duties within the EU since 1968, there were still obstacles to the movement of goods, services, capital and people; and it was these non-tariff barriers that member states wished to address. The Commission's final plan contained over two hundred points, identifying measures to be taken and a detailed timetable for achieving completion of an internal common market throughout the EU by the end of 1992.

The plan identified three sets of non-tariff barriers which were to be removed. These were classified as physical, technical and fiscal barriers.

Physical barriers. These were barriers to cross-border travel and trade; they involved such matters as restrictions on the movement of people, varying rules on health and safety standards, and 'red tape' in moving goods from one country to another.

Technical barriers. These involved differences in technical standards and testing procedures, which had developed over time and were now seen as a considerable cost barrier to intra-EU trade.

Fiscal barriers. These barriers included differences in sales taxes (VAT) between countries, and also considerable variations in excise duties imposed by individual member states.

Expected consequences of the Single Market

These three types of barrier were considered to have resulted in fragmentation across the EU, and a number of studies were conducted both by the Commission and by others in the 1980s to try to quantify the expected gains from completing the common market. The results of these studies suggested that considerable gains were likely to be made in cost savings (for example, from the removal of frontier formalities alone); and that companies operating within the EU were likely to gain at least £35 billion a year from harmonisation of national standards and technical regulations. The Cecchini Committee set up by the Commission also looked at overall economic effects, and suggested that the GDP of the EU as a whole was likely to increase by a minimum of 4.5% in the medium term. It predicted that increased competition would have a significant effect on consumer prices, with a minimum anticipated fall of 6.1% in prices overall; and expected significant employment effects, with the likelihood of at least 1.8 million new jobs being created solely as a result of the removal of non-tariff barriers.[13]

For companies, the consequences were expected to be a significant reductions in costs, arising from economies of scale and the necessary reorganisation of businesses to operate more effectively within the single unified market. Although potentially all companies were expected to benefit, the greatest gains were expected to be made by larger firms which adopted a regional approach, and by those firms which were prepared to rethink their organisational structures and operations to deal with the new market.

> ✎   CASE STUDY
>   Japanese carmakers and the EU
> The size of the EU, together with the fact that it is a mature consumer market,
> means that it is seen as a primary market for carmakers. Companies operating within
> the bloc are in a position to take advantage of the opportunities offered by the bloc
> itself, and more recently the introduction of the Single Market. Ford had already
> developed a regional strategy in Europe and was developing the idea of a 'European
> car', with a sourcing and marketing strategy which treated the area as a whole and
> not as a set of separate domestic markets. Other companies were at a disadvantage
> without a manufacturing base within the EU. This was particularly so for Japanese
> producers. The European market was a major one for Japanese car exports – so
> much so that quota systems were in operation to limit the number of cars that could
> enter the EU.
>
> These quota systems and the common external tariff were a major incentive to pro-
> duce within the EU. Britain in particular was seen as a good base, as a result of the
> incentives offered by government, and because English is often thought of as the
> second language of the Japanese. Japanese manufacturers of other products had
> located in Britain since the 1950s. The main method chosen has been foreign direct
> investment on greenfield sites, although there are also technology licensing arrange-
> ments with local manufacturers. The main fear was of 'screwdriver' plants, only con-
> cerned with assembling imported components. To overcome this concern,
> companies such as Nissan agreed a package with government whereby locally pro-
> duced components were progressively introduced over a period of time. With com-
> panies such as Nissan, Toyota and Honda operating production facilities in Britain
> for local consumption and for export to Continental Europe, Japanese car manu-
> facturers now form a significant segment of the car industry in Britain.

The Treaty on European Union

With the completion of the 'common market' stage of integration under way, to keep
the momentum going the member states decided to push forward to plans for economic union. The Treaty on European Union, which is more usually known as the
Treaty of Maastricht, was signed in 1991; it outlined the steps towards economic
union, and the process by which it might be attained. The main provisions of the
Treaty concern increased economic and monetary union between the member states;
steps towards a common currency; a 'social chapter' concerning employment relations;
and proposals for a common foreign and security policy. These are scheduled to be
phased in over a number of years.

The main Treaty provision of interest to international firms is that which details steps
towards economic and monetary union (EMU). This involves three essential elements.
The first is the creation of a European Central Bank. This then leads to the formulation of common monetary policy, particularly with regard to price stability and interest rates; and to the introduction of the ECU as a common currency for all member
states.

Convergence criteria

Member states wishing to participate in EMU will have to meet the 'convergence criteria'. These criteria take the form of targets that economies must meet in order to start the process. The first requires that a member state must have a record of inflation no more than 1.5% above the average of the three best-performing member states. The second is that domestic exchange rates must have been within the narrow bands of the Exchange Rate Mechanisn (ERM) of the European Monetary System for two years. Third, interest rates should be no more than 2% above those of the three best-performing member states for the previous year. Fourth, the budget deficit must be within 3% of GDP. Fifth, public sector debt must be no higher than 60% of GDP.

EMU

EMU has three stages. In stage one governments are to implement policies to achieve convergence. Once a member state has achieved the convergence criteria, it will be eligible to join the monetary union.

Stage two is concerned with the setting up of the European Central Bank. This started in 1994 with the establishment of the European Monetary Institute (EMI). The role of the EMI is to create the appropriate conditions for the third stage, complete monetary union. The EMI was given until December 1996 to identify a framework for a new system of European System Central Banks (ESCB). The Council of Ministers would also decide at that date whether a majority of member states met the criteria for convergence. Until this happened, stage three could not begin. If there was a majority, then a date would be set for the implementation of a single currency across the EU; if not, the plan was to establish the ESCB by July 1998, with a move to a single common currency by 1 January 1999.

Under stage three the currency in use in the EU for companies, individuals and EU transactions becomes the ECU, rather than national currencies. From this time national currencies have an agreed conversion rate against the ECU, which is a fixed rate. Also at that stage, the European Central Bank replaces the EMI and takes on the role of implementing monetary policy across the EU, with the control of inflation as its main objective.

It is not necessarily the case that all member states will participate in all aspects of EMU. Britain, for example, has concerns about national sovereignty, and has negotiated an opt-out from the Treaty whereby there is no obligation to move to stage 3 of EMU without a separate decision to do so by its national Parliament. However, Britain does retain the option to move to stage 3 at a later date, provided the convergence criteria are met.

International firms and EMU

For international firms, EMU represents the possibility of significant decreases in foreign exchange transaction costs, through the introduction of a common currency. For a firm currently doing business in two or more EU countries, there will only be the cost of transfer into or from the ECU, rather than between different national currencies. This, it is expected, will generate a more stable business environment, as volatility of exchange rates will be reduced. For firms only doing business within the EU, the cost savings are likely to be considerable, as there will be no need to deal in foreign currencies at all. In addition, a common monetary policy with a commitment to maintaining price stability and common interest rates will reduce uncertainty in business planning, and may well lead to cost savings for companies.

The North American Free Trade Agreement

The North American Free Trade Agreement (NAFTA), signed in 1993, is a free trade agreement which aims gradually to eliminate all trade and investment restrictions between the US, Canada and Mexico, over a period of fifteen years. It is an extension of the US-Canada Free Trade Agreement which became effective on 1 January 1990. This Agreement had as its aim the elimination of all tariffs on trade between the USA and Canada by 1 January 1998. The extension of the Agreement to Mexico occurred as a result of Mexico's wish to enter into a free trade agreement with the USA. NAFTA is described in greater detail in Chapter 9, and only the main issues are outlined in the following paragraphs.

The main agreement has provisions concerning tariff reduction and the lifting of restrictions on cross-border investment, with side agreements covering employment legislation and the enforcement of environmental legislation. The tariff reduction provisions require tariffs to be removed in most sectors within ten years, with all tariffs on agriculture lifted within fifteen years. Investment restrictions are to be lifted in most sectors, the exceptions being oil in Mexico, culture in Canada and airline and radio communications in the US.

Any country can leave at any time, giving six months' notice of their intention to do so; and there is a provision allowing enlargement of the Agreement to cover additional countries in the future. It is expected that Chile[14] will be the first additional country to sign it. A panel of independent arbitrators has been set up to resolve disputes arising between participating countries over matters dealt with in the Agreement; and there is provision for 'snap-back' tariffs to be re-imposed if the Agreement generates a marked rise in imports in any participating country, which has a detrimental effect on that country's domestic producers.

Effects of NAFTA

Static and dynamic effects

It is anticipated that the main gains for participating countries are likely to come from static effects such as trade creation and increased productivity. However, there may also be elements of trade diversion, as new producers become available within the tariff-free area, producing at new lower costs. There are also likely to be dynamic effects on participating countries from higher growth and changes in investment rules.[15]

It is anticipated that Mexico will gain most initially from NAFTA,[16] because about three quarters of its trade is with the USA, and its economy is much smaller than that of either the USA or Canada. In addition, there are expected to be benefits from the liberalisation of investment rules, with the financial sector to be opened up gradually; all US and Canadian barriers are scheduled to be eliminated by 2007. Canada is most concerned with ensuring its continued importance to foreign investors as a base for entry into the North American market as a whole.

Particular concern has been expressed about the effects on employment[17] in the three countries. It is likely that in the restructuring process all three countries will initially experience company closures, and there have been worries that companies will relocate from the USA to Mexico in order to take advantage of cheaper wage rates. However, it has also been argued that this effect may not be as great as initially feared, because although it is possible that low-skilled labour-intensive companies may relocate, the overall effect may be to create a new and mutually beneficial division of labour in the longer term. Moreover, there is some protection from the side agreement on labour laws, to ensure that companies do not take advantage of any shortcomings on enforcement; and the trade panel has powers to arbitrate in any disputes in this area, and to apply sanctions.

Rules of origin[18]

Free trade areas are faced with problems arising from rules of origin. The free trade provisions are intended to eliminate tariffs on goods produced within the group. This presents problems as to the degree of local content in finished items. Within NAFTA, concern has been expressed that the rules of origin applying in certain sectors – particularly textiles and vehicle production – may force suppliers within the group to source from less efficient producers, and thus create trade diversion.

Impact on the EU

A study by the European Commission published in 1993 identified various areas where it believed the NAFTA agreement could lead to loss of market share for European companies, particularly in the US and Canada. There were particular concerns about financial services and insurance, where there were fears that the benefits NAFTA could bring would be limited only to companies with majority holdings based inside NAFTA and not to the subsidiaries of companies based in the EU. The rules of origin – particularly those applying to cars and textiles – require more local content than within the EU and concern was expressed that this could cause difficulties for European producers involved in these sectors. With respect to agriculture the Commission considered that exports in some sectors such as milk products, sugar and meat exports might be affected owing to the raising of Mexican tariffs against their import as part of the Agreement. However, overall the Commission considered that the NAFTA agreement would be likely to lead to a significant increase in trade with the European Union.[19]

Latin American regional integration

There have been many attempts at regional economic integration in Latin America in recent years. A major problem in the region is that of relatively small home markets, and regional integration has often been seen as a means of generating the benefits of economies of scale. These attempts at integration have often been accompanied by severe region-based restrictions, consistent with the inward-looking approach of the import substitution development strategies adopted by the individual countries.

The first major attempt at regional integration came in 1960 with the formation of LAFTA (the Latin America Free Trade Area), which was formed by all the countries of South America and Mexico. Its main goal was to to try to achieve a common market. However, this grouping experienced a variety of problems, particularly owing to the diverse size and nature of the economies concerned; and it achieved only small increases in trade between its members. LAFTA was abandoned in 1980, and a new grouping was developed under the name of ALADI (the Latin American Integration Association). This had much looser aims than LAFTA, and mostly comprised a set of bilateral free trade arrangements between members. Another regional group which developed from LAFTA was the Andean Pact, which included Bolivia, Ecuador, Peru, Colombia and Venezuela. The Pact was formed in 1969 with the intention of developing home industry within the region. The members of the group have agreed to form an Andean common market by 1996, and some progress has been made towards this, with tariffs between participants being phased out from 1993.[20]

MERCOSUR

The latest regional economic grouping is that of MERCOSUR,[21] whose members are Argentina, Paraguay, Brazil and Uruguay. This was established in 1991 by the Treaty of Asuncion, which aimed at forming a customs union and a common market by the end of 1996. The intention was that internal tariffs would be eliminated for the larger economies of Argentina and Brazil by 1994, and for Paraguay and Uruguay by the end of 1995. The Treaty was revised by the Protocol of Ouro Preto signed in December 1994. This Protocol has precedence over the Treaty, and adds to it in three main areas.

The first main area covered by the protocol is specification of the form and nature of the institutional arrangements for the bloc, and delineation of their respective roles. It deals first with the three main institutional bodies. The MERCOSUR Council, the most important in terms of decision-making authority, has a membership comprising the foreign and finance ministers of the four countries, with the presidency initially being held by each country in turn on a six-monthly rotating basis. The MERCOSUR Group, the main executive body for the bloc, is made up of officials from the four governments. Finally, there is the Trade Commission, which has the task of reviewing trade policy and examining complaints arising from trade between the four countries. Other institutions, which are primarily consultative forums, include a parliamentary commission representing the parliaments of the participating countries, and a grouping for private sector businesses and trade unions. Administration of the bloc is undertaken by the MERCOSUR secretariat, based in Montevideo in Uruguay.

The second main area in the Protocol is concerned with transitional arrangements for the free trade aspects of MERCOSUR, and the setting up of the common external tariff (CET); and in particular with product categories to be temporarily exempted from these aspects of the bloc. Each country negotiated its own lists of product categories which it felt had local strategic significance, or for which it considered temporary protection from competition was required.

This element of the Protocol formalises a slower progress towards freeing trade and establishing the customs union than was initially anticipated in the Treaty of Asuncion. Thus although by January 1995, for example, only about 90% of products were tariff-free and about 85% of product categories were covered by the CET, the remainder are covered by special provision in the Protocol, with negotiated arrangements for establishment of free trade in all goods for Argentina and Brazil by 1999, and for the remaining countries by 2000. It is not expected that the common external tariff will be fully in place until at least 2000.

The third main area in the Protocol is that which ascribes 'international' status to the bloc. This allows negotiations to take place between MERCOSUR and other international groups, as well as individual countries. Following this, it was expected that initial negotiations would begin in 1995 towards an accord with the EU, aimed at reducing trade barriers between the two blocs. In the mid-1990s, about 25% of participating countries' trade was with EU countries. It was also anticipated that Chile would join the bloc, as an associate member within a free trade grouping, at some later date. This left Chile free to become a full member of NAFTA. In addition it was expected that free trade arrangements might well then be expanded to include the countries of the Andean Pact, to form a South American free trade zone.

This new trading bloc still has specific problems to overcome, relating to the differences in size of the economies of the participating countries, and to infrastructure difficulties which may initially impede the growth in trade expected. As far as size is concerned, Argentina and Brazil dwarf the two other participants, as may be seen in Figure 6.1 below. However, it is possible that these differences in size have been overemphasised, as if the bloc is successful the smaller countries will also share in that success. In terms of infrastructure, the major problem appears to be inadequate road and rail links, leading to substantial differentials in transport costs which are likely to persist for some time.

	GDP ($bn) in 1993	Population (million) in 1993
Brazil	456.0	159.2
Argentina	255.3	33.5
Uruguay	13.1*	3.2
Paraguay	6.4*	4.6

* 1992 figures

Source: The Financial Times, 25.1.95

Figure 6.1

Nevertheless, in general MERCOSUR is expected to be more successful than previous attempts at integration in the area – particularly because of the Enterprise for the Americas Initiative discussed below.

Enterprise for the Americas

It is expected that regional groups in Latin America will benefit from the Enterprise for the Americas initiative which was announced in 1990 by the then President of the United States, George Bush. This involves plans for investment and other measures which it is hoped will eventually establish free trade arrangements covering the whole of the Americas, from Canada to the tip of South America. These plans were reinforced at the Summit of the Americas in December 1994, where a commitment was made to further economic integration and free trade, progressively eliminating barriers to trade and investment by means of the creation of a new free trade area, to be known as the Free Trade Area of the Americas (FTAA). It was agreed that negotiations to this end would be completed by the end of 2005.[22]

AFTA

AFTA (the ASEAN Free Trade Area) was set up on 1 January 1993 with the aim of cutting tariffs between participating countries. Its establishment was agreed by the members of ASEAN (the Association of South East Asian Nations), which had been formed in 1967 by Brunei, the Philippines, Indonesia, Malaysia and Thailand. The general objective of AFTA is to increase exports by participants, with collaboration when it was in the interests of participating countries to do so. AFTA is often viewed as only a partial attempt at a free trade area. Although it is committed to reducing tariffs in general, in practice this has been rather piecemeal, and many categories of goods are exempted from its provisions. In addition, some participants continue a policy of strong protection for certain industrial sectors; Malaysia, for example, protects its car industry.[23]

Apec

In the mid-1990s initiatives began, under the aegis of the Asia Pacific Economic Cooperation (Apec) summit, which might lead to wider free trade groupings. The summit involved most countries of the Pacific Rim, including the USA, Australia and New Zealand. The initiatives were initially most concerned with considering ways in which trade liberalisation might be increased within the region as a whole. In November 1994, for example, a new code on foreign direct investment was agreed by officials representing the countries involved, and plans have been put forward for full liberalisation of trade in the Asia Pacific area by 2020.[24]

International business in regional blocs

For international firms, regional blocs offer many opportunities arising from larger tariff-free markets and the potential for more efficient use of resources. For companies within the bloc there is an increased risk from the changed competitive environment; the home market is now expanded to include other participating countries, and there is no longer protection from more efficient producers through tariffs. For companies outside the bloc, the emergence of common external tariffs (involving possible increases in existing tariffs) may present additional risks to existing business activities, or require a redesign of strategies to deal with changed conditions. The result may well be increased foreign direct investment, in order to have a base within the bloc which can serve its markets and avoid tariffs.

All companies doing business in countries participating in a new regional bloc may well find it necessary to conduct a review of their operations. The agenda could include the following items: consideration of how business is organised within the bloc, and awareness of ongoing business practice;[25] the location and staffing of the corporate headquarters; distribution and transport arrangements; considerations concerning the size and location of manufacturing plants and warehouses; marketing networks; the scope for joint ventures, mergers and acquisitions and cross-border strategic alliances; and the recruitment, training and development of staff, together with employment relations issues.

Summary

International companies cannot afford to ignore the growing impetus towards regional economic integration throughout the world economy. Such integration can take a variety of forms, depending on the degree of interdependence participating countries wish to have. The benefits of integration can be classified under the headings of static effects and dynamic effects. The EU is the longest established and most closely integrated trading bloc in the world today; it has the form of a common market, and is negotiating towards closer union. Elsewhere it is commoner to find free trade areas, although MERCOSUR in Latin America is moving towards becoming a common market by the end of the century. There are now established free trade areas in North and South

America, and plans for an Asia Pacific free trade zone. Each of these blocs, in line with the EU, has plans for expansion and for establishing free trade between the blocs.

It is easy to anticipate that in the next century there may well be a coming together of these expanded blocs and their associate members, establishing the largest free trade zone of all – one that is truly global. These developments will bring greatly expanded opportunities for international business in terms of access to markets, resources and investment opportunities; but for all firms there will be new competition risks as protection of domestic markets fades. The most successful firms in this new climate are likely to be those which prepare for the new opportunities by exploring new ways of doing business, and developing appropriate strategies in advance.

CASE STUDY
Mazda in Europe

In March 1993, the Japanese car producer Mazda abandoned negotiations with Ford (which owned a 25% stake in Mazda) to set up joint venture production in Europe. This meant that Mazda alone of the top five Japanese car makers had no production base in the EU. Three of the Japanese producers had chosen direct investment as their entry strategy – Nissan, Toyota and Honda establishing plants first of all in the UK. Mitsubishi, on the other hand, chose to develop joint car production with Volvo in the Netherlands.

The breakdown in negotiations followed similar non-productive discussions with Saab of Sweden. Mazda commented that local sourcing in Europe remained an important strategic consideration. In the light of this Mazda planned to examine its options without Ford of Europe, and to consider possible co-operative ventures with other European manufacturers. Talks had also been held with Chausson of France. Ford said that its talks with Mazda broke down over the issue of potential profitability of a co-operative European venture.

The *Financial Times* of 4 March 1993 commented that the lack of a European production base was likely to act as a serious brake on Mazda's growth in Europe in the 1990s. Without local production it would be unable easily to circumvent the quota restrictions on direct exports from Japan which were scheduled to last until the end of the century. The EU was pushing Japan to cut its export shipments in the light of the steep decline forecast in new car demand. Mazda was also studying the shipment of cars to Europe from its joint venture assembly plant with Ford in the US.

Source: adapted from the *Financial Times*, 4.3.93

Questions for discussion

I Critically evaluate the possible impact of the completion of the Single Market on foreign-owned companies operating in the EU, such as Ford and Toyota. How does this differ from the impact on locally-owned international companies operating within the EU?

2 Do locally-owned international companies operating in Europe have more to gain from the introduction of a common currency than firms which are based in countries outside the EU?

3 Why do Japanese carmakers see the EU as an important market?

4 Explain what is meant by 'local sourcing'. Why is this preferred to exporting as a means of servicing the European market?

5 What options for European operations were available to Mazda after the talks with Ford had broken down?

Further reading

Richard Brown, *Managing in the Single European Market*, Butterworth Heinemann, 1993.

J.D. Daniels and L.H. Radebaugh, *International Business Environment and Operations* (7th edition), Addison-Wesley, 1995.

Financial Times Survey, 'MERCOSUR', 25 January 1995.

Phil Harris and Frank McDonald, *European Business and Marketing*, Paul Chapman, 1994.

P. Herbig and K. Day, 'Managerial Implications of the North American Free Trade Agreement', pp 15–35, *International Marketing Review*, Vol. 10 No. 4, 1993.

The Times Guide to the Single European Market, Times Books, 1992.

R. Welford and K. Prescott, *European Business: An Issue-Based Approach* (2nd edition), Pitman, 1994.

Notes

1 See David H. Blake and Robert S. Walters, *The Politics of Global Economic Relations* (3rd edition), Prentice Hall, 1987, page 12.
2 For discussion of global free trade and regional blocs see *IMF World Economic Outlook* (May 1993), pages 106–15.
3 James K. Weekly and Raj Aggarwal, *International Business: Operating in the Global Economy*, The Dryden Press, 1987, page 192.
4 *Ibid* pages 198–9.
5 *Ibid* pages 200–4.
6 J.D. Daniels and L.H. Radebaugh, *International Business: Environments and Operations* (7th edition), Addison-Wesley, 1995, page 262.
7 Weekly and Aggarwal, *op cit*, page 202.
8 *Ibid*, page 202.
9 *Ibid*, page 204.
10 Jill Preston (ed), *Cases in European Business*, Pitman Publishing, 1992, page 19.

11 *Ibid*, page 22.
12 *Barclays Briefing*, No. 76, April 1988.
13 P. Cecchini, *The Benefits of the Single Market*, Wildwood House, 1988.
14 'Nafta aims for swift Chilean entry', *Financial Times*, Weekend December 10/11 1994.
15 'Free trade deal bewitches economists', *Financial Times*, 8 April 1991.
16 *Financial Times* Survey 'North American free Trade', 12 May 1993.
17 *Ibid*.
18 See Daniels and Radebaugh, *op cit*, pages 256–7.
19 'EC positive about Nafta agreement', *Financial Times*, 11 May 1993.
20 Daniels and Radebaugh, *op cit*, pages 264.
21 The material on MERCOSUR in this chapter draws on a survey in the *Financial Times* of 25 January 1995.
22 'A promise to advance in prosperity and democracy', *Financial Times*, 12 December 1994.
23 'Asean under pressure to speed the pace of trade liberalisation', *Financial Times*, 22 November 1994.
24 'Apec urged to broaden global trade role', *Financial Times*, 14 November 1994.
25 See *Barclays Briefing, op cit*.

7 Emerging markets: characteristics and opportunities

Objectives

By the end of this chapter, you will be able to:

- understand some of the main common aspects and differences among those economies known as 'emerging markets'.
- understand some of the different methods of analysing emerging markets for investment purposes.
- appreciate the importance of emerging markets within the world economy.
- understand some of the different policies that have been followed by different emerging markets as they have striven to integrate with the world capitalist economy.
- show detailed knowledge of some of the main characteristics of, and developments in, several of the most important emerging markets.

Introduction

✎ CASE STUDY

It is the largest country in the world, with the third largest population. It has the world's largest reserves of bauxite, chromium, gold, manganese and platinum. It is a leading producer of copper, coal, oil, titanium, tea, cocoa and coffee. It is a major exporter of crops, from vegetables and flowers to fruit and nuts. Its scenic beauty makes it one of the world's most attractive tourist destinations. Where is it? Africa.

The above is paraphrased from a report by Barings' Africa specialist Michael Power. It captures the essence of emerging markets – lands of opportunity where potential growth is enormous, but infrastructure, legislation, banking systems and equity markets are at an early state of development. In spite of its enormous wealth, Africa south of the Sahara, says Michael Power, has a collective gross national product (GNP) smaller than that of the Netherlands. But following Nelson Mandela's victory, could South Africa provide the opportunity for the private and the institutional investors to share in the continent's growth? Could the countries of Central and Eastern Europe, of Latin America, of Asia manage to unshackle themselves from poverty and become more prosperous economies?

The answers to these questions depend upon the success of the so-called emerging markets or emerging economies, and their systems of economic and social development; systems which have many similarities and many differences. These are countries which represent both tremendous opportunities and considerable risks for investment.

Which markets and economies in the world are considered as emerging? The International Finance Corporation defines emerging markets as those which have low or middle per capita incomes; this covers 80 per cent of the world's population. However, when one tries to be more specific than this, one finds there are almost as many different definitions and classifications as there are authors. Some call the most advanced type of emerging market – Mexico is an example – the 'newly industrialised countries' (but there is no single definition of these countries either). Those that have only just begun to develop (e.g. Morocco) are then described as 'embryonic' or 'submerged' countries; leaving countries such as China and South Africa in a middle category[1].

This approach implicitly divides the world into three types of economy: the 'established', or 'efficient', or 'developed' economies of the rich countries of the world; the emerging markets, otherwise called 'emerging countries', or 'developing countries'; and finally the 'less developed countries'. We will broadly adopt this classification; but it is important to be aware that other authors use different methods of classifying or defining emerging markets.

Financial analysts in New York, writing for investors, recently listed the existing emerging markets continent by continent, as shown in Figure 7.1:

Real GDP growth; % change from year before

	1993	1994
AFRICA		
Algeria	NA	NA
Côte d'Ivoire	−1.1	1.7
Morocco	−1.1	11.5
Nigeria	2.9	0.0
South Africa	1.1	2.2
Zimbabwe	NA	NA
ASIA		
China	13.4	11.8
Hong Kong	5.8	5.9
India	4.3	5.3
Indonesia	6.5	7.0
South Korea	5.6	8.5
Malaysia	8.5	8.7
Philippines	2.0	4.5
Singapore	10.1	10.1
Taiwan	6.2	6.5
Thailand	7.8	8.5
Vietnam	8.5	8.5

EUROPE		
Bulgaria	−4.2	−0.8
Czech Republic	−0.3	2.6
Greece	0.0	0.8
Hungary	−2.3	−2.8
Poland	3.8	5.1
Portugal	−0.5	1.4
Russia	−12.0	−8.0
Slovenia	1.0	2.9
Turkey	7.5	−6.0
LATIN AMERICA		
Argentina	6.4	5.9
Bolivia	3.2	NA
Brazil	4.1	5.7
Chile	6.3	4.3
Colombia	5.2	5.8
Costa Rica	6.1	4.5
Dominican Republic	5.0	NA
Ecuador	2.0	3.9
Jamaica	2.6	NA
Mexico	0.4	3.5
Panama	5.9	NA
Paraguay	3.5	NA
Peru	6.5	12.9
Uruguay	0.8	NA
Venezuela	−1.0	−3.3

Source: *Economic Research*, JP Morgan, Morgan Guaranty Trust Company, New York, 7.4.95, p.11

Figure 7.1

We can see that among the economies the financial analysts considered as 'emerging' are several which are part of the 'newly industrialised country' group in Asia; others are full members of the European Union; and a third group, if we were to use the classification of the World Bank, are among the low-income countries. However, the term 'emerging markets' is mainly used by financial analysts writing for foreign investors, and their usage is independent of the official country classification used by the World Bank.

Since the beginning of 1995, many experts have taken to describing emerging markets as 'submerging'; they are suggesting that the top two tiers of emerging markets are tending to slide back towards the third level. This probably exaggerates the situation; nevertheless, in the mid-90s investors in stock markets in many parts of the developing world found themselves suffering losses, as markets such as Mexico, the Philippines and Hungary sank under the weight of their own success. Pumped up by money from abroad, many of the globe's most promising young stock exchanges shot up so furiously in the frenzied first quarter of 1995 that a fall became inevitable. The biggest 'winners' of the previous year   Thailand, Turkey, Poland, and Indonesia − dropped 25% or more.

Offsetting those risks is the enormous growth potential of emerging markets, in which economic reforms are taking hold, and GDP growth rates are averaging two to three times those of developed countries. One emerging market, Turkey, was the world's best performer in the first quarter of 1995. Israel also did well during that quarter. While investors will probably never see another year like 1993, when emerging markets delivered an average return on investment of 67–68%, those with steely nerves and a good eye for value can still expect to outperform the mature markets by a wide margin.

Reasons for international interest in emerging markets

Motives for being interested in emerging markets vary. For some, they provide an opportunity to make huge, quick returns on purely financial investments. (It can be argued that this particular motive is a significant cause of instability.) For others, emerging markets represent an exciting sales opportunity for a wide range of consumer goods. Others again see an opportunity for providing much-needed infrastructure. Many small and medium-sized European firms, under intense competitive pressure in their domestic markets, have found that their particular skills (perhaps in the provision of specialised computer software, or financial services, or management consultancy) can be exploited within the context of a large consortium project in Brazil or Chile, or a joint venture in Bulgaria, Russia or India.

European manufacturing firms see many emerging markets, with their relatively low costs and potential for economic growth, as attractive locations for production facilities – as is happening in Vietnam and China, for example. Often, the attractiveness of an emerging market for foreign direct investment arises partly from the proximity of the chosen country to other markets which offer sales potential for the final products. Produce in Vietnam to exploit cheap skilled labour, and you can sell not only to Vietnam but also to its Pacific Rim neighbours including China and Japan.

> CASE STUDIES
> Unilever everywhere
> Competition and cost pressures in its mature markets have motivated Unilever (which has a strong presence in the EU) to move into East Europe, Latin America, India and China in recent years. It has spent $200 million in China forming eight joint ventures, and has set up ice cream factories in Beijing and Shanghai.
>
> Source: *Marketing Week*, 16.6.95
>
> Environmental Resources Management (ERM) in Chile
> At the start of 1995 ERM, based in London, had 70 offices in 20 countries including Chile, Brazil and Mexico. *Overseas Trade* reported in March 1995 that the UK's Overseas Development Agency had commissioned ERM to manage a major environmental improvement project in Chile. ERM would be overseeing the development of a regional and environmental management plan for the north of the country; environmental auditing and pollution control at the Ventanas copper smelter in central Chile; and economic assistance in the south for Chile's Ministry

of Forestry (CONAF). Both the public and private sector were involved in all three of these areas. The overall project cost would be £1.2 million, and the project was likely to last two years. It included the development of financial mechanisms to control environmental impacts, as well as environmental impact assessement and auditing. Within the region is the largest open cast copper mine in the world (Chuquicmata), and the Atacama desert, parts of which have been without rainfall for a century.

Source: *Overseas Trade*, March 1995

Approaches to the study of emerging markets

As we have already begun to see, there is no single widely-accepted model, or theory, or method, or approach for analysing emerging markets. It is very important to keep this in mind, and we will stress the fact in different ways throughout this chapter. Moreover, no one knows for sure what economic policies should be adopted by a particular country striving to integrate with the world capitalist economy. What seems to work for some countries has not worked elsewhere; and policies that have seemed to be working extremely well for a specific emerging market – even to the extent of encouraging many commentators and practitioners to announce that this is the model for others to follow – can suddenly and spectacularly fail, as happened recently in Mexico.

We shall make some generalisations, but it is important to warn that all generalisations on this topic are suspect. If the development of the economies of the world's poorer countries were an easy subject, then by now there would be no poor countries in absolute terms. It is desirable to offer at least some explanations and analytical tools for approaching countries not yet fully capitalist in their economic structures; but even the world's most experienced experts have made mistakes, as the events of 1995 illustrated.

The published literature on emerging markets approaches the subject from a range of quite different viewpoints – for example:

- from the point of view of political economy and the theory of development economies
- from the point of view of the changes in Central and Eastern Europe (this is quite a narrow view, because the economies in this region are very different from those of Latin America or Asia, for example)
- from the point of view of investment theory (particularly the modern portfolio investment theory) or securities investment.

As already noted, the majority of the publications do in fact concentrate on the investment interest of emerging markets, which are generally regarded by stock market investors as a 'special case'. It may take years of trading before their pricing behaviour can be reliably tested. A key consideration therefore is the cost to investors of making incorrect assumptions. It is variously assumed that the emerging markets:

- present unusual growth opportunities
- have useful diversification properties.

- exhibit above-average risk characteristics
- are characterised by high transaction costs.

The implication of the first two assumptions is that emerging markets are potentially attractive to informed investors; and of the second two, that such markets are probably best avoided by those who lack specialist local knowledge, or do not possess a high tolerance of risk. It is fair to describe the emerging markets as a quite new phenomenon (even the *Economist* did not begin to publish regular statistics on them until the autumn of 1994). There is no widely-held theory which explains the operation of these markets. Economic theory is struggling to keep pace with advanced capitalism, and we lack proven economic models for the successful transition from other forms of economic organisation to the capitalist system in its present form. It is even difficult at this stage to imagine that a single theory or model could ever explain markets as different as those of, say, Poland, Thailand and Peru.

The 'efficiency' of a market

This chapter attempts to provide an economic explanation of the rise of the emerging markets, especially those in Asia and Latin America, and a description of their characteristics. We will make some comparisons with the so-called 'efficient markets' (i.e. the established markets of the developed world). From a stock market investor's point of view, the term 'efficient' can be used to describe several characteristics of a market:

- the existing institutional infrastructure
- the costs of transacting
- the financial disclosure system
- the market's pricing behaviour.

Explaining these characteristics will enable us to gain a clearer focus about the efficiency of the emerging markets.

Infrastructural efficiency

The institutional infrastructure of a market can be described as efficient if:

- the local culture and political environment are sympathetic to a market economy
- a sophisticated and well-informed investment analyst profession exists
- there are no significant capital inflow-outflow restrictions.
- an effective regulatory framework and investor protection system is in place.
- market participants generally have realistic expectations about the risks and returns from investment
- investment dealing is systematically policed
- the taxation system is consistent with accepted international practice.
- the efficiency of stock price behaviour is rigorously and regularly researched and reported.

Transactional efficiency

The market is efficient with respect to security transactions if:

- the market has depth, breadth and resiliency
- the transaction process makes full use of current technologies
- issue and transaction costs are low.

Informational efficiency

The market is informationally efficient if:

- a well-regulated accounting and auditing profession exists, which gives credibility to the contents of corporate reports and statistics
- the overriding philosophy is one of full and timely disclosure of relevant financial data
- information is disseminated widely and speedily.

Pricing efficiency

In the standard classification of pricing efficiency, three levels of efficiency are identified, each level representing the market's response to a particular set of information, with the sets becoming progressively more comprehensive. The market is defined as efficient:

- **at the weak level**, if it reflects the information contained in past prices
- **at the semi-strong level**, if it reflects all publicly available information
- **at the strong level**, if it reflects all available information, including information not yet in the public domain.

The efficiency of emerging markets

It is obvious that a market's degree of efficiency needs to be determined by rigorous empirical testing. In this sense, we can make only some preliminary conclusions about emerging markets at this stage. First, an emerging market lacks sufficient history to provide the necessary empirical data for conducting a convincing test of its pricing efficiency. Investors have no alternative but to form a view on the basis of imperfect information. Second, although there may be some variation in the degree to which emerging markets in Eastern Europe, Asia and Latin America fall short of established markets' infrastructural, informational and transactional standards, it is probably fair to describe them collectively as inefficient in these respects.

These conclusions could create serious doubts about emerging markets (though some of the established markets might also have difficulty in meeting all the efficiency criteria). After the collapse of the Mexican peso at the end of 1994, and the following explosive reaction in Latin America, Asia and Eastern Europe, such doubts in fact increased. But a general belief in the inefficiency of emerging markets is not enough. It cannot be overemphasised that the rationale for active investment is not confidence in the market's pricing efficiency, but rather confidence that a particular strategy will generate abnormally high returns after adjusting for risk.

Frameworks for evaluating emerging markets

Many of the largest multinationals in the world (both banks and other companies) are using analytic frameworks for evaluating and monitoring emerging markets. Such frameworks tend to concentrate on five fundamental aspects of the reform process in these economies:

- Political environment
- Economic stabilisation
- Structural reforms
- External debt burden
- Supply/demand factors.

Political environment

Some key factors for evaluation are:

- Extent of enthusiasm for reform in the government
- The strength of the popular mandate for reform
- The degree of popular participation in the political process
- The ability of a government to implement its goals
- The composition and policies of potential future governments.

Obviously, the raw statistics cannot capture the political side of country risk. Elections, unstable governments, and the degree to which monetary policy is independent of political control will all make a country more or less capable of pursuing policies which are sustainable in the long term. (See also 'Relations with governments' later in the chapter.)

Economic stabilisation

Three areas are crucial for responsible management of a stable price environment and for sustaining long-term growth:

- Monetary policy
- Currency policy
- Fiscal policy.

There is more on stabilisation programmes a little later in this chapter.

Structural reforms

The following areas are the most important in the transitional period:

- Privatisation
- Tax policy and collection
- Foreign investment regulation
- Foreign trade policy.

External debt burden

The analysis has to reflect trends in a country's ability to generate foreign exchange, and in its fiscal and external balances which affect debt-servicing capabilities over the medium and long term. The country's vulnerability to external shock, such as movements in interest rates and flows of foreign capital, also needs to be assessed.

Supply/demand factors

The analysis has to evaluate underlying factors affecting the supply of, and demand for, a country's debt which may cause its prices to diverge from the levels implied by its economic fundamentals.

Important economic indicators

Figure 7.2 tabulates some basic economic indicators specialised investors should monitor (it is used by the World Bank's Institute of International Finance). Taken together, these indicators show whether a country is vulnerable to a change of heart by investors. If they are available when needed (a big if), they ought to provide a fair indication of a country's vulnerability to a loss of investor confidence, and the resources it has to withstand such a loss.

Emerging markets: Indicators for an economic health check

I. Balance of payments:

- Current account balance (as % of GDP)
- Foreign Direct Investment (as % of GNP)
- Reserves: months of payments for imports & interest

II. Debt position:

- Total external debt (as % of GDP)
- Total external debt (as % of exports)
- Short-term external debt (as % of total external debt)

III. Macro-economic stance:

- Budget balance (as % of GDP)
- Inflation rate (%)
- Savings (as % of GDP)
- Investment (as % of GDP)
- Real GDP growth (%)

Figure 7.2

A current account deficit – the natural counterpart to a net inflow of foreign capital – need not present a problem in itself. Even a relatively large deficit may be sustainable in the medium term. The bigger it is, however, the more important it is to know what is causing it, and how it is being funded.

The root of all current account deficits is low domestic saving, relative to domestic demand. If foreign money is being invested in profitable private investment, the deficit ought to be sustainable. The worry comes when the inflow is being used to finance excessive consumption. In theory, only government can get away with borrowing beyond its means. The budget deficit will tell you whether inflows are merely financing government over-spending.

However, deficit figures as published by governments are sometimes unreliable, and not always directly comparable. If we take the Mexican economy as an example, it had a current account deficit of more than 8.6% of GDP in 1994. The Mexican government's own numbers for that year masked big rises in lending by state-owned banks. All the same, the roots of much of the crisis were in the private sector: in 1994 foreign money was increasingly being lent on a very short term basis, to finance private consumption.

The level of foreign reserves can show how well the government could cope with a sudden fall in confidence. A low level of reserves is a fairly good sign that things have been going wrong for some time. Falling reserves are an even better signal. It is usually more important to know the way things have been moving than the current state of play. It is fairly easy to keep up with daily changes in the rate. Other key variables are often only available months later. In the Mexican case, lack of clear and timely information about the level of reserves and – critically – domestic monetary growth exacerbated the shock of devaluation.

Stabilisation programmes

Often emerging markets are required to undergo a stabilisation process to rescue the economy from low growth and high inflation; such stabilisation programmes are frequently followed by various policy and structural reforms to open the economy to international markets. As already indicated, these processes and programmes – and their timing and sequencing – vary from country to country. Perhaps the best abstraction of them is provided by Michael Bruno in his excellent book *Crises, Stabilisation and Economic Reform: Therapy by Consensus*[2]. While this chapter uses some of his empirical findings, it adopts for the most part a different approach to explaining and describing emerging markets. Nevertheless, his summary of the components of stabilisation and structural reform is helpful, and a slightly adapted version is shown in Figure 7.3.

I **Real fundamentals ('orthodox' stabilisation)**
Objective: Achieve internal and external balance.

    a) Establish permanent budget balance (usually includes substantial cut in direct and indirect subsidies, and increase in taxes).
    b) Devalue (usually followed by pegging the exchange rate).
    c) Promote central bank independence.

d) Obtain external stabilisation fund (and/or debt rescheduling).
e) Establish social safety net within constraint of 1(a).

2 Multiple nominal anchors ('heterodox' stabilisation)
Objective: Conditional on 1 above, achieve rapid synchronised disinflation of all nominal variables.

a) Initial exchange-rate peg.
b) Money and/or credit ceilings.
c) Wage freeze or tax-based incomes policy.
d) Price controls.

3 Extra nuts and bolts
Objective: Facilitate quick move to new macro-equilibrium.

a) Interest-rate conversion rules for nominal assets (to prevent excessive initial increases in real interest rates).
b) Introduce new currency.
c) De-indexation.
d) Internal debt rescheduling (between firms, banks and government) and/or public debt write-off subject to constraint 1(a).

These first three groups deal mainly with the stabilisation process.

4 Structural reforms
Objective: Remove micro-distortions to enhance efficient growth.

a) External current account liberalisation (remove quotas etc.)
b) Fiscal reforms (tax, expenditure and internal transfer).
c) Deregulation of domestic financial and capital markets.
d) Deregulation of labour markets.
e) Privatisation.
f) Deregulation of the external capital account.

5 Political reforms
Objective: Establish full-fledged democracy.

Figure 7.3   Components of stabilisation and structural reform

Clearly not all emerging markets have gone through all of the stages shown in Figure 7.3, nor would it be appropriate to do so in all cases. Nevertheless, there is enough similarity in the programmes of many emerging markets to make this a useful list.

Relations with governments

Government policies continue to be of critical importance in most emerging economies, and many companies are preparing special government-relations strategies. There is a trend worldwide for multinational firms to seek to reduce risk by making deals with governments, but this is particularly the case in emerging markets. A government-relations strategy should have regard to the following:

- Judicious use of intermediaries to assist in interacting with governments.
- Understanding of governments' priorities, and of how the decision-making process

is structured (including the structure of political power) in different countries.

- A framework for structuring incoming information about new or changing business-government issues.
- Use of former government employees in key negotiating roles.
- Continuing involvement of senior management.

Possible host-government actions in the emerging markets, which need to be monitored or even influenced by some of the above-mentioned methods, include the following:

- Regulation of international movements of capital and foreign exchange.
- Tariff and non-tariff barriers to trade.
- Incentives for international business (subsidies and grants).
- Tax incentives in some sectors of the economy, or for some activities.
- Rules regarding transfer prices.
- Licence regulation and practice.
- Land property regulation.
- Codes of conduct (of business activities).
- Regulations regarding the repatriation of profits.

Looking at specific markets

Having stressed the variety of prescriptive and analytical approaches to emerging markets, it is perhaps also necessary to comment briefly on the choice of examples in this chapter. If we tried to cover the whole spectrum, unavoidable limitations of space would mean that only a few brief points could be made about each country. Instead, we shall go into some depth in the analysis of several emerging markets, and aim to get somewhat briefer insights into a few others. The choice of specific countries is designed to illustrate the variety of conditions that apply; the focus is on Latin America and Asia, and several emerging markets from each region have been analysed so that contrasts and comparisons may be made between countries which have cultural and historical similarities. (Central and Eastern Europe have a chapter to themselves, Chapter 8.)

Key regions

Asia

Divided by culture, splintered by religion, riven by political and ideological differences and impoverished by war, for much of this century Asia was a wretched place. Yet over the past 15 years the three-fifths of the world's five billion people who live there have come to share a goal: to make themselves richer. By pursuing wealth, not war, they now account for about a quarter of gross world product. If they can keep up the pace, on a measure of purchasing power, early in the next century theirs could be the world's richest region.

In the mid-1990s the region continued to be the fastest growing in the world, but with a quite important volatility in year-on-year growth rates in export and industrial production. Also, the economic growth of the region as a whole was slowing – led by China and Hong Kong. A destabilising 20% inflation rate in China raised concern that the government would have to take harsh measures to slow things down. In fact, rising inflation was the main negative risk in Asia. Questions were raised about which Asian countries might suffer the same problems as Mexico. While some indicators and criteria were similar – Thailand, for example, had a high level of short-term debt, a rigid currency system, and a large current account deficit – the economies of Emerging Asia were still enjoying a high domestic savings rate, and thus did not rely on external capital in quite the same way as the Latin American economies. For most, 1994 had been a year of struggle against excessive capital inflows. Any abatement, therefore, was probably welcome relief, rather than any kind of major problem.

Latin America

In the mid-1980s Latin America was a quagmire of debt and dictatorships. A decade later, government accounts were improving, most economies had tamed hyperinflation, and many countries were inching closer to full democracy. It seemed that Brazil, one of the slowest to adopt economic reform, might finally be pulling things together. The market turmoil following the Mexican devaluation at the end of 1994 had cut economic growth prospects right across the region, apart from Brazil, but in a range from mild to extreme. Regional real GDP was expected to rise only 1.6 % in 1995, well down from the average rate of 4% in recent years. Brazil's economy, however, entered 1995 with considerable upward momentum (growth had reached almost 10% year-on-year in the fourth quarter of 1994), just as Argentina and Mexico might be tipping into recession.

Mexico's recession was likely to be particularly sharp – the economy was projected to shrink at an annual rate of about 5% in the first half of 1995. The key reason for the slowdown in the region overall was the sudden need to adjust current accounts rapidly to the new reality of sharply reduced net capital inflows. The need for adjustment was most severe in Mexico, where the current account deficit reached more than 8% of GDP in 1994, and net private sector capital flows had been outward rather than inward since the December 1994 devaluation.

Emerging Europe

By 1994, the world's newest open markets in the Eastern European countries of Poland, Hungary, the Czech Republic, Bulgaria, Slovenia and Russia were following Western Europe into a phase of quite important economic expansion; they continued to derive a major growth stimulus from surging exports to Western Europe. These economies will be analysed in more detail in the next chapter.

Southern Europe was softer. The Turkish economy had plunged into recession in the first half of 1994, and struggled to recover in the second half of the year. Growth was expected to strengthen in 1995 and 1996, but remain anaemic in the face of the need to run policies tight enough to meet IMF targets. Greece, too, was constrained by the imperative of fiscal discipline in order to get on top of its huge budget deficit (still about 12% of GDP in 1994). Portugal's recovery had been surprisingly weak, reflecting a determination to drive inflation lower.

Some key emerging markets

China

Whether the Asian economic boom continues, or eventually turns to bust, depends on how well the countries of Asia learn to manage its most troublesome power. The 'big dragon' which is emerging as the economic power to reckon with in the region is Greater China – the 1.3 billion citizens of the People's Republic, plus those dazzling entrepreneurs, the 55 million Overseas Chinese.

Sources of foreign direct investment in Asia (excluding China)	
	1993 ($ billion)
Singapore	2.5
Taiwan	4.4
Japan	3.7
Hong Kong	19.1

Foreign reserves (excluding China)	
	1993 ($ billion)
Hong Kong	43.0
Singapore	77.9
Japan	106.4
Taiwan	91.0

Source: Louis Kraar, *The New Power in Asia*, October 31 1994, p. 41

Figure 7.4

As Figure 7.4 reveals, the three small nations where the Overseas Chinese predominate – Hong Kong, Singapore, and Taiwan – have together eclipsed Japan as the primary source of capital and foreign investment for the region with the world's fastest growing economy. (For the period 1988-1992, according to the *Economist* in November 1994, China was the biggest recipient of foreign direct investment in the world, with a total of $25.6bn.)

Add in the assets controlled by Chinese businessmen in countries where they are a minority, such as Indonesia (3% of the population) and Thailand (10%), and this ethnic group's clout grows even larger. In 1994 the Overseas Chinese were conservatively estimated to control some $2 trillion in liquid assets (*Fortune*, 31 October 1994, p. 42). If all these enterprising people lived in one country, its gross national product would total at least $500 billion – larger than the $410 billion GDP of mainland China. Now combine the People's Republic's exports and imports with those of Hong Kong and Taiwan, and Greater China already accounts for a larger share of world trade than those arch-exporters, the Japanese (see Figure 7.5).

Trade: exports plus imports

	1993 ($ billion)
US	1,068.2
Germany	723.5
Greater China	634.2
Japan	603.9

Souce: Louis Kraar, *The New Power in Asia*, October 31 1994, p. 42

Figure 7.5

That lead can only grow. Drawn by China's capable pool of low-cost labour and its growing potential as a market that contains one-fifth of the world's population, foreign investors continue to pour money into the People's Republic of China (PRC). Some 80% of that capital comes from the Overseas Chinese, refugees from poverty, disorder, and communism, who in one of the era's more piquant ironies are now Beijing's favourite financiers and models for modernisation.

Partially as a result of this, China's economy, which advanced at a torrid 13.4% pace in 1993 and by 11.8% in 1994, has become a potent tonic for the entire Pacific Rim. In a report[3] issued by the Pacific Economic Cooperative Council, an organisation of government officials, business people, and academics, the economist Lawrence B. Krause commented: 'Even Australia and the United States find China the fastest growing market of any size. ... With Europe still mired in recession and Japanese imports either stagnant or declining, dependence on China for growth of export markets is unlikely to be reduced very soon.'

Economic transition in China

The modern history of that ancient country China dates from the beginning of this century. The fall of the Qing dynasty in 1911 freed China from almost two millennia of despotic monarchy, only to plunge it into a century during which it has endured (so far) a revolution, a short-lived republic, a descent into warlordism, a partial occupation, a civil war, a second revolution and a communist dictatorship. A brief summary of key moments in the recent political and economic history of China is presented in the box below.

Chronology of background events in China	
Period	**Main political/economic events**
1911	Outbreak of the National Revolution
1921	Chinese Communist Party has its first Congress in Shanghai
1924	First National Congress of the Kuomintang (Nationalist) Party
1925	Foundation of the All-China Federation of Trade Unions

1934–35	The Communists' 'Long March'
1945	End of the Second World War: the Japanese surrender
1949	The 'Liberation': the Communists take power, and People's Republic of China established under Mao Zedong
1949–52	Economy centralised under a new communist government Emphasis on heavy industry and 'socialist transformation'
1951	Outbreak of the Korean War
1953/57	First Five-Year plan
1958/60	The Great Leap Forward: an economic reform plan based on labour-intensive production methods
1960	Sino-Soviet split: Moscow recalls technical advisors
1966	The Cultural Revolution: years of strife follow
1976	Deaths of Premier Zhou Enlai and Chairman Mao
1978	Start of New Economic Reforms in Sichuan Province Deng Xiaoping's reforms: liberalisation of agriculture and introduction of individual incentives
1979	Enterprise reforms extended to other areas
1980	Trial of the 'Gang of Four'
1981	Rise of Deng Xiaoping, and Sixth Five-Year Plan (1981–85) Growth rates accelerated
1982	Workers' Congresses set up in 95% of large enterprises
1983	Substitution of taxation for profit remittance in state enterprises
1984	New Law on enterprise management in urban factories
1985	Enterprise Responsibility Contract System approved
1986	Seventh Five-Year Plan (1986–1990)
1987	Food prices increase substantially
1988	Zhao Ziyang approved as Party General Secretary; Li Peng as Premier
1989	Tiananmen Square student demonstration Imposition of Martial Law, and fall of Zhao Ziyang
[2000]	Target year of 'Four Modernisations' goal that per capita GNP should reach $1,000 (at current prices)

Deng Xiaoping's economic reforms

Two years after the death of Mao Zedong, in 1978, the new Chinese leader Deng Xiaoping proclaimed major economic reforms. Collectivised agriculture was abolished, and agricultural land was distributed among households on long-term leases. In exchange for a lease, a household agreed to pay a fixed tax and contracted to sell part of its output to the state. But the household made its own decisions (a difference from the previous system) on cropping patterns and the quantity and types of fertilisers and other inputs to use, and also hired its own workers. Private farm markets were liberalised, and farmers received a higher price for their produce. Also, the state increased the price that it paid to farmers, especially for cotton and other non-grain crops.

The results of Deng Xiaoping's reforms were astounding. Annual growth rates of output of cotton and oil-bearing crops increased a staggering fourteen-fold. Soybean production, which had been declining at an annual rate of 1 per cent between 1957 and 1978, now started to grow at 4% a year. Growth rates in yields per hectare also increased dramatically. By 1984, a country that six years earlier had been the world's largest importer of agricultural products became a food exporter! The reforms did not merely produce massive expansion in the agricultural sector; increased rural incomes led to an expanding rural industrial sector that, by the middle 1980s, was employing a fifth of the rural population.

China has gone even further, and is encouraging foreign investment and joint ventures. In addition, it is experimenting with formal capital markets, and now has quickly growing stock markets.

Motivated partly by political considerations, China is proclaiming the virtues of what it calls a 'one country, two systems' approach to economic management. The political source of this movement is the existence of two capitalist enclaves in which China has a close interest: Taiwan and Hong Kong. China claims sovereignty over Taiwan. Part of Hong Kong, a UK crown colony, is currently leased by the United Kingdom from China. When the lease expires in 1997, it has been agreed that the whole of Hong Kong will become part of China. Anxious not to damage the economic prosperity of Hong Kong, China is proposing to continue operating the territory as a capitalist economy.

The results of the transition towards a free-market economy in China are dramatically summarised in the country's real GDP growth statistics. Between 1982 and 1988, real GDP per person grew at a staggering 9.7 % a year, almost doubling in a six-year period. China is not only experiencing rapid growth of real income per person, but is also increasing its international competitiveness. Its exports grew during the 1980s at a much faster rate than GDP, and by 1990 stood at 17% of GDP.

How has this dramatic success been achieved? The following characteristics of the reforms are probably among the main factors:

- A massive rate of creation of new private and cooperative firms, mainly in the rural areas.

- Large increases in the productivity and profitability of the state enterprises, as a result of their increased economic independence and the new economic stimulus.

- The creation of the Special Economic Zones.

- An efficient taxation system.

- Gradual price deregulation.

- Opening of the economic borders and increased competition.

- Favourable climate for foreign direct investment and joint ventures.

- Positive trade relationships with neighbouring economies.

- Decreased role of the Central Plan in the development of state-owned enterprises.

China's economic situation in the mid-1990s
The main economic indicators for 1993 and 1994 are shown in Figure 7.6.

	1993	1994
Real GDP, % change	13.4	11.8
Consumer prices index, Dec/Dec	17.0	25.4
Exchange rate, units/$	5.80	9.10
Balance of payments, $ billion	−12.1	5.6
Current account balance, % of GDP	−2.5	1.0
International reserves, $ billion	22.4	52.9
Import coverage of reserves, number of months	2.2	4.7
Total external debt, $ billion	79.7	105.0
Short term	12.8	12.5
Total external debt, % of GDP	14	19
Total external debt, % of exports	69	65

Source: *Emerging Markets Economic Outlook*, J. P. Morgan, Morgan Guaranty Trust Company, *Economic Research*, May 1995

Figure 7.6

In 1994–95 China continued its reform programme of gradual introduction of market elements into its economy. Calming any 'overheating' of the economy is likely to remain the government's top policy priority for the coming years. Stabilisation efforts cut industrial output growth from the peak of 26.4% to 15.5% in February 1995. Correspondingly, the 12-month consumer price index inflation dropped from a high of 27.7% to 22.4% in February 1995. The central government was planning to continue tightening credit and curbing its own spending and capital investment in the property sector. To contain food prices, in early 1995 it banned grain exports, began importing large amounts of farm products, and imposed domestic retail price capping. These steps to rein in inflation, however, were confronted with mounting contrary pressures from the state sector and the high number of unemployed, which were likely to force the central bank to loosen credit selectively.

Structural reforms continued to proceed gradually. The main price being paid for macroeconomic tightening was the slowing of planned privatisation and other microeconomic reforms. Before the latter could resume, the government needed time to expand the new social welfare system, stabilise the macro environment, and improve its monetary management.

Exports continued to prosper, with rising demand from Japan, the United States and Hong Kong, thanks to the relative weakness of the RMB (China's national currency) against major OECD currencies. Slower import expansion could be explained by weakening domestic capital spending, although foreign direct investments continued to surge. The main tasks of the Chinese government were continuation of political reform, improvement of the legal and taxation system, and further opening of internal markets.

✎ CASE STUDY
British firms in China
Between April and July 1995 *Overseas Trade* reported on the activities of a number of British firms in China.

AVP Baker Ltd. had a £150,000 contract to supply refrigeration equipment for new chilling, blast-freezing and cold storage for poultry processing. The order had been placed through FES International Ltd. and the Chinese main contractor, as part of a £2 million deal. AVP Baker would be providing single screw compressors and associated products. Complete containerised plant rooms for the five sites were being engineered, built and commissioned by FES International.

Railko Ltd. had entered the Chinese marine market by first signing a distributor agreement with the Jiangnan Shipyard, Shanghai. This was followed by an order for bearings to be fitted to bulk carriers being constructed by the shipyard for foreign owners.

Hanson Transmissions had supplied 48 drive packages for conveyors and elevators to be installed at the Minsheng Grain Terminal, Shanghai. Valued at £500,000, the drive assemblies incorporated the latest design Hansen P4 gear units with Brook Crompton motors. This was part of an overall £8.5 million handling and storage project. Hanson Transmissions had also completed a contract with GEC Alsthom Engineering Systems, valued at more than £330,000, to supply 22 packaged drives for the Shajiao C power station in Guangdong. The power station was being built for Hopewell Energy, a subsidiary of Hong Kong-based Consolidated Electric Power Asia, by a consortium led by GEC Alsthom in association with ABB Combustion Engineering and Slipform Engineering. It was a turnkey project which included all handling facilities for riverside coal deliveries.

The newly-formed Systems Integration Group of Bristol Babcock Ltd. had won a major Chinese project worth over £200,000. It would supply the control system for a water treatment plant at Daya Bay, Guangdong Province in southern China, built by Thompson Kennicott and serving a nuclear power station built by GEC Alsthom at Daya Bay. Bristol Babcock were providing the engineering, process plant control and documentation for two identical streams. A second contract had also been awarded to this firm, for the provision of local housings for instruments and analysers.

The Mouchel Group based in Surrey, England, had been appointed to manage, coordinate, design and supervise construction of the extensive civil engineering works associated with the new Yuehuang Power Station situated on the Yangtze River in Hunan Province, some 1,200 km south of Beijing. Mouchel also designed a vast dry coal store for this coal-fired power station, and apparently enjoyed excellent cooperation with Chinese engineers, four of whom spent many months in the UK helping with the detailed engineering design of the power station.

Source: adapted from *Overseas Trade*, April to July 1995

The *Financial Times* of 11 April 1995 reported that twelve small and medium sized UK machine tool manufacturers (such as Crawford Swift of Halifax) began exporting to China under a scheme launched by the UK's Department of Trade and Industry in March 1995. If successful, the scheme would be replicated in other industries and sectors and for other countries. The idea was to use a Chinese consultant to provide local market knowledge, and for this information to be distributed to the twelve UK firms, thus dramatically cutting down on their market research costs. The companies could then either begin direct exporting or operate through an agent.

Source: adapted from the *Financial Times*, 11.4.95.

Analysing the Chinese economic and business environment in the mid-1990s, we can identify the following general opportunities:

- Enormous market of 1.2 billion customers
- Rapidly growing purchasing power
- Cheap, well-educated labour
- A wealth of raw materials
- Opportunities for provision of components to customer industries (e.g. car manufacturers).

The problems existing within this environment are the following:

- Unstable political situation
- Bureaucracy and corruption still strong
- Shortage of hard currency
- Difficult 'stabilisation' climate after first deficit
- Undeveloped tax and banking system
- Rising inflation
- High unemployment, particularly in the urban areas
- Inadequate infrastructure (transport, energy)
- Productivity still low by western standards
- Lack of technical personnel (skills, mobility)
- Inefficient procurement of raw materials
- Weak legislation and legislative infrastructure in the field of technology protection, copyrights, etc.
- China is not a member of GATT
- Continuing violation of human rights.

1995 was a pivotal year for economic reform, and to a certain extent for political reform. The country was facing big challenges in curbing inflation, salvaging faltering state-owned enterprises, and maintaining agricultural production. Changes in the political direction of the country were absolutely necessary: the era of Deng Xiaoping was at an end, and the Chinese Government had to deal with increasing international pressure to improve its human rights policies, and to continue with democratic political reforms.

Vietnam

Vietnam was ruled by China from 208 BC until 939 AD, when it defeated and expelled the Chinese and became independent. For the next ten centuries up to 1858, China intermittently waged war with Vietnam, sometimes successfully. On 2 September 1858 the French occupied Vietnam, and began exploiting the peasants as slave labour. The Japanese displaced the French during the Second World War, and when Japan was defeated Vietnam was handed back to the French. Some two million peasants died of starvation while producing crops for export to the French empire.

The Vietnamese fought the French for seven years, and finally defeated them in 1953, at which point the country was divided, with a Communist government in the North in conflict with a Saigon government supported militarily by the USA and Australia. The North won in 1975, but it was not long before the reunited country was invaded once more by its oldest foe, China, in 1979. Again Vietnam was successful. Meanwhile, in 1978, it had also had to deal with another adversary threatening its borders: the notorious Pol Pot regime, which had taken over Cambodia and which was in effect supported by both China and the USA. Vietnam prevailed, setting up what was virtually a client government in Phnom Penh.

In addition to these armed conflicts, the country also had to endure an American-led trade embargo from 1975 to 1994. Not only did the USA refuse to trade with its 'enemy', but it also threatened economic sanctions against other countries seeking to trade or invest in Vietnam. The USA used its power within the international agencies to ensure that Vietnam was denied development funding and (to a large extent) other financial assistance from the World Bank and IMF. The government was forced to default on payments on an IMF facility in 1985, and became ineligible for further funds. It improved its repayment record subsequently, but IMF and World Bank funding was not restored, principally because of persistent pressure from the USA[4]. (Aid and low interest credits to the value of $2 billion have been forthcoming since November 1994.) After all this, the surprising thing is not that Vietnam is among the poorest countries of the world, but rather that it exists at all.

For nearly twenty years Vietnam was Communist, and it was no more successful with this discredited form of political and economic organisation than anyone else. Like communist regimes elsewhere, it tended to give high priority to physical production targets at the expense of macroeconomic stability. In 1986, under the newly appointed General Secretary Nguyen Van Linh, the country began a liberal economic reform programme (known as *'doi moi'* and analogous to *'perestroika'* in the USSR), and became an emerging market. Initially the liberal reforms were of the 'market socialism' type, which represents a compromise between socialist control and free markets.

Market socialism does not appear to work, and in Vietnam as elsewhere it was associated with blackmarkets, corruption, bureaucracy, inefficient firms and low growth. More radical reforms were introduced in 1989; there was a devaluation to the market rate, only a dozen prices remained controlled, family farms replaced collectives, state subsidies were abolished, and the formation of private companies encouraged. Inward foreign investment (portfolio and foreign direct investment) increased each year from 1989 to 1994, and many of the newly industrialised countries of the Pacific Rim are using Vietnam for 'offshore production'. (In the mid-1990s, labour costs were 80% lower than in neighbouring Thailand.)

Since 1989 the country has become the world's third biggest exporter of rice, and inflation was reduced from around 900% to around 10% (although in the first quarter of 1995 inflation appeared to be headed upward). It is still the sixteenth poorest country in the world, but a 1994 World Bank report drew attention to good standards of health, education and employment, a relatively long life expectancy, low crime rates, relatively even distribution of income and other long-term advantages, and suggested that Vietnam was likely to join the Southeast Asian NICs in about 20 years, barring major setbacks. The country was due to join the ASEAN trade bloc in July 1995. Meanwhile, oil has been discovered off the coast, and initial estimates suggested that these fields will yield between 1 and 2.5 billion barrels.

Figures for inward foreign direct investment for 1992, quoted in the *Fortune* issue of April 1995, indicated that there were 600 contracts worth $4.6 billion, which included:

Taiwan	$790 million
Hong Kong	$606 million
France	$475 million
Australia	$404 million
UK	$305 million

According to the *Financial Times* of 4 April 1995, many American companies were showing interest in the Vietnamese market, including Boeing, Chrysler, Citicorp, Coca-Cola, Pepsico, General Electric, Holiday Inn, Hyatt, IBM, Mobil, and airlines such as Delta, Northwest and United. Ford, Chrysler, Daimler-Benz, Toyota, Suzuki and a consortium of Indonesian and Japanese concerns had applied to set up car manufacturing plants, and this represented an investment of almost $600 million. Joint venture deals with indigenous firms in the automotive industry were expected later in 1995.

CASE STUDY
APV & Allied Domecq in Vietnam

APV, which is based in Peterborough, England, manufactures biscuit-making equipment. *Overseas Trade* reported in early 1995 that the Bien Hoa Sugar Refinery Company had commissioned a complete plant to make a wide variety of moulded biscuits. The plant included mixing, moulding, panning, baking, cooling and packaging technology. The contract included technical support and training. Vietnamese staff had visited APV in Peterborough for hands-on training. Vietnam was joining the list of 80 countries using APV biscuit-making technology.

Overseas Trade also reported that the first fast food chain to enter the Vietnamese market was the British company Allied Domecq's, which had opened its first Baskin-Robbins store in Ho Chi Minh City. The store operated under a franchise arrangement; the franchisees were two former Vietnamese refugees. Baskin-Robbins was originally a US brand but is now owned by Allied Domecq.

Source: adapted from *Overseas Trade*, January and March 1995

Clearly a great deal has been achieved since 1989. However, potential foreign investors still have much to consider. As of 1995, the country was still run by a one-party communist regime. Monetary policy and inflation were not yet stabilised, nor was the currency (since 1 October 1994 the authorities had been implementing policies to diminish the role of the US dollar in favour of the Vietnamese dong). The country's infrastructure and technological base required massive investment. The balance of trade ran a small deficit in 1993 and a large one in 1994. The Goverment continued to run a large internal budget deficit. China and Vietnam had territorial disputes over the recent offshore oil discoveries. There is also the lesson of Mexico, which similarly appeared to have achieved much in a short time until the currency collapse in December 1994.

Indonesia

The Republic of Indonesia has a population of 179,140,000. This is the world's largest island chain with about 13,000 islands, of which less than half are inhabited. The total area of Indonesia is 735,354 square miles. Indonesia proclaimed its political independence in 1945; the political system is a unitary multi-party republic, with a bicameral legislature. It is the world's largest Muslim country: 87% of the population are Muslims, 10% are Christians, 2% Hindu and 1% Buddhist. The capital of Indonesia, Jakarta, is the largest city in Southeast Asia with a population of over 7 million. Another interesting feature of Indonesia is that there are 360 ethnic groups, speaking over 250 languages and dialects.

Foreign investment: opening of the economy

With more than $5.8 billion in foreign investment committed to Indonesia between 1989 and 1993, almost four times the $1.5 billion committed in 1987, Indonesia is one of the largest recipients of foreign investment among the nations of Southeast Asia, and indeed among all the world's developing nations.

The additional investments of 1989-93, which involve more than 300 projects, amount to 21% of the total foreign capital attracted since Indonesia first invited investment with the Foreign Capital Investment Law of 1967. A substantial proportion of the funds invested in 1989-93 came from small- and medium-sized companies attracted by low costs, a large labour pool and economic deregulation. The chemical industry received the largest share of foreign investment, accounting for $2.6 billion of the $5.8 billion. Also high on the list of sectors receiving substantial funds were the textile industry with $585 million in commitments, metal products with $293 million, and food processing with $224 million worth of investment.

The strong growth of investment in Indonesia reflects both its natural attributes – an abundance of resources and labour, a huge domestic market, and a strategic location in Southeast Asia – and its stable and deregulated economy. Faced with declining prices for its principal exports of oil and natural gas, and growing global competition for investment capital, the government began in the mid-1980s a major overhaul of its regulatory environment to create a more attractive business climate.

Since 1985, investment opportunities have been greatly expanded; administrative requirements drastically reduced; the minimum investment capital requirement lowered; foreign equity ratios raised; divestment periods extended; export/import constraints and barriers reduced; restrictions on foreign participation in wholesale distribution dropped; and import monopolies eliminated.

These reforms, in combination with a streamlined taxation system, a fully convertible currency (the rupiah) and the total repatriation of profits, have established Indonesia as a strong and growing participant in the global marketplace. The growing inflow of investments is the strongest testimony to the effectiveness of these policies.

Foreign trade

1987 marked the transition from an economy primarily reliant on the commodities of oil and gas to one whose growth is increasingly dependent on value-added manufacturing. Oil and gas exports played a significant role in the GDP growth rate of 8–10% for the period from 1971 to 1981; but in the early 1980s the government embarked on a programme to promote economic diversification, in order to maintain economic growth while reducing its dependency on oil and gas. Although Indonesia suffered from a decrease of well over 50% in the price of oil in 1986, with export-oriented diversification already under way the economy rebounded; and in 1987, for the first time in modern Indonesian history, non-oil and gas products surpassed oil and gas as the main source of export revenue.

Exports are essential to the continued growth of the Indonesian economy. Reforms and deregulation undertaken in the trade sector have included:

- dropping import quotas
- eliminating non-tariff barriers in favour of flat tariffs
- abolishing import and export licensing
- simplifying port and customs procedures
- dismantling import monopolies
- removing duties on products used in manufacturing goods for exports
- allowing foreign investors that produce 65% for export to invest in virtually any sectors of the economy.

In addition, a floating currency has ensured that Indonesian goods remain competitive in the world economy.

According to the Ministry of Trade of Indonesia, the contribution of the non-oil economy to the gross domestic product is in excess of 60 per cent, with industrial exports making up more than three quarters of this percentage. Leading the category of industrial exports in dollar value is the plywood and wood products group; other export product sectors which have demonstrated fast growth were chemical products (petrochemicals and plastics) and electrical goods. The other major categories – agriculture (mainly rubber, coffee, cocoa beans, tea, shrimps, fish and spices) and mining – account for the remaining quarter of the non-oil and gas products.

While it is establishing itself as a growing exporter of basic manufactured goods, Indonesia is also moving into the exportation of more advanced products such as aircraft and aircraft components, electronic goods and measuring instruments. The restructuring of Indonesia's export base has brought new areas of growth to offset the weak commodity prices of recent years. Growth in manufacturing and wholesale and retail trade contributed to a permanent GDP growth rate for the last 4 years of more than 6.5% per year. Tight fiscal and monetary policies have kept inflation under 10% since 1984. (It was 9.9% in 1991, 5.0% in 1992, 10.0% in 1993 and 9.0% in 1994.) A tax reform of 1983 replaced sales taxes with a value-added tax, and combined and simplified taxation of individuals and corporations into three brackets – 15%, 25% and 35%.

The financial sector reforms of 1988–1990
In 1988, the Indonesian government implemented a series of sweeping measures aimed at reinforcing and augmenting the growth and advancements achieved up to that time. The goals of the financial sector reform, begun in October 1988, were:

- to mobilise private funds.
- to develop the capital markets in order to stimulate foreign investment and the general liquidity and mobility of funds.

- to attract additional offshore funds into Indonesia for investment and capital expansion, and to support the export drive and the further development of the non-oil economy
- to increase competition within the banking sector – leading to increased efficiency, broader public participation, reduction in the cost of money and greater confidence in the rupiah.

Through new measures aimed at increasing liquidity, new banking instruments and the freeing of domestic and foreign banks to expand throughout Indonesia, the banking sector has experienced unprecedented growth in the early 1990s. This transformation has caused banks to become more efficient and competitive, and has allowed the industry to tap into much-needed sources of financing for private sector economic growth.

The first package of reforms (PAKTO), initiated in October 1988, was comprehensive and far-reaching. The PAKTO measures, designed to complement earlier economic deregulatory actions, included:

- Permitting the opening of new private domestic banks.
- Allowing existing domestic banks to open branches throughout the country.
- Relaxing the requirements on deposits by state-owned enterprises, thereby permitting up to 50% of the funds of such enterprises to be deposited at private commercial banks.
- Permitting existing foreign banks to open sub-branch offices.
- Allowing foreign banks to enter into joint ventures with domestic banks.
- Establishing a legal lending limit of 20% of a bank's own equity to finance any one individual client, and a maximum of 50% to finance a company group.

Changes were also made to improve the implementation of monetary policy:

- The minimum reserve requirement for banks was lowered from 15% to 2%.
- The liquidity requirement of 2% was also applied to Non-Bank Financial Institutions (NBFIs), in view of their new freedom to issue Certificates of Deposit.
- Confidence in Indonesia's currency, the rupiah (Rp), was reinforced by allowing the official dollar swap rate to be set by a market-based formula, based on the differential between domestic and international rates.

Measures announced in March 1989 provided further clarification of the deregulatory measures of October 1988:

- Ceilings on foreign borrowing by foreign exchange banks and NBFIs were abolished.
- The central bank (Bank Indonesia) introduced a maximum limit for a bank's net foreign exchange position, which was set at 25 percent of its share capital.
- Banks were permitted to borrow money abroad at rates lower than those charged in Indonesia. This makes a greater amount of money available for domestic borrowers, and has led to lower domestic interest rates because of increased competition.
- In October 1989, Bank Indonesia officially allowed foreign banks to open an unlimited number of sub-branches in Jakarta and in six other provincial capitals: Medan, Bandung, Semarang, Surabaya, Denpasar and Ujung Pandang.

Rewards of reform

Like so many areas of the economy affected by the reforms of the 1980s and early 1990s, Indonesia's banking sector has undergone a far-reaching transformation, and has become more dynamic, flexible and efficient. A few examples clearly show that this growth is solid and continuing:

- Total deposits rose nearly 50% between 1989 and 1991.
- In 1991, the savings deposits in private banks exceeded those in state banks by 74%.
- The deregulation measures of 1988 allowed new foreign banks to set up joint ventures with local banks. Since then more than 18 new joint-venture banks have been created. In Surabaya, one of the fastest growing cities, the Bank of Tokyo, Deutsche Bank, the Hong Kong and Shanghai Bank, ABN-AMRO Bank and Daiwa have all established operations.

The capital markets

While Indonesia has one of the world's oldest stock trading traditions, dating from the days of the Dutch colonial era, the Jakarta Stock Exchange of the modern era was only reactivated in 1977. Between 1977 and 1987, however, the stock exchange was virtually dormant. As a result of the economic resurgence after the oil shock of the mid-eighties, and the comprehensive set of economic reform measures implemented in 1988–1990, the stock market experienced a rebirth, and the early 1990s saw explosive growth. By the middle of the decade total capitalisation of the market had risen to $20 billion, more than 15.4% of GDP; the average daily value of share trading was about $10–12 million.

Substantive foreign interest in the Indonesian capital markets has primarily taken the form of portfolio investment. Over the past three years, an increasing number of foreign brokerage houses has been purchasing securities on the Jakarta Stock Exchange, as they quickly recognised the importance of this emerging market, and secured a firm foothold through the establishment of country funds.

Indonesia's economic situation in the mid-1990s

The main economic indicators for 1993 and 1994 are shown in Figure 7.7.

At 7% in 1994, real GDP growth had already nudged up against the higher end of historical experience. Yet the outlook in 1995 was for even faster growth, thanks to a host of factors, not least the continuing successful restructuring of the economy.

On the external side, non-oil exports had recovered from a very tough first semester in 1994. Firming global oil prices were also expected to help boost export revenues; oil and gas still accounted for 28%-30% of export revenues (depending on price), and as the average oil price was expected to be 7%-8% higher in 1995, this would add significantly to revenues. A rupiah that fell 7% over the course of 1994 was also expected to boost exports in 1995. In the domestic economy a certain monetary laxity dominated the years after the reforms, particularly in 1993 and most of 1994. In this sense, fiscal policy could be characterised as neutral-to-positive for growth.

As huge foreign inflows inundated the entire ASEAN region in 1993, real interest rates in Indonesia fell sharply. They recovered only gradually; in early 1995 real rates were still more than 300 basis points below long-run averages. The legacy of 18 months of

	1993	1994
Real GDP, % change	6.5	7.0
Consumer prices, Dec/Dec	10.0	9.1
Exchange rate, units/$	2110	2200
Balance of payments, $bn		
Merchandise trade balance	8.2	8.6
Exports	36.6	42.5
Imports	−28.4	−33.9
Current account balance	−2.0	−4.2
% of GDP	−1.4	−2.5
International reserves, $bn	11.3	13.2
Import coverage of reserves, number of months	3.1	3.0
Total external debt, $bn	95.6	98.9
Short term	21.7	22.0
Owed to commercial banks	38.4	39.5
Total external debt, % of GDP	64	59
Total external debt, % of exports	222	201
Interest payments, % of exports	16	14
Debt service ratio	30	27

Source: *Emerging Markets Economic Outlook*, March 1995, J.P. Morgan, Morgan Guaranty Trust Company, Economic Research, New York, p.35

Figure 7.7

low interest rates was likely to have its effect in 1995, adding significantly to overall demand in the economy.

The main problem of the Indonesian economy in the mid-1990s was inflation. Given that the economy was already close to the upper limits of its potential, further demand stimuli were likely to boost inflation as much as, or more than, real growth. Inflation increased in the second half of 1994, due mainly to rapidly rising food prices, and seemed likely to accelerate in 1995 because of underlying factors other than food. It appeared probable that it would be especially difficult to keep overall inflation below President Suharto's perennial year-end request of 10%.

Nevertheless, from the point of view of foreign investors, the Indonesian economy promises even more growth in the medium term.

India

India is one of the new economic giants of Asia, with a population of 870 million people, living in an area of 3,288,000 square km. The country is the world's second largest emerging market, and has some advantages over China: a developed banking system, a western-style legal code and a large number of English speakers. However, it has traditionally been reluctant to admit foreign capital; a government ban on foreign portfolio investment was not lifted until late 1992. Real economic reform started at the end of 1991, and by the mid-1990s India was beginning to enjoy the first fruits of the economic transformation.

Foreign investment and exports were rising fast, the stock market was up, and long-stagnant industrial output was starting to recover. After six years of good harvests, the richer farmers were content – and spending money as never before. The political situation was stable, and the position of the government seemed stronger than at any time since the Prime Minister, Narashimha Rao, took over the ruling Congress party from the assassinated Rajiv Gandhi in 1991. India had avoided the deep-rooted social unrest which hit many of the neighbouring countries struggling with pro-market reforms. As the Prime Minister of India said in an interview in early 1994 (*Financial Times*, 30 March 1994, Special Survey): 'The best thing is to show people that reform works. ... Perhaps in many other countries it has taken a longer time, therefore people have lost their faith and all kind of difficulties are threatening to come. In India fortunately we have been able to convince the people though, of course, much more remains to be done.'

Results in 1993 and 1994 showed that India could achieve the government's target of a steady growth rate of 5-6 per cent over the next few years. However, this aim was quite modest, given that India grew at an average rate of 5.5% in the Gandhi era of the pre-reform 1980s. To reach a significantly higher rate, India might need to undertake the radical reforms it had so far largely avoided – notably organising large-scale investment in infrastructure, and cutting its bloated public sector. Moreover, as many experts acknowledged, without a growth rate of above 6% the country was unlikely to create jobs for its unemployed and underemployed masses, or generate sufficient resources for education, health care and other development spending.

Foreign investment

For foreign investors, India looked more promising in the mid-1990s than at any time since independence. With some signs of the Chinese economy over-heating, many international investors looking for alternatives among developing countries were turning to India and its vast unexploited market of 870 million people. Between mid-1991 and 1995, India approved foreign direct investments totalling more than $5bn, including over $3bn in 1993-4. Much of it was concentrated in the energy sector, a top government priority. The amount actually flowing into India was also growing – from $148m in 1991–92 to an estimated $1.5bn in 1993–94. Foreign financial investment mushroomed after India opened its stock market to foreign institutions in late 1992, and eased rules for Indian companies issuing paper overseas. Investment from these sources soared to an estimated $3.6bn in 1993-94, from virtually nothing three years before. The growth was so fast that it clogged the Bombay market's settlement machinery.

India's economic situation in the mid-1990s

The main economic indicators for 1993 and 1994 are shown in Figure 7.8. 1995 seemed very likely to bring a further acceleration of real GDP growth – provided agriculture (a sector that still contributed nearly one-third of GDP) remained healthy. Vigorous business investment, surprisingly strong exports, and fast-growing imports (consistent with an overall rapid growth of domestic demand) showed an economy in a cyclical growth surge – and perhaps in a period of structural growth too. The news on trade was not all positive. The dollar's depreciation against the yen and DM perhaps implied that at least some of the increase in India's nominal trade growth in the second

	1993	1994
Real GDP, % change	4.3	5.3
Consumer prices, Dec/Dec	8.6	9.5
Exchange rate, units/$	31.4	31.4
Government balance, % of GDP	−7.3	−6.7
Balance of payments, $bn		
Merchandise trade balance	1.1	0.4
Exports	22.7	26.9
Imports	−21.6	−26.5
Current account balance	−0.3	−1.8
% of GDP	−0.1	−0.6
International reserves, $bn	15.1	19.0
Import coverage of reserves, number of months	5.7	5.9
Total external debt, $bn	85.6	91.0
Short term	8.9	9.5
Owed to commercial banks	9.9	11.0
Total external debt, % of GDP	33	30
Total external debt, % of exports	268	242
Interest payments, % of exports	13	13
Debt service ratio	27	29

Sources: *Emerging Markets Economic Outlook*, J.P. Morgan, Morgan Guaranty Trust Company, Economic Research, March 17, 1995, New York, p.34; the *Financial Times*, Investment in India, 30 March 1994, p.II from the Survey.

Figure 7.8

half of 1994-95 had been in prices, not volumes. Moreover, the trade and current account deficits were widening rapidly.

Further, inflation had taken a turn for the worse. In early 1995 the wholesale price index rate was more than 11% above that of a year earlier, and the official aim of 7%-8% for the year was at risk both from domestic pressures and from the dollar-linked rupee's relative weakness (though any weakness would help trade competitiveness). It was obvious that the government needed to continue its drive for reform with extra vigour and effectiveness (and maintain political support for it, with national elections due by 1996). Poor infrastructure remained an even greater hurdle. While India was making progress in trying to attract private investment into power projects, it will be the late 1990s before these new schemes make much of an impression on the general shortage. The inadequacy of telecommunications facilities was equally acute, with investment delayed by a combination of legal disputes over contracts for mobile telephone networks and political argument about privatisation policy. The liberalisation of investment in roads, rail and ports was even further away – though domestic air travel had quite successfully been opened up to privately-owned carriers.

In the mid-1990s the inefficiency of publicly-owned services and industries remained a strong drag on the economy, accounting for nearly half the nation's capital but producing only about 27% of its output. The government had sold stakes in leading state-owned enterprises, including banks, steel operations and electronics manufacturers, but ministers opposed selling more than 49% per of a unit for fear of losing control. Government was also reluctant to liberalise India's restrictive labour laws, which seriously limited employers' rights to make surplus workers redundant. While companies could find ways around the law, through voluntary schemes and redeployment, large-scale dismissals were virtually impossible. Finally, India's progress might be held back by the low educational standards of much of its population. Only 52% of Indians could read, compared with about 75% of Chinese. It would take time to integrate the remainder, or even their children, into a modern economy.

Nevertheless, none of these medium and long-term problems was insoluble. India was firmly on the path of transition – but at its own steady pace.

Argentina

UK's market share in Latin America compared to main EU rivals	
	%
Germany	6.2
Italy	3.9
France	3.1
UK (less than)	2.0

Over 900 European firms have operations in Latin America; by comparison, the USA has less than 300 firms. 40% of the total European FDI in Latin America comes from the UK. Exports from the UK to this region in the first quarter of 1995 were up 30%, compared to the same quarter in the previous year.

Argentina's transition from an agricultural to an industrial economy gained its main impetus early in the twentieth century. Its meat-packing industry, as well as the utilities (electricity, gas and water), stem from developments at the end of the nineteenth century. Today the country boasts not only a range of heavy industries such as coal, oil, steel, petrochemicals, iron and aluminium, but also a comprehensive array of consumer products (including automobiles) and services (including financial services), in addition to its agricultural and agro-industries sectors. Apart from shortages caused by the First World War (particularly in imports of machinery – although the War also stimulated some industrial sectors), and the period of the Great Depression, industrialisation grew quite rapidly up to 1937. From that year on, however, Argentina's industrial development slowed; there were many bankruptcies, and many factories shed labour. The Second World War provided a boost to capital-intensive industries, and an even more significant one to those which were labour-intensive. The food processing industries tended to modernise and grow, substituting machinery for labour, while the larger textiles factories tended to remain labour-intensive until the end of the War.

By 1945 Argentina had become Latin America's leading industrial nation. To some degree this transformation was due to 'import substitution' and protectionist strategies adopted in the 1930s, enabling the indigenous food processing and textile industries to expand sufficiently to satisfy domestic demand by 1945. However, manufacturers did not keep pace with technological innovation, and failed to achieve the economies of scale that accrue to larger organisations. As a consequence they were dependent upon the government continuing to provide protection and subsidies, and failed to emerge in the second half of the twentieth century as efficient, competitive, entrepreneurial organisations.

Privatisation and an influx of foreign capital, including inward foreign direct invest-ment and takeovers by multinational companies, also contributed to modernisation. This foreign investment had a detrimental impact on many Argentinian firms, espe-cially in the automobile, cigarette, metallurgy, chemical, machine tool and paper man-ufacturing sectors. Most of the foreign investment came from the USA, and was concentrated in the auto-parts and cigarette industries. French, Dutch, Spanish, German and Swiss concerns were in the forefront of investors from Europe. To a large extent, foreign investors were avoiding the various barriers which prevented them exporting to Argentina; they were also acquiring cheap assets, selling into established and often under-served markets, and operating in a business environment where the main local competition lacked the resources and knowhow for significant marketing activities, or investment in new plant and equipment.

Instead of facilitating an increase in the investment, productivity and competitiveness of its indigenous firms, the government responded by subjecting proposed foreign investment to lengthy bureaucratic and political procedures and evaluations. Dow Chemical applied to build a large plant at Bahia Blanca in 1966, but gave up its efforts to get permission in 1971. Predictably, the flow of inward foreign investment virtually dried up; and established investors sought to withdraw from an increasing restrictive environment. These reverses for foreign investors created opportunities for their Argen-tinian counterparts – opportunities of a risk-taking type in the consumer markets, and of a long-term industrial empire-building type in the heavy industries.

In other words, if Argentinian entrepreneurs had been like many in the USA (prepared to take risks), or those in Japan (planning long-term), they might well have seized the opportunity to make their own fortunes while propelling their country's economy into the top rank of industrial nations. However, they turned out to be more like those in Britain; they were not risk-takers, they were more concerned with short-term profits, and they tended to put their money into property and to play the stockmarket. Also like the British, Argentinians consumed more than they saved, and short-termism became institutionalised as part of the business culture.

Unlike firms in the USA and most of Europe (although not Italy), Argentinian firms tended to remain family businesses; they did not develop into publicly-owned corpo-rations. This meant that the stock market was relatively undeveloped, and local firms were at a disadvantage compared with foreign ones when it came to raising finance. Also, the government was in competition with the private sector when it came to rais-ing finance; government bonds were increasingly used as an alternative to taxation through the 1960s and 1970s. Most of the banks were foreign owned, and preferred lending to the relatively few large corporations; the typically small, family-owned local manufacturing firms were in a weak position when seeking funds. The blackmarket, tax evasion, flight capital and tight banking credit all ensured that industry was starved of finance. Added to this was the cost of corruption and political violence during and after the Peron administrations.

The public sector grew, the private sector was squeezed, unemployment increased and inflation grew out of control. Defence expenditure and the national debt soared. Bankrupted companies were taken into the public sector, and private capital became increasingly concentrated in a few large monopolies, which colluded with a military government in what became from the 1970s a corporatist state. Many foreign-owned firms either collapsed or closed down, and local firms had interest repayments on their debt which exceeded their profits. Wages had failed to keep up with the cost of living, and strikes and absenteeism were common. There was also a banking crisis in 1980; and the Falklands War in 1982, which left Argentina with a democratically-elected government, but with inflation in three figures.

In 1985 the Argentina government implemented the IMF-inspired Austral Plan to tackle inflation. A new currency, the austral, was issued. New taxes were introduced. Prices and wages were to be controlled, government expediture was to be reduced, and state enterprises were to be made more efficient and their budgets subject to political control. Foreign investment and exports were to be encouraged. Against the wishes of the IMF, foreign debt repayments were suspended. The Plan was only partially implemented, and outstanding among the failures was the government's pledge to curb its own expenditure: it was reduced by less than 4%. By April 1986 all efforts to curb wages and prices were abandoned, and by February 1987 the annual rate of inflation was once more over 100%. By 1990 real GDP was not only lower than any time during the 1980s (a decade of negative growth), but right back to its mid-1970s level.

Probably the main reason for the failure of the Austral Plan was a lack of political and social consensus. The average term of an Argentinian president since 1930 has been just over two years; that of an economy minister has been just over one year (in 1981 there were six!) Viewed from today's perspective, it seems that it was necessary for things to get even worse before they could get better.

The New Economic Model
1991 saw the beginning of a startling reversal in Argentina's economic fortunes, with nearly every economic indicator showing a positive trend. Real GDP grew by 5%, and investment by 30%. Foreign investment was ten times greater than in the previous year, and some of the estimated $50 billion of domestic money that had sought safer locations abroad during the 1980s began flowing back. The stockmarket boomed, largely due to an increasing number of privatisations, and the foreign debt was reduced by billions of dollars. Inflation was reduced to less than that of the UK. Further economic success and reform continued in subsequent years. Success was due to the Government's stabilisation programme; this was introduced in 1989, but for full effect required further measures such as the Convertability Law (Law 23938, passed on the first of April 1991), which fixed the exchange rate, prevented the Central Bank from financing the Government's defict, ended the system of indexation, and legalised contracts in US dollars.

Argentina has an unusual system, in that the peso is fixed at parity with the dollar and the government cannot print more local currency unless it is backed by an equivalent amount in foreign exchange reserves. The result of this is that outflows of foreign capital reduce the domestic money supply and threaten the domestic economy with recession. President Carlos Menem and his economy minister Domingo Cavallo had been in office for six years by 1995 – in itself something of a record. They found that nothing succeeds like success. Between 1991 and 1995 only China enjoyed a larger growth rate in GDP. Investment in Argentina increased 30% a year during the same period, and consumer demand grew 10% a year. In the mid-1990s industrial output, including that part which was exported, was continuing to increase. Domestic demand was concentrated in the automobile and housing sectors, serviced by indigenous firms. Investment was particularly strong in telecommunications, power generation, air and land transport, health services and, from 1994, the minerals sector. The country was actively seeking foreign multinationals to help exploit its massive reserves of gas, petroleum and other resources.

Other key features of the successful stabilisation programme introduced in 1989 include improving tax collection; rationalising the tax system to reduce distortions; reducing government expenditure; deregulating the economy, ending protectionism where possible and opening the economy to international competition; and increased privatisation and a general reduction of the role of the state, increasing the autonomy and importance of the private sector. The government and its economic reform programme enjoy wide public support, despite high levels of unemployment and the sluggish agricultural sector which appears to have been left behind by the rapidly-expanding industrial and service sectors.

On a more negative note, the labour market is still highly protected; this often results in expensive litigation and a lack of flexibility. Also, a traditional lack of protection for intellectual property inhibits high-tech investment; pirating by local firms is still quite common. While intellectual property rights (and especially patents) are currently being strengthened by legislation, the Government still has some tough political battles ahead on both labour protection and intellectual property. There is still a degree of protectionism in some sectors, such as automobiles and electronic equipment (higher tariffs and preferential trading incentives), some textiles and paper pulp and athletic footwear. However, quotas and tariffs are the exception rather than the rule.

All restrictions on capital movements were swept away in 1989. Foreign exchange is freely available from local banks at market rates in whatever quantities are required. Exporters may use profits for whatever purpose they wish at home or abroad. Argentina is not a cheap labour location like Mexico; in fact, it is one of the most expensive countries in the world. Its attraction for foreign investors lies in the relative political and economic stability achieved in recent years (assuming this lasts); its natural resources; the extent to which it is deregulated; its increasing integration with the world economy; and its membership of the regional trade block MERCOSUR (established in 1995 with Brazil, Paraguay and Uruguay) which is a customs union with a common external tariff. It may also become a full member of NAFTA. (There is further information on MERCOSUR and NAFTA in Chapter 6 and – for NAFTA – Chapter 9.)

In the mid-1990s it seemed likely that, assuming Argentina withstood the potential domino effect of the crisis in Mexico (see later in this chapter), and continued with its political stability, economic reform and integration, foreign investors would look favourably on the country as a location from which to serve the other markets within MERCOSUR and NAFTA. Japanese firms have tended to show a particularly strong aversion to political risk, and while they were not yet a significant presence in Argentina by the middle of the decade, they were actively considering its market opportunities.

Specific sectors and main national players
Telecommunications equipment. The Argentinian telecommunications sector was fully privatised in 1991. The former state firm ENTEL was divided into two companies, Telefonica and Telecom, which share the country. In 1994 cellular telephony was licensed throughout the country. CTI, a consortium headed by GTE and AT&T, won the contracts to provide a cellular service everywhere except Metropolitan Buenos Aires, where MOVICOM, a consortium headed by Bell South and Motorola, is among those providing a similar service. Figure 7.9 provides some recent statistics for this sector.

| | (Figures are US$ million) | | |
	1993	1994	1995
Total market size	1,300	1,450	1,600
Total local production	927	1,043	1,158
Total exports	7	8	8
Total imports from USA	65	75	85

Figure 7.9

Health care. About half of the total market is served by imports, with the USA as by far the greatest source and Japan, Germany, Italy and Switzerland providing most of the rest.

Avionics and aviation. Nearly the whole of this sector is served by imports; the USA provides some fifty per cent, France about twenty per cent and German and Canadian firms provide smaller shares.

Electrical power systems. Some seventy-five per cent of the market is imported. Japan is the main player, followed by Germany, the USA, Spain and Italy.

Computer software. Imports comprise over half of the market, with the USA dominating; Germany and Spain have smaller shares.

Computers and peripherals. Nearly the whole market is supplied by imports. Over sixty per cent is from the USA, with Germany and Japan as relatively minor players.

Laboratory and scientific instruments. Again imports dominate, with forty per cent coming from America, followed by companies from Germany, Italy and France.

Airport development. The USA, France, Israel, Germany and Canada all have more than ten per cent of the import market for this sector.

Construction industry. Imports are less than ten per cent of the market, with Italy, Spain and Brazil as the main players; the USA has a very small market share.

Apparel. Most of the market is served by imports; Taiwan has the largest share with thirty per cent. The USA, Korea, China, and Brazil between them have well over fifty percent of the import market in this sector.

Entry methods for foreign firms

Exporting. Most exporters use a local agent/distributor. Relations between exporter and agent/distributor are subject to Argentinian law, in particular the Civil and Commercial Codes; the application of foreign law is excluded. If a contract is agreed in a foreign country to avoid Argentinian law, it will not be recognised by Argentinian courts. There is no special legislation to regulate the termination of contracts between exporter and agent/distributor. The Civil and Commercial Codes permit a principal to terminate an agency agreement at its discretion, but it may be liable for damages resulting from a wrongful termination. The original contract the exporter makes with the local agent/distributor should include an agreed termination clause. Toys, games and educational products (all tending to be high-tech) are currently fast-growing sectors for imports (with Brazil and the USA the front runners), as are autoparts from Europe.

Foreign direct investment. Some sectors are still protected (e.g. automobiles), but generally speaking the market for inward foreign direct investment is very liberal (as explained above), and actively encouraged by the host government. Foreign firms generally choose to establish a separately incorporated subsidiary, as opposed to a branch of their operations; if a branch is used, all of the foreign corporation's assets throughout the world may be subject to potential liability. If the foreign investor uses a subsidiary, then liability is generally limited to the assets owned by that subsidiary. The general legal requirements require careful attention – in particular the labour laws, tax laws, and laws relating to standards and intellectual property.

Joint ventures. There are few restrictions on joint ventures with foreign firms. A contract must be signed and registered with the Commercial Registry. The contract must contain a number of specific clauses, and must also provide for the appointment of a legal representative in charge of management.

Franchising. The Argentine Commercial Code protects franchising contracts. Franchisor and franchisee are able to secure protection on virtually every aspect of their contractual obligations, including service, shared production, commercial trade market/name, methods, systems, know-how, supplies, quality and ultimate control by the franchisor of the various elements included in the licence, as well as the specific contractual elements. In the extreme case of franchisor bankruptcy or other commercial failures, Argentinian law is not always specific about the obligations regarding the franchisor; the foreign investor should therefore seek legal advice before finalising a contract. During 1993 the number of franchising firms doubled. The main sectors so far are wearing apparel, fast food, shoes, bakeries, ice cream and tyre repair, all of which are likely to be dominated by the USA.

Licensing. Argentinian Law 22,426 deals with transfers of know-how, patents or trademarks from a foreign to a local firm or individual. This law differentiates between transfers involving related companies and non-related companies. The former are subject to prior governmental approval, and a levy of 27% withholding tax if the prior approval is not obtained. Registration is the only requirement for transfers between non-related companies.

Registration procedures

Registration of a corporation requires at least two legal or natural persons, foreign or Argentine. A corporation may not be a partner in a parnership (although limited and general partnerships are allowed in Argentina, they are not subject to the same legislative requirements as corporations). The corporation can usually be established within a few weeks if the capital is supplied only in cash. If the capital is supplied in kind, it usually takes around two months to establish the corporation. The administrative costs of incorporation are between US$1,000 and US$2,000, including fees and stamp tax. The initial capital must be at least US$12,000, except for firms in the financial sector.

Mexico

At the time of writing Mexico was in deep trouble, and the USA was attempting to prevent complete collapse of that country's currency. This was particularly alarming because Mexico's heterodox stabilisation and reform model was regarded as the most successful, and an example for others to emulate. The economy had been relatively healthy and stable in the 1950s and 1960s. In 1969 student protests announced the beginning of a period of political and economic upheaval. The government tried to avoid the threat of left-wing insurrection by increasing public expenditure; then came the series of OPEC oil price shocks and the collapse of commodity prices. Determined to maintain high levels of profitability, western commercial banks threw money at less developed countries including Mexico.

The revenues from Mexico's oil helped finance a public spending spree, but the cost of imports soared, while the bottom dropped out of commodities exports. As interest rates floated upwards Mexico found itself with its worst-ever economic crisis. Foreign debt doubled and doubled again, so that by 1981 it reached $74 billion. Inflation reached 100%, there was a massive devaluation and massive flight of capital out of Mexico, the oil price boom ended, import controls were imposed, and the Government sent shockwaves around the international financial sector by announcing that it was ceasing interest repayments on its national debt.

The IMF and Mexico's new President de la Madrid introduced a severe orthodox stabilisation programme which created massive and violent social protest. Ending government programmes and subsidies at a stroke put many families below the subsistence level. These measures met with some economic success, but the 1985 earthquake and a 1986 fall in oil prices resulted in another devaluation, a dramatic increase in inflation, the collapse of the stock market and other economic problems which signalled a need for the additional corrective measures of a heterodox programme.

In December 1987 the Mexican government signed the 'Pact de Solidaridad' with the workers and business community. The exchange rate, money, wages and to some extent prices were fixed. Import controls had been somewhat liberalised during the initial reforms of the early 1980s, and significant further liberalisation occurred in 1988. Also, by the end of 1990, 80% of the state-owned industries had been privatised, and Mexico's economic indicators suggested that the country had regained economic stability. The crash of December 1994 appeared to take everyone by surprise, and understandably 1995 did not seem likely to be a good year for the country. Even a $50 billion emergency loan agreement from the USA seemed for a time to depress the dollar rather than strengthen the peso. However, the USA showed no signs of abandoning its NAFTA associate, and it is possible that in time December 1994 will be regarded as a necessary correction to a period of explosive growth, serving as a warning to other emerging markets against trying to do too much too quickly.

At the time of writing the analysis of what went wrong had only just begun. An IMF World Economic Outlook report in early 1995 blamed a combination of policy mistakes, political unrest and external economic shocks. The report argued that Mexico had to reduce its dependence on foreign finance and continue with structural reforms. Floating the peso in December 1994 was said to be a sudden change in exchange rate policy which created panic in the financial markets. The Mexican authorities should have raised exchange rates, the report said. While the IMF was busy criticising the Mexican government, other governments were criticising the IMF for not giving warning of the peso's collapse; it seemed probable that the IMF would soon have increased powers and responsibilities in this regard, in the hope that this debacle would not be repeated elswhere. However, attempting to maintain the confidence of the international financial markets is always going to be difficult in the high risk, high gain atmosphere engendered by emerging markets. (See Chapter 9 for further information on Mexico.)

Brazil

> ✎   CASE STUDY
>   Semco SA
> 'When I took over Semco from my father 12 years ago, it was a traditional company in every respect, with a pyramidal structure and a rule for every contingency. But today, our factory workers sometimes set their own production quotas and even come in on their own time to meet them, without prodding from management or overtime pay. They help redesign the products they make, and formulate the marketing plans. Their bosses, for their part, can run our business units with extraordinary freedom, determining business strategy without interference from top brass. They even set their own salaries, with no strings. Then again, everyone at Semco will know what they are, since all financial information at Semco is openly discussed. Indeed, our workers have unlimited access to our books (and we only keep one set). To show we are serious about this, Semco, with the labour unions that represent our workers, developed a course to teach everyone, even messengers and cleaning people, to read balance sheets and cash-flow statements.'
>
> Ricardo Semler is president of Semco SA, Brazil's largest marine and food processing machinery manufacturer. Since 1990 one in three capital goods manufacturers has gone bankrupt, while over the same period Semco have maintained their level of profitability. Cash flow, orders and invoices are controlled by the managers, but virtually all other decisions are taken democratically by the workers. Semco has plans to allow the workers to set their own wages. All the managers set their own salaries, and every six months the workers have a chance to evaluate their managers' performance and decide whether to continue with the manager at the same salary. People work in groups, up to a maximum of ten per group.

Semco encourages its workers to leave and set up their own businesses; they are given financial, technological and managerial help to do this. Semler says that anyone is welcome to take some of the fixed assets and set up his or her own company. In return, these satellite companies sell to the central unit on terms favourable to Semco. The workers who have accepted this challenge run their satellite companies in the same manner, and often recruit workers from Semco. The managers (six at Semco) take it in turns to be Chief Executive, and all offices are open plan, with everyone having access to everyone else. Semler says that nothing else will work except groups of ten.

Semco is one of Latin America's fastest-growing companies, acknowledged to be the best in Brazil to work for; it has waiting lists of thousands of potential employees, and has been studied by numerous other foreign companies interested to learn if this Brazilian firm could serve as a model for their own organisations. 'Large, centralised organisations foster alienation like stagnant ponds breed algae,' says Semler. 'In massive corporations, an employee will know few of his colleagues. Everyone is part of a gigantic, impersonal machine, and it is impossible to feel motivated when you feel you are just another cog. Human nature demands recognition. Without it, people lose their sense of purpose and become dissatisfied, restless, and unproductive.'

Clearly it is not only Japanese management practices and Japanese firms which might provide models for firms from other parts of the world. Indeed, many managers of European firms have visited Semco with a view to adopting some of its management policies and structures.

Source: Ricardo Semler, *Maverick! The Success Story Behind the World's Most Unusual Workplace*, Century, 1993

Brazil and Mexico achieved a greater degree of industrial diversification than most emerging markets, and this is even more true of Brazil than of Mexico. In addition to this, Brazil's industrial development began some ten years earlier than Mexico's, and its inward foreign direct investment came more from Europe than from the United States. Well over thirty per cent of Brazil's total industrial growth came from import-substitution activities in which foreign investment played the major role. (For a comprehensive analysis of the similarities and differences of Mexico's and Brazil's economic development, see Hewlett and Weinert, 1984[5].) Between 1945 and 1980 Brazilian industrial production grew at over 8% a year on average (Fritsch and Franco, 1991[6]). The country was said to experience an 'economic miracle' between 1967 and 1973, and nearly 80% of the inward flows of capital went into manufacturing.

A great many of the foreign subsidiaries established in the twenty years after the Second World War were in the form of joint ventures with local concerns – including, especially in the petrochemical sector, 'triple alliance' joint ventures between foreign multinationals, state enterprises and private firms. Foreign firms control some sectors such as transport equipment, rubber products (tyres), pharmaceuticals and tobacco; and they lead other sectors such as electricity generating equipment, motor manufacturing and paints. The presence of foreign firms in over 40% of the sectors of the Brazilian economy contributed greatly to the country's successful export performance.

Brazil is not only the largest country in Latin America, it is also the most industrialised. It is a democratic, intermediate-income developing nation with the ninth largest economy in the world. It has a diversified industrial, agricultural, and services base; it possesses a wealth of resources, both human and material. Brazil's current economic structure breaks down into roughly 54 per cent of GDP from services, 35 per cent from industry, and about 11 per cent from agriculture.

In recent years, a relatively sophisticated capital goods industry has emerged, with greater emphasis placed on indigenous technological development. The evolution of Brazil's industrial sector was orchestrated by the government through a system of incentives for production and export. Industry represents a growing percentage of Brazil's GDP. Principal industries are agriculture (coffee, soybeans, and orange juice), minerals, steel, automobiles, footwear, textiles, capital goods, electronics, and petrochemicals. In 1991, Brazil's global trade reached almost $53 billion; $31.6 billion in exports, and $21.0 billion in imports. The USA is Brazil's major trading partner, absorbing approximately 21% of Brazil's exports during 1991.

Economic difficulties, aggravated by the oil shock of the early 1970s and Brazil's debt crisis, led the Brazilian Government to pursue a policy of import substitution and export promotion. To foster domestic production, the Brazilian government established incentive programs to stimulate exports and to assist import substitution. However, after several decades of following an inward-looking economic development model, most of the incentive programs have ben abandoned as costly and inefficient in recent years. Brazil has changed its approach to favour policies aimed at attaining greater economic competitiveness, incorporating the country more fully into the world economy. To accomplish this, the Brazilian government is implementing an ambitious program of economic and trade liberalisation. In recent years, most of Brazil's non-tariff barriers to trade, such as import quotas, import prohibitions, restrictive import licensing, and local content requirements, which for many years were the hallmarks of its restrictive trade regime, were eliminated or drastically reduced. Import duties have been massively reduced. (However, they still remain high in comparison with most other countries, and Brazil imposes several other taxes and fees on imports that add significantly to the product's landed cost.)

Geographically, industrial growth in Brazil has been very uneven. It is heavily concentrated in the Southeast region, principally the states of São Paulo, Rio de Janeiro, and Minas Gerais. Though primarily agricultural, the southern states of Paraná, Santa Catarina and Rio Grande do Sul are considered among the more developed, technologically advanced, dynamic and productive states in Brazil. North and central Brazil have great potential for agroindustrial development, but large capital investment will be required. The Government of Brazil has encouraged heavy agroindustry investment in this area. It also has toughened zoning restrictions in the state of São Paulo in an attempt to force industry to locate in the North. However, foreign firms should also be aware that there are restrictions concerning the amount of rural land that foreigners and foreign companies can own. Exceptions to this may be made on a case-by-case basis.

Economic activity in the Northeast is primarily agricultural, notwithstanding periodic droughts in the semi-arid areas. The Northeast has received considerable aid from the Brazilian government, including special fiscal incentives designed to promote development of new industries. While establishment of an industrial centre and a petrochemical area near Salvador has enhanced economic growth in the state of Bahia, income in the region as a whole still remains well below the national average. Brazil's development plans aim to stimulate activity in agriculture and mining in certain selected areas of the North.

Under the development policies of previous Brazilian administrations, the government established a tradition of being the dominant force in shaping economic growth by means of planning and management. Its influence was felt not only directly through the day-to-day activities of government entities, but also through governmental wage, price, and credit policies, and subsidy and fiscal incentive programmes. While the central government still retains an important economic role, the policies of the current administration focus on reducing the role of the government in economic activities, and concentrating government activities on more traditional roles such as improving public health, safety and education. As a result, the government is emphasising the creation of greater economic opportunities for the private sector through privatisation, deregulation, and removal of impediments to competition. However, in April 1995 the Brazilian Government, like Mexico, was warned by the IMF to get its finances under control.

After entering office in March 1990, the Collor Administration made an effort to implement a sweeping programme of privatising state-owned companies. The programme had broad public support, but got off to a slow start because of opposition from labour and certain vested interests. However, in 1991 with the sale of a major steel mill, it began to gain momentum. Firms in the steel, transportation equipment, fertiliser and petrochemical sectors have been successfully auctioned. The scope of the privatisation programme is limited by provisions of Brazil's 1988 Constitution which established government monopolies for basic telephone and telegraph services, electric energy production, and petroleum extraction and refining. These constitutional provisions effectively prevented privatisation of Telebras (the telephone company), Electrobras (the electric utility holding company) and Petrobras (the petroleum company). Constitutional amendments were introduced to allow privatisation in these sectors.

In an effort to attract more foreign investment, the government has amended the rules for foreign participation. The rules governing privatisation limit foreign ownership to 40% in the first sale of the state enterprise, but foreign companies can buy up to 49% of the privatised firm during a subsequent resale. Foreign capital invested in a privatisation must stay in Brazil for six years before it can be repatriated.

Potential exporters to Brazil should take into consideration the vast geographic size of the country, as well as its demographics and diversified industrial base. In Brazil, these market factors have traditionally been overshadowed by political and economic uncertainties. However, since the advent of the Collor presidency in 1990, a policy has been in effect to stabilise the domestic economy and resolve the external debt issue, as well as to liberalise the market to allow for greater imports. With a marketing campaign focused on medium to longterm growth, experienced exporters and investors will benefit not only from Brazil's sheer size but, as the market evolves, from the country's increased need for capital equipment and foreign technology. To enter this changing market, it is essential that firms establish a relationship with a well-qualified Brazilian partner. The Brazilian representative should have proven knowledge not only of the sector marketplace but of current government policy and IMF analysis.

> ✎ CASE STUDY
> **British firms land contracts in Brazil**
> *Overseas Trade* reported in February 1995 that the systems division of Cheadle-based Peek Traffic was part of a consortium that had won a £20 million contract to supply computerised traffic systems to São Paulo, the largest and most congested of Brazil's cities. The other members of the consortium were Metodo, a Brazilian telecommunications and civil engineering company, which would handle the roadworks and cable installation; Autotrol, an Argentinian electrical engineering firm which was providing project management; and Sonda, a Chilean company which was providing systems, communication and traffic engineering skills.
>
> In August of the same year, *Overseas Trade* reported two further British successes. The Brazilian airline Transbrasil had chosen Rolls-Royce Trent 800 engines to power three Boeing 777 wide-bodied airliners for operation on routes to North America; and Sheffield-based Land Infrared had sold five thermal imagers to the state-owned Brazilian electricity company, Furnas Centrias Electricas, to monitor electrical connections on its power plants and sub-stations. Furnas generates and distributes power for the South-east.
>
> Source: *Overseas Trade*, February and August 1995

Under a special regional trade initiative, Brazil has extended preferential import duty rates and other benefits to certain imports from members of the Latin American Integration Association (ALADI), formerly the Latin American Free Trade Association (LAFTA). Under ALADI, Brazil has had bilateral trade agreements with each of the other 10 members (Mexico and the nine South American republics), and participated in many of ALADI's multilateral industry agreements.

In July 1988, the Brazilian government approved legislation to establish export processing zones (ZPEs) – free trade areas to encourage production of goods for export in the Northeast and other priority development areas. Law 8037 of 30 December 1991 created a ZPE in the new state of Amap. The free trade area is in the city of Macap, capital of the state. Legislation regarding ZPEs establishes requirements that firms operating in the zone export at least 90% of production. Up to 10% of production can be sold in the domestic market, and is subject to a duty of 75% ad valorem on the final price, minus the cost of imported inputs. Normal corporate income taxes apply to profits generated in the zones; firms operating there will be exempt from foreign exchange regulations.

Import channels
All the customary import channels exist in Brazil: agents, distributors, import houses, trading companies, subsidiaries of foreign firms, etc. The typical import transaction is the importation of capital goods or raw materials by an individual firm for its own use. Brazilian import firms do not generally maintain stocks of capital equipment or raw materials. This is partly due to a shortage of working capital.

As in other countries, the selection of an agent in Brazil requires careful consideration.

A unique factor in the Brazilian situation is that a prospective agent may not be able to cover the entire country adequately. A regional orientation still prevails in Brazil, despite improved internal transportation and communications. A São Paulo-based agent, for example, may want to split the commission with a subagent in Porto Alegre who would cover southern Brazil. This kind of arrangement is not always attractive to an agent in Porto Alegre, who is accustomed to operating independently.

The ability of an agent to cover the country depends in large part on the item being sold; certain types of sophisticated machinery may have only a dozen or so potential buyers in Brazil, making marketing relatively simple. On the other hand, less expensive equipment with a wide potential market and the need for countrywide service facilities puts much greater organisational demands on an agent.

Once the agent-principal contract is signed, a Brazilian agent is protected by law from unilateral termination of the contract by the foreign principal without 'just cause'. The definition of just cause is limited to the following: the agent's negligence; the agent's breach of contract; acts by the agent damaging to the principal; and conviction of the agent for a serious criminal offence. The legislation governing contract stipulations and conditions for termination of agency agreements in Brazil is contained in Articles 27-39 of Law Number 4886, of 10 December 1965.

The trading company is another type of import marketing organisation in Brazil. Although principally designed as an export promotion tool, trading companies may play a role in importing through direct purchase or countertrade activities. The operation of Brazilian trading companies is open to foreign as well as national interests. Brazilian trading companies were modelled to some extent after foreign trading companies, principally German and Japanese. They are set up to give small and medium-sized manufacturers the same operational flexibility as large manufacturers in promoting Brazilian exports, especially of non-traditional exports. Trading companies may act as principals, acquiring goods from Brazilian producers for the specific purpose of exporting, assuming all commercial risks and exporting under their own names.

Alternatively, trading companies may act as intermediaries. In this role, they operate as commercial agents, utilising their functional structure to provide complementary services.

Summary

In this chapter, an overview of emerging markets was provided, and it was explained that while definitions varied somewhat, the term could be taken to describe those economies that had middle to low GDP on a per capita basis. These ranged from countries which were just beginning to develop to the more advanced emerging markets known as 'newly industrialised countries'. Much of the published material available analyses emerging markets from the perspective of portfolio investment (i.e. money which is invested in financial products such as shares, bonds, bank deposits etc). However, these markets are also important to international firms as potential markets for goods and services, and as locations for FDI. There is no single widely-held theory which explains how countries have 'emerged', or should set about doing so, and integrating into the world capitalist economy. However, this chapter has offered several different methods of analysing emerging markets, as well as descriptive accounts of how some of the main countries achieved this status. Included in the empirical information on such countries were important facts relevant to European firms considering entering or selling to these markets.

CASE STUDY
Business Applications Software

BAS was founded in Reading, England in 1994 by five recent graduates. Three of the graduates are specialists in computing; one took a Business degree with Spanish, Portuguese and French; and one specialised in International Business and Finance. BAS produces customised business software programmes. It began by servicing a number of banks and insurance companies in London, Reading and Basingstoke. Within months it had won contracts to provide software to a number of manufacturers in the north of England. By September 1995 BAS was also selling its software to manufacturing and retailing firms in France and Spain. The work involves spending a few months getting to know the company and its needs, and then developing comprehensive software packages to cover most – sometimes all – aspects of the business. BAS continues to work with these companies for at least one year after the software has been installed, to ensure that any unforeseen problems are resolved.

Because of the expansion of the business in France and Spain, and anticipated future expansion, BAS has recruited another ten staff, all computing experts. While waiting for a plane in Madrid airport, one of the original founders of BAS gets into conversation with an Argentinian businessman. He owns a car component manufacturing plant in Buenos Aires. He expresses considerable interest in BAS, and suggests that a representative visits him soon and brings some samples of software.

Meanwhile, one of the Spanish firms that BAS does business with has opened a manufacturing plant in Brazil, and has suggest that BAS might help configure their operations with some software suitable for the Brazilian business environment. The firm makes office equipment. The five founders of BAS are all equal partners, and they meet to discuss whether they should expand the firm's operations in either Argentina or Brazil, or in both of these countries.

Questions for discussion

1 Draw up a summary of the pros and cons (a Strengths, Weaknesses, Opportunities and Threats analysis if you wish) of following up (a) the Argentinian opportunity and (b) the Brazilian opportunity.

2 Assuming BAS did successfully proceed with at least one of these opportunities, how might it further expand its business in that country? What strategies could it adopt to minimise the risks involved in its expansion?

3 What are the advantages and disadvantages of BAS setting up facilities in one or both of these Latin American emerging markets? What type of facilities do you think they ought to consider?

Further reading

Some recently published general textbooks on international business include a few pages, or perhaps a chapter, on emerging markets; but the scope tends to be limited, and there is not always very much empirical data. For example, students may wish to read Chapter 10 in Czinkota, Ronkainen and Moffett, *International Business* (International Edition, 3rd. edition), Dryden Press, 1994. This chapter contains some good material on state-owned industries and privatisation in Central and Eastern Europe and China, but it hardly mentions Latin America.

More advanced students who have a good background in economics should read Michael Bruno's books (listed below), especially the 1993 reference. As yet there are very few sources for students on this interesting and important topic.

Colin I. Bradford (ed.), *Mobilising International Investment for Latin America*, OECD, 1993.

M. Brookes, *Measuring World GDP*, Goldman Sachs, 1994.

Michael Bruno, *Crises, Stabilisation and Economic Reform: Therapy by Consensus*, Clarendon Lectures in Economics Series, Clarendon Press, 1993.

M. Bruno et al (eds.), *Inflation Stabilisation: Argentina, Israel, Brazil, Bolivia and Mexico*, MIT Press, 1988.

Thomas Clarke and Christos Pitelis (eds.), *The Political Economy of Privatisation*, Routledge, 1993.

R. Dornbusch and S. Edwards, *The Macroeconomics of Populism in Latin America*, University of Chicago Press, 1991.

Economic Intelligence Unit, *Emerging Markets 1995*.

'Emerging Markets, Where Next?', *Financial Times* Quarterly Review of Personal Finance, Spring 1995.

John Ellis and David Williams, *International Business Strategy*, Pitman, 1995.

W. Fritsch and G. Franco, *Foreign Direct Investment in Brazil: Its Impact on Industrial Restructuring*, OECD, 1991.

Neil Harvey (ed.), *Mexico: Dilemmas of Transition*, The Institute of Latin American Studies and British Academic Press, 1993.

S.A. Hewlett and R.S. Weinert, *Brazil and Mexico*, Institute for the Study of Human Issues, 1984.

Internet, US Department of Commerce.

Hans Jansson, *Transnational Corporations in Southeast Asia: An Institutional Approach to Industrial Organisations*, New Horizons in International Business, Edward Elgar, 1994.

Paul R. Krugman and Maurice Obstfeld, *International Economics: Theory and Policy* (3rd edition), Harper Collins, 1994.

Simon Keane, *Emerging Markets: The Relevance of Efficient Market Theory*, *Occasional Research Paper No. 15*, Technical and Research Committee, The Chartered Association of Certified Accountants, 1993.

Paul Lewis, *The Crises of Argentine Capitalism*, Chapel Hill, 1990.

OECD, *Economic Surveys: Mexico 1991/1992*.

Michael Parkin and David King, *Economics* (2nd edition), Addison-Wesley, 1995.

C. Rodriguez, 'The Argentine Stabilisation Plan of December 20th', *World Development*, No. 10, pages 226–38, 1982.

'Russia's Emerging Market', *The Economist*, Special Survey, 8 April 1995.

Ricardo Semler, *Maverick! The Success Story Behind the World's Most Unusual Workplace*, Century, 1993.

Vietnam: Industrial Policy Reform and International Cooperation, UNIDO Industrial Development Review Series, 17 January 1991.

Notes

1 See John Ellis and David Williams, *International Business Strategy*, page 92, Pitman, 1995.

2 Michael Bruno, *Crises, Stabilisation and Economic Reform: Therapy by Consensus*, Clarendon Press, 1993)

3 Lawrence B. Krause, report issued by the Pacific Economic Cooperative Council.

4 See United Nations Industrial Development Review Series, *Vietnam*, 1991.

5 S.A. Hewlett and R.S. Weinert, *Brazil and Mexico*, Institute for the Study of Human Issues, 1984.

6 W. Fritsch and G. Franco, *Foreign Direct Investment in Brazil: Its Impact on Industrial Restructuring*, OECD, 1991.

8 Doing business in Central and Eastern Europe

Objectives

By the end of this chapter, you will be able to:

- understand the transition from a central planning economy to a free-market economy.
- describe the process of political, economic and business changes in Central and Eastern Europe.
- describe the economic, legal and cultural problems confronting the countries of Central and Eastern Europe.
- understand the business environment in these countries, and the advantages and disadvantages of doing business there.
- describe and analyse the factors, and the existing problems in the business environment in the region, which influence the choice of market entry strategies for these countries.
- understand when and how strategic alliances can be formed with companies from the region.
- obtain a better understanding of the investment behaviour of Western companies, wishing to invest in Eastern Europe, so as to learn from their successes and their mistakes.

Introduction

The common language we speak today is not the language of the West, now adopted by the East. It is an intrinsically universal language which belongs to nobody in particular and therefore to everybody. The countries of East-Central Europe have not shed their communist system in order to embrace the capitalist system – whatever that is. They have shed a closed system in order to create an open society. The open society, to be exact. For while there can be many systems, there is only one open society. If any creed has won in the events of last year, it is the idea that we are all embarked on a journey into an uncertain future, and have to work by trial and error within institutions which make it possible to bring about change without bloodshed.

Ralf Dahrendorf, 1990

At the end of the 1980s, the air was thick with notions of a new Europe, as the East threw off communism and the West celebrated its cold war victory. Talk of new Marshall Plans and European integration flourished amid the triumphalism. Five-star hotels rose swiftly in Prague, Budapest and Warsaw to accommodate the armies of western consultants, bankers and advisers arriving on every flight. Since then, the Euro-euphoria has turned sour for the East Europeans.

The European Union has opened up to the budding market economies, except in sensitive areas where the East Europeans are most competitive: steel and steel products, coal, meat, agricultural products, and wine. The West has profited, flooding the East with goods and generating a widening trade gap in the West's favour. In 1989 the rallying cry across half the continent was 'Back to Europe', a conviction that the collapse of the Soviet Bloc, the Warsaw Pact, and the Comecon trade regime would trigger a reintegration of East and West. The painstaking work towards realising this vision has created some remarkable transformations. In 1989 more than half the foreign trade of the most advanced quartet in the bloc – Poland, Hungary and what are now the Czech and Slovak republics – was with the Soviet Union and its clients. By the mid-1990s more than half was with the EU.

Nonetheless, Brussels' attitude towards the East left the aspiring members bitter. The main grumble concerned West European barriers to free trade. While western politicians preached the merits of the market economy to the post-communist countries, the EU erected stringent non-tariff barriers in the areas of farm produce, steel and textiles. These sectors accounted for more than half of East European exports to the EU in 1993. 'The main threat to Eastern European exports and investment comes from actual, threatened and "latent" trade remedy action employed for purposes of managing trade to support industrial policy objectives in the EU,' the European Bank for Reconstruction and Development said in October 1994. Although these trade restrictions protecting vulnerable industrial sectors were due to be dismantled or reduced over the next few years, they still left East Europeans dismayed, particularly because the net beneficiary of the radical shift in trade patterns in the early 1990s was the West.

In 1989, Eastern Europe had a billion dollar trade surplus with the OECD countries, mainly the EU. By 1994 this had turned into an $8 billion deficit. The imbalance was harder to bear for the East because the EU was by far its biggest export market. By contrast, EU exports to Poland, Hungary, Slovakia and the Czech Republic comprised 2 per cent of EU exports in 1994. 'The widening trade and current account deficits are widely regarded as the major obstacles to sustained economic recovery for the East Europeans,' noted Vienna's Institute for Comparative Economics, which monitors the post-communist economies. The 1989 revolutions took Western Europe and the world by surprise. Rather than freezing its deliberations on West European integration to digest the implications for the continent, Western Europe burrowed more deeply into the Maastricht trenches. The East Europeans were made to feel like unwelcome gate-crashers at the EU party.

Half a decade or so after the fall of the Berlin Wall, could the West be said to have failed Eastern Europe? 'I don't think you can say there has been a failure,' was the view of Andrzej Wroblewski, editor of Warsaw's financial newspaper, *Gazeta Bankowa*. 'But there's been disappointment here. The initial hope was that our western allies would finally liberate us if not in 1945, then in 1989. It hasn't turned out that way. We on this side of the wall underestimated the problems and so did the West.' The East Europeans knew that it would be years, perhaps more than a decade, before they could afford either EU or NATO membership. What they were looking for were target dates to aim for, and road maps showing how to get there.

The East European economic transition as a concept

By the mid-1990s, the reforms in Eastern Europe were coming to a critical point. Governments which came to power offering a shock therapy model were forced to resign. This was the case in Poland (Mazowiecki-Balcerowicz and Bielecki), Bulgaria (Philip Dimitrov) and Russia, where Gaidar was forced to resign and Yeltsin to some extent changed course; 'Saiudis' in Lithuania also lost power. In the middle of the decade Hungary and Bulgaria became the latest East European countries to return the Socialists to power.

An immense gap in expectations, anticipating easy success and wholehearted western support, has not been filled. Comparisons between the current situation, with all its problems, and life during socialism have not helped the changes. Responding to public discontent, new governments have had to come up with new policies – the beginning of a new, different stage in the East European transformation. Shock stabilisation programmes have been replaced by a policy of more pragmatic economic transformation, in which the main accent is on national industrial competitiveness. National priorities have been reviewed in an attempt to reverse the slowdown.

As we have seen, the political and intellectual leaders of Eastern Europe's revolution of 1989 described their aim as a 'return to Europe'. Their overwhelming judgment was that the postwar division of Europe into East and West was artificially imposed by the Soviet Union with the help of the Allies, at enormous human and economic cost. They underscored the artificiality of the division by referring to their region as East Central Europe (or Middle Europe), rather than Eastern Europe, thereby stressing their countries' place in the mainstream of European history, politics, arts, and economy.

For the political 'fathers' of the East European revolution the road of change was clear and definite: a free market economy and the creation of political and economic institutions in the style of Western Europe. (Of course, even Western Europe offers a wide array of alternative economic models from which to choose, but in practical terms there has been little reason yet for the Eastern European countries to choose among the variants of Western European political economy.) Following this Western European model, their countries were directed toward the creation of multi-party parliamentary democracies and market economies with large private sectors. With amazing rapidity, the post-communist politicians of Poland, Czechoslovakia, and Hungary dropped any support for an economic 'third way' – that is, some form of market socialism – and were intent on moving instead to a full-fledged market economy based on private property.

The ideal model for the Eastern European reformers in the turbulent winter months of 1989/90 was Reagan's liberal economic philosophy and Thatcher's market ideology as experienced in Britain. They never discussed or considered the differences between the ideological background of this freemarket model and the various real examples of attempts to operate it in actual economies.

For many years the IMF and the World Bank have tried to apply a similar approach in various countries, and for all those years the results have been quite controversial. Moreover, it is important to remember that all the countries in question already had long-established institutions and other elements characteristic of a market economy. The economies of Eastern Europe had been very differently organised; yet almost the same 'effective' medicine was offered as a panacea.

The goal was to transform centrally-planned economies into a free market system, including an appropriate ownership structure. It is very important to emphasise that in 1989–1990 there was not a single historical example of a transition from a centrally-planned economy to a free-market economy. Even if we take as an example previous privatisations in other economies, these were small by comparison, and implemented in the context of economies which were already largely private-sector. Indeed, in no country which has experienced privatisation has the share of public sector output in GDP approached that in Eastern Europe. It has varied from 1% in Guatemala, through 5% in Austria, to 37–38% in Zambia. Britain privatised, at most, less than 10% of its economy over about ten years. Other countries have had even less success. Moreover, western countries have had the benefit of private markets, stock exchanges, meaningful accounting records, labour markets, and a substantial number of individuals with extensive assets who could purchase a significant number of shares in new companies. None of these conditions was valid in 1989–1990 for countries attempting to throw off Marxism.

In fact, in 1989 the countries of Central and Eastern Europe were in the tenth year of an unprecedented social, economic and political crisis (see Figure 8.1 at the top of the next page).

Elements of the transitional model

Such was the economic environment in these economies in 1989–1990, when the concept of a transition to a free-market economy was introduced. The 'parents' of the transitional model were the IMF and some American advisors, of which the most famous was the Harvard professor Jeffrey Sachs. Among the main elements of the concept of 'transition' were the following:

- Liberalisation of the behaviour of economic subjects, starting with a freeing of price formation.
- Opening of the national borders of these economies to 'free' trade with the rest of the world.
- Introduction of national currency convertibility (which included its adjustment against the main hard currencies, and devaluation, with additional impact on other standard of living features).
- Establishment and promotion of an economic and business environment conducive to competition, through an anti-monopoly policy and liberalisation in setting up new enterprises (under the principle of pluralism and equal opportunity for all existing forms of ownership).
- Reduction of state participation in the economy, and substantial limitation of public spending.
- Restructuring of the financial system and creation of a non-penalising tax system.

Essential features of the socio-economic crisis in Eastern Europe before 1989

1. **The durability of the crisis.** The earlier trend of high economic growth (particularly in the period 1966–1976) had been broken after the Second Oil Shock in 1978. Since the beginning of the 1980s the economic growth in the region had fallen below 2 per cent (with zero per cent growth in Hungary and in Poland).

2. **Foreign debt**. In 1989 the foreign debt of all the Soviet Bloc countries had reached unprecedented levels. At the end of that year the total net debt of the six East European countries (including the former Soviet Union) was around $130 billion. A number of these countries had serious liquidity problems, and two of them – Poland and Romania – had been forced to reschedule their debts in the early 1980s.

3. **Decline in investment activity.** The general restriction of investments due to the liquidity crisis was characterised not only by a slowdown but sometimes even by an absolute decline in investment activity in each of these countries. There was an absolute decline in Hungary for seven years (between 1980–1986), in Poland for five years (1981–1986), in Czechoslovakia for four years (1983–1987), and in East Germany, Romania and Bulgaria for three years (1986–1989).

4. **Weakening of the national currencies.** Because of the factors already mentioned, and of a growing deficiency in raw materials, production and consumer goods (due to a lack of hard currency), improvements in the standard of living over the two preceding decades had turned into stagnation, and then to a rapid deterioration. In Poland and Hungary the phenomenon of open inflation (as distinct from the more common hidden or repressed inflation) reappeared in 1985–86 after many decades.

5. **Progressive alienation from labour.** As a result of the persistent deterioration of the standard of living and the lack of free market business opportunities, alienation, apathy and cynicism appeared at all levels of society. Social confidence and social and moral values were undermined.

6. **A falling share of world trade for the Central and Eastern European economies.** The foreign trade of the countries from the Soviet Bloc expanded fairly rapidly after the devastation of the Second World War and a period of isolation during the Cold War; their share of world trade peaked in the mid-1960s, reaching 10.5% of world exports and imports in 1965. After that time a slow but steady loss of market share occurred; their total share was 8.8% of world exports and 7.9% of world imports in 1986. By 1989–1990 it had contracted to around 3.5% of both world exports and imports.

Figure 8.1

- Reform of the banking system and establishment of appropriate capital market institutions.

The main aim of the proponents of this concept was a fast and efficacious surgical operation – in other words, shock therapy. It had three main directions:

- Changing signals: introduction of price and trade liberalisation.
- Changing incentives: introduction of bankruptcy legislation and procedures, privatisation of the state sector and creation of a labour market.
- Creating an infrastructure: establishment of a legal and institutional framework, similar to those in the free-market economies.

Two different approaches to transition

In the realisation of this transitional model, the Central and Eastern European countries followed two different approaches. The full shock therapy model was applied in Poland, Bulgaria and to a certain degree in Russia, while a more step-by-step (or gradual) approach was used in Hungary and to a certain extent in Czechoslovakia. (Romania started a little later than the other countries.)

The shock therapy model was based on a rapid and strict stabilisation of the existing macroeconomic imbalances (and initially, as in Poland, hyper-inflation and massive shortages) and liberalisation, together with a speedy reconstruction of fundamental institutions. The first two changes were more important that the third one. Herein lies the danger of this approach: it is far more difficult to foresee the reaction of the economy to tough stabilisation and liberalisation measures, particularly because this reaction is usually worse than in an already restructured economy.

Poland and Bulgaria applied a 'big bang' approach to liberalisation of the formation of prices; all prices were liberalised except for a few consumer basics. In Hungary and Romania there was 'step-by-step' price liberalisation in phases; machinery and consumer durable prices were liberalised first, and prices for consumer basics last. Czechoslovakia had 'managed markets' liberalisation: many prices were subject to ceilings or review by the central authorities, while prices of consumer basics were increased, but not liberalised.

The Polish and Bulgarian shock therapy stabilisation programmes included the following measures:

- Adoption of the rule that the budget deficit cannot be financed by interest-free central bank credit. The deficit can be covered only through treasury bills (public debts) and/or credit taken outside the Central Bank, on commercial terms.
- The Central Bank's strict observance of the rule of adjusting the volume of money supply according to the requirements of the anti-inflationary programme.
- Application of a full market mechanism in setting prices, i.e. freedom of price-setting and elimination of rationing and mandatory intermediaries.
- Elimination of all subsidies to enterprise investment projects, and visible reduction of subsidies for energy products and main food products.
- Introduction of attractive forms of long-term savings, by adjusting the interest rates to inflation level.
- Creation of 'internal' convertibility of the national currency – with a free-floating exchange rate, established every day by the Central Bank.
- Stricter fiscal and financial discipline for the state enterprises, especially those which were late in meeting their liabilities to the state budget.
- Establishment of an environment conducive to domestic and international competition, through an anti-monopoly policy and full liberty in setting up new enterprises.
- De-monopolisation of state industry – breaking the large monopolistic manufacturing firms into smaller enterprises.
- Decentralisation of the large management structures of the state enterprises.
- Establishment of a labour market.
- Opening of the economic borders to international competition, and establishment of an investment climate attractive to foreign investors.
- Large-scale privatisation of state-owned enterprises.
- Agreements with the London and Paris Clubs of bank creditors for the reduction of the existing foreign debt .

In 1992 the governments in favour of a shock-therapy approach resigned almost everywhere in Eastern Europe. The stabilisation policies which continued have been changed to respond to the political and social discontent in these countries.

Reasons for the failure of shock therapy

More and more articles attempt to identify the main reasons for the failure of the shock therapy approach; however, the reasons remain less than fully clear. Undoubtedly there is more than one single explanation, and further serious study on this topic will certainly be worthwhile. What is irrefutable, however, is that a complex web of specific conditions, circumstances and settings in the countries involved made them rather different from the previous clients and 'patients' of the IMF; and it can be argued that the programme, in the form it took, was condemned to failure from the beginning.

No doubt a leap forward (a 'jump', as Jeffrey Sachs has called it) sounded attractive; people wanted immediate changes, and believed they could be made with little or no suffering. It fairly soon became obvious, however, that economies could not 'jump' in that way, even symbolically or theoretically; nor could they be changed in a few months by wishful thinking.

Even more important were two further considerations: the point from which Eastern Europe started its transition, and the right direction to move in, whether for a leap or for more gentle movement! From the vast amount of documentary evidence, interviews, articles, etc., one may form the conclusion that professional economists, politicians, businessmen and ordinary people in the West all had a very imprecise picture of the real situation to the east of them.

The rational and the real

The typical socialist economic structure consisted of large state-owned enterprises, with 'monopoly positions', producing mainly for the huge Soviet (and East European) market. It is important to make it clear that those monopoly positions were on a rather limited national (or at most a Comecon) scale. This needs emphasising, because it may have been crucial in the failure of the original transition programme.

The implementation of the IMF's economic concept in the East European economies raises some epistemological questions. Liberalising prices, the key element of the concept, in economies where each sector was represented by a single large state enterprise could have only one result: huge, uncontrollable and unjustified increases in those prices. (In Poland the average price level soared by about 85% in January 1990; in Bulgaria, it rose 200–300% in February–March 1991.)

Prices were still formed in the context of an economy closed to international competition, and thus could not fully perform their main task of providing signals and spreading information on demand and supply patterns through the market, to direct producers towards more effective and efficient production. (Of course, there is no empirical guarantee that the blind 'groping' of the market produces a set of rational prices.) In Eastern Europe, 'price liberalisation' became a euphemism for price increases whenever the government or the individual monopoly producers needed more income to fill the ever-present gaps in their budgets. Consequently, wages did not reflect market competition and market power either. Thus, even the initial problem – curbing inflation and correcting the prevailing imbalance between consumer demand and existing stock – was not solved in the best way.

Generally, as we saw earlier, the economic axioms of the IMF were directed toward countries with a limited state sector, forming not more than 25–30% of the whole economy. In Eastern Europe, the state sector represented 95–98%, and it remains the more competitive element of these economies.

It is not possible to reconstruct a whole economy, or to privatise it, in one year. But the IMF concept did not take account of the immense state sector; in fact, it was totally neglected. It is important to emphasise the considerable scope for efficiency gains in firms likely to remain in the state sector in Eastern Europe for several years yet. If state firms continue to be important economic players, then the approach to economic transition needs to be changed; in the first place, industrial policy should go well beyond privatisation. (In fact, Hungary did apply a more flexible approach of this kind.)

The IMF concept included 'de-monopolisation' of the state sector. This could happen 'naturally' if subsidies to the state firms were cut, leaving them to market forces. If the latter were not effective enough, 'command' administrative measures would be applied in order to dismantle and abolish the existing 'elephants' of those economies. There is, however, another side to this problem. All of those countries had 'national champions' in some sectors and subsectors, at least on an East European level; and indeed some of them were able to compete internationally. Most of them were in branches which – perhaps contrary to conventional wisdom in the West – were using (and transferring) relatively advanced technologies. By lowering their competitive ability, this source of income, employment and knowledge was artificially and unnecessarily destroyed. In situations where privatisation could not yet even begin, the domestic 'jewels in the crown' – admittedly few in any given country – were deliberately sacrificed in the childish hope that others might appear later.

The IMF concept cherished the idea of fast growth of a viable private sector. Such hopes, however, were premature. Private firms could not replace the state sector even in Poland, which had most previous experience – there had been a private sector of about 25% in the Polish economy since the end of the Second World War, compared with only 1 to 2% in countries like Bulgaria or Czechoslovakia. Not surprisingly, in all the countries such firms became involved mainly in trade, pursuing the opportunities for faster and relatively easier accumulation of profits and capital which trade always presents, especially in distorted markets such as the present ones of Eastern Europe.

A confusion of results

The inefficient restructuring of the state sector, and particularly the damage to large state fiirms previously competitive internationally, pitched the Eastern European economies into a vicious circle of diminishing outputs, increasing unemployment, and insoluble financial, social and political problems.

Poland and Bulgaria employed the shock therapy approach in its purest form, and it is therefore useful to consider some of their economic indicators. These are set out, with comparative figures for other Eastern European countries, in Figure 8.2.

	Per capita GNP in $(PPP) (1992)	Monthly wages in $ (1993)	Inflation (1993) %	Unemploy- ment (1993) %	Fiscal balance (as % of GDP, 1993)	Real GDP growth (1993) %	Share of agriculture in GDP (%, 1992)
Bulgaria	5130	114	72.8	16.4	−15.1	−4.2	16
Czech R.	7160	221	20.8	3.5	0.5	−0.3	6
Slovak R.	5620	201	23.0	14.4	−7.5	−4.1	6
Hungary	5740	317	22.5	12.1	−7.0	−2.3	7
Poland	4880	194	35.3	15.7	−6.7	3.8	8
Romania	2750	82	256.1	10.2	−0.1	1	20
G7 group (for comparison)	19600						2.5

Source: EBRD and World Development Reports, 1995

Figure 8.2   Economic indicators for Poland and Bulgaria

There have been some attempts recently to present the end results for the Polish econ-omy as the first turnaround success story in the Eastern bloc. Certainly, the Polish example does show a number of important results[1]:

- The inflation rate has been radically lowered, from 40% per *month* in August 1989 to 40% per annum in 1992–1993. It should be remembered that much of the infla-tion in the period 1990–1992 was corrective inflation – i.e. the price paid for attain-ing better relative prices.
- A rapid and radical elimination of queues and shortages has been achieved. This has been very important, not only for the consumers' welfare but also for the increased efficiency of enterprises.
- Buyers can now choose from a considerably broader range of goods and services, thanks to the greater availability of imports and – after a certain time lag – thanks to the increasing appearance of newer and better goods produced in Poland.
- The role of foreign trade has radically widened, despite a collapse of bilateral and multilateral trade within the former Comecon countries. Polish exports to, and imports from, Western countries have increased substantially, especially as far as the EU is concerned.
- Finally, there has been an extremely fast growth of the private sector, and a related rapid privatisation of smaller units.

This phenomenal growth in the private sector, and the increasing signs of adjustment by some state enterprises, made Poland (in 1993) the first post-socialist country to reg-ister a positive rate of GDP growth. However, despite these obviously encouraging results, there have been some quite important negative side-effects:

- Growing unemployment which, at the end of 1994, stood at almost 16.4 per cent.
- Decreased output in certain important sectors of the economy.
- A continuing high rate of inflation – 30 per cent at the end of 1994.

These imbalances cause concern, because they are mirrored in all the other Eastern European countries which adopted the shock therapy model. Even Jeffrey Sachs could not deny that unemployment continues to be higher than expected in his model; the budget remains in chronic deficit, and its financing becomes ever more expensive; and privatisation of large-scale industrial enterprises is almost completely paralysed. In the widely advertised area of the newly born Warsaw stock market, quite controversial points also arise. A meteoric rise in share prices in Poland in 1993 cannot hide the fact that small unsophisticated investors (mostly households) dominate the market; and the recent very high returns have encouraged speculative holdings. The Warsaw Stock Exchange is mainly attracting cash-rich individuals and entities building largely unregulated speculative portfolios – to the possible long-term detriment of a stable and smooth-functioning savings and investment process for the economy.

It is not surprising that people should try to present the Polish reforms as a success, given the amount of effort and resources put into them and the many reputations at stake, from Harvard professors to international institutions. However, it is important to remember that in fact the Polish transition started at the beginning of the 1980s. Poland, too, is the country which was treated best by the international financial, banking and business community; more than 50% of its debt was reprieved. Moreover, it enjoys what are perhaps the best export conditions, comparatively speaking.

Even countries like Czechoslovakia and particularly Hungary, which adopted a more gradual model than that followed in Poland and Bulgaria, are not able to show significantly better results. This shows that the problem does not lie only in the pace of the reforms. In fact, the whole economic concept applied since 1989 in Eastern Europe may prove to be not a great deal more than a convenient fiction emanating from the political and economic ideology which dominated the Western world in the 1980s; even as a fictional ideal, it is inherently problematical.

The East European reforms – problems of implementation

By 1993–94 most of the countries in Eastern Europe had completed the first (stabilisation) stage of their economic changes, and were starting on their structural reforms. Yet considerable parts of the initial programme had not yet been put into practice, or had proved inadequate. Among the most important practical problems were the following:

- The financial and tax system was far from reaching its targeted structure. Private business was thriving on the inability (or, as many suspected, the unwillingness) of government to collect taxes. This had a double – even a treble – impact: first, the government could not gather the required amounts to keep to budget targets; second, the state sector was put in an unfavourable situation because it did pay taxes; and third, private companies could experience acute and perhaps fatal cash crises when they were, finally, forced to pay up.

- Bad debts were one of the greatest problems for state firms. Such debts had been accumulated during long years of extending easy loans to insolvent state enterprises, with implicit state approval. In 1989 they were officially transferred to the present commercial banks. Sharply higher interest rates and the general economic environment made them absolutely unserviceable, and in only two years they grew to enormous levels. This put most of the state firms on less than equal terms with private business. Even worse, it was a substantial barrier to privatisation. Governments have been forced to excuse the debts of some state firms, but only rather selectively, with decisions resulting mainly from lobbying by pressure groups.

- The authors of the reforms had clearly underestimated the flexible and creative response of endangered enterprises. Most of the state firms had employed defensive strategies – based on the reserves they had accumulated in recent years, and making use of high interest rates (a reflection of high inflation) – to remain in existence and make a contribution to overall employment which was much higher than predicted for that stage of the reforms. Surviving for so long, they could press their cases on the government, exerting additional social and political pressure on it (and thus on its stretched finances).

- Private business frequently did not pay tariffs – even if it was 'contributing' to the 'salaries' of the border control officials! Again the budget suffered as a result, but potential export revenues were lost too, since many of the goods officially destined for foreign markets were in fact sold within the country.

- Many important market institutions were not yet in operation – including, for instance, things like the stock market which in theory should be the place where the real value of firms offered for privatisation could be determined.

- Austerity programmes, supposedly a cornerstone of the first stages of reform, were never completed. Real wages, which dropped sharply in the first months of implementation, quickly recovered to unhealthy levels; this, in turn, did not allow inflation to be kept down to an acceptable level.

- A consequence of the high interest rates on deposits was that people with money to invest preferred to take advantage of the safer and relatively higher returns such deposits offered; productive investment was condemned to play second fiddle from the beginning. (Everyone knows that in a severe depression monetary policy is ineffective, because of the 'liquidity trap' – the desire of savers to hold on to the money they have.)

- The energy infrastructure, and associated environmental problems, provided an even heavier burden for the economies of Eastern Europe. Since, in most of the countries, the 'green' movements were among the first officially to turn against socialism, they had obtained quite a significant place on the political scene. However, their claims could not easily be met in such financially-stretched economies. A dispute between Hungary and Slovakia was a showpiece case of tradeoff between political and economic concerns, and debates about nuclear power stations in Bulgaria and Czechoslovakia were another aspect of the same situation. The Gulf War only made things worse, contributing to higher energy prices and thus to general price increases.

- There was a general lack of competence, knowledge and experience in free market conditions. Training up new management, designing new competitive products, building clever financial strategies, devising comprehensive marketing campaigns –

all these require time, especially when coping with difficult conditions. Moreover, many able people had emigrated, and in the name of removing former socialists too many 'flexible' and 'adaptive' – but incompetent and ignorant – people found themselves in positions of unexpected power. This is not only a serious moral problem, but one with direct economic consequences as well.

Investing in Central and Eastern Europe

Between 1990 and 1993, total private capital flows to the non-OECD world almost quadrupled; the largest component was foreign direct investment. (The figures include portfolio equity investment, which we will ignore for the purposes of this analysis.)

What is quite clear is that the old attitude to foreign investment and transnational corporations has gone. Previously there were restrictions on the industries in which such companies were allowed to become involved; they could not have a majority of the equity; and the transfer of profits was restricted. (See, for example, Poland's previous foreign investment laws of 1982, 1986 and 1988.) Now all this has gone, at least in most countries, as they try to attract foreign investment. The governments in the region understand that foreign direct investment (FDI) brings capital, technology, management skills, and access to export markets. These crucial inputs are needed both for privatising existing enterprises and for creating new 'greenfield' production facilities.

As many countries have learned, FDI brings much more than just new machinery and/or finance. To produce goods or services that other companies and individuals will buy, enterprises in the region will need to be able to make continual progress in technology and design, reaching standards competitive in world terms. Management skills need also to include elements that are scarce today in Eastern Europe, such as development of marketing strategies, sales management and financial planning.

By bringing foreign companies with such skills into ventures where their profits depend on the success of their enterprises in Eastern Europe, FDI can provide these inputs. Each country's position in the transition towards the free market naturally varied, but in the mid-1990s the Czech and Slovak Republics, Hungary and Poland had the major share of the investment; the Czech Republic, Hungary and the Slovak Republic between them accounted for two thirds of the total.

However, the region only captured a 3% share of world-wide investment flows in 1993. Even on a country-by-country rather than a regional basis, the picture was not much better; no country from the region featured among the top ten countries for 1994 investment flows, or for 1994 total investment stock. This was perhaps not surprising, since most of the countries that did feature have been active in seeking foreign investment for much longer, and are not post-socialist economies. One exception to this was China, but this is probably in a class by itself because of its sheer size (see Chapter 7 for an analysis of that emerging market).

The bulk of the growth in FDI worldwide has in fact gone to Asian and Latin American countries – particularly China, Argentina, Mexico, Malaysia and Indonesia. China alone has attracted more than three times the amount going to all the countries of Central and Eastern Europe. Over half the investment going into Central and Eastern

Europe has gone into privatisation transactions. This can now be expected to tail off, as investment becomes directed more at greenfield operations and strategic alliances.

However, investment flows will not necessarily continue to increase. Indeed, there are predictions that they will fall off – in part due to the effect on confidence of the Mexico crisis.[2] The attempts to attract investment have undoubtedly produced a response, but not as much as the governments in question had expected. Almost all the countries in the region have enacted foreign investment legislation, but legal inconsistencies and a lack of clarity in implementation continue to cause problems for investors. The main risk factors identified by a 1993 survey from the EBRD,[3] in order of importance, were:

- Lack of clearly defined legislation
- Lack of property rights
- Lack of a developed market economy
- Lack of a capital market
- Uncertainty with respect to price trends.

If that survey were to be repeated today, the first item would probably retain its top position, although there would now be substantial differences between the countries with respect to the other risk factors. Despite the generally positive attitude of governments in the region and the surge in FDI in 1993–94, foreign investors are concerned with the overall impact of a wide range of policies and institutions. Several significant problems in the current climate for FDI in the region need precise consideration and analysis:

- First, the value and yield of investments is affected not only by foreign investment laws but also by the level of the exchange rate, the extent of convertibility in practice, and the local fiscal regime.
- Second, many investors will be affected by macroeconomic policies, often in contradictory ways depending on their particular circumstances.
- Third, investors will be concerned about institutional aspects of market functioning and regulation other than privatisation – e.g. competition policy, price and border controls.
- Fourth, they will in most cases require a wide range of goods and services which cannot readily be imported, and whose supply often remains ostensibly under state control.

In short, foreign investors are concerned with the whole range of policies and institutions which governments in the region, whether 'big bang' proponents or gradualists, are having to construct. There are also signs of increasing public concern about foreign ownership. In this sense, there is an obvious need for a more cautious approach in entering these markets, many of whose features are quite different from those of markets in the Western world or on the Pacific Rim.

Nevertheless, many firms are entering risk-sharing contracts, licensing agreements, co-production arrangements, management contracts, minority investments, joint turnkey activities and joint ventures to profit from the opportunities available. It is estimated that 70% of major western companies have changed their investment programmes following the introduction of reforms in the former Eastern bloc. (A survey by business advisers KPMG in May 1990 of the activities of major companies in the United States and Europe showed that interest was moving away from the Western European countries, as companies concentrated their investment plans on the Eastern bloc.)

Around the world, such strategic alliances are justifiably hailed as the competitive weapons of the 1990s. But because alliances are distinct from more familiar activities such as acquisitions and standard distribution arrangements, designing and using them can present a substantial challenge. Given the tremendous business potential involved in the emerging markets, it is worth appreciating what makes alliances succeed. While the principles are the same for all alliances, those with Eastern European companies deserve special consideration.

Why strategic alliances?

By fostering strong joint commitments, alliances make possible activities that are not feasible when companies take risks alone. They consequently provide extensive opportunities to build strength, involving an exceptionally wide set of organisations including customers, suppliers, competitors, distributors, universities, local authorities, and firms in other industries. Alliances may involve any task of interest to both organisations – product development, marketing operations, logistics, and more. And unlike acquisitions, an alliance only has to involve those parts of each firm's culture and functions which will work together.

Certainly, there are other possible strategies for entering Central and Eastern European markets; but several factors explain why the creation of strategic alliances is often the preferred option. Let us look briefly at each.

The characteristics of these markets
These are markets which represent tremendous opportunities from an investment point of view, but also considerable risks. A key consideration is the cost to investors of making incorrect assumptions; a strong local partner will be helpful in avoiding these.

New policies in Central and Eastern Europe
'The honeymoon has come to an end', Mr Andrei Kozyrev said in Geneva in March 1995. The US and Russia had entered 'a sobering period', but their post-Cold War honeymoon had ended 'not in divorce but in a growing ability to resolve problems that we face.'[4] In mid-decade, some politicians and local investors in Eastern Europe were beginning to ask how far privatisation should go, and how much foreign investment should be permitted. This time it was not only a political exercise. East European producers withdrew from some markets for political reasons, but Western companies immediately replaced them. Sectors such as defence and telecommunications were left helpless in the political euphoria after 1989, but these were precisely areas in which foreign investors expressed particular interest.

This situation little by little brought about a different view of foreign investment, particularly among the new local investors in these countries. Internal competition is becoming stronger, and more domestic firms are in a position where the foreign investor is considered a competitor, and no longer to be encouraged. In such an environment, obviously the creation of an alliance with a local player may be a safer and more effective penetration strategy.

Of course, in principle, involvement of foreign companies might seem ideal for the restructuring of old firms. They bring in new management techniques, new technology and access to new markets; they even increase the depleted capital stocks. But they also have two big drawbacks. First, they are unlikely to invest more than a marginal amount; and second, they skim the cream, making it harder to restructure the rest of industry. This is already happening in Hungary, which is why, after calling the Czech privatisation scheme a fake, the government is considering one of its own.

A strategy for continued successful participation in privatisation
Although the benefits of privatisation of inefficient state-controlled industries cannot be denied, the speed of privatisation has been slow in most Central and East European countries. This has been partly due to difficulties over the valuation of assets, as a result of price controls which have distorted prices. East European citizens remain largely sceptical about selling off state assets, especially as few ordinary people can yet afford to buy stakes in the larger enterprises. In addition, many employees in existing public enterprises are naturally afraid of future redundancies. In every case, the preference (formal and informal) is for domestic rather than foreign buyers. Such a preference is quite strongly shared by all the responsible authorities in these countries. In this situation, the creation of an alliance could be a successful strategic learning step toward a further privatisation of the same company.

Recent regulations in many of the Central and Eastern European countries allow foreigners to form wholly-owned companies and subsidiaries, and the mid-1990s have seen a considerable increase in foreign equity investment; but strategic alliances, and particularly joint ventures, are still the best investment option. Throughout Eastern Europe, joint ventures have proved to be the most popular form of market entry, because they offer the greatest control, less risks and the opportunity to benefit from reliable Eastern European partners with good connections and access to raw materials and equipment. Moreover, there is no shortage of companies wishing to create a serious link with a Western partner.

Strategic alliances in Eastern Europe: trends and examples

Statistics on foreign direct investment in the region are extremely unreliable, because both private and governmental records of FDI commonly fail to distinguish between agreements and their implementation, and between overall agreed future investment commitments and the actual flow of funds. The most useful source of official data is the United Nations Economic Commission for Europe's *East-West Investment and Joint Ventures News*, but the analysis in this section relies mainly on press sources, and the information for the created strategic alliances may not be totally accurate.

Western investors poured some $15 billion into Eastern Europe in the five years sfter the Berlin Wall came down, but not everyone was happy. Here are some contrasting examples[5]:

- General Electric had to put an additional $400 million into its Hungarian light bulb maker, Tungsram, before it saw any profit at all.

- Dow is reported to have pulled out of a $200 million deal in the Czech Republic after accusing the Czechs of grossly overstating assets.
- Negotiators from Germany's industrial giant Siemens had little to show for a marathon 28-month negotiating session with the heavy engineering arm of Skoda, the Czech industrial group.
- ABB Asea Brown Boveri became the most important investor in the former Warsaw Pact countries. Through shrewdly managed joint ventures and acquisitions (again via joint ventures), by the mid-1990s it controlled 58 companies with 20,000 employees in 16 countries, and was looking for more. Most of ABB's companies – from turbine makers in Poland to a full-scale power plant assembler in Russia – had already been integrated into ABB's global production network.
- Siemens had an equal number of joint ventures, but it was operating in four fewer countries.

Strategic alliances in Russia

By the mid-1990s there were more than 19,000 strategic alliances (mainly equity and industrial joint ventures) in Russia, and more than $10 billion in foreign investment in the country. The number of US–Russian joint ventures increased from 625 in January 1992 to 2,800 in January 1994.

The numbers vary, but the author's own research suggests that around $1 billion in US investment flowed into Russia from October 1992 to December 1993. Large US industrialists are on the scene, including IBM, GE, Ford, Hewlett-Packard, Eastman Kodak, Playtex, Chevron, and AT&T. In 1993, PepsiCo signed a $3 billion multiyear trade pact, and in 1989 and 1990, McDonald's invested $50 million in a food-processing plant and a restaurant in Moscow. Thousands of small and middle-size ventures have also arrived.

Most of the joint ventures have been in software, heavy industrial production, tourism, and hotels. There has also been an explosion in the growth of research and development. Companies like Bell Labs are working with Russian scientists to study space, electronics, optics, lasers, and nuclear energy.

Strategic alliances in Hungary

When the political changes in the region were beginning, Hungary was the first country to attract the attention of international capital. There were good reasons for this. First of all, Hungary was the earliest to establish the legal framework of a market economy; and the country was politically fairly stable – in recent years there have been less strikes in Hungary than anywhere else in Europe. Furthermore, it offers a relatively cheap and extremely well trained work force. It is no accident that some $7.2 billion in capital (more than the total amount invested in Poland, the Czech Republic and Slovakia) was injected into Hungary between 1991 and 1994, mainly in the form of foreign direct investment.

Figure 8.3 shows the ten largest joint ventures involving Hungarian and foreign companies.

Rank	Investor	Nationality	Partner	Sector	Share	Investment
1	US West	US	Westel	Telecom	49%	$330m
2	GM	US	GM Hungary	Cars	67%	$300m
3	Suzuki, C. Itoh	Japan	Magyar Suzuki	Cars	60%	$250m
4	PTT Netherlands, Telecom Denmark	Various	Pannon GSM	Telecom		$250m
5	Allianz	Germany	Hungaria Biztosito	Insurance	67%	$220m
6	Alcoa	US	Kofem	Aluminium	51%	$165m
7	Prinzhorn Group	Austria	Halaspack, Dunapack	Paper	40%	$160m
8	Guardian Glass	US	Hunguard	Glass	100%	$110m
9	Banca Commerciale Italiana,	Italy	Central European	Banking	64%	$87m
	Bayerische Vereinbank,	Germany	Intnl. Bank			
	Sakura Bank	Japan				
10	Columbian Chemicals	US	TVK	Carton black	60%	$55m

Sources: *Financial Times*, 14 April 1994; Hungarian Chamber of Commerce; Credit Suisse First Boston

Figure 8.3   Hungary: the top ten strategic alliances

Strategic alliances in Poland

The almost $3.6 billion which flowed into Poland between 1991 and 1994 compares poorly with Hungary, which has a domestic market only a quarter the size of Poland's nearly 39 million. At least another $4.9 billion had been promised in investment programmes proposed by foreign investors. At the same time, the value of investments on a cash basis had probably not even reached $1 billion by 1994.

Companies with foreign capital participation, including joint ventures and wholly-owned foreign companies, have continued to be the fastest-growing category of companies in Poland. By the end of September 1994, 18,599 companies with foreign capital were registered in Poland, almost 50 per cent more than in mid-1993. The number of fully foreign-owned joint ventures was estimated at 850, and the number of companies with foreign participation equal to or exceeding 50 per cent was reckoned to be 1890. German companies have been the most active in Poland, although those from the United States lead in the large investor category.

The two biggest foreign investors to date are Fiat and Coca-Cola. Fiat (which started with a pure licensing agreement) has committed $2 billion to expanding output and building up the country as the sole source for Europe-wide sales of its new Cinquecento model. In 1991, Fiat finalised an industrial joint venture agreement with FSM, whereby Fiat gained a majority 51 per cent share of the Polish car company. The Polish Government maintained a 29 per cent share, and the workforce bought the remaining 20 per cent of equity shares. Coca-Cola has already invested $170m, and has committed another $50m in fierce rivalry with PepsiCo.

The Japanese car makers have been major rivals of Fiat in the Polish car market. Toyota formed an equity joint venture agreement in 1990 with the Nissho Iwai Co. (one of the nine famous *shogo shoshas*) to form the Toyota Motor Poland Co., setting up twenty sales points in Poland for the distribution of its cars. Mazda has established a joint venture with C. Itoh (another *shogo shosha*) and Polmot for the sale of its models in Poland. The USA has not been left out; General Motors succeeded in establishing an international subcontracting alliance with Fabryka Samochodow Osobowych (FSO) in 1992. The Polish car manufacturer has agreed to build General Motors' Opel Astra family cars and Vectra models from imported parts; GM has invested $75m in the FSO factory in Poland for this project.

Western companies have also formed consortia. In 1991, the French-owned BSN and the Swiss company Nestlé joined forces to buy 51 per cent of the formerly state-owned confectioner Cokoladovny. This had a 60 per cent share of the growing Czech and Slovak confectionery market.

As the market is still very young, the true effectiveness and ultimate success of Western firms entering it cannot be accurately measured; no studies have as yet been done, and information has been difficult to collate.

Strategic alliances in Romania

By the mid-1990s, over 5,000 joint ventures have been set up in Romania, of which 440 are with Italian capital.

Motives of Western investors

There are two main motives for Western companies wishing to enter the emerging markets of Central and Eastern Europe. The first is the possibility of using the area to source products – either independently produced or sub-contracted items. The second is the opportunity to increase turnover, and perhaps (in the defence and electronics sectors) also to use the new markets to absorb the over-capacity created by a reduction in defence contracts at home.

Strategic alliances for market growth

One important and obvious category for investment is branded consumer non-durables[6] such as cigarettes (BAT, RJR, Phillip Morris), detergents (Henkel, Proctor and Gamble, Unilever), jeans (Levi Strauss, VF), razor blades (Gillette) and food (Nestlé, Parmalat, PepsiCo, Unilever, United Biscuits).

In Poland, for instance, the fast-expanding list of consumer goods companies attracted by the prospect of rapid growth from a low base in a large market now includes the leading detergent and household ware companies, among them Unilever, Proctor and Gamble, Henkel, Benckiser and Cussons; the big fast food chains from McDonald's to Burger King and Pizza Hut; and a growing number of chocolate, confectionery and food processing companies and breweries. These include Nestlé, which paid $25m for a 45% stake in the Goplana confectionery factory near Poznan; and Heineken, which at the beginning of 1994 paid $40m for a 25% stake in Zywiec, the recently privatised brewery.

In consumer durables, on the other hand, many sectors have little prospect of significant regional market growth, because ownership levels are already high and incomes insufficient for regular replacement purchases. The main exceptions here are cars (GM, Volkswagen, Fiat, Suzuki, and most recently Rover) and furniture (IKEA and some other Finnish companies).

However, other areas of considerable importance (and notoriously poorly provided for in the region) are business, financial and personal services such as insurance (Aegon, American International, Allianz, Sedgwick), airlines (Air France, Alitalia), retailing (Delhaize, K-Mart, Tengelmann, and more recently Marks and Spencer and Sainsbury), fast food (McDonald's, Burger King, Pizza Hut) and advertising (Lintas, Leo Burnett, Ipsos in Hungary, the old Saatchi and Saatchi). Numerous Western banks, management consultants, and accounting and law firms have established alliances with local partners.

There are also relatively backward industrial and infrastructure sectors in which there is a large prospective market for modern technology to upgrade processes and products, or which supply rapidly-growing final products industries. Here, local interests may block imports or even foreign acquisitions, while strategic alliances offer a better chance of good results. Examples are telecommunications (Alcatel, AT&T), power engineering (ABB, Siemens), lifts (Otis, Schindler), steel (Voest-Alpine, Mannesman), glass (Glaverbel, Pilkington), chemicals (Cabot, Columbian Chemicals, Rhone-Poulenc) and trucks (MAN, Mercedes, Renault, Scania).

Lastly, environmental improvement investments include water treatment plant (E. Allen), chemicals (Great Lakes Chemical Corp.) and water management (Halcrow).

Strategic alliances for low-cost production

Many firms are looking for low-cost labour or other resources with which to supply global markets, usually involving a long-term commitment. In labour-intensive sectors wages are a fraction of German levels and levels of skill comparatively high; hence *Business Week's* headline proposition, 'All simple production will go East'[7]. Examples are furniture (IKEA, Schneider), white goods (Electrolux, Whirlpool), consumer electronics (Philips, Samsung) and car components (Audi, Ford, Loranger).

Originally, one of the main aims of joint ventures in Eastern Europe was to reduce labour costs by using local personnel. But now expatriates also tend to cost less. Soon after the changes of 1989, a manager sent to an Eastern European country was given a 'hardship' bonus of 10–15% on top of his or her salary; but today such incentives are disappearing. In cities such as Prague, Budapest or Warsaw, living conditions have considerably improved and Western produce is easily obtainable. However, it still remains necessary to compensate managers going to Russia, particularly those going to destinations outside Moscow or to the other Republics of the former Soviet Union.

It is important to note that in textiles, clothing and footwear, which are extremely important in the region's cheap-labour exports to the West, Western producers, wholesalers and retailers mostly use contractual arrangements rather than other forms of strategic alliance. This is typical of the global sourcing in this sector, and arises because the Western partners' firm-specific advantage lies in market access, rather than in proprietary technology or production management.

Also significant are those sectors in which cheap capacity is available in the context of the global market strategies of particular firms, regardless of world-market recession: examples are acrylic fibres (Dow Chemical), steel (Voest-Alpine), ball-bearings (SKF) and machine tools (Dorries Scharmann).

Lastly, many raw materials and semi-manufactured goods are available cheaply in the region, often because of chronic regional over-supply, and although typically these can be purchased from trading companies, strategic alliances may be the best way to ensure access and product quality, as in non-ferrous metals (Alcoa) and construction materials (Wimpey, Ciment Français).

The 'crown jewels'

Certain sectors or individual investment targets are especially attractive from the standpoint of the dominant global strategy of Western multinationals operating in that particular sector – especially where they can be seen as having a double strategic role, combining attractive local or regional markets with production costs competitive in world markets.

The most important of these sectors are the following:

- the motor industry
- financial services
- white goods
- confectionery
- tobacco
- power engineering
- the defence sector (mainly telecommunications, aerospace, physics research and computing).

Non-equity alliances

A major factor in many investments in the region since 1989 has been the past experience, on both sides, of non-equity forms of strategic alliance. It is important to realise that many Western firms (mainly German) have simply continued to use long-standing cooperation agreements, both for local marketing and for sourcing, where no significant benefit is seen in switching to other forms of equity alliance.

Motives of Eastern European partners

The motives for, and benefits of, joint ventures for Eastern European companies are:

- access to Western technology and know-how

- application of Western management techniques.
- investment in replacing outdated technologies
- opening-up of new markets
- links with an international name, and more prestige even in the domestic market.

The investment climate: legislation and other characteristics

The newly created legislation for joint ventures and other forms of foreign investment is in general sufficiently flexible, and offers many effective opportunities. Obviously, investors will want to seek protection against erratic changes and risks from political upheavals in countries that are still undergoing far-reaching institutional change. Contracts between states and investors containing stability clauses and guarantees against retroactive changes in laws and policies could offer a degree of security. Expanding the network of Bilateral Investment Treaties (BITs) that many countries – Hungary, Poland and Bulgaria, for example – have initiated will also help provide protection and improve confidence among foreign investors. Legally binding on both parties, BITs spell out rights, obligations and rules of behaviour on essential issues for both foreign investors and host governments. BITs are often a prerequisite for financial support of investors by their home countries. Combined with treaties to avoid double taxation, they are a stimulant to investment.

Typically, foreign investors are able to choose between the creation of joint ventures; the establishment of companies they own entirely; and holding a minority stake in the equity of an indigenous firm. There are often only a few restrictions on the legal form of the investment, as long as it is legally incorporated in the host country. Basic legal rules for business activities – such as corporate organisation, codes defining and regulating commercial activities, and entrepreneurship and bankruptcy laws – are frequently already in place. Free repatriation of profits, of the salaries of expatriate workers, and of capital gains is usually granted, although intellectual property rights are not yet fully protected. Domestic legislation and a network of BITs usually provide for compensation in cases of expropriation, and procedures for settling disputes.

Most transition economies follow broadly the principle of national treatment, by which the host country undertakes to treat foreign-controlled enterprises operating on its territory no less favourably than domestic enterprises. Some, like Hungary, include the principle in their domestic laws. There are, of course, still exceptions that limit the freedom of foreign investors by comparison with nationals – in, for example, the financial sector, real estate, and arms production; and restrictions on the ownership of land and fixed property exist in many transition economies. Here, medium- or long-term leasing offers a temporary alternative.

Joint ventures with Western partners are encouraged by the new legislation in almost all Central and Eastern European countries. New legislation in Russia, Hungary, the Czech Republic, Slovakia and Bulgaria allows foreign capital to hold up to 100% of a company in these countries.

Salaries for local employees vary tremendously in Eastern Europe. Hungary, Slovenia and Poland have the highest paid employees, while Russia and Romania have the lowest paid. In most countries, employees can be paid in local currency. However, in Russia, because of the rampant inflation, many employees prefer to be paid in foreign currency, although this is forbidden by law. One alternative is payment in goods purchased with hard currency through stores or mail order, although there may be complaints about limited choice. However, roubles remain the official method of payment for Gillette, which has formed a joint venture in St. Petersburg. It considers that companies should adhere to the local currency for the long-term good of the Russian economy.

The EU has a special financing programme called JOPP (Joint Venture Phase Programme), which has the task of promoting small joint ventures between companies from Central and Western Europe.

Remaining obstacles

Despite a relatively favourable legal framework, foreign investors sometimes confront extreme difficulties in Central and Eastern Europe. The most severe problems arise during the initial investment process. Some of the most troublesome aspects of investment procedures arise where the venture involves a public sector partner, and there is a possibility of subsequent privatisation. Obviously, procedures must be developed to secure the interests of private parties in joint ventures if the public party is privatised. In principle, the private partner should have the right of first refusal to purchase the public company. Unless this right is guaranteed, the private partner may find that the public half of the joint venture is purchased by an unfriendly buyer, or perhaps even a direct competitor.

The right of first refusal must be contained in more than just the joint venture contract. The contract is signed with the public partner, but that partner cannot obligate itself in the event of its own privatisation. Privatisation is the decision of the owner or ministry/committee, and the seller (a Privatisation Agency or an investment fund under mass privatisation). Therefore, a new legal or regulatory instrument is needed to protect the rights of private parties in joint ventures. This should be enacted immediately to remove any uncertainty.

Another important obstacle concerns the valuing of non-monetary contributions when registering a new company or joint venture. Modern investment frequently includes non-monetary contributions, such as intellectual property rights and good will. Many countries permit companies to register a self-declared worth of non-monetary contributions. Poland and Hungary, for instance, allow this – they permit investors to perform their own valuation, and then impose tough penalties if these values are later discovered to have been inflated. It would be helpful if the other countries in the region could follow this model and amend their commercial laws as a matter of top priority.[8]

Some practical recommendations

The comparatively low level of flows of foreign direct investment into the Central and Eastern European countries and the CIS is disappointing, in view of the attractive opportunities for large-scale FDI that many of these countries offer. It may be useful at this point just to summarise some of the main advantages and disadvantages of investing there by means of a strategic alliance. Among the main advantages are:

- Relatively large, sometimes even vast, internal markets that urgently require an efficient consumer-goods industry.
- In some cases, enormous natural resources.
- Low structural costs.
- Opportunities for risk reduction.
- The creation and exploitation of synergies.
- Lower financial investment than is needed for wholly owned subsidiaries.
- Long-term market penetration resulting from the local market knowledge provided by the host country partner.

The potential disadvantages include:

- Political risk.
- Legislative uncertainty.
- Excessive dependence on agents with strong political knowledge (contacts, etc.)
- Serious logistical problems for some products.
- Poor 'visibility' in the marketplace.
- Lack of an indirect or direct distribution channel.
- Conflicting objectives of the partners.

Political risk is still obviously the biggest type of risk in this region. Foreign investors are using a variety of different political risk strategies. The most effective, particularly for these countries, are the following:

- Increasing a joint venture's bargaining power.
- Improving a joint venture's political role.
- Building other local alliances.
- Achieving a good citizenship status.

Much has been written about the crowded McDonald's restaurants in Moscow and in Budapest – and little about what is most significant about them. The joint ventures are succeeding (of course in differing degrees) because their terms have been tailored to the emerging new facts of the Russian and Hungarian political and business environments. Deciding where to invest and how to structure a deal, however, can be fraught with problems. Westerners would do well to learn from their predecessors' mistakes. Several questions need very special attention:

- **Choice of the right partner.** One point that must be stressed is the necessity and importance of a careful and thorough screening process.

- **Choice of the right location.** The question arises as to which of the emerging markets are sufficiently developed, and in other ways most suitable. Choices will vary according to the criteria and motives for investment. (The Czech Republic may well emerge as a prominent candidate. It was the most technically advanced of the former communist countries, and the most industrialised.)

- **Foreign exposure risk**, and related questions.

- **Government relations strategy.** The role of governments in the region is still a very powerful one, and almost every important investment decision or procedure depends on a government body or officials. Government policies continue to be of critical importance in most emerging economies in this region, and many companies are preparing special government-relations strategies. In this sense, an identified source of 'superior insight' must be properly authenticated by rigorous procedures which are now recognised as essential by successful multinational companies, especially if they operate in Eastern Europe.

- Extensive delegation.
- Establishment of friendly relations with local leaders.
- Anticipation of possible shortages of materials.
- Establishment of brand loyalty and differentiation.

Summary

This chapter has focused on the transition of Central and Eastern European countries from central planning to free-market economies. It has analysed some of the economic reasons for the collapse of the socialist system in 1989, and described the structure of the process of transition towards a market economy. This process had three main directions: changing signals, with the introduction of price and trade liberalisation; changing incentives, with the establishment of a legal framework for bankruptcy, privatisation and unemployment; and creation of an infrastructure, with the legal and institutional framework which market economies need. We saw that transition in Eastern Europe in practice followed two different approaches: the shock therapy model, and the gradualist approach. The results of the first stage of economic reform, the so-called stabilisation reforms, are controversial – some important positive results have been achieved, but other macroeconomic aspects are still in quite bad shape.

Foreign investment in the region is increasing, but not with the speed expected by the governments of these countries. A lack of necessary stability in the existing legislation, and the remaining political risks, are among the main factors still worrying foreign investors. In an analysis of viable market entry strategies for Central and Eastern Europe, it was emphasised that the creation of strategic alliances with local partners is still the best option for doing business in the region. Despite the general welcome given by Eastern European governments to foreign investors, and the surge of FDI in the last few years, by the mid-1990s there were signs of increasing public concern about foreign ownership in Eastern Europe. In this new investment climate, the creation of coherent business and cultural bridges, and long-term strategic alliances, between Western and Eastern European firms remains the best possible choice.

Strategic alliances and other bridges between companies can only be built if Western and East European investors fully understand and appreciate each other's cultures, interests, advantages and disadvantages. Another culture (and its business practices) can only be instinctively absorbed by direct experience over an extended time period. No amount of advice, teaching, or consultancy can adequately cross this cultural gulf.

The creation of strategic alliances between Western and East European investors and companies is an important problem for international management (and, indeed, international politics), and one which is likely to become increasingly prominent in the near future.

✎ CASE STUDY

You work for a British company operating in the defence sector. You have informal relationships with one of the largest Russian state-owned companies, a manufacturer of rocket launchers. This Russian company has developed a very valuable new product using its unique technological know-how, and it is trying to decide how best to sell this product. You know from your informal contacts in the company that it is also commencing a major internal restructuring programme, and it needs some additional capital. It believes that its choices are:

a) to manufacture the product at home, and let foreign sales agents handle marketing (mainly in the Middle East and Africa).
b) to manufacture the product at home, and set up wholly-owned subsidiaries in Syria and in Zimbabwe to handle marketing.
c) to enter into a strategic alliance with a large European firm active in the defence sector, and use the marketing base, international prestige and financial resources of that other firm.

Questions for discussion

1 Are the three choices quoted the Russian firm's only options?

2 Your company is interested in entering into some form of cooperation with the Russian company.

  a) What will your advantages be in any negotiations?

  b) How will you approach the Russians?

  c) What kind of cooperation arrangement would you prefer to make with them, and why?

  d) Why might they eventually agree to your proposal?

3 Prepare a report for your Board, outlining a plan for a joint venture with the Russian company. The report should identify the criteria used for the selection of this particular partner; specify the motives for, and objectives of, the joint venture; indicate how the joint venture is to be structured and managed; and outline the policies needed to minimize the risk of failure.

Further reading

All the following are worth consulting:

A. Berg and J. Sachs, 'Structural Adjustment and International Trade in Eastern

Europe: The Case of Poland', in *Economic Policy: a European Forum*, Cambridge University Press, 1992.

Samuel Brittan, 'Post-communism: the Rival Models', p. 17, *Financial Times*, 24 February 1994.

Commissariat Général du Plan, *L'Expérience Française d'Economie Mixte*, 1991.

Ralf Dahrendorf, *Reflections on the Revolution in Europe*, Chatto, 1990.

J.S. Flemming, 'Price and Trade Reform: The Economic Consequences of Shock Therapy and Possible Mitigating Measures, or, Why Liberalisation is not Enough', pp. 4–12, *National Westminster Bank Quarterly Review*, May 1993.

R. Gilmour, 'America's Unknown Enemy: Beyond Conspiracy', *American Institute for Economic Research*, Vol. XXIV No. 5, 1991.

J. Gray, *Post-Communist Society in Transition*, Social Market Foundation, 1994.

D. Ivanov, 'Strategic Analysis of the Investment and Privatisation Opportunities in Bulgaria' – paper given at a conference on 'Enterprise development in Eastern Europe', Manchester Business School, September 1992.

D. Ivanov, 'Strategies of Transition in Eastern European Economies: the Case of the Balkans', *European Business and Economic Development*, Vol.1 Part 5, March 1993.

D. Ivanov, 'Analysis of Management Culture and Practices in Eastern Europe and Their Impact on Foreign Investment and Privatisation', *Proceedings of the Second Biennial International Conference on Advances in Management, Calgary, Canada*, Vol. 2, pp. 35–36, 1994.

S. Jones, 'The Road to Privatisation', *Finance and Development*, March 1991.

Ivo St. Kovachev, 'Japan as Role Model for Eastern Europe', p. 16, *The Japan Times*, 19 June 1994.

Ivo St. Kovachev, 'Privatisation in Bulgaria: A Revolution that never Happened' and 'Evolution that is Sweeping Everything Around', *Reform Round Table Document 18*, International Center for Economic Growth, San Francisco, August 1994.

D. Lipton and J. Sachs, *Creating a Market Economy in Eastern Europe: The Case of Poland*, Brooking Papers on Economic Activity, No. 1, Brooking Institution, 1990.

M. Mejstrik, O. Kyn, Z. Blaha and J. Mladek, 'The Three Knots of Voucher Privatisation', *Respect*, February 1992.

Stanley J. Paliwoda, *Investing in Eastern Europe: Capitalizing on Emerging Markets*, Addison–Wesley, 1995.

K. Prescott and R. Welford, 'Production and Marketing Strategies for East European Firms in the EC', *European Research*, Vol. 2 Part 3, May 1991.

Hugo Radice, *The Role of Foreign Capital in the Transformation of Eastern Europe*, Research paper, School of Business and Economic Studies, The University of Leeds, 1993.

J. Sachs, 'Time for Japan to Help Lead World Community', p. 6, *The Daily Yomiuri (Tokyo), 25 October 1992.*

J. Sachs, *Poland's Jump to the Market Economy,* MIT Press, 1993.

T. Sawa, 'After the Bubble Economy', p. 18, *The Japan Times,* 19 October 1992.

K. Suzuki, 'Economy in Eastern Europe After CMEA System', *Japan Society of Slavic and Eastern Europe Studies Annual Journal* (Tokyo), 1992.

J. Svejnar, 'Microeconomic Issues in the Transition to a Market Economy', pp. 123–138, *Journal of Economic Perspectives,* Vol. 5 No. 4, Fall 1991.

A. Vining and A. Boardman, 'Ownership Versus Competition: Efficiency in Public Enterprise', pp. 205–239, *Public Choice,* 73, 1992.

Notes

1 Leszek Balcerowicz, 'Transition to Market Economy: Central and East European Countries in Comparative Perspective', p. 39–40, *British Review of Economic Issues,* Vol. 15 No. 37, October 1993.

2 Report issued by the Institute of International Finance based in Washington, April 1995.

3 *Private Investment in Central and Eastern Europe: Survey Results,* Working Paper No 7, EBRD, London, 1993.

4 *Financial Times,* 23 March 1995, p. 2.

5 *Fortune,* 2 May 1994, pp. 24–30.

6 See Hugo Radice, *The Role of Foreign Capital in the Transformation of Eastern Europe,* Research paper, School of Business and Economic Studies, University of Leeds, 1993.

7 *Business Week,* 14 September 1992, p. 46.

8 See *The Climate for Foreign Direct Investment: Diagnosis and Recommendations,* Foreign Investment Advisory Service, The World Bank, February 1994.

9 European Business in North America

Objectives

By the end of this chapter, you will be able to:

- appreciate the business environment in North America (including Mexico).
- understand the business operations of companies in the USA, Canada and Mexico (with a particular focus on small businesses).
- analyse and describe the North American Free Trade Agreement (NAFTA).
- understand the regional diversity within each of the three countries.

Introduction

CASE STUDY
Nashville Tea Party

John Skoley was the Marketing Director of a small tea distributor located in Liverpool. The company purchased and packaged a high quality tea which they sold to small retail outlets throughout Merseyside and also on a home delivery basis, using their distinctive vehicles, which had a large teapot on the van roof. A combination of factors was causing a decline in their traditional markets, not least the competition from high-quality own brand teas in the supermarkets. John had recently received some literature from the Liverpool Chamber of Commerce inviting him to an export seminar, and decided that possibly the export market was the answer to the difficulties being experienced by the company. His enthusiasm was heightened by the seminar, and he contacted his brother who had previously emigrated to Toronto in Canada. He also contacted his neighbour who worked for a freight forwarding company, and discovered that they would undertake all the export documentation, shipping and insurance of the tea.

His brother was able to put him in touch with a friend who was a local importer of foodstuffs in Toronto, and very quickly John found that he had a steady volume of exports. Indeed, he was amazed how easy it appeared to be to break into this new market. Confident after this success, and having been informed that a lot of tea was drunk in the Southern states of the United States, he decided that this would be his next target export market. He was encouraged in this by the other directors, who noted his initial success and believed that there were essentially no differences between Canadian and US consumers. They had no doubts that this would also be a success.

Unfortunately John had no contacts in the area, but being a fan of Country and Western music he decided to make Nashville his initial target. He therefore contacted the local Chamber of Commerce in Nashville, and on their advice placed an advertisement in the *Nashville Chronicle* for an importer for his teas. He received several replies, of which three appeared very promising. John therefore booked a flight to Nashville and arranged to meet the three importers.

John arrived in Nashville in the evening, and chose to have an early night prior to the important meetings with the importers the following day. After breakfast, and before the meetings, he decided to visit some local supermarkets to research the competitor's brands and drove to the nearest shopping mall. It was here that reality struck when he discovered that the only tea being purchased in the supermarkets by most customers or drunk in the Mall's restaurants was iced tea, for which his product was totally unsuitable. John caught the next flight home!

One of the most sophisticated and competitive trading areas in the world is to be found in North America. Traditionally this term has been used to describe the countries of Canada and the United States of America. Many perceived these two countries as a huge market of consumers who, because of their European origins and associations (whether these were with Northern, Southern, or Eastern Europe), were particularly favourable to European products and services. The short case study at the beginning of this chapter illustrates how these preconceptions might be false, and may cause disaster for the inexperienced exporter!

Most recently Canada and the United States have been joined by Mexico in the North American Free Trade Area. Although located geographically in the Central American region, for trade purposes Mexico can therefore now be considered a part of North America.

This chapter attempts to give an understanding of the various North American markets. It is split into three major sections; the first gives a brief introduction to the recent trends within the three countries. The second section then investigates the free trade agreement that welds the three countries into one trading relationship, namely the North American Free Trade Area (NAFTA). The final section considers the key elements of doing business in each of the three countries, and looks in depth at important questions confronting businesses (particularly foreign companies) in each of the markets.

In 1995 the stability of the Mexican economy was threatened by economic and political pressures that resulted in an economic crisis, requiring large international loans to be arranged. This has led to questions, by both political and business leaders within the United States, regarding the wisdom of a free trade agreement with an emerging nation. Despite this instability, discussions have already started on extending the Agreement to include the whole of Latin America, with a target completion date early in the next century. The present chapter will not consider this possible expansion, but further discussion of some of the nations concerned may be found in Chapter 7.

Such a trade area will have major implications for the operation of businesses worldwide, and will complement the probable growth of the European Union to include the former nations of the Comecon pact in Eastern Europe, in addition to the possible membership of Turkey, Cyprus and Malta.

An overview of the three nations

Canada

The nation of Canada is the second largest country (following Russia) in the world, with an area of 9,976,139 square kilometres. Canada consists of ten provinces plus two federally governed territories. From East to West these are Newfoundland, Nova Scotia, Prince Edward Island, New Brunswick, Quebec, Ontario, Manitoba, Saskatchewan, Alberta and British Columbia. The two territories, namely the Northwest Territories and the Yukon Territory, lie to the north of the provinces.

Within this area, the country contained in 1991 only 27,296,859 inhabitants, making it also one of the least densely populated countries. In practice this is slightly misleading, since most of the population live in a strip of land, adjacent to the United States border, which is around 4000 miles in length and 100 miles wide. Even this is an over-simplification, with the population being heavily concentrated within this strip towards the two extremes, consisting of parts of Quebec and Ontario in the east, and British Columbia in the west. This concentration of population is partly for economic reasons, but importantly also because of the harshness of the Canadian climate and geography. Parts of the land are snow-covered throughout the year, and even within the populated strip the winter temperature regularly can fall to −30 degrees Celsius.

The colonial history of Canada is one of conflict between the British and the French, with final control gained by the British in 1763. Confederation was established in 1867, when a policy of national development was given greatest prominence. Resulting from this objective, one may see a variety of economic policies that have both welded the nation and influenced the direction of its development. Most important within these policies are those relating to communications in order to ensure cross-Canada links (e.g. the trans-Canada railroad); and the imposition of the Canada tariff, a protective tariff that enabled domestic industry to develop a competitive advantage within the national markets. Both these policies had a common theme: a concern with being partially or totally annexed, economically or politically, by the United States.

Another major historical factor that has influenced the development of present-day Canada was the colonial dispute between the French and the English. This has resulted in a bilingual policy being adopted, together with continual political friction between provinces. As a consequence of this, 26% of the population has a first language that is French, whilst over 60% have English as their first language. More important from a business perspective is the fact that a large proportion of the French-speaking population is concentrated in the province of Quebec. Finally, with respect to population density, there are seven metropolitan areas each with a population of more than half a million inhabitants (Toronto, Montreal, Vancouver, Ottawa, Edmonton, Calgary and Winnipeg); the two largest, Toronto and Montreal, have over three million inhabitants each.

Canada has traditionally been viewed as a resource-based economy, and within its territorial borders may be found quantities of most of the world's minerals and raw materials. Consequently Canadian industry has a strong competitive advantage in this sector, and Canadian companies in the sector compete strongly throughout the world. This is reflected in the Canadian trade statistics. With respect to location, businesses in the primary sector are found at the source of the minerals, raw materials or other primary products. The fishing industry is located on both coasts, as is the important forestry (lumber) industry.

Manufacturing companies do not enjoy such a global competitive advantage, although (as stated above) the Canadian external tariff, imposing duties on imported manufactured items, has given them protection within Canada's domestic markets. Further details of this protection and its implications are given in a later section of this chapter. The location of manufacturing industry is highly concentrated, with 80% being found in either Ontario or Quebec. With respect to the service sector, the financial services segment is probably the most competitive, and Toronto has become a major challenger to London, Frankfurt, New York and Tokyo as a world financial centre.

EXPORTS		
Country	Value (in US$ million)	Percentage
United States	103,860	77.8
European Union	9,315	7.0
Japan	6,073	4.6
Mexico	613	0.5

IMPORTS		
Country	Value (in US$ million)	Percentage
United States	79,294	62.5
European Union	11,897	9.4
Japan	8,914	7.0
Mexico	2,207	1.7

Source: *IMF Direction of Trade Statistics Yearbook*, 1993

Figure 9.1   Canada's external trade, 1992

Figure 9.1 shows the importance of trade with the United States for Canadian companies. Although the total value is distorted by the automotive trade that originated under the Auto Pact (see later in the chapter), there is a high concentration of United States-Canada trade, which was a major factor in the development of a first free trade agreement creating the Canada-United States Free Trade Area (CFTA). By contrast, the level of trade with Mexico is fairly small, comprising only 0.5% of exports and 1.7% of imports. A similar pattern is found with respect to Foreign Direct Investment, where there is also a dominance in the statistics by the United States. Indeed, Canada is the main destination for United States foreign investment, as the United States is for Canadian foreign investment.

Politically Canada has experienced a degree of stability at Federal level, with power transferring between the two major parties, the Liberals and the Conservatives. This, however, disguises political tensions between provinces that have resulted in the rise of a strong nationalist party in Quebec, which has threatened to secede from the other provinces. The impact of this was seen in the most recent general elections, which resulted in a larger spread of political opinion gaining representation and the decline of the Conservative party to a small rump.

Mexico

Compared to the economies of either the United States or Canada, the Mexican economy is less stable and less highly developed. Until the mid-1980s Mexico was typified by a vast array of restrictions and regulations governing economic policy. There were import tariffs and quotas, restrictions on foreign investment and foreign ownership, and controlled exchange rates, together with a large amount of state intervention within business. The aims of such a set of policies were to achieve self-sustained growth, largely based upon self-sufficiency. The 1970s had appeared to herald an era of growth based upon a successful oil economy. The oil price rises of these years produced a high level of optimism, and foreign loans were obtained to finance investment projects and consumer spending.

This optimism started to fade as the decade progressed, and during the 1980s the business climate changed to one of pessimism. Falling relative oil prices, unserviceable levels of foreign debt, the cessation of loans by foreign banks in August 1982 and the major earthquake in Mexico City in 1985 all contributed to a need for a change of direction in economic policy. In 1987, with inflation at almost 160%, a foreign debt equivalent to 76% of Mexico's GNP, little output growth and falling real per capita income and wages, the Government decided to act. In December 1987 the Pact of Economic Solidarity was announced, imposing severe fiscal and monetary constraints. This was followed in January 1989 by the second stage of the reforms, known as the Pact for Stabilization and Economic Growth, which was introduced by the new President Salinas.

Alongside the controls, the Government made a determined effort to diversify the economy away from the petroleum industries and thus reduce the dependency upon this sector. President Salinas also imposed a strategy of liberalising the economy, reducing the level of state involvement, and opening up areas of the national economy to foreign investors. In 1991 a Mexican Investment Board was set up to attract foreign investment, targeting a range of countries including the United States, Japan and Germany. The level of tariffs was gradually reduced, and by the time of the introduction of the NAFTA agreement almost 50% of imports from the United States were entering Mexico duty-free. However, import restrictions in the form of import licences still operated for numerous goods. Despite the liberalisation the rate of economic growth was restricted by these various controls, and fell continuously in the early 1990s, from 4.6% in 1990 to 0.4% in 1993 – although there was a slight upturn in 1994 to 2.4%, coinciding with NAFTA's introduction.

The manufacturing sector, excluding the Maquiladora companies (see later in the chapter), has been weak in recent years; this weakness is reflected in the trade statistics with a balance of trade deficit standing at $17.5 billion US dollars. Contrasted with this is the growth in the infrastructural industries, and also in some areas of the service sector. As with Canada, the prime trading partner is the United States, which accounts for around 75% of both exports and imports. The rate of expansion of US trade was slowing down in the early 1990s after very rapid growth in the 1980s, but is expected to increase once again as companies adjust to the new NAFTA business environment. The 1990s have also seen a shift from a Mexican trade surplus with the United States to a deficit of 1.7 billion US dollars in 1993.

Alongside the economic weakness, which led to a major crisis in 1995 with the collapse of the Mexican currency, there has also been political weakness. The country has been ruled since the Revolution by the Institutional Revolutionary Party (PRI) which has given an air of political stability. There have been sporadic demonstrations against this political domination, and there has been a gradual opening up to opposition parties and groups. The stability was severely shattered in 1994 with the eruption of a full-scale revolt in the southern state of Chiapas which continued into 1995, together with the assassination of a Presidential candidate. This political instability fed the economic crisis of 1995.

EXPORTS		
Country	Value (in US$ million)	Percentage
United States	32,624	76.4
Canada	2,207	5.2
Japan	1,130	2.6
European Union	3,340	4.6
IMPORTS		
Country	Value (in US$ million)	Percentage
United States	40,598	76.0
Canada	613	1.1
Japan	3,805	7.1
European Union	7,305	13.7

Source: *IMF Direction of Trade Statistics Yearbook*, 1993

Figure 9.2   Mexico's external trade, 1992

United States

Compared to Canada, the United States is a country of far greater diversity with respect to culture, the economy or geography. It consists of fifty states, forty-eight of which are contiguous, with Alaska and Hawaii being the exceptions. As well as the states there are also offshore territories, such as the Mariana Islands and Puerto Rico, which have been incorporated following wars or other political events. Like Canada the country is extremely large, but with a population of 260.3 million in July 1994 there is a much higher density of population. Also contrasting with Canada, the population is spread throughout the 50 states, with over 31 million in California alone. As a consequence of this spread of population, there are excellent communication networks which utilise the river system as well as including road, rail and air links. There are, however, important regional variations within the United States, requiring businesses to consider the country in terms of a series of regional markets; this is discussed in more detail later in this chapter.

The industrial structure of the United States is typical of that of many advanced industrial nations, with a decline of manufacturing industry, which is being replaced by the fast-growing services sector. This has resulted in a change in the location of the industrial base within the United States, away from the traditional industrial heartland (Pennsylvania, Illinois, Ohio etc.) to the growth foci in such states as Texas, Arizona and Colorado. At the same time there still exists a strong primary base, in particular the agricultural sector, which although small in relative terms retains an important role in the economy. One most significant factor of the United States economy is its resilience, which many commentators link to the vitality of the small business sector. Again this is explored in more detail later in the chapter.

The United States Government has attempted economic management during the recent past, utilising theoretical concepts and ideas from different economic philosophies. Monetary policies focusing upon several monetary indicators have been attempted, as well as fiscal and supply-side policies, but none has had the desired effects and achieved the objectives set by the government; the steady non-inflationary growth of the 1980s changed to the recession of the early 1990s.

This was one of the factors that led to political change in 1992 with the election of a Democratic President, Bill Clinton. Since that date the economy has gradually begun to move out of recession, but the impact on employment, income and levels of taxation was still being felt by the majority of the United States population in 1995. Again, this was partly responsible for the second major political change of the 1990s, with the Democratic-controlled House of Representatives and the Senate both being won by the Republicans in 1994. The consequence of this latter change was most likely to be seen in budgetary policies, with the Republicans calling for tax cuts and demanding a target date for the achievement of a balanced budget. It was also possible that more emphasis might be given to domestic as opposed to foreign policies.

Coinciding with these economic and political changes were equally dramatic changes in the business sector. Most noticeably, companies were downsizing, shedding layers of management, and re-engineering themselves to get closer to the customer and offer a more customer-orientated, quality service. This change was facilitated by the dramatic changes in communications technology that allowed company supply chains to be shortened and stocks and warehousing needs to be reduced. Further changes were occurring in the employment area, with the growth of part-time contracts, and with employees working from their homes and connected to their fellow workers through computers and modems. The effect of all of these changes, noticeable particularly in the smaller companies, has been to make United States businesses more cost-effective, despite higher wage costs than in some of their competitor nations, and consequently more competitive in global markets. The overall effects of greater competitiveness may be seen in Figure 9.3.

EXPORTS

Country	Value (in US$ million)	Percentage
Canada	90,156	20.2
Mexico	40,598	9.1
European Union	102,851	23.0
Japan	47,764	10.7

IMPORTS

Country	Value (in US$ million)	Percentage
Canada	101,292	18.3
Mexico	35,886	6.5
European Union	97,110	17.6
Japan	99,481	18.0

Source: *IMF Direction of Trade Statistics Yearbook*, 1993

Figure 9.3   The USA's external trade, 1992

Figure 9.3 also shows that, compared to either Canada or Mexico, the degree of domination of trade by the other nations of North America is much smaller. Although Canada is the most important source of imports (18.3%) and destination for exports (20.2%), the relative proportions are much smaller. More importantly, the second (single-country) trading partner – again for both exports (10.7%) and imports (18.0%) – is Japan. Japan has the highest level of trading surplus with the United States; by 1994 it had risen to 65.7 billion US dollars. The trading surplus that Canada had for the same period, by comparison, was only 14.5 billion US dollars. The third most important trading partner, and a major reason for its inclusion in the new North American Free Trade Area (NAFTA), is Mexico, the destination for 9.1% of United States exports and the source of 6.5% of its imports. A major difference, however, is that of these three trading partners only Mexico has a trade deficit with the United States. (In 1994 it was 1.3 billion US dollars.)

Overall, the United States had a growing balance of trade deficit in goods and services during the first half of the 1990s, and had large deficits with not only Japan and Canada but also Germany and the People's Republic of China. This has naturally focused United States Government attention on these four nations, and there has been a strenuous campaign for many years to enable US manufacturers more easily to penetrate Japanese markets. In January 1995 a minor trade war erupted with another of these nations, namely China, over the protection of Intellectual Property Rights. United States manufacturers claimed that many of their products (video and audio tapes, computer software and compact discs) were being pirated by Chinese manufacturers and no license fees or royalties were being paid.

North American trade

Background

The Canadian Government and the Canadian people have retained suspicions, as already mentioned, about the motives of the United States with respect to both their economic and their political sovereignty. As a consequence of this mistrust, the Canadian Government levied a protective tariff against United States products (but not *exclusively* those of the United States) at the onset of independence. This was combined with a policy of creating a national identity by integrating the East and West coast markets, eventually resulting in the building of the trans-Canada railroad. Early political attempts to alter the policy of protectionism resulted in electoral defeat for the party proposing the change – for example, the Liberals lost both the 1911 and 1953 elections when they included a form of free trade agreement as an important manifesto commitment. Economically, however, the trading relationship between Canada and the United States was steadily increasing, as may be seen in the statistics relating to both the trade in goods and services, and the levels and sources of foreign investment.

Whilst the general level of tariffs between the two countries was gradually reduced as a result of the successive rounds of international discussions within the General Agreement on Tariffs and Trade (GATT), the first real breach in the protective external tariff was achieved by the 1965 Auto Pact. This pact arose from the concerns expressed by US car manufacturers about alleged export subsidies being offered in Canada to car manufacturers there, and the fear that they might be exploited by the growing number of Japanese manufacturers seeking a North American base. In a complex agreement the big three US car manufacturers achieved sectoral free trade for their products and related items, whether they were produced or assembled in the USA or in Canada. In return the Canadians were offered assured levels of production and hence employment within Ontario. Other safeguards (side agreements) were included which gave the US car companies some protection from their Japanese competitors.

The next watershed in the movement towards the development of a regional free trade area was the election in Canada of the Conservative Government headed by Brian Mulroney in 1984. At that time the Conservative party was still espousing a policy of resisting a free trade agreement. During their period of office, however, this policy was quickly reversed and the 1988 election was primarily fought on the basis of the introduction of a negotiated Canada-United States Free Trade Agreement which the Liberal party opposed. The reasons for the reversal of policy by the Conservatives were several, but of particular significance were the following:

- The personal experiences of Brian Mulroney, who had been closely involved in trade liberalisation discussions prior to becoming Prime Minister.
- The proposed changes within the then European Community, and its closer integration after 1992. It was generally believed that this would result in further concentration of trade between the member countries of the European Community (and associated states) to the exclusion of non-members. Some even foresaw a similar pattern occurring within Asia, which would leave a very isolated group of countries in the Americas.
- The growth of the trading relationship between the United States and Canada (over 60% of imports to and exports from Canada were with the US), which led many

Canadians to believe that a special relationship existed between the two countries. (This myth was shattered with the 'Nixon surcharge', when Canadian exports to the US were treated no differently from those from other countries, and attracted the same penalties.)

The election success by the Conservatives was quickly followed by the introduction of the first North American free trade agreement, known as the Canada-United States Free Trade Area (CFTA) agreement, which became effective on 1 January 1989. The CFTA, as its name suggests, was a free trade area agreement and not a customs union. The key distinguishing feature of the former type of trade agreement is that member countries allow the free passage of goods and services from their partners covered by the treaty into their national markets. This should result in increased trade between the partners, as a consequence of lower border taxes encouraging exports, but also it may result in the diversion of trade from third countries towards partner countries (see Figure 9.4).

CASE ONE

Initial position

Country A levies a 10% tariff on all imports.
Country Y sells cutting machines at $100,000.
Country B sells cutting machines at $105,000.
Country A imports 100 cutting machines from Country Y.
Consequently the price of cutting machines in Country A is $110,000.

Free trade agreement between Country A and B

Country A levies no tariff on goods from Country B.
Country A levies a 10% tariff on all imports except those from Country B.
Country Y sells cutting machines at $100,000.
Country B sells cutting machines at $105,000.
Country A imports 100 cutting machines from Country B.
The price of cutting machines in Country A is $105,000.

CASE TWO

Initial position

Country A imposes a tariff of 10% on all imports.
Country B imposes a tariff of 20% on all imports.
Country X manufactures milling machines at $100,000.
Both countries import these machines from Country X.
The price of milling machines in Country A is $110,000, and in Country B $120,000.

Free trade agreement between Country A and Country B (without rules of origin)

Country X will export their milling machines directly to Country A, and with the tariff of 10% will sell the machines in that country at $110,000.
Country X will export their milling machines to Country B via Country A. They will face a tariff of 10% when entering Country A but none between Country A and Country B. They will therefore sell their machines in Country B also at $110,000.

Free trade agreement between Country A and Country B (with rules of origin)

Country X will export their milling machines directly to Country A, and with the tariff of 10% will sell their machines at $110,000 in that country.
Country X will also export their milling machines directly to Country B, because under the rules of origin the machines would not enter freely into Country B from Country A. The selling price will be $120,000.

Figure 9.4   *Implications of a free trade agreement*

Members of a free trade area are, however, allowed to maintain differing tariff barriers towards third nations. (In the case of a customs union the member nations agree to impose a common external tariff towards third countries.) Consequently, for example, a manufacturer of soft toys in Europe faced different tariff barriers from the two members of the CFTA. Such a manufacturer might therefore attempt to enter the country where it faced the higher tariff by diverting its goods; that is, by initially exporting its toys into the market with the lower tariff, and then using the free trade agreement to enter the chosen market (see Figure 9.4). In order to prevent this occurring, a free trade area agreement will normally introduce a 'rules of origin agreement' which defines the goods eligible to enter the other member nations' markets with preferential treatment. In most cases, a figure of 50% value added within the partner countries must be observed if the product is to be eligible for treatment under the duty-free regulations; and this was the figure in fact adopted for the CFTA. (The 50% figure may be varied for certain economically sensitive products such as textiles.)

The Canada-United States Free Trade Area agreement

A summary of the content of the CFTA is provided in Figure 9.5.

Part 0	Preamble
Part 1	Scope and objectives
Part 2	Rules for trade in goods
	- including: Rules of origin
	Customs treatment
	Tariffs and non-tariff barriers
	Agriculture products
	Energy
	Automotive products / Autopact
Part 3	Rules on government procurement
Part 4	Rules for trade in services
	- including: Services
	Business travel
	Investment
Part 5	Administrative procedures
	- including: Avoidance of disputes
	Countervailing duties
	Anti-dumping
Part 6	Various items not covered elsewhere
Part 7	Rules for trade in financial services
Part 8	Final provisions and Annexes

Figure 9.5

Since the year 1935, Canada has gradually reduced the level of its external tariff, requiring its domestic industry and commerce to compete globally without protectionism. This process has been hastened by the various rounds of the General Agreement on Tariffs and Trade (GATT) talks, which have had the effect of reducing tariffs on goods (but not agricultural produce or services, prior to the Uruguay Round of the 1990s) between member countries. The effect of the CFTA was to continue this tariff reduction process, with the aim of achieving a zero level between Canada and the United States by the year 1999 at the latest. It has often been stated that 80% of United States products entered Canada duty-free prior to the enactment of the Agreement, and therefore the CFTA covered only the other 20%. More specifically, a target of 1 January 1999 was agreed for the elimination of tariffs unless industry representatives agreed an earlier date.

The United States Customs User Fee, equivalent to 0.17% of the value of the imported product, was to be eliminated immediately, and other non-tariff barriers such as quotas and minimum price requirements were also to be included in these targets. The phasing out of two important trade distortions, namely duty drawbacks and duty remissions, was to be achieved by 1998. Export taxes, however, were to be permitted provided they were within the GATT guidelines.

The only exceptions to the above were to be for specific well-defined purposes, e.g. measures against such activities as anti-dumping, which were generally agreed to be anti-competitive. Problems of true competitiveness remain in dispute, because of the existence of different social policies that contribute to product cost. There was also an attempt to achieve compatibility of product standards between the two countries, to prevent them being used as a non-tariff barrier to trade.

As in many other free trade area agreements, a rules of origin figure of 50% was adopted. In practice a distinction was drawn between goods containing imported items that were substantially transformed during manufacture, and those containing imported goods that were not transformed. The 50% of value applied only to the latter. Consequently the thrust of the Treaty ensured that a principle of national treatment existed. Under such a principle, whilst countries are allowed to follow their own individual policies with respect to national development, they are prevented from using such policies to discriminate between domestic goods and those from their partners. The agreement also looks towards the future, with the principle of non-discrimination applying to new laws rather than those in existence, unless those existing laws are specifically included within the scope of the agreement.

The inclusion of agricultural products within the agreement was not as substantial as that for goods. This was not surprising, given the important role that agriculture plays in both countries and the numerous distortions that are present in many agricultural produce markets. Significantly, though some agricultural items were covered by the agreement, this was to become an area of continuing dispute between the two countries, and an area where both GATT and the Disputes Settlement Procedures were called into operation.

The services sector coverage was also not as comprehensive as that of the goods sector, and was essentially restricted to business and consulting services, insurance, tourism, computer services including data transmission, real estate and wholesale distribution. A separate section was directed towards the financial services sector. Telecommunications, transportation and (importantly for Canada) the cultural industries sectors were excluded, along with others not specifically mentioned, such as education and health care. Whilst the inclusion of part of the services sector in the agreement was indeed a major breakthrough, the exclusion of transportation and telecommunications was disappointing.

Furthermore, there were no strong obligations for future policies to avoid certain types of discrimination, such as sector subsidies or access to the government procurement of services. This was in contrast to the government procurement of *goods*, where Canadian and United States companies were permitted to compete for government contracts. One enlightened provision that applied to business travellers was the lifting of restrictions on temporary entry for work purposes.

The greatest movement towards liberalisation of market access in the services sector was reserved for financial services. This was a reflection of global changes whereby restrictions were being eliminated and markets opened to global competition. The agreement covers a range of financial intermediaries from commercial banks to trust and loan companies. Interestingly, in this case the liberalisation and deregulation applied to existing regulations as well as, naturally, to future market access issues. Examples of the effects of the agreement were seen immediately; one was the removal of ownership restrictions on the nationals of the partner countries.

One sector that was always regarded as a crucial part of the Canadian economy, needing to be protected from foreign ownership and control, was energy. This was naturally related to the competitive advantage of the nation, previously mentioned. A different perspective was evident in the United States at the time of the negotiations, and President Reagan was heard to emphasise that one of the major benefits of the treaty would be access to Canadian energy sources. This was an area of the agreement that was subsequently highlighted in the political campaign of those opposing the CFTA in Canada. The Canadian Government was also forbidden to use energy prices as a indirect subsidy for Canadian industry. Similarly, export taxes and export restrictions (outside of the GATT framework) were forbidden.

The US Government agreed to exempt Canada from various restrictions imposed upon other countries relating to the direct export of oil from Alaska, the enrichment of uranium, etc. Canada by contrast retained a large amount of control over ownership within the energy sector.

This latter aspect was reflected in the treatment of foreign direct investment within the CFTA. Once again, national treatment was to be extended to investment by nationals from the partner country, together with a guarantee not to impose a local content, export or import substitution requirement. Existing practices and policies that were not in accordance with this policy were allowed to be retained, provided they did not contravene international obligations. Both governments operated a variety of policies that would be classified under the last item, and it was acknowledged that a gradual liberalisation of these restrictions would occur over time. The cultural industries were once again specifically excluded from the agreement.

Possibly one of the most significant aspects of the CFTA, but one which at first sight appears insignificant, is that relating to the disputes procedure. Canadian governments had considered Canada to have a special relationship with the United States, and had therefore been shocked that the Nixon surcharge was applied to Canada. The Disputes Settlement Procedures enshrined this special relationship within the heart of the CFTA. It was also significantly better than similar mechanisms in other free trade area agreements, and importantly avoided the use of the GATT multilateral facilities. Trade disputes relating to the interpretation of the CFTA were referred to a Canada-United States Trade Commission, which could choose from a variety of methods for resolution that would culminate in either arbitration or settlement by a panel of experts.

In practice, however, the operation of the disputes mechanism did not match the lofty aspirations, and several trade complaints raised by the Canadians were unilaterally rejected by the United States Government.

The impact of the Canada-United States Free Trade Area agreement is difficult to estimate, because the introduction of the agreement coincided with world-wide recession and the introduction of the General Sales Tax (GST) in Canada, raising prices and reducing consumer demand. Consequently, the closure of several US manufacturing companies' operations in Canada could have been the result either of the recession or of a change in operational policy, with the companies choosing to access the Canadian market through exporting rather than manufacture in the country. Canada has also been stricken by a divisive debate concerning the degree of provincial independence, and the future of Quebec within a unified federal state. Finally, the expansion and renegotiation of the CFTA to include Mexico took place before many of the clauses within the original agreement could be enacted.

As expected, and despite the recession, one positive trend has occurred – namely an intensification and concentration of the trading relationship between the two countries. A negative element is the growing number of trade disputes between Canada and the United States, and the rancour that has accompanied them. Such disputes have included the elimination of the Canadian patent law that allowed the transfer of patents to Canadian companies at low royalty rates, and countervailing duties imposed by the United States on pork, softwood lumber, etc. Overall, however, the CFTA was a crucial stage in the creation of a regional trade bloc within the continent of the Americas, and one that will be a major challenge to the growing segmentation of the world's trading nations.

Moves for extension of the treaty

In June 1990 President Bush of the United Sates announced that he wished to start discussions with the Mexican Government with a view to extension of the CFTA to include Mexico. He was also involved in wider discussions, which had the long-term aim of creating a broader free trade area throughout the whole of the Americas, meanwhile in the shorter term developing a series of bilateral free trade areas involving the United States and other individual Latin American nations. The Canadian Government therefore had little choice but to join the Mexican discussions with a view to extending the existing CFTA. The alternative would have been to allow the United States to obtain a dominant position in trade within the Americas, and to reap the advantages of bilateral free trade arrangements which might not be offered to third countries.

Hence in February 1991 it was announced that negotiations would formally be opened; and they were subsequently concluded with a draft treaty in 1992. Although agreed by the negotiators, the contents of the treaty had to be ratified by the three governments; this proved to be a more difficult proposition for the newly elected President

Clinton than he had expected. In a series of last-minute meetings various side agreements were eventually agreed by the President, enabling him to put together a majority to pass the Bill.

The underlying reasons for the extension of the treaty were primarily related to the objectives of the United States and Mexican governments. These were not solely economic in origin, but also politically motivated. Economically both countries expected to gain from enhanced access to markets, and from the reduction of the considerable market restrictions that existed in Mexico; for United States businesses there was concern about the restrictive foreign investment laws that existed in Mexico outside of the Maquiladora sector. But the United States government was also concerned about potential political instability within Mexico, and believed that it could be counteracted through the provisions of the treaty which would aid economic prosperity. Similarly, the Mexican government headed by President Salinas also believed the treaty would give support to its free market economic policies and to its liberalisation and privatisation legislation. This was severely threatened soon after the treaty was brought into force by insurrection in the southern part of Mexico and by the financial crisis that arose in 1995, requiring United States financial aid.

The Canadian government took the opportunity to seek to widen the scope of the CFTA to the advantage of Canadian companies. The actual amount of Canada-Mexico trade was small, and although there were hopes that the treaty could lead to an expansion, there were also concerns that Mexican goods and services would replace Canadian goods and services in the United States.

North American Free Trade Area agreement

The North American Free Trade Area agreement was signed in November 1993; it was an extension of the previous Canada-United States Free Trade Area agreement, but with the addition of a new partner, Mexico, and with a content that was broader in scope. Figure 9.6 summarises the content of the agreement; what follows is a consideration of the key differences between the two agreements.

As was the case with the CFTA agreement, the new agreement is a free trade treaty and not a customs union. Consequently the first major chapter of the agreement considers the rules of origin regulations. It clearly defines the goods and services eligible for preferential treatment under the terms of the NAFTA. The rules have been drawn up with a view to ease of interpretation as well as minimisation of administrative burdens. Eligible items are those with a regional value content of either 50% (if calculated by the transaction-value method) or 60% (if calculated under the net-cost method); they must also satisfy other criteria if applicable.

The rules governing automotive products are slightly harsher, and specify a figure that rises to 62.5% local content by the year 2002 under the second of the two methods of calculation. In order to ensure a minimisation of administrative costs, the agreement specifies a common certificate of origin to be used in all three countries, and common customs procedures.

0	Preamble and objectives
1	Rules of origin
2	Customs administration
3	Trade in goods
4	Textiles and apparel
5	Automotive goods
6	Energy and basic petrochemicals
7	Agriculture
8	Sanitary and phytosanitary measures
9	Technical standards
10	Emergency action
11	Anti-dumping and countervailing duties
12	Government procurement
13	Services trade
14	Land transportation
15	Telecommunications
16	Investment
17	Competition policy etc.
18	Financial services
19	Intellectual property
20	Business travel
21	Institutional disputes procedures
22	Administration of laws
23	Exceptions
24	Final provisions
25	Environmental provisions

(Note: The ordering of these chapters varies from that of some drafts of the agreement.)

Figure 9.6   Chapter headings of the NAFTA agreement

With respect to trade in goods, the NAFTA builds on the Canada-US treaty, and tariffs will be reduced in stages within ten years for all but the most sensitive goods, where a period of fifteen years has been agreed. A similar understanding applies to other forms of border restrictions affecting goods, and a new category is created which allows the duty-free temporary admission of goods for business purposes. Another new element within the treaty is to distinguish and recognise the uniqueness of certain alcoholic drinks, e.g. Tennessee whisky.

Chapter 4 of the treaty focuses upon the trade in textiles and apparel, where the tariffs are again to be reduced to zero over a period of ten years, with the proviso that import quotas or tariffs may be erected within this transitional period (primarily against Mexican produce) to give temporary safeguards to the domestic industry in the two other partner countries.

With respect to the energy sector, contained within Chapter 6 of the treaty, the provisions of the previous treaty are extended to Mexico where a strong protectionist policy was previously in force. The obligations are also made more stringent.

The agreement with respect to agriculture is structured differently from those dealing with either goods or services. The NAFTA agreement sets out three bilateral agreements, the first giving undertakings on US-Mexico agricultural trade, the second on US-Canada trade, and the third on Canada-Mexico trade. The provisions that encompass all three countries concentrate upon regulations relating either to agricultural export subsidies or to domestic support for agricultural goods.

The US-Canada provisions are primarily a restatement of the previous CFTA agreement. The provisions relating to US-Mexico border agricultural trade require the elimination of all non-tariff barriers, although this will often be achieved initially by their conversion to tariffs. The tariffs themselves will then be phased out over a period of fifteen years, with half of the bilateral trade being tariff-free immediately and only the most sensitive produce such as corn, orange juice or sugar taking the full period before elimination. Finally, the provisions relating to Mexico-Canada bilateral agricultural trade have a ten-year phasing-in period for the elimination of almost all tariffs, with only a few exceptions such as poultry and eggs.

Other important changes within the NAFTA treaty, as compared to the CFTA equivalent, include new sections on intellectual property rights, land transportation and speciality air services, and environmental measures. The chapter dealing with service industries extends the coverage of the agreement to the trade in nearly all services, as compared to only 150 in the previous treaty; the opening up of government procurement contracts is extended in coverage and lower financial thresholds are set; and finally, a broader coverage of sectors is also contained within the chapter on foreign investment.

The new chapter on intellectual property rights extends patent protection to 20 years, limits compulsory licensing (importantly in the pharmaceutical sector), strengthens trademark protection, and extends the definition of copyright to cover new products such as satellite signals, computer programmes etc.

The regulations contained within the chapter on land transportation allow for the removal of existing restrictions on transportation in cross-border trade. This will enable the competitiveness of the sector to increase, and take advantage of the expected growth in cross-border trade. The provisions are phased in over six years, with a gradual increase in the geographical area covered by the provisions in each country.

The final new set of provisions relates to the environment; the countries have agreed to implement the NAFTA provisions consistent with environmental protection, and also to promote sustainable development. Consequently the whole of the NAFTA treaty contains references to the environment.

There is also an important change in the Disputes Settlement Procedures. As already mentioned, Canada was most concerned that disputes should be settled by the treaty partners rather than being referred to a third party. There was, however, disappointment over the operations of the procedures of the previous treaty. The new NAFTA procedures establish a Trade Commission that meets in those cases where consultation between the disputants fails. The Trade Commission, which includes members from all three nations, will attempt to solve the dispute using whatever means are most applicable. If a settlement still cannot be reached, the dispute may either then be referred to a third party such as the World Trade Organisation (WTO) or to panel proceedings involving only the three partners. The panel will arbitrate on the dispute, and recommend a course of action for settlement, but has no powers to enforce the settlement. If the recommendations are rejected, the complaining partner may suspend equivalent benefits to the value of the dispute until a settlement is reached.

The NAFTA agreement will shape economic relations between the three partners in the future, and will therefore dominate trade relationships within the continent of the Americas. It is highly likely that it will also form the basis of future trading relationships between the existing partners and the other nations of both Central and South America. Whilst the treaty is confined to trade relationships, the broader political and social interaction between the United States and existing and future members should not be underestimated. Naturally this is already covered in numerous declarations and conventions, but it will be cemented within this framework.

Comparisons with the European economic treaties are often made by commentators who suggest that the North American nations will follow a similar path, towards a North American Union or Federation. Whilst this may occur in the distant future, the political momentum for such a development in the near future is absent. Major reasons for this are the domestic politics of the United States and the related factor of superpower status. Indeed, an important contrast with the European Union is the domination of North America by the United States; in Europe no one country has that kind of domination.

Doing business in North America

This section considers practical aspects of business operations in the North American continent. It offers a broad picture of business operations in each of the three countries, together with a more detailed consideration of key elements in each of those markets.

Canada

In many respects comments relating to the United States have a great many parallels in the conditions experienced in Canada. There are strong regional differences throughout the country, accentuated in Canada's case by the bilingual environment. Small business growth is important. There are also many differencesbetween the US and Canada, and the intention of this section is to highlight some of these.

Marketing in Canada

> ✎   CASE STUDY
>   A North American licence
> During the 1980s Montreal was recognised as a cultural hotspot and attracted people from both Canada and the Northeastern United States. Amongst the immigrants were a couple from New York City who decided that for them Montreal had far more attractions that New York. With sufficient funding of their own available,

they decided to start a small business selling indoor gardens by post. This enabled customers to cultivate flowers in an indoor flower box, and have them flowering whilst outside the harsh Canadian winters offered a bleak outlook. The business prospered, and they chose to expand their product range with related items. They travelled to various craft fairs where they contacted potential outlets to sell their products, but also made contact with the manufacturers of possible new products.

One item that attracted their attention was a decorative candle that had a luminous design included in the wax. They discovered the product was manufactured in England, and therefore contacted the producer. Unfortunately they were informed that a North American licensee had already been appointed, but that it would be possible to sub-license from that person. Whilst this would involve additional cost and possibly reduced margins, they felt elated that they now had the possibility of including the product in their range. The next stage would be to meet the local licensee and agree terms.

They therefore telephoned the number that they had been given, to discover to their horror that the North American licensee was located in San Francisco – further from Montreal than the original English manufacturer!

CASE STUDY
Belgium's Interbrew bids for Labatt

Until recently, Belgium's Interbrew epitomised many of the beer industry's most venerable traditions. Beer connoisseurs cherish Interbrew's more than 40 brands, including the lager Stella Artois, the cloudy white Hoegaarden, and an unusual raspberry-flavoured malt. In June 1995, *Business Week* reported that this bastion of tradition was suddenly emerging as one of the industry's most aggressive global players. Early that month, Interbrew had offered to pay almost $2 billion for the Canadian brewing giant John Labatt Ltd. This deal followed on the heels of Interbrew's forays into China, Hungary, and Romania. If it was approved by Labatt shareholders, it would turn Interbrew into the world's fourth-largest brewer, up from just sixteenth in 1994, when it had earned $100 million on sales of $1.7 billion. Moreover, Interbrew would be 'far more international' than the US giants Anheuser-Busch Inc. and Miller Brewing Co.

Faced with mature domestic markets, leading brewers must go global. But Interbrew would need years of costly marketing to take its main beer, Stella Artois, worldwide. The only option, said *Business Week*, was to buy growth. Labatt would give Interbrew a formidable springboard for further expansion. A North American presence was essential 'if you want to be an international beer mogul,' according to Robert S. Weinberg, a St. Louis beer consultant whose clients included Miller and Anheuser. Labatt would give Interbrew 45% of the Canadian market, a rapidly growing US specialty-beer business, and a 22% stake in Mexico's second-largest brewer, Femsa Cerveza.

These businesses, said *Business Week,* had enormous growth potential. In the USA, Labatt was already among the top three players in specialty beers, the most promising market segment. Since 1987, its US sales had zoomed ahead at 21% annually, while the market as a whole managed just 1%. Labatt believed it could boost its US sales a further 85% by 2000. And that was without counting the addition of Stella Artois, which Interbrew chief Hans H. Meerloo now hoped to position as an upmarket drink in US bars. In Mexico, Femsa was likely to enjoy strong growth, once the peso crisis subsided. And analysts were speculating that Interbrew might team up with Quilmes Industrial, Argentina's No. 1 brewer, to expand into the rapidly growing South American market. Quilmes had been a major player in a hostile bid for Labatt led by Onex Corp. the previous month.

In Europe, Labatt owned Birra Moretti, which had an 11.6% stake in the Italian market; and Interbrew would also get Labatt's 533 British pubs, which would consolidate Stella Artois's position as Britain's top premium beer.

That would leave Interbrew with Labatt's beer businesses. In 1994 the core Canadian brewery had had an operating profit margin of 22.8% – more than Heineken, Carlsberg, or Anheuser. It was likely that Interbrew could boost margins even more, simply by cutting Labatt's marketing budget. It made one wonder, commented *Business Week,* why other beer giants had hesitated in making a play for Labatt. Now they were likely to copy Interbrew's recipe.

Source: William C. Symonds and Linda Bernier, `A Belgian Brewer's Plans Come To a Head',
p. 22, *Business Week,* International Edition, 19.6.95

The first part of this section discusses the phenomenon of Canadian regionalism, and its regional markets. This topic is considered in greater detail, within the United States context, in the discussion of the United States markets. Consequently, we need only note at this stage that there exist within Canada several distinctive regional markets. Indeed, many marketers would strongly argue that there are effectively five major regional markets within Canada, separated by geography, language, industrial structure, history and regulations: these are the Atlantic Provinces, Quebec, Ontario, British Columbia and the Prairie Provinces. In the mid-1990s the Atlantic Provinces were economically depressed, with their traditional industries suffering from recession. The prosperity of the Prairie Provinces, as their name suggests, is very much dependent on grain crops; whereas Ontario is more diversified, and contains traditional industries linked with minerals extraction and processing, but also manufacturing. In addition, it has a growing strength in the services sector; particularly important in that context are the financial services industries in the Greater Toronto metropolitan area. British Columbia, with its westward-looking coastline, has traditional industries such as logging but has also been a key location for many newly-established Asian manufacturing and service companies.

Possibly the greatest difference between markets, however, relates to language differences – especially in the French-speaking Quebec regional market. The difference in language overshadows other important distinctions; the Quebecois have a historical distinctiveness, with different cultural traits and expenditure patterns, a strong Catholicism, and an alternative legal system based upon the French Civil Code.

Just as in the United States, the choice of regional market is crucial to business success. The contrast with the United States, however, is that the choice is simpler because of the concentrated location of a vast percentage of the population, and the sparseness of the rest.

Once a regional market has been chosen, the other components of the marketing mix with respect to Canadian operations must be considered. The first of these is the product itself. As with most overseas markets, it is necessary to adapt the product or its associated features to local customer requirements. The first of these adaptations relates to the need for specific language use in advertisements, on packaging, in manuals and so on. This will differ according to whether a French-speaking market is chosen, for instance in Quebec, or an English-speaking market in, say, the Prairies. Consumer tastes are also often believed to differ in the different language markets, and again will require the product to be adapted.

A second reason for adapting the product is to meet the various legal requirements that relate to product safety, compliance with Canadian standards and regulations, and Canadian intellectual property laws. In the case of trademarks and copyright protection, registration with the Canadian authorities is necessary. Patent protection is provided through the Federal government. Trade secrets are not protected by any form of registration, but require the signed agreement of persons who may come into contact with that secret. Trading and technical standards are imposed by a variety of bodies, both public and private, although the former have no legal status unless incorporated into federal, provincial or local legislation. Examples of such legislation are the Food and Drugs Act Regulations and the Consumer Packaging and Labelling Act. Products should also be manufactured to accord with the general regulations relating to product liability, which because they are a provincial responsibility may vary throughout the ten provinces of Canada. Other requirements are that all imported products should display their country of origin, and that measurements be given in metric units. Finally, care must be taken to ensure compliance with the environmental requirements detailed in the Environmental Protection Act.

Pricing within the different Canadian markets is seen as a major factor in achieving competitiveness, although low margins cannot normally be compensated for by sales volume in Canada because of the size of the Canadian markets. In making the choice of final price, it should also be borne in mind that Canadian goods are subject to sales taxes, imposed by both Federal governments and provincial governments, that vary from province to province and may result in the product being sold at differential prices throughout Canada. Although the federally imposed goods and services tax (GST) is currently applied at a rate of 7% throughout the country, the provincial variations range from 4% to 12%, with Alberta not levying a tax at all. As well as sales taxes, imported products may also be affected by import taxes. The combined effect is to raise the price of goods and services sold in Canada. This may be significant in the future, when United States exports have completely duty-free access to the Canadian markets.

Distribution within Canadian markets is strongly affected by the concentrated nature of businesses in Canada. The size of the market, the geographical spread, protectionist policies such as the Canadian Tariff and branding, and possibly weaker anti-trust legislation than in other comparable countries have led to this concentration. Consequently, many industrial sectors have relatively few businesses in particular Canadian markets, or at least domination by a few businesses. This does enable suppliers to sell directly to these companies more easily, with a resulting possibility of shortened distribution chains and reduced costs. This occurs not only in producer goods markets but also to a certain extent in consumer goods markets, where retail chains such as The Bay and Eaton's have considerable market share. Food retailing is similarly affected by supermarket chains with high market shares, such as Canada Safeway and Loblaw.

If direct sales are not possible, the exporter must consider the use of a local representative – normally an agent (or broker) or a merchant (distributor). As in the other North American nations, persons or companies can act simultaneously as both an agent and a merchant for different products. The choice of agent or merchant will depend upon industry custom, product and potential sales volume. Agents will, however, often require an exclusivity agreement giving them sole representation rights within the market and consequently a position as the only direct contact with the customer. The choice will depend upon the usual criteria, and different agents or merchants may be required for different Canadian markets. Some companies may choose to use their own sales staff. This will be more likely for companies which have their own premises within Canada, but may also be attractive to the exporter if technical knowledge relating to the product is necessary, or if a technical after-sales service is offered.

An alternative to the distribution methods listed above is the possibility of direct sales by mail order. This may be undertaken either from within Canada itself or from overseas; either way, because of the isolated geographical location of many Canadians catalogue sales remain an important sales technique. The newer electronic catalogues and home shopping television channels are also attracting growing numbers of customers, because of the readiness Canadians have to accept new communications technology.

Direct sales are only one element of the marketing communications programme that businesses must consider. Other forms of direct selling are available to companies within the Canadian markets. All of these are also available in European markets, but the code of ethics relating to such sales is often considered to be more lax in Canada. Also, the sophistication of the target customer lists used by direct mail companies in the Canadian market is poorer, resulting in many mailshots being sent to inappropriate potential customers. Consequently, greater use is made of inserts in magazines and free newspapers, together with a higher usage of couponing. Toll-free numbers are also a feature of direct selling, but are not as numerous as in the United States per head of the population.

The more traditional forms of promotion such as advertising are an essential feature of Canadian markets, and the range of media available is wide. Because of the two-language policy, care must be taken to address all Canadians in their own language. All advertising in Quebec must be in the French language by law. This prevents the use of global advertising throughout the Canadian markets. Furthermore, Canadian television advertising – like its US counterpart – relies on a hard sell approach rather than the more oblique or humorous advertisements seen in Europe. Overall there is plenty of choice within the media, with 70% of the Canadian population having both terrestrial and cable television receivers and access to the hundreds of local radio and television channels and networks. Newspapers and magazines offer businesses a more targeted approach to reaching potential customers, but there is only one national news-paper, the others being local or regional. There is a wide variety of free publications. Careful choice of communications policy for businesses' Canadian operations is essential.

Foreign investment and government intervention

An interesting aspect of the Canadian business environment has been the significant role that the federal and provincial governments have played. This has been seen both directly in the operation of various businesses themselves, and more indirectly in regu-lation of the market. A typical example is the requirement for most alcohol to be sold through government-owned stores in many provinces.

Most governments either regulate or intervene in the free market for a variety of rea-sons – whether to protect certain groups within society, or to improve the workings of the market process, or to offer an advantage to one group over another. In the case of the Canadian governments at both provincial and federal level, all of these motives and others have been used to justify intervention in the market. This has resulted in vari-ous pieces of legislation which have both helped and hindered business activity in Canada. At times different justifications have been used to change or reverse policies that were introduced by previous governments, introducing a certain degree of insta-bility within the business environment. This will be seen in the policy towards foreign investments detailed below.

The most far-reaching of these policies has probably been the protection given to com-panies located within Canada by the Canadian Tariff. This had the effect of imposing an import surcharge on most items entering the country, and during the CFTA and NAFTA negotiations still applied to 20% of imported products from the United States. Although the effects of the tariff have gradually been eroded, primarily in the various GATT Rounds, a protectionist policy still applies against non-NAFTA nations. Simi-larly, there are various non-tariff import (and export) controls in Canada which are specified in the Export and Import Permits Act. These often arise from supply man-agement policies undertaken in the domestic economy, such as in the agricultural sector.

As well as border impediments, businesses operating within Canada may also be faced by internal protectionist measures imposed by provinces to protect their own provincial industries. These apply to domestic and foreign companies alike. This has been highly publicised in the brewery sector, where only beer that is produced in a certain province may be sold there. These and other inter-provincial trade barriers are gradually being withdrawn, and a freer market is emerging which will be backed by federal legislation. The effects of all of these policies have made their contribution towards the high levels of concentration in some areas of Canadian industry. Greater competition, with the reduction of trade barriers under the CFTA and NAFTA, is reducing this factor.

One result of the Canadian Tariff is the large number of foreign companies that have set up plants or establishments within Canada. This has resulted in a fairly active, yet changing, policy towards foreign investment by successive Canadian governments. Until 1985 the Foreign Investment Review Act gained notoriety as a fairly restrictive policy discouraging foreign investment in Canada. Under this legislation the federal government undertook a review of each major proposed investment. Policy was liber-alised in 1985 with the introduction of the Investment Canada Act which recognised the advantages that can accrue from foreign investment. Consequently the purpose of the Act was to encourage such investment, but it also aimed to regulate it, using a review and notification threshold. The Act laid down criteria that must be met if the investment required review, and was targeted at large investments that might or might not involve an existing Canadian-owned company or investments in certain sensitive areas. All investments must, however, be reported.

As well as the federal legislation, there is often provincial legislation which creates further restrictions, often with respect to land purchases for either speculative or agricultural reasons. At the same time as this legislation is being applied, foreign investment is also subject to a series of provincially-based incentives that offer loans and grants for companies, either Canadian or foreign, to invest in areas of slow economic growth.

In some areas of the economy there remain strong restrictions on any foreign investment or ownership. These areas include the financial services sector, cultural industries, media, transportation and certain types of commercial fishing. Furthermore, at a provincial level there are often additional barriers relating to liquor distribution, real estate and professional services. An example of such a provincial restriction is in Saskatchewan, where regulations control the sale of farm land to non-residents – whereas no such restrictions apply in Newfoundland.

Mexico

As previously mentioned, the Mexican Government has been making great strides in the direction of liberalisation and deregulation of the Mexican economy, allowing greater access for foreign companies, together with reduced restrictions on foreign ownership and the privatisation of many state enterprises. The most impact will be felt by companies located within the other NAFTA member countries. It is likely, however, that within a short period of time, these same opportunities will be made available to companies from nations outside the NAFTA region. (Mexico has already signed free trade agreements with Chile, Venezuela, Costa Rica and Colombia.)

Marketing in Mexico

> ✎   CASE STUDY
>   Subtronic in Mexico
> Subtronic is part of the Morgan Collins Group, which is part of Thames Water. In April 1995, *Overseas Trade* reported as follows: 'In what may be the world's largest single sewerage and water supply mapping project, currently underway in Mexico City, British software is being produced by Subtronic...[which] has supplied 18 copies of its SUS25 mapping software to IASA, part of Severn Trent International, and Agumex, in which North West Water International is a shareholder. The two companies have been commissioned by the Federal District Council of Mexico City to carry out the study, and they are using the SUS25 software for site survey and data processing of both the water supply and sewer networks for an area covering almost half the city. Subtronic is now pursuing other similar projects in Mexico where it is hoped the tremendous investment in environmental infrastructure will require their systems and expertise.'
>
> Source: *Overseas Trade*, April 1995

> ✎ CASE STUDY
> Cementation Piling & Foundations in Mexico
> This Croydon-based firm (part of Trafalgar House Construction) has provided some of the foundations and infrastructure for the Hilton Hotel in the centre of Mexico City. Grupo Sitra, a joint venture company which is 50% owned by Trafalgar House Construction, is the main contractor for the project which will help create a seven-level carpark beneath the 30-floor hotel and office tower.

Companies wishing to market their products in Mexico will find that a vast range of opportunities exist, but that care must be taken to ensure adherence to the local customs. The traditional pattern of entry to the Mexican market has been via direct exporting. The first possibility is that of direct sales to retail stores, government agencies, or other institutions. Whilst this type of activity is important, its growth is hindered by the size of many retail establishments which are small and unwilling to hold stocks, preferring small orders delivered rapidly to meet customer demand. The state enterprise sector, which accounted for around 17% of total imports in the early 1990s, will decline in importance with privatisation.

In the future exporters will normally enter the Mexican market using the skills of a local agent or distributor (sometimes referred to as importing distributors). Often the same person will operate in both roles, preferring an agency agreement even for the more sophisticated and expensive products (the more typical type of agency agreement, for capital products, is also found). Care must be taken in the choice of agent or distributor, because they will be the key representative for the company as far as its customers are concerned. More technical aspects also need to be noted, such as exclusivity arrangements, geographical coverage, contractual arrangements including commission, and so on.

For consumer goods the retail sector is changing gradually, but according to statistics provided by the National Association of Retail and Department Stores in Mexico, 80% of such stores are still small family-owned enterprises. These stores rely upon availability of the product and/or price for their competitive edge, and therefore demand a high level of service with respect to delivery schedules. More recent developments have been a growth of larger stores, such as the Cifra chain, in the more populated cities; and the appearance of US companies such as Wal-Mart Inc. Large cost-cutting factory outlets are not yet common in Mexico. Exporters need to be aware of the range of taxes that will affect their product, before agreeing a final price.

A more recent phenomenon has been the rapid growth of international franchise outlets, at a rate of around 25% per annum. Many of these are naturally of United States origin; few domestic Mexican franchise chains – for example Video Centro, Diversiones Moy or El Farolito – predate the late 1980s. Franchising as a method of market entry was relatively unknown prior to 1990, because of the strict regulations surrounding the operation of such companies. These governed all aspects of the business from royalties to duration. Deregulation in the 1991 Law for the Promotion and Protection of Industrial Property triggered the recent growth. The likely pattern is that this growth may slow as the Mexican consumer becomes more product-discerning, with a greater need to adapt the product to Mexican culture. Entry into the market through either joint ventures or foreign direct investment will be considered a little later in this chapter.

Adaptation of the product to the Mexican market is of great importance. Adaptation applies not only to the associated elements of the product such as manuals, where Mexican Spanish is required, but also to the core product – with a need for spicier food, for example, or shorter office furniture. Without such changes, acceptance of the product or service by the Mexican market is made extremely difficult. The issues of standards, product testing, certification and related matters were previously considered to be a formidable barrier to entry into the Mexican market, but with the adoption of the 1993 Standardisation and Metrology Law there has been a dramatic reduction in the number of product standards regulations, now reduced to just over 300.

Promotion of the product or service in Mexico also needs to be adapted to the local culture, at the minimum requiring translation of the promotional materials into Mexican Spanish. A wide variety of media, both of a general nature (e.g. regional and national newspapers) and also industry- or product-specific, is available within Mexico for advertising products or services. Similarly there are various radio stations, and two terrestrial television channels plus two cable services, although all these are not available throughout the country. In all cases, however, the prospective advertiser should be aware of the costs involved, which are presently higher than in many comparable markets. Tele-marketing has had little impact to date within the Mexican market, nor has the direct marketing sector. A major feature of marketing in Mexico remains the personal contact between buyer and seller. Similarly, the importance of personal relationships in business success must also be stressed.

The final aspect of marketing in Mexico relates to location. As in the other North American nations there are a series of regional markets, although the country is much smaller than the other two. The infrastructure system, including the transport network, is being rapidly developed, but there are still problems with respect to communications, although the number of major investment projects is growing. Hence some areas of the country are still relatively difficult to access. The greatest concentrations of population are to be found within the major metropolitan areas: Mexico City, which alone contains a quarter of the Mexican population; Guadalajara, the major financial and commercial centre in western Mexico (also nicknamed the Mexican silicon valley); Monterrey, located in the northern region and the second industrial city, with a strong manufacturing bias; and lastly Puebla, another important industrial centre.

Foreign investment in Mexico and the Maquiladora sector

Recent legislation has changed the foreign investment climate in Mexico dramatically from the regime of strict limitations imposed by the 1973 Law to Promote Mexican Investment and Regulate Foreign Investment. Under this law, all foreign investment was required to be registered with the Mexican Government, and ownership was limited to 49% of an enterprise. The effect of the law was naturally to discourage such investments, despite the growing domestic market (with the exception of those in the border areas – see below). The repeal of the restrictions began in 1989 when a series of criteria was stipulated (such as a maximum limit to foreign investment of $100m, and the meeting of environmental criteria) which if met would give investors automatic approval for their investment. In other cases government approval is still necessary. There are still some sectoral restrictions upon foreign investments, including forestry and air transportation. Other sectors have a restriction upon the degree of foreign ownership within enterprises; these include areas such as auto parts and carbon deposits. In total, however, over 75% of the economy is now open to foreign investment. In all cases the normal company incorporation criteria apply, as well as the national regulations that apply to Mexican-owned companies. Figure 9.7 shows the origin and sectoral composition of foreign direct investment in Mexico.

	Cumulative total (in billions of $)	Percentage share
Origin		
United States	19.1	63.0
Germany	2.0	6.6
United Kingdom	1.9	6.3
Japan	1.5	5.0
Switzerland	1.3	4.3
Other	4.5	14.9
Total	30.3	
Sector		
Industry	18.9	62.3
Services	8.8	29.0
Commerce	2.1	6.8
Extractive industries	0.5	1.6
Agriculture	0.1	0.3

Source: Table 4.3 in G.C. Hufbauer and J.J. Schott, *North American Free Trade*, Institute for International Economics, 1992

Figure 9.7   Mexico: foreign direct investment, 1990

A related market entry mechanism is that of joint ventures. Again, this has been encouraged by the liberalisation measures that have been taken by the Mexican government. Of specific importance for this activity, and also for licensed production, has been the changes in the laws relating to property rights. These were strengthened considerably in 1991 and 1994, and affected all elements of intellectual property rights. Patent protection was extended in both the number of years and the range of products and processes covered; copyright regulations were extensively revised to bring them into line with those in the United States; and trademark protection was given for ten-year renewable periods. Alongside the legal changes, there has been a clampdown on breaches of the laws, with US companies claiming widespread pirating of items such as audio and video tapes.

The exception to the previous restrictions with respect to foreign investment was under the Maquiladora programme, which was established originally under the title Border Industrialisation Programme (BIP) in 1965. The objective of the BIP was to reduce the level of unemployment and poverty in Mexico by allowing foreign companies to establish in the region bordering the United States (20 kilometres originally). An additional aspect of interest to both countries was the related reduction in migration across the border. (In some of the towns covered by this programme open unemployment was as high as 70%, leading to the desire to migrate across the Rio Grande.)

The programme has allowed foreign companies to take advantage of the low level of Mexican wages and assemble products duty-free from imported parts and components. The level of wages has been estimated at around one tenth of the levels found in the United States or Canada, and has even been quoted as half of the South Korean level. The products in these industries would then normally be exported, and this has contributed strongly to the growth in US-Mexico trade. These companies now are the second largest source of foreign exchange earnings for Mexico after the petroleum sector. If the goods were sold in the domestic market, they would lose their duty-free status and be eligible for various taxes.

The majority of Maquiladora companies are US-owned, but this disguises the fact that the US companies themselves may be subsidiaries of Japanese or South Korean companies. These wholly-owned firms are the major form of Maquiladora company. Others are either contract manufacturing operations, or wholly Mexican-owned in-bond assembly operations that can avoid various costs of business operations in Mexico and are popular amongst small and medium-sized companies. Recently the law has changed, allowing Maquiladora companies to be established throughout much of Mexico; but over 80% are still located in the border region. This is of course related to access to the United States and lower transportation costs.

United States

It is difficult to generalise about the various issues concerned with doing business with the United States, because of the great regional diversity that exists within the country; the suggested success factors for companies in one area may be very different from those that apply to another area. Consequently, the first issue that will be considered within this section is the regional diversity of markets.

Regionalism in the United States

The North American market is often considered by many exporters to consist of the markets of the three countries, namely the United States market, the Mexican market and the Canadian market. Furthermore, they have viewed each of these markets as a single unit in which the consumers have common tastes and consume similar products. In practice, as we have already seen, each of these countries contains a range of distinct markets with major differences in product choice and consumer behaviour. This may be illustrated by the accompaniments that consumers in the United States might choose with their hamburger. Typically the cola drunk in the South would be Coca Cola, whilst that in the North would be Pepsi Cola. Similarly, the northern consumer would choose Kraft Miracle Whip salad dressing, while those of the South would choose the blander Hellman's Mayonnaise – see Michael J. Weiss[1].

Typically markets are segmented initially on a geographical basis, which for an exporter has the obvious advantage of minimising logistical costs. It may well be cost-effective to concentrate sales activity in one region or state, rather than attempting to market to the whole of the United States or even to urban America. Transportation costs will be reduced, as will warehousing, distribution and even communications costs. This may be reinforced by varying consumer tastes and behaviour, as already shown in the cola and mayonnaise examples. The official geographical regional segmentation is given in Figure 9.8.

NEW ENGLAND	Connecticut, Maine, Massachusetts, New Hampshire, Rhode Island, Vermont
MIDDLE ATLANTIC	New Jersey, New York, Pennsylvania
EAST NORTH CENTRAL	Illinois, Indiana, Michigan, Ohio, Wisconsin
WEST NORTH CENTRAL	Iowa, Kansas, Minnesota, Missouri, Nebraska, North Dakota, South Dakota
SOUTH ATLANTIC	Delaware, District of Columbia, Florida, Georgia, Maryland, North Carolina, South Carolina, Virginia, West Virginia
EAST SOUTH CENTRAL	Alabama, Kentucky, Mississippi, Tennessee
WEST SOUTH CENTRAL	Arkansas, Louisiana, Oklahoma, Texas
MOUNTAIN	Arizona, Colorado, Idaho, Montana, Nevada, New Mexico, Utah, Wyoming
PACIFIC	Alaska, California, Hawaii, Oregon, Washington

Source: US Government Department of Commerce, *United States Census*, 1994

Figure 9.8   Geographical regions of the USA.

Such a geographical approach to market segmentation, whilst appealing in locational terms, may not be appropriate for the marketing manager; it certainly does not demonstrate the true diversity of the United States. For a better understanding of this diversity, alternative segments may need to be considered. This is best shown by consideration of particular aspects of this diversity. These may be initially viewed in some of the official statistical tables produced by the United States government departments, and reproduced in part below.

State	Area (sq. miles)	Land (sq. miles)
Alaska	656,424	570,374
Texas	268,601	261,964
California	163,707	155,973
•		
•		
Delaware	2,489	1,955
Rhode Island	1,545	1,045
Washington D.C.	68	61

Source: A. Carpenter and C. Provorse, *The World Almanac of the USA*, Funk and Wagnalls, 1993

Figure 9.9   Diversity of the states: the land

Figure 9.9 clearly illustrates the diversity of state land areas, ranging from the enormous Alaska to the minuscule Washington D.C. – a factor which has a direct impact upon logistical decisions. This is further complicated by the geographical features of the various states, with again a wide diversity ranging from the flat desert landscape of the Southwestern states (e.g. in parts of Arizona and New Mexico) to the mountains of

Colorado and Wyoming. Another important geographical feature for businesses that varies throughout the United States is the access to the important river traffic, for example on the Mississippi river.

State	Highest	State	Lowest
Arizona	105.0	Alaska	−21.6
Nevada	104.5	North Dakota	−5.1
California	98.8	Montana	−2.9
•		•	
•		•	
Vermont	80.5	Arizona	38.1
Maine	78.9	Florida	38.9
Alaska	71.8	Hawaii	65.3

Source: A. Carpenter and C. Provorse, *The World Almanac of the USA*, Funk and Wagnalls, 1993

Figure 9.10   Diversity of the states: climate (monthly average temperature)

Table 9.10 demonstrates a further element of the regional diversity of the United States, namely climatic variation. The impact that this will have upon consumer demand is self-evident, but less recognised is the impact that the climate has upon production. Climatic extremes either limit the locational decisions of companies, or alternatively have an impact upon energy costs, both heating and air conditioning.

Further climatic variation is shown by the statistics on vulnerability to earthquakes, cyclones, tornadoes and hurricanes. Again, this has a direct cost impact upon businesses, with building regulations in the affected areas which certainly reduce the impact of the climatic disturbance, but also increase the cost of construction and rents for businesses.

State	Total	State	Annual Growth
California	31.4	Nevada	5.4%
Texas	18.4	Arizona	3.3%
New York	18.2	Idaho	3.0%
•		•	
•		•	
North Dakota	0.6	Maine	None
Vermont	0.6	Connecticut	−0.1%
Wyoming	0.5	Rhode Island	−0.3%
United States	260.3	United States	1.0%

Source: A. Carpenter and C. Provorse, *The World Almanac of the USA*, Funk and Wagnalls, 1993

Figure 9.11   Diversity of the states: population (millions, July 1990)

From Figure 9.11 the wide variations in the population of the different states can be observed, together with the trend with respect to population growth. This is also reflected in the data if the official regional groupings are considered, as may be seen from Figure 9.12.

Region	Total
New England	13.3 mill.
Middle Atlantic	38.3 mill.
East North Central	43.4 mill.
West North Central	18.6 mill.
South Atlantic	46.9 mill.
East South Central	16.1 mill.
West South Central	28.6 mill.
Mountain	15.6 mill.
Pacific	41.9 mill.

Source: US Government Department of Commerce, *United States Census*, 1994

Figure 9.12   Diversity of the states: population by region

Once again, the areas of fastest population growth are the mountain areas of the Rockies and the Southern states, which will result in further variations in the regional populations. Exporters must, however, be cautious in using these regional classifications as their sole method for market segmentation, because although a population of 41.9 million in the Pacific region may appear to have greater market potential than the 13.3 million in New England, the latter region is tightly concentrated geographically compared to the Pacific region, which stretches along the whole of the west coast of the United States and also includes Alaska and the Hawaiian islands.

Two other important attributes of the population must be considered within the context of market choice – namely income levels and ethnic composition. Both these items will naturally affect consumer choice, and consequently market demand. The American population has often been described as a huge melting pot which continuously absorbs ethnic groupings from throughout the world. Indeed, the history of the United States is one of continuous immigration for either economic or political reasons (this would include religious persecution as well as asylum seekers), causing the original native Americans to become a minority race. The process has continued into the 1990s with fast-growing Asian and Hispanic communities. Figure 9.13 below attempts to encapsulate some of these differences by considering the states with the greatest proportion of certain ethnic groupings.

State	Percentage
MOST WHITE	
Vermont	98.64
Maine	98.41
New Hampshire	98.03
MOST BLACK	
Washington D.C.	65.84
Mississippi	35.56
Louisiana	30.79

MOST HISPANIC

New Mexico	39.42
California	25.83
Texas	25.55

MOST NATIVE AMERICAN

Alaska	15.58
New Mexico	8.87
Oklahoma	8.02

Source: A. Carpenter and C. Provorse, *The World Almanac of the USA*, Funk and Wagnalls, 1993

Figure 9.13   Diversity of the states: ethnic composition, 1990 (as a percentage of the state population)

The second consideration with respect to population that is important for marketers to consider relates to income levels. Again, a wide variation may be seen throughout the United States, which is illustrated in Figure 9.14.

State	Income per capita (dollars)	Household income (dollars)
Connecticut	20,189	41,721
Washington D.C.	18,881	30,727
New Jersey	18,174	40,927
●	●	
West Virginia	10,520	20,795
Arkansas	10,520	21,147
Mississippi	9,648	20,136

Sources: US Government Department of Commerce, *United States Census*, 1994; A. Carpenter and C. Provorse, *The World Almanac of the USA*, Funk and Wagnalls, 1993

Figure 9.14   Diversity of the states: income per capita and household income, 1989

Finally with respect to income differences across the different regions and states, Figure 9.15 considers the household income by ethnic group.

Ethnic grouping	Connecticut $	Mississippi $	USA $
All races	41,721	20,136	30.056
White	43,407	24,940	31,435
Black	28,011	11,625	19,758

Source: US Government Department of Commerce, *United States Census*, 1994

Figure 9.15   Diversity of the states: household income by ethnic origin, 1989

Figure 9.15 clearly illustrates not only the disparity of income levels between states, but also the disparity within states. In Connecticut and Mississippi the difference between the average household incomes of the two racial groupings is $15,396 and $13,315 respectively, whereas that for the United States as a whole is slightly less, at $11,677. More importantly, the variation between the household incomes of the two ethnic groups in Mississippi is over 100% whilst in Connecticut and in the USA as a whole it only averages around 55% to 60%. The importance of this for companies is naturally related to the level of potential demand for their products.

Each of the preceding tables illustrates different aspects of the variation and regional diversity that exists in the United States. Great care and much research is therefore necessary before doing business within the country. Products that are acceptable and have a strong demand in one geographical region may have little demand in another. An additional consideration is that the legislation of the states varies – a factor that has partly been responsible for the changing location of domestic industry within the United States. This is perhaps typified by the decline of the traditional manufacturing sector located in the East North Central and Middle Atlantic regions, and consequent loss of employment there, contrasted with the growth of the newer manufacturing industries in the Pacific and Mountain regions. A similar but less pronounced pattern may be seen in the services sector.

An alternative approach to market segmentation adopted by many marketers, which may be used either as a substitute for or in conjunction with geographical segmentation, is customer segmentation. This relies upon the identification of certain characteristics of customers, ranging from their income levels or racial groupings to their personal tastes and preferences. The most commonly identified characteristic on which market segmentation is undertaken is household income. This may either be considered in its own right, or used as a substitute for some other item for which data is more difficult or expensive to collect. In the case of the United States, as already suggested, this measure would commonly be used in conjunction with geographical segmentation. If necessary, a third characteristic relating to ethnic origin is also commonly used in studies, alongside the geographical and income-related segments. Age and sex information may then be used to refine the study further.

The use of customer segmentation in relation to magazine readership may be seen in Figure 9.16.

Magazine	Target reader
Car and Driver	Male; aged 34/35; professional
Cosmopolitan	Female; aged 18/34; middle-income
Esquire	64% male; aged 30/49; upper middle income
Penthouse	Male; aged 18/34; upper income
Sassy	Female; aged 13/19

Source: Adapted from L. Eckert, J.D. Ryan and R.J. Ray, *Small Business* (3rd edition), Dryden Press, 1993

Figure 9.16

A more interesting approach has been adopted by other marketers, who have extended this analysis and attempted to segment Americans using a cluster of identifiable lifestyle characteristics. A. Mitchell[2] adopts this method, and identifies nine distinctive groups or clusters within the American population, associated with particular lifestyles and values. These he categorises as Survivors, Sustainers, Belongers, Emulators, Achievers, I-Am-Me, Experientials, the Socially Conscious and finally the Integrated. The first three categories. he suggests, are need-driven with low levels of income; the next two groups are outward-directed, as opposed to the inward-directed lifestyles of the following three groups. The final category, the Integrated, have reached a physiologically mature state and are both tolerant and understanding.

An alternative methodology for clustering may be seen in the portrait of the United States drawn up by Michael Weiss[3]. He identifies forty clusters in his original text, ranging from the Blue Blood Estates through the Old Yankee Rows and the Golden Ponds to the Public Assistance cluster. Again, each of the clusters has been constructed using a series of demographic, lifestyle and value indicators. The larger number of indicators enables business organisations to identify their potential target cluster more readily. For example, compared to the average American, the high income Blue Blood Estates cluster is more likely to read *Barron's* magazine, drive a Rolls Royce, drink bottled water and watch David Letterman. Conversely, it is less likely to read *Ebony* magazine, drive Dodge Diplomats, drink powdered fruit drinks or watch American Bandstand. Contrasted to this cluster are the low-income Tobacco Roads people, who are more likely to be seen reading *Southern Living* magazine, driving Pontiac Bonnevilles, drinking canned tea and watching American Bandstand than the average American. Conversely they are less likely to be found reading *Rolling Stone* or *Ms.* magazines, driving Ferraris, eating Mexican food or watching the Tonight Show.

Not only does this type of segmentation method again demonstrate the diversity of the American population, but it has the added advantage that, because of the larger number of clusters identified by Weiss, a geographical linkage may also be made. Hence the Blue Blood Estates cluster is most likely to be found in the states of Maryland and Virginia, whereas the Tobacco Roads cluster is most likely to live in the Carolinas, Georgia, Mississippi and Arkansas. Further, it should be noted that whilst each of these clusters has a relationship with levels of income data, several clusters may have a similar average household or per capita income and yet exhibit different characteristics. For instance the Hard Scrabble cluster, who have a similar average income level to the Tobacco Roads cluster, nevertheless show different characteristics – preferring to watch Wheel of Fortune, use dried milk and drive Mercury Marquises more than the average American; they are concentrated in the states of New Mexico, the Dakotas, West Virginia and the southern part of Texas, amongst others.

All the preceding information clearly indicates the rich regional diversity to be found within the United States and the importance of treating the country as a combination of contrasting markets. This is further reinforced if consideration is given to the non-contiguous states of Alaska and Hawaii, which exhibit profound differences from the rest of the United States.

Marketing in the United States

> CASE STUDY
> Endorsement advertising
>
> Winning the baseball, basketball, football or hockey finals in North America results in the earning of large sums of money for the most highly prized players. Indeed, many players earn more off the field of play than on it, via product endorsements. One of the latest stars of basketball, Shaquille O'Neill of the Orlando Magic, may be seen in advertisements endorsing Pepsi Cola, All Sport drinks and most importantly Reebok sports shoes. Many teenagers may be seen wearing Reebok trainers with the legend SHAQ emblazoned around the back of the shoe. These endorsements, it is estimated, earned Shaq O'Neill more than $12 million in 1994. This, however, was estimated to be only half of that earned through endorsements by Michael Jordan, who appeared endorsing Nike sports shoes, McDonald's and Hanes underwear.
>
> Similar patterns may be seen in the other major North American sports; baseball, hockey and football stars may be seen on most television channels. Endorsement advertising, however, is not confined to sports stars, and 1995 saw Pizza Hut being endorsed by the famous entrepreneur Donald Trump and his ex-wife Ivana. A similar pattern may be observed in other countries, with their sports stars – such as Gary Lineker in the United Kingdom – or even ex-politicians being featured!

Once the regional location of the proposed business or export market has been chosen, it is appropriate to consider the other elements of the marketing mix. The first of these is the distribution methods needed to ensure that the goods or services produced will reach the potential customer. Normally, for exporters, the mechanism requires the use of a representative, whether this may be an importer (distributor), agent or broker. The broker would act as a facilitator between the seller and purchaser, without having a formal contract with either party.

Beyond the broker, companies may have a well-developed wholesale and retail network. In the case below, Laura Ashley established a network of retail outlets, backed up by licences to local manufacturers to supply goods under the Laura Ashley brand.

> CASE STUDY
> The growth of Laura Ashley in the United States
>
> In the United States, Laura Ashley, the British clothing and furnishing business, is seen by the customer as a high-quality exclusive designer label with a special English and romantic appeal. In the period to 1985, sales of clothing represented around two-thirds of total Laura Ashley sales by value in the United States, a much higher proportion than elsewhere in the group. This reflected a difference in consumer habits in the United States, where a higher proportion of furnishing consumers than in the United Kingdom use the services of professional interior designers and decorators. The group responded to this difference by establishing decorator collection showrooms, which sold to the interior designers in specialist centres. Consultancies were also established to provide a complete interior design service for clients in their own homes.

Rapid expansion in the United States was facilitated by the relatively low capital costs of establishing shops, compared with the United Kingdom. More than two-thirds of Laura Ashley shops were located in modern shopping malls. Rentals were generally turnover-related, and Laura Ashley was attractive to mall developers as a tenant because of its high sales per square foot.

The catalogues used in the United States were similar to those issued in the United Kingdom. They were made available to generate interest in the shops, and also to increase general consumer awareness of the Laura Ashley name. The catalogues were also used for mail order activity in the United States.

The group granted a number of licences to United States manufacturers. The major licence was with Burlington Domestics, which had exclusive rights in the United States to manufacture and sell bed linen and bathroom accessories, the design of which was under the full control of the group. These products were sold in major department stores throughout the United States as well as in Laura Ashley shops. Other licences were arranged with Henredon Furniture Industries Inc., which manufactured and sold in the United States a range of furniture upholstered in Laura Ashley fabrics; and with Raintree Designs Inc., which produced a range of furnishing fabrics, vinyl and other wall-coverings sold through interior design stores in the United States, Puerto Rico and Canada. The group also had an agreement with the McCall Pattern Company for the production of dress patterns to Laura Ashley designs which were sold world-wide by the group.

The company also made a temporary, less successful, foray into the acquisition of domestic American businesses, including Willis and Geiger, an outdoor clothing specialist, and Revman Industries Inc., a home furnishings company. Willis and Geiger was rapidly divested, having failed to integrate into the Laura Ashley brand. Further, more successful, US expansion came with a segmentation strategy reflected in the opening of a chain of mother and child shops to add to the company's direct and licensed clothing and furnishing operations.

Together with the marketing of a perfumery range through its retail outlets, these operations resulted in a US turnover in excess of £130 million in the early 1990s.

Source: adapted from G Johnson and K Scholes, *Exploring Corporate Strategy*, 1993, p. 501

Few overseas companies will employ their own sales staff without a substantial investment having previously taken place within the country. Even if this has occurred, there is still a strong likelihood that a representative will be chosen rather than company sales staff, because of the costs of employment compared to commission. Exceptions to this principle are those companies which sell their products to an exporter management company that purchases products on behalf of specific clients (e.g. large department stores); and those that sell direct to the customer through catalogues or through their own outlets (such as IKEA), or are selling large producer goods. As in the other North American countries, the rules relating to representatives allow for multiple agencies to be held, and for individuals or companies to act as both importer and agent for different products. The choice of representative is therefore an important aspect of business in United States markets. One further aspect of this choice is that many importers and agents are unwilling to become involved in warehousing and onward distribution from locations in the USA; this may require the company to involve itself in these activities.

Normally manufacturers must not assume that products successful within Europe will automatically be suitable for the US markets without adaptation; and even when they prove successful in one geographical area or region, this will not necessarily mean acceptance throughout the nation. A crucial aspect of product adaptation will be to meet the technical and legal standards and requirements of the United States. Not only is it necessary to register certain items such as pharmaceuticals with the federal agencies, but a myriad of safety standards and testing regulations need to be met. This has led to the need to use standards and benchmarks developed in both public and private sector bodies. Trademark, patent and copyright legislation is a well accepted aspect of US business operations, and it is often found that the coverage is broader and more comprehensive than in similar European legislation, giving firms like Laura Ashley the brand protection they need. Trade secrets may also be protected, although this is done at a state level and varies across the nation. The definition of trade secret is any information that is not generally known, has value to the business and is kept secret in any reasonable circumstances.

Probably the legislation that most concerns many companies operating in North America is that dealing with product liability. Examples are rife throughout the world of companies losing many million dollars in legal cases relating to product liability, and this factor is generally held responsible for the collapse of the General Aviation manufacturing sector in the United States. Recently a further item has begun to affect business operations, and has been featured widely in the discussions on the admittance of Mexico to the NAFTA agreement; it concerns environmental compliance regulations and the related code of conduct for business ethics. Both these items are very likely to continue to be important into the foreseeable future.

Markets in the United States are often considered to be the most price-sensitive consumer and producer markets in the world. Whether this reputation is correct or not, it is certainly true that markets within the United States are highly price-sensitive. A high level of customer service is also emphasised, with many retail outlets operating a policy of meeting the price that competitors charge, and also of changing items previously purchased without question. Consequently pricing is a key determinant within the marketing process in the United States markets. Profit margins are often reduced to low levels, with a preference for a strategy that relies upon a large volume of sales. Both importers and retailers will often expect automatic discounts on bulk purchases, and customers are very often attracted by direct price reductions or couponing techniques. Exporters must, however, be careful to avoid price reductions that lead to a suspicion of dumping, a most sensitive aspect of business operations in the United States.

Finally, the choice of marketing communications media in the United States is extremely broad and at times confusing to the overseas sales manager. Whether direct marketing, selling or advertising is considered, the possible options are numerous. For Laura Ashley, catalogues sent by direct mail were an important means of promotion. Also, the legal restrictions that apply to these choices are less than in many European countries; the visitor should not be surprised to see large billboards alongside a freeway (motorway), or a large number of negative political advertisements at every state and national election.

Whilst media availability is similar to that found in Europe, it is useful to outline a few differences. Taking newspapers first, the regional diversity of US markets is reinforced by the fact that only two newspapers (the *Wall Street Journal* and *US Today*) out of the 1600 available have a national distribution. Second, the large number of television and radio stations again tend to offer only local geographical coverage. A third difference is the much greater use of direct marketing techniques such as tele-marketing (which has a long history of use within the USA), direct mail shots and catalogues, and mail order sales. Recently new forms of direct marketing have begun to appear, with electronic shopping malls featuring on the Internet (the so-called electronic highway), and home shopping television channels. Direct marketing applications have importance because of the low geographical population density.

Foreign investment and the small business sector

CASE STUDY
Mail order success

1994 was an important year for Fanfare Enterprises because the two owners, Marty and Carolyn Singer, were chosen as Runner-up New Hampshire Small Business Administration Persons of the Year. They had managed in the space of thirteen years to develop from a business idea to a $22 million company. Marty and Carolyn had dreamed of running a small business, and following numerous discussions decided to go for it. They launched their mail order music and performing arts-related gifts business in 1982. Both had an interest and background in the arts, and believed that their business would serve a niche in the market. During the early years they faced difficult circumstances, as do many mail order businesses.

The development of an appropriate database of names and addresses is crucial to success and low costs. Therefore money spent on purchasing or renting existing customer databases is not always effective. Similarly, large mailings of catalogues to the wrong people are also extremely costly. Not only did the couple have to face these difficulties, but they also met the further obstacle of a global recession in the late 1980s. Despite these adversaries, the couple enabled their business to grow, and by 1995 had 75 full-time employees and over a hundred seasonal workers. They believe a major factor in their success is their belief in people making it happen. They have followed this philosophy, and now have a dedicated work force.

Source: adapted from text on the Small Business Administration World Wide Web home page

CASE STUDY
Pasta growth

Advice and assistance from the Small Business Administration's sponsored programme in central Virginia (the Small Business Development Centre) have been credited as important in the rise of Pasta by Valente. The company was started 12 years ago by Mary Ann Valente and her mother Fran Valente. They believed their own traditional pasta was better than that available locally, and started selling home-produced pasta at the local farmer's market each weekend. This developed into a pasta and pasta sauce business, and soon demand was increasing. With the purchase of a new pasta machine, they were able to start increasing output and sold their produce further afield. The business continued to grow, and with the purchase of newer machines and a network of independent sales representatives they had by 1995 expanded their output to 12,000 pounds of pasta a month. A far cry from the original five pounds a week!

Source: adapted from text on the Small Business Administration World Wide Web home page

It is important to recognise that the legal system in the United States is different from that in Europe in many respects, and that the business environment includes a large number of legal restrictions at both federal and state level. One must realise too that not only will this legislation be used by the public bodies to ensure compliance, it will also be used by competitors. Consequently, it has sometimes been suggested that far from being a free market economy, the US economy has a strongly regulated environment. Whilst this latter view is greatly exaggerated, there are numerous regulations that businesses should be aware of, if they wish to undertake operations in the United States. It is therefore advisable to use a legal adviser, and such people are commonly employed by companies of all sizes in the United States.

In keeping with the description of the United States as the epitome of a free market economy is the attitude of the US government to foreign investment. The government has been in the forefront of the demands for greater worldwide openness to direct foreign investment. At the federal level, the government itself has operated a policy that accords with this philosophy; it offers foreign companies investing in the US the same treatment as that offered to national companies. Furthermore, the federal government encourages such investments, although no special incentives (or disincentives) are offered. The same policy broadly operates at the state level, but there are numerous cases where states have introduced specific legislation limiting foreign investment in selected sectors. An example is Hawaii's recent restrictions limiting foreign ownership of real estate, which are aimed primarily at the Japanese. Exceptions to the general open door policy also apply to specific sectors – most importantly financial services, farmland and mineral land; and certain restrictions are applied in the interests of national security.

Small business is crucial to understanding the dynamics of, and change within, the United States private sector as a whole. The number of businesses is difficult to calculate because of the statistical definition adopted, which relates closely to the reason for the collection of the statistics. Tax returns give a very high count of businesses, around 21 million, whereas other counts only total around 5 million – a major difference being whether the business is a part-time or full-time occupation. Whichever statistic is chosen, most sources agree that there are fewer than 8,000 companies with more than 700 employees in the United States, and 98% of businesses employ fewer than 20 people. A recent report to the President[4] suggests that small business has played a crucial role in the creation of new jobs; 75% of new jobs come from new businesses. Small business is responsible for 58% of employment outside of the farm sector, is important in the introduction of new goods and services, and is at the forefront of organisational changes – leading the way, for competitive reasons, in customer service.

Each year there are more than 500,000 business incorporations in the United States, alongside which must be placed around 90,000 failures every year. The half-life of the typical small business has been calculated at only just over 4 years – i.e. half of all new small firms fail within four years. Despite this mortality rate the share of small business employment in total employment is growing, because the industrial sectors that are growing most rapidly have a high proportion of their employees within such businesses. This demonstrates the role that such companies have in growth and innovation. The pattern has been reinforced during the recession of the 1990s, with these companies showing great resilience.

A related aspect is the acceptance of business failure, and the culture of entrepreneurship, that is evident in the United States population. Less stigma is attached to a failed business executive, and there is a strong infrastructure to aid companies and prevent failure, as evidenced by the Small Business Administration which operates numerous programmes to help and advise small business managers. Examples of such programmes include Small Business Investment Companies (SBICs), which provide venture capital, and the Minority Business Development Agency (MBDA) which offers assistance to minority groups.

✎ **CASE STUDY**
   Disaster means success

The threat of earthquakes and other disasters has led to a successful business idea for Karen Hicks of Southern California. Karen graduated from a management programme and chose to set up a business producing emergency preparedness kits. Working from her home, she raised an initial capital of $10,000, and so began Red Suspenders. During the first year sales amounted to only $2000, but demand was growing. She soon realised that further growth would require new equipment, which would mean a loan. She also realised that to obtain the loan she would need a professional business plan. To help her compile such a plan she enrolled on a course offered by the Coalition for Women's Economic Development (CWED), which also offers loans for micro-businesses from funds provided by the Small Business Administration. This enabled her to write a successful plan, and she received a loan from CWED for $5000. A report on the Internet said that she expected her 1994 sales to double to $50,000.

Source: adapted from text on the Small Business Administration World Wide Web home page

---

Some of the programmes offered operate through local agencies which provide a variety of help either to specific communities or to industries. This leads to differences in the support infrastructure and business facilitation that small businesses may receive throughout the nation, as Figure 9.17 indicates. The figure shows part of a chart produced by the Corporation for Enterprise Development, classifying suitability for location by state for an entrepreneur starting a small business.

Rank	State
1	Colorado
2	Idaho
3	California
4	Utah
5	New Mexico
•	
•	
46	New Jersey
47	Rhode Island
48	Oklahoma
48	Louisiana
50	New Hampshire

Source: Corporation for Enterprise Development, *Report on Small Business*, 1993

Figure 9.17   Entrepreneurial location by state

The compilers of the chart, the Corporation for Enterprise Development, are a non-profit research group. They drew up the classification according to the following criteria:

1 State economic performance
2 Business vitality
3 Development capacity
4 Small business culture
5 Small business assistance environment
6 Balanced tax/fiscal system

This demonstrates yet again the regional diversity with respect to business operation in the United States.

Small businesses may take a variety of forms, but one of the most successful in terms of survival is the franchised operation. Franchising is often viewed as synonymous with United States fast food outlets. This, however, is a misrepresentation of the true picture; most service businesses have their franchised outlets, with growth most recently in the area of professional services. These would include educational, legal, architectural, accountancy and dental services. The importance of franchising within the United States may be seen from the following statistics quoted by Hodgetts and Kuratko[5]. Franchising has been estimated by the US Department of Commerce to account for 34% of all retail sales, totalling $813.4 billion in 1992 from a total of almost 570,000 outlets. Furthermore, a survey of US franchises by the same authors[6] published in the *Wall Street Journal* showed that 97% of them remained in business after 5 years, with 86% owned by the original franchisee.

CASE STUDY
Niche markets

The entrepreneurial motive is encouraged by governments throughout the world, although the support given to small businesses varies dramatically. One of the more well-known of these agencies is the Small Business Administration in the United States. Despite the existence of such agencies business success can never be guaranteed, however much support is given. One factor that increases the likelihood of success is the choice of a unique product or service.

Where a unique product is impossible, it is still possible for small businesses to prosper in the most competitive of markets by choosing a niche segment. Examples of these are numerous. In the retail sector more and more products are being sold through low price general stores such as Wal-Mart, or specialist superstores such as Tower Records, or national/regional franchised outlets such as Wendy Restaurants. In all of these product sectors small retailers survive and are profitable by choosing a niche within the sector. A walk through any shopping mall will illustrate this example. Amongst the franchised or chain outlets such as FootLocker, Gap or Radio Shack you will find the independents. These may be retailers of shareware software, crafted native American jewellery or specialist music. Each is within a market sector occupied by major players, but each can prosper by choosing a niche.

Success can, however, bring difficulties along with it, as competitors search for new profitable markets and choose to compete directly. Bookshops such as Borders have opened coffee bars, Blockbuster Video have specialist music sections, and COMPUSA computer superstores sell all types of software alongside computers and computer parts.

Summary

To conclude this chapter, it is enough to state that the North American nations offer a range of diverse opportunities to potential exporters or foreign investors; but that the choice of market is critical. Market research must be undertaken to gain a knowledge of this diversity, and to understand better the opportunities that exist.

CASE STUDY
The Internet shopping mall

1994 saw a huge growth in both the ownership of personal computers within the United States and the linkage of these computers to the Internet, termed the electronic highway. (It has been estimated that in 1994 there were over 2.5 million hosts connected to the Internet.) This growth interested many companies, and several retailers believed it to be an alternative to either personal or catalogue shopping. The possible cost savings of such an idea were enormous, with no need to maintain costly stores with sales employees, nor large stocks for customers to peruse. The electronic shop required only a site on the Internet, the contents of which could be updated on a daily basis; a batch of telephones together with staff to answer them;

and good supplier contacts that enabled items to be delivered direct from the manufacturer.

Retailers believed that ordering through the Internet rather than via telephone would be the next step in the reduction of costs, with the computer system itself transmitting the customer's orders to the suppliers. Unfortunately, few customers at that point trusted the electronic mail system enough to allow their credit card details to be transmitted. However, *USA Today* reported in March 1995 that this reluctance might change with the latest application developed by the Wells Fargo group. Wells Fargo had developed software designed to lock credit card data in a computer-encoded electronic envelope that prevented their contents being intercepted and read by unauthorised users. KPMG Peat Marwick had reported that with a safety feature installed into the computer system, electronic sales could become a $600 billion business by the year 2000.

Source: adapted from *USA Today*, 14.3.95

Questions for discussion

1 What do you consider to be the potential for sales via the Internet in each of the three countries of NAFTA? How far has electronic payment via the Internet developed since the *US Today* report quoted in the case study?

2 Assume the role of an adviser to a company considering exporting to North America. Using a product of your choice, explain to the potential exporter how regionalism might affect the market for its products.

3 Write a short report for a popular business journal that predicts the likely effects of NAFTA on each of the present three member countries, five and ten years into the future.

Further reading

There are few books on North American business available in the UK. The list below comprises a variety of texts which address issues related to North American business topics, together with official documents. It is worth noting also that a variety of materials is now available on the Internet.

I.A. Bryan, *Canada in the New Global Economy*, Wiley, 1994.

D. Cameron (ed.), *The Free Trade Deal*, Lorimer Press, 1988.

A. Carpenter and C. Provorse, *The World Almanac of the USA*, World Almanac (Funk and Wagnalls), 1993.

J. Crispo (ed.), *Free Trade: The Real Story*, Gage Educational Publishing Co, 1988.

L. Eckert, J.D. Ryan and R.J. Ray, *Small Business* (3rd edition), Dryden Press, 1993.

R.M. Hodgetts and D.F. Kuratko, *Effective Small Business Management* (5th edition), Dryden Press, 1995.

G. C. Hufbauer and J.J. Schott, *North American Free Trade*, Institute for International Economics, 1992.

H. Noponen, J. Graham and A.R. Markusen (eds.), *Trading Industries Trading Regions*, Guilford Press, 1993.

A.M. Rugman and R. M Hodgetts, *International Business*, McGraw Hill, 1995.

United Kingdom Department of Trade and Industry, *Trading with Canada*, 1993.

United Kingdom Department of Trade and Industry, *Trading with the United States*, 1993.

United States Government, *The North American Free Trade Area Agreement*, 1993.

United States Government Department of Commerce, *Country Commercial Guide: Canada*, 1994.

United States Government Department of Commerce, *Country Commercial Guide: Mexico*, 1994.

United States Government Department of State, *Background Notes: Canada*, 1992.

United States Government Department of State, *Background Notes: Mexico*, 1993.

United States Government International Trade Administration, *Overseas Business Report: Canada*, 1993.

United States Government, *Report to the President – The State of Small Business*, 1992.

United States Small Business Administration, *Opportunities in Mexico – A Small Business Guide*, 1992.

United States Small Business Administration: various information sheets on programmes

M.J. Weiss, *The Clustering of America*, Tilden Press, 1989.

Notes

1 M.J. Weiss, *The Clustering of America*, Tidlen Press, 1989.

2 A. Mitchell, *Nine American Lifestyles: Who Are We, and Where Are We Going?*, Warner Books, 1983

3 See note 1 above.

4 United States Government, *Report to the President – The State of Small Business*, 1992.

5 R.M. Hodgetts and D.F. Kuratko, *Effective Small Business Management* (5th edition), Dryden Press, 1995.

6 R.M. Hodgetts and D.F. Kuratko, *Wall Street Journal*, 15 October 1993.

10 European business in Japan

Objectives

By the end of this chapter, you will be able to:

- show basic knowledge about the Japanese economy and industries.
- have insight into Japanese management styles.
- understand the Japanese consumer market and distribution system.
- understand how European firms should go about entering the Japanese market.

Introduction

> ✎ CASE STUDY
> Tibbett plc
>
> Sitting behind his plain desk in a clean, modest office in the modest company he has built virtually from scratch, the chairman and managing director of Tibbett plc does not appear to be wholly content. The company ships 50 per cent of its production of quality outergarments to the Japanese market place, where they are sold almost as fast as they arrive, but Abe Tibbett feels that he has still not achieved what he would like. Tibbett plc, based in Wellingborough, Northamptonshire, has quietly become a model of how a small company can enter the Japanese market place, compete with some of the biggest names in quality clothing, and succeed.

The company's marketing strategy in Japan is based on developing direct business with large retailers and manufacturers. This policy allows it to secure bulk orders and follow-on orders, while allowing the customer to take care of the entire consumer-oriented promotional and marketing side of the business itself. Typically, a senior Tibbett executive will visit Japan five or six times a year. Tibbett has found that this approach is very effective in the Japanese market; close attention to detail pays off handsomely in Japan. As Chairman of one of the UK clothing industry's real success stories, Abe Tibbett is far from sanguine about his exporting triumphs to date. With half of his export sales to the Japanese market, he knows that success has to be earned.

Source: adapted from Stephen Kremer, `Quality Exports: Tibbett Targets Japan', *Anglo-Japanese Journal,* Vol. 6 No. 2, pp. 16-18, 1992

To succeed in the Japanese market, Western companies not only need quality goods, but must also understand Japan's culture, history, management styles and economic development path, as well as its policies on technological development.

The early history of Japan is shrouded in mythology; it is believed that large numbers of people migrated from the Asian mainland to the Japanese archipelago via Korea. Japan probably began to become something like a nation at the beginning of the fourth century AD, and the first permanent capital was founded at Nara, not far from Kyoto, in 710. The country was greatly influenced by Chinese culture and by Buddhism. Until the mid-19th century Japan was a feudal society governed by a military ruler. The restoration of the authority of the Meiji emperor in 1868 was followed by the setting up of a parliamentary system, though with very limited power. During the US occupation (1942-1952) after Japan's disastrous defeat in the Pacific War, a radical land reform programme was undertaken and the *zaibatsu* (business conglomerates) were nominally broken up. Under the guidance of the occupation authorities, the 1947 constitution reduced the emperor's role, previously regarded by many Japanese as god-like, to being merely a symbol of the state. This has had a profound impact on Japan's economic 'miracle'.

The country comprises four main islands: heavily populated and industrialised Honshu; forested and mountainous Hokkaido in the north; the southernmost of the four, Kyushu; and the smallest, Shikoku. While the emperor remains head of state, legislative authority resides entirely with the Parliament or Diet, the upper house of which is the House of Councillors (252 members) and the lower house the House of Representatives (512 members). The prime minister is head of government.

The Japanese economy and industry

Since the immediate post-war reconstruction period, the Japanese economy has been characterised by high levels of savings and investment, a high rate of productivity growth, and rapid economic expansion. During the 1950s and 1960s the average annual rate of real GDP growth was 10 per cent, with investment in plant and equipment growing at an annual average rate of 22 per cent. In 1965 Japan's nominal GNP was only 10 per cent of that of the USA, but by 1990 it had reached 53.3 per cent. Whereas the annual real GNP growth rate in 1987-1991 averaged 1.9 per cent for the US economy, it was 4.9 per cent in Japan. Today, Japan's economy is the second largest of the OECD group. It is also one of the fastest growing, and is catching up with the USA as the major trading economy in the world.

Many observers believe that the role of industrial planning and state intervention has been important in Japan's success. Others look elsewhere to account for that success. In comparison with other developed industrialised economies, Japan has its own unique characteristics. The major elements are as follows:

● It has enjoyed low inflation and a muted business cycle.
● It saves more and invests more.
● It has a marked preponderance of smaller firms.
● It has unusual (and interconnected) economic customs and institutions, including

a tradition of co-operation between management and labour; life-time employment; a corporate alliance among many members of *keiretsu* groupings (conglomerates with a key company surrounding smaller firms within the group) and a financial system that in various ways lowers the cost of capital for industry.

- It had the great advantage of being a 'late developer'. It could acquire proven manufacturing technologies from the other developed countries.

During the early 1980s Japan's trade surplus rose rapidly, from $18 billion in 1982 to $96 billion in 1987. This trend has carried on into the 1990s. The Japanese twelve-month trade balance figures ending June 1994 showed a surplus of $144.9bn. The performance of Japan's export industries was encouraged by the strength of the dollar, and weakness of the yen, until 1985 when the 'Plaza Agreement' led to a rapid and dramatic appreciation of the yen. Against the dollar, the yen rose by about 80 per cent to a rate of ¥133 by September 1988, before levelling out to an average rate of ¥138 during 1989. Against sterling, it appreciated rather less rapidly, by about 40 per cent to a rate of ¥225.

Initially, the effects on the Japanese economy were far-reaching. Real GNP growth fell from 5.1 per cent in 1984 to 2.5 per cent in 1986. The appreciation of the yen had a severe impact upon traditional industries, such as coal mining, steel and shipbuilding, which were already facing intense competition from abroad. Other export industries, such as motor vehicles, electronics and other consumer goods also faced intense cost pressures. However, Japanese companies moved swiftly to adjust to the effects of yen appreciation, by diversifying into other products and markets, cutting costs and margins in order to maintain export volumes, and in some cases setting up manufacturing or assembly operations in overseas countries which could often lower costs.

The broad structure of Japan's economy does resemble that of other large OECD nations. Manufacturing accounts for 29% of nominal GDP, and services (including distribution) for just over half. By contrast, agriculture, mining and related activities between them accounted for only 2.6% of GDP in 1991. As a result Japan's major imports have been oil and food, although these are now exceeded by manufactured imports. Whereas in 1984 manufactured imports were still worth less than 30% of the total value of Japanese imports, by 1992 their share had risen to over 50%. In 1975 about 13% of those in work – defined as employees, the self-employed and family workers – were in the agriculture, forestry and fishing sectors. By 1992 the figure had fallen to 6.4%. Manufacturing employment in the manufacturing sector, as a percentage of the total employed, was 25.8%. By 1983 the figure had slipped to 24.5% but, with some fluctuations, has since fallen only slightly to 24.4% in 1992.

Recent developments

Recessionary conditions following falls in asset prices, as Japan's 'bubble' economy collapsed, brought Japan's real GNP growth rate down to only 1.5% in 1992. Most of the top 10 Japanese firms had lost money in 1992 (see Figure 10.1). With the sharp rise of the yen (to below ¥100/dollar) more and more Japanese firms have been shifting production abroad, as the plunge of asset prices and slow-down of the Japanese economy have dented corporate profits. This is causing a serious threat to employment at home.

At the same time, the need to reduce costs substantially in order to maintain cost competitiveness has also led to increased purchases of components from cheaper sources outside Japan. Those moves may help to maintain the competitiveness of the large manufacturers, but the worry is that they are hurting the vast number of Japanese component makers which have been a crucial factor behind the country's industrial might. While moving out their low-technology production, the large companies have been focusing on energy and on R and D in high-tech areas.

Rank	Company	1992	1991	Rank	1990	Rank
1	Toyota	3,758	5,743	1	7,338	1
2	NTT	2,488	3,528	2	4,143	2
3	Sanwa Bank	1,953	2,073	4	2,267	6
4	Nintendo	1,637	1,562	10	1,403	18
5	Tokyo Electric Power	1,583	1,468	12	1,282	21
6	Fuji Photo Film	1,512	1,689	6	1,602	15
7	Mitsubishi Heavy Industry	1,407	1,554	11	1,526	16
8	Shimizu Construction	1,326	1,244	17	1,157	24
9	Mitsubishi Bank	1,306	1,688	7	1,840	10
10	Kansai Electric Power	1,235	1,415	14	1,097	28

Source: The Wako Research Institute of Economics

Figure 10.1   Top 10 Japanese companies by pre-tax profits (¥00m)

The key industries

Japan's performance in a number of industries illustrates her position in the world economy. Japan's manufacturing sector is the backbone of the economy; it is mostly privately owned, and almost all domestically owned. Most firms are very small, and the relatively few industrial giants account for an overwhelming share of total output and employment.

The Japanese car industry is Japan's major export earner and one of its success stories. Japanese car production is the largest in the world (9 million passenger cars and 4 million commercial vehicles in 1989). Among the 30 largest world auto manufacturers, there are eight Japanese firms – from Toyota, the third largest, to the 21st largest, Isuzu[1]. Until 1990, strong domestic demand made up for exports, which had been gradually falling since 1987 because of their displacement through local production elsewhere. But in 1991–1992 domestic sales declined for two consecutive years. In the face of what appeared likely to be a prolonged slump in exports, the Japanese automobile industry has been seeking both to stimulate domestic demand and to evolve a strategy of heavy outward investment in production facilities to cut costs and avoid protectionism.

Japan is one of the foremost producers of electronic and electrical products. Despite slackening domestic demand for electronic products in the early 1990s, the industries which have been showing the best growth prospects in recent years are high-value-added areas, such as electronics and precision machinery. Japan's output of electrical appliances is the largest in the world. In the domestic PC market, Japanese PC makers' dominance has for the first time begun to be threatened by foreign competition, with the arrival of Compaq and Dell on the scene.

The Japanese steel industry was inspired to diversify after the rapid appreciation of the yen and a slowing of domestic demand following the Plaza Agreement in 1985. Steel production fell from 105m tonnes in 1985 to 98m tonnes a year later, and the leading makers slipped into the red during 1987. Nevertheless, production of crude steel in 1989 was the second highest in the world, after that of the USSR. There is growing competition from imports, and slower economic growth in the early 1990s reduced domestic demand for steel products, with the result that 1992 output was only 98.1m tonnes.

The country's shipbuilding industry, despite recent dramatic cutbacks in capacity, is still the world's largest, representing half of the world's shipping tonnage in 1989. The shipbuilding industry has engaged in radical rationalisation and improved its competitiveness, but there has been only a small revival in output, to 6.8m tonnes gross weight in 1992.

Japan is also a leading producer in the field of chemicals and in other high-technology industries. In response to competition from the newly-industrialised countries and elsewhere, the country has for several years been following a policy of switching from high-energy and high-labour intensive industries such as shipbuilding and textiles to high-technology, high-value-added industries such as semiconductors, industrial robots and computers.

New technologies

In order to remain competitive in international markets, Japan has for several years been focusing on R and D in key technologies. If in previous decades there was some justification for the criticism of the Japanese as 'copy-cats', those days are over. High-definition television (HDTV), video phones and electric cars, which are based on new technologies, were expected to become widely available in the second half of the 1990s. Japanese companies have been pushing towards development of 1 gigabyte dynamic random access memory chips (D-RAMs) and other ultra-large-scale integrated circuits. R and D in the area of liquid crystal display (LCD) technologies has also been actively pursued in the expectation of rapid market growth for large-screen wall-mounted televisions. Industrial giants such as Toyota are now investing more in R and D than in plant and equipment (see Figure 10.2). The private sector in Japan finances virtually all its own R and D. The government contributes only a fifth of Japan's US$60 billion total annual bill for R and D – and that fifth goes to the universities and its own research institutions.

	R and D Yen bn	Capital expenditure	R and D as % of capital expenditure Yen bn
Toyota	275	225	120
Matsushita Electrical Industry	271	66	410
Hitachi	262	103	255
NEC	250	172	150
Toshiba	190	109	175
Fujitsu	184	119	155
Nissan	155	74	210
Sony	128	134	95
Mitsubishi Electric	122	59	205
Canon	75	45	165

Source: *Japan Company Handbook*, cited in Survey of Japanese Technology, *The Economist*, 2 December 1989.

Figure 10.2   Japan's top ten in R and D, 1988

Japan and Western Europe

The first contact with Europeans came in the sixteenth century; the Portuguese arrived in 1542 at Tanegashima off the coast of Kyushu. Christianity was first introduced to Japan by Portuguese and Spanish missionaries. Ironically, it was a rebellion by Japanese Christians – the Shimabara rising, beginning in 1637 – which confirmed the decision to close the country, when Japan cut herself off from the rest of the world[2]. Japan reopened to the outside world during the Meiji era (1867–1912). European contributions towards the 'modernisation' of Japan were obvious. For example, gas lamps, newspapers, schools, the letter post and steam-boats were introduced from the West. A legacy from European influence on Japan's entry into the modern world in the second half of the 19th century is still widely present in Japanese language and customs.

Historically, 'Europe' has not been conceived of by Japan as a political and economic entity. Rather, Japan has viewed the area simply in its geographical context, and as a cultural model which it has wanted to follow to some extent. Until the late 1980s, official contacts between Japan and European countries were – as with almost all of Japan's external relationships – essentially one-dimensional, concerned only with trade and economic relations. In spite of a gradually developing mutual understanding, there have been constant trade frictions between the two sides. The first major criticism of Japan from the EC has been that of 'dumping' its exports on to world markets, of 'unfair competition' in pricing and marketing practices. In 1991, Japanese exporters were the subject of six definitive anti-dumping decisions, compared with only three in 1990. In the same year, Japan's trade surplus with the EC rose to $27.4 billion, an increase of 48 per cent. The second European complaint specifically about bilateral trade matters has been that Japanese exports are too concentrated on sensitive industrial product lines. In the past, those industries included textiles, steel, ships, cutlery and cameras. More recently, the focus has shifted to passenger cars. After years of testy negotiations, the EC won agreement to restrict Japanese car imports until 1999. These complaints too may have their roots in the consistent Japanese trade surplus with the EC.

From time to time, anti-Japanese sentiments can surface in Europe. For example, the former French prime minister Edith Cresson's description of Japan as a nation of ants shows that some circles at least still recently had serious anxieties about a Japanese threat. Recent complaints have been concentrated on exclusive business practices in Japan, the distribution system and technical barriers to imports into Japan, especially for pharmaceutical and food products.

For the Japanese, the intensity of European dissatisfaction concerning the overall trade imbalance hardly seems warranted. Japan consistently, throughout the 1970s, argued that the EC should liberalise progressively and completely, and in particular should end all 'discriminatory' quantitative restrictions maintained selectively against Japan. The Japanese government has been trying to alleviate the huge Japanese trade surplus with the EC. It has put into effect a comprehensive programme amounting to $63 billion which emphasises public works, for which the Bank of Japan has reduced the official discount rate. One aspect of the Japan-EC relationship noted by the Japanese side has been an 'attention gap'. Japanese attention to the EC has been much greater than that of the EC to Japan.[3]

In the area of direct investment, the EC (and now the EU) has been the second largest recipient of Japanese outward FDI, just behind the USA. In 1992 investment between Europe and Japan came to $73 billion, whereas US-Japan investment totalled $170 billion. As Europe and North America are roughly on a par in terms of the size of population and GNP, there seems to be considerable scope for improvement in the Japan-Europe figures. Nevertheless, more and more Japanese firms have relocated in the EU in response to the Single Market. The UK is the number one destination of such an economic 'invasion' of Europe. In 1991, 41% of Japanese investment in the EU was made in the UK (see Figure 10.3).

Region	1987	1988	1989	1990	1991
Europe	6.6	9.0	14.8	14.3	9.4
North America	15.4	22.3	33.9	27.2	18.8
Asia	4.9	5.6	8.2	7.1	5.9
Latin America	4.8	6.4	5.2	3.6	3.3
Others	1.7	3.6	5.4	3.6	4.1
World total	33.4	47.0	67.5	56.9	41.5

Source: Japan's Ministry of International Trade and Industry, reported in the *Financial Times*, Survey of Japan and the European Community, 13 November 1992

Figure 10.3   Japanese Foreign Direct Investment (US$ billion)

Although European investment in Japan cannot be compared with the Japanese investment in the EC (and now the EU), European firms have been increasingly active in the Japanese market. Both in 1990 and 1991, European firms surpassed their US counterparts in investing in Japan. Some of them have been doing extremely well. For example, the European car makers have established a niche market in Japan, beating their American competitors. After getting nowhere with Japanese dealers or import agents, the Europeans began setting up their own dealerships in the early 1980s. BMW (with 120 outlets in Japan), Audi, Volkswagen and Citroën are coming up fast[4].

Country	1987	1988	1989	1990	1991
UK	2.5	4.0	5.2	6.8	3.6
Netherlands	0.8	2.4	4.5	2.7	2.0
Luxembourg	1.8	0.7	0.7	0.2	0.3
Germany	0.4	0.4	1.1	1.2	1.1
France	0.3	0.5	1.1	1.3	0.8
Spain	0.3	0.2	0.5	0.3	0.4
Belgium	0.1	0.2	0.3	0.4	0.2
Ireland	0.1	0.0	0.1	0.05	0.1
Italy	0.1	0.1	0.3	0.2	0.3
Portugal	0.01	0.01	0.1	0.1	0.0
Greece	-	-	-	0.0	0.0
Denmark*	-	-	-	-	-

* Figures for Denmark are unlisted. Historically, Japan's foreign direct investment in Denmark has been the lowest of the twelve, amounting to a cumulative total of US$50m over the period 1951-1989.

Source: Japan's Ministry of International Trade and Industry, reported in the *Financial Times*, Survey of Japan and the European Community, 13 November 1992

Figure 10.4   Japanese investment in the twelve EC countries (US$ billion)

Region	1987	1988	1989	1990	1991
Europe	0.5	0.8	0.6	1.4	1.4
US	0.9	1.8	1.6	0.7	1.3
Others	0.6	0.3	0.4	0.5	1.0

Source: Japan's Ministry of International Trade and Industry, reported in the *Financial Times*, Survey of Japan and the European Community, 13 November 1992

Figure 10.5   Foreign Direct Investment in Japan (US$ billion)

	1987	1988	1989	1990	1991
UK	0.05	0.1	0.08	0.05	0.4
Germany	0.05	0.2	0.1	0.3	0.2
France	0.02	0.03	0.03	0.07	0.05
Netherlands	0.07	0.2	0.3	0.7	0.3

Source: Japan's Ministry of International Trade and Industry, reported in the *Financial Times*, Survey of Japan and the European Community, 13 November 1992

Figure 10.6   Investment in Japan by principal EC countries (US$ billion)

Japanese management

Japanese management has been widely regarded as one of the backbones of Japanese economic growth. Many Western firms are 'Japanising' themselves, following the principles of Japanese management. Lifetime employment, consensus decision-making, and hierarchical organisations based on seniority are commonly known as the three pillars of Japanese management. The three are entwined with each other. For example, lifetime employment can facilitate the consensus decision-making process. As employees are assumed to work in the same company for the rest of their working life, they ares obviously interested in taking part in the decision-making, as the future of the company will directly affect their own future.

Lifetime employment

The present lifetime employment practice took root in Japan after World War Two. Under this system, when university graduates or school leavers are recruited, they are guaranteed permanent employment with the firm. The firm will not resort to methods such as redundancy and voluntary early retirement, except in extremely rare circumstances. While some have argued that the system has deeper roots in Japanese history and culture, and stems directly from Confucianism and the feudal legacy[5], others strongly disagree and argue that the system is by no means traditionally Japanese, but evolved simply as a response to market conditions.[6] This system is more relevant among large firms than among small firms. Less than 30% of the workforce enjoys lifetime employment, but the idea permeates the whole system, even if it does not guarantee all jobs. Lifetime employment is a psychological contract between company and regular employees that is not taken lightly[7].

There are many advantages in this system. It can create a high degree of commitment and loyalty to the organisation. Loyal employees over time develop contacts and friendships across many far-flung divisions and operations. They also cultivate an intimate knowledge of the company's operational idiosyncrasics. Guaranteed employment enables a company to retain qualified and skilled workers. As employees are supposed to work in the same company for the rest of their working life, they have a strong personal interest in the future of their company. This reinforces the social norm of seniority, as work experience in the company counts towards the individual's promotion, wages and other welfare.

However, the conventional wisdom will often be questioned at a time of difficulty. Life time employment has been criticised as being at the root of today's management problems[8]. The immobility of employees means that if someone fails to adapt to a new environment or does not share the view of the management, he or she will feel trapped. This will result in employee dissatisfaction and low productivity. The system can produce unwieldy bureaucracies staffed by uniformly mediocre 'generalist' managers who are ill-suited to today's fast-changing world marketplace. The lack of individualism can hinder creativity and innovation. For foreign firms operating in Japan, hiring skilled workers is a headache. The lifetime employment system has greatly reduced the chance and motivation for employees to go 'job hopping'.

Changes are taking place, but not without encountering resistance. In December 1992, an announcement of planned redundancies at Pioneer Electric Company created a furore in Japan. Pioneer wished to release 35 'lifetime' employees, all over 50, from among its 9,000 employees in Japan. The 35 had no subordinates and few responsibilities. They were members of the 'window-gazing tribe', a term used to describe ageing white-collar employees who have nothing to do but admire the view. Pioneer proposed to pay them up to two year's salary as part of compensation for leaving early. Faced with enormous opposition from other employees and the union, Pioneer backed down in January 1993.[9]

Decision-making

Understanding the Japanese decision-making process is vital for the Western business-man who wants to be successful in business relationships with the Japanese. The *Ringi* system of organisational decision-making in the Japanese firms was used before indus-trialisation and modernisation started in the middle of the 19th century. The word *Ringi* means obtaining approval on a proposed matter through the vertical, and some-times horizontal, circulation of documents to the company members concerned. The system can be regarded as a confirmation and authorisation process. A proposal is usu-ally initiated by middle management; it is then written on a form and circulated to all affected individuals for review and confirmation; they affix their seals to the document and add comments if they have different ideas and suggestions for improvement. After this the proposal is sent to top management for final approval or, in some cases, veto.

Some people argue that the system is tediously time-consuming; in today's world, they say, swift and decisive decision-making is the order of the day. The system is often regarded as outdated in Western countries. However, it can often be as efficient as, if not more so than, the Western top-down process. It is worthwhile to spend sufficient time on generating plausible and workable ideas and consulting those concerned, as it can not only improve the probability of successful implementation but also reduce the potential problems, such as lack of co-operation from those affected by the decisions but not consulted. It does seem time-consuming to provide for greater input from those affected prior to commitment to a change; but it helps to meet the basic human desire to have a voice in shaping one's destiny.

The function of top executives is to approve the proposal. Although it seems that these executives are sometimes redundant in such a process, their position and seniority are the backbones of any major decision. Another principal idea behind such a process is that if the proposal does not work, no specific person can be blamed; hence, no one will lose face. Harmony and co-operation are thus preserved. However, how well the system works depends on an individual firm's culture. Sometimes, it can be merely a formal-ity. What Western businessmen have to remember is that they need to work both ways. During business negotiations, while it is important to convince those one is negotiat-ing with, one should not neglect those behind the scenes. Very often, they are more important than those who appear to be the chief negotiators.

Trade unions

Japanese unions are different from those in Western countries. It is therefore extremely important for any Western firm which intends to undertake operations such as setting up a subsidiary in Japan to understand how Japanese unions work.

The flexibility in the labour market provided by the two-tiered structure of lifetime and contract employment would not work effectively without the institutional support of trade unions. The majority of unions are affiliated to the labour federation, Rengo. Although a small number of 'joint' unions have been formed to represent employees in a particular trade from a number of different companies, most trade unions in Japan are limited to employees of one particular company, This encourages the unions to be co-operative with management, because it is not in their interest to push high wage claims, or to oppose plant closures if they are needed to improve the financial position of the company. The smaller the enterprise, the less likely it is that there will be union representation; those enterprises employing less than 100 workers are approximately 95 per cent non-union.

In a Japanese 'enterprise' union nearly everyone is a union member, including younger management members. In addition to this, most company managers are sincere supporters of their firms' union. An 'enterprise' union has its office provided by the management and acts as if it is a welfare department of the firm. Overall, union leaders and management in Japanese companies cooperate closely to maintain harmony within the firm. At the same time, the Japanese employees are closely and intimately bound to the company; they are therefore less likely to take any drastic action against it. Japanese unions are just as concerned about how to increase production, improve safety and upgrade quality, as they are with job security and higher wages. Lifetime employment strengthens this unique characteristic.

Virtually all foreign firms of any size in Japan are unionised, and many have very serious difficulties with their unions. The problems are frequently the result of cultural barriers and failure to adapt to the Japanese environment; foreign firms often try to install their own management style to which Japanese employees are not accustomed.

The Japanese consumer market

Not long ago, the conventional thinking was that Japan was a nation full of savers and producers. Advocates of this line of thinking have suddenly gone quiet; increasing affluence is changing Japanese consumer behaviour. New types of consumer group are emerging. For example, the Japanese are fascinated by European luxury goods such as French jewellery, German sedans or Italian suits. 1989 and 1990 were the years of the EC brand names. Although the Japanese consumer used to purchase the brand rather than the product, quality has become the most important consideration, and competitiveness in price is another key factor. Japanese consumers have rapidly matured in their buying habits; they still want brand-name products, but at a cheaper price.

Some 60% of Japanese people alive today were born after 1945. More and more people tend to live in cities. The life expectancy has greatly increased (to 76 years for males and 81 for females), resulting in an increased proportion of people of pensionable age. Some distinctive key consumer groups are emerging:

- **City Single.** More and more young people living in cities are marrying late. This has led to a growing number of people with high disposable income. At the same time, because of high house prices, people are spending on consumables rather than on property.
- **Double Income No Kids.** While a growing number of young people prefer to marry late, more married couples are choosing to have no children. This group, with lower incentives to save, coupled with good pay and bonuses, has emerged as another group of high spenders.

- **Office Lady.** Although this group overlaps with City Singles and Double Income No Kids, its distinctive spending patterns make it worth considering separately. Members are more likely to spend more on consumer goods and services. In most cases, they are the decision makers at home.
- **Double Income With Kids.** An increasingly affluent market consists of households with a double income and children. Housewives in their late 30s and 40s returning to work, even if on a part-time basis, are keen to contribute to the prosperity of their family by using their additional income to purchase items such as cameras, videos and other products to enrich family life.

Other consumers' groups include the 'Silver Market', consisting of elderly people aged above 60. These are increasingly becoming more healthy, and intend to enjoy the rest of their life. They also have the means, because they belong to a generation of savers.

The changing consumer life styles provide a much easier market for Western companies intending to serve Japanese consumers. However, while cultural values in Japan are changing rapidly, and these changes are having a direct impact on the market, the latter is still very much Japanese despite a surface patina of Westernisation. In socio-economic terms, the Japanese population remains remarkably homogeneous, despite growing affluence and recent moves towards a more individualistic life style. Therefore, Western firms should not take it for granted, and close analysis of the market is still required.

Distribution systems

The complexity of distribution channels has frequently been cited as one of the most visible barriers to entry into the Japanese market. Everything a consumer bought – made in Japan or imported, whether personal computer, razor, ball bearing, or man's suit – had to wend its way through the books of as many as half a dozen middlemen. Some of them even never took possession of the products, but all extracted a toll, creating the world's most exorbitant prices.

For foreign firms, the basic question is why Japanese have permitted such underdeveloped conditions as far as distribution is concerned. Some have come to its defence, and argued that the system has nothing to do with backwardness; it is basically linked with Japanese culture. A difference in culture creates a different distribution system. Efficiency cannot be the only yardstick to evaluate the performance of a distribution system. The Japanese system does provide consumer convenience.[10] Japanese consumers demand prompt after-market service; the large number of wholesalers and retailers can fulfil this requirement.

In the traditional distribution network, manufacturers concentrate mainly on production and national promotional activities. Intermediates (wholesalers) interact closely with both the manufacturing and the retailing level; their work extends far beyond pure break-bulk or product assortment activities. Retailers in turn focus on selling and promotional activities aimed at consumers within their area of business.

One of the characteristics of the Japanese distribution system is the existence of large number of middlemen – wholesalers. Japanese wholesalers consist of three different groups: primary wholesalers, secondary wholesalers and tertiary wholesalers. Altogether, there are approximately 230,000 registered primary wholesalers in Japan, and several thousand unregistered ones.

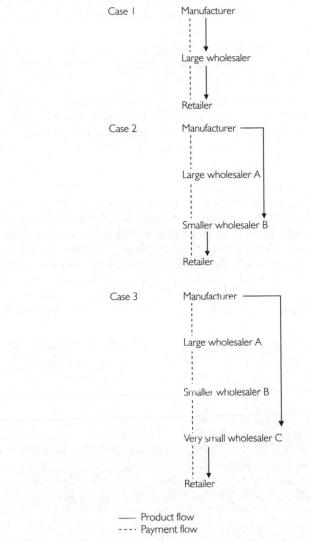

- —— Product flow
- ---- Payment flow

Source: Michael Czinkota & Jon Woronoff, *Unlocking Japan's Markets*, Probus Publishing Company, 1991

Figure 10.7   The variety of distribution alternatives – the channels for soap

The Japanese distribution system is characterised by very close ties, both at social and at business level, between the participants in the distribution process. The bonds do not discourage competition. Wholesalers are expected by their retailers to be actively involved in business development, and pressures are exerted via them on the manufacturers to remain competitive in their product and price offerings. Most of the retailers are family-owned and handle only a single line of goods. Many are affiliated with a primary supplier – one of Japan's industrial behemoths or a specialised wholesaler – which provides advertising, signs, and inventory financing, as well as most of the merchandise. In return, the owners strictly observe suggested retail prices. Because these shops are too tiny to keep extra inventory, the owners order small quantities of goods from suppliers almost daily. To handle all these transactions and shipments, secondary and tertiary wholesalers evolved, linked through other larger distributors to manufacturers or to Japan's giant trading companies.

Retail regulations make it extremely hard for developers of large stores to displace existing family shops. Other laws restrict the size of buildings that retailers can erect, or dictate store lay-out and even construction materials. Most department stores and other traditional retailers generally buy merchandise on the condition that they can return whatever does not sell.

We are now witnessing a revolution in the Japanese distribution system. Several factors lie behind this revolution, but one of the most important is a direct result of the increasing liberalisation of the Japanese economy. As imported goods become increasingly common in Japanese stores, wholesalers and retailers alike are having to respond to the changed conditions, and new distribution patterns are gradually being established. Manufacturers are starting to reach out directly to consumers, and some retailers are eliminating wholesalers. The wholesalers are integrating both horizontally and vertically. The Japanese market is operating more like that of its Western industrialised counterparts. As a result, it is much easier now for Western firms to operate in Japan.

CASE STUDY
An SME firm's long road to the Japanese consumer

Export Today reported in 1992 that up to that point Mulberry Company Ltd. had established nine Mulberry shops in Japan. This was an essential part of their strategy for establishing their designer brand of clothing and accessories in the Japanese market. Sales to Japan began in the seventies, and their first serious customer was the Ginza, a subsidiary of the leading cosmetics giant Shiseido. The three year contract with the Ginza resulted in good sales growth; but it became apparent to Roger Saul, Mulberry's MD, that their objective seemed to be to develop the Ginza brand, and that the Mulberry name was barely visible to the general public. So Mulberry looked for a new partner to help them open retail stores, to extend the Mulberry image to a wider public. They were soon offered a contract for a series of 'Mulberry corners' by a leading department store.

Unfortunately Mulberry had negotiated through the department store's London office, and when they met their partners in Japan they found they had been allocated to the woman's handbag division, so that they could not sell fashion, menswear or men's accessories. Two corners were still opened, and did give Mulberry a high profile. But problems followed when the yen weakened and their prices became astronomical. This led to pressure to license manufacture in Japan, which Roger Saul resisted. Mulberry found a new partner, a medium-sized trading company, and signed a new contract with a commitment to establish two Mulberry shops. Unfortunately, it turned out that the new partner had little experience in the wholesale or retail areas. A shop was finally opened in the third year of the contract.

Almost all designer brands that have succeeded in Japan have formed joint ventures, according to Roger Saul. Mulberry found a new partner and established a joint venture. They then set out a five year business plan to open 15 shops, backed by strong wholesale business. They also found a chief executive who understood their design and brand philosophy and has built a team of committed Japanese personnel, according to Roger Saul.

Source: *Export Today*, 1992

Market entry strategies

The Japanese Ministry of International Trade and Industry (MITI) has encouraged leading Japanese firms in sectors such as automobiles, electronics, machine tools, semiconductor manufacturing equipment and trading to draw up and implement voluntary plans to expand imports at home, to increase local procurement abroad and to promote inter-corporate co-operation through direct investment, joint ventures and technical co-operation. A recent survey, conducted by AT Kearney, of 340 leading US companies with operations in Japan revealed a marked improvement in the environment for foreign companies doing business in Japan, though some obstacles still existed[11]. Companies deciding to enter the Japanese market have a wide choice of possibilities open to them, including arrangements with Japan's major trading companies; using specialist agents; setting up joint ventures or wholly owned subsidiaries; or even going for take-overs.

Among the most successful companies are the German car makers Volkswagen/Audi, BMW, and Mercedes Benz – who together account for a disproportionate 59 per cent share of the imported car market. They are successful in part because of the many years they have devoted to burnishing the image of their products. VW and Audi together claim 23 per cent of the market; BMW 16 per cent, and Mercedes 17 per cent.

Exporting to Japan

The average level of Japanese tariffs on industrial products is lower than that imposed by either the United States or the EU. Non-tariff barriers (NTBs) against manufactured imports (though not against agricultural produce) are lower than in most OECD economies, though it is widely believed that the Japanese market is well protected by the government. Uniquely among the world's trading nations, Japan has a government programme for the increase of imports through credits and through the supply of information and services to foreign exporters, using the offices of the Japan External Trade Organisation (JETRO) all over the world. JETRO was set up in 1958, initially to promote exports; now its role is largely to promote imports, with around US$70m allocated annually to import promotion. The Japanese Export/Import Bank is responsible for a range of credits promoting imports. Import credits are provided to Japanese business, including subsidiaries of foreign corporations, for the import of resources and manufactured goods vital to the development of the Japanese economy. The bank also supplies credits to foreign corporations for the development and export of natural resources deemed essential to the Japanese economy, as well as credits for the long-term funding needs of foreign firms in order to increase exports of manufactured goods to Japan.

Major efforts have also been made by both the EU and the individual member states to narrow the trade gap with Japan. For example, the Executive Training Programme funded by the EU makes it possible for European Union companies with a sound marketing strategy and a clear commitment to Japan to send young businessmen and women to study and work in Japan for 18 months. Individual countries have also been active in helping their firms export to Japan. In the UK, the Department of Trade and Industry (DTI) has been promoting exports to Japan through various means, notably the establishment of an Export to Japan Unit specialising in providing export-related services to British exporters, supported by programmes such as the Priority Japan Campaign and trade missions to Japan. Evidence has shown that foreign firms committed to the Japanese market and with high quality goods and services can make an impact in Japan.

Import control and exchange control regulations

Most goods enter Japan unrestricted; however, some are subject to an Import Quota (IQ) system. Under this system, the importer must first obtain an IQ Allocation Certificate from MITI, which entitles it to receive an import licence on application to an authorised foreign exchange bank. An import licence is valid for 6 months. Liberalised commodities of interest to UK exporters include cheese (IQ abolished 1 April 1989) and fruit juices (IQ abolished 1 April 1990). A Tariff Quota system is also in existence for leather and leather footwear, as provided for in the 1986 EC-Japan Agreement.

Customs duties and taxes

The Japanese Customs Tariff is based on the Harmonised System (HS) of classification. Except for certain raw materials, essential items of industrial equipment and antiques, as well as agricultural tractors, machine tools, cars, home appliances, books, etc., imports are generally liable for customs duties. On most dutiable items there is a GATT rate; some items have temporary reduced rates of duty. Most goods are subject to *ad valorem* customs duty based on the CIF value. From 1 April 1989 the commodity tax, which was levied mainly on luxury goods, was abolished; and a consumption tax (three per cent on all goods sold in Japan) was introduced.

Documentation

Certificates of origin are not required for goods for which conventional or beneficial rates of duty are claimed, i.e. goods which are entitled to GATT or Most Favoured Nation (MFN) rates of duty. A declaration of origin in the commercial invoice is sufficient for this purpose. For coffee, woven fabrics, silk and certain sea products, a certificate of origin is required, however. Two copies of the commercial invoice are required which should include the mark, number, name description, quantity and value of the goods, the HS number, place and date of the invoice, names and addresses of the consignor and consignee and conditions of contract relating to the value of the goods. To obtain a GATT or MFN rate of duty, a signed declaration of origin should be made on the invoice by the shipper.

Export and import channels
Japan has some 8,000 trading companies, of which the nine largest '*sogo shosha*' are well known as general trading companies handling a wide range of goods and services. Some *sogo shosha* belong to large business conglomerates, although their trading is not exclusively within the group. They are strong in high volume or high value imports and in co-ordinating international projects, and are all represented in major European cities such as London and Paris. Some Japanese manufacturers also act as importers/distributors for imported goods. In addition, there are a number of European trading firms based in Japan which can be quite helpful. As export volume increases, at a appropriate stage an agent may be appointed. The selection of a suitable agent is particularly important in Japan. For some European firms, department stores in Japan can be the bridge to the Japanese retail markets. There are about a dozen department store groups in Japan. The stores are the most important outlet for high quality consumer goods imported from Europe. Buying is done both through the Japanese distribution system and in many cases direct from European suppliers.

Licensing

Although Japan is no longer a nation of copy-cats, its thirst for foreign technology is ever-growing. Licensing agreements have often been considered a good way into the Japanese market, but careful consideration needs to be given to the nature of the product, market conditions and the state of Japanese technology in the area. Licensing agreements are approved automatically and in theory without restriction, excluding certain areas of technology such as computers, aerospace, nuclear energy and defence equipment; all agreements are, however, still subject to anti-monopoly law. The government appears to encourage the importation of foreign technology. Licensing can be a stepping stone for direct investment in Japan. It can provide not only a potential future partner for a joint venture, but also valuable knowledge of manufacturing and marketing before making any significant equity commitment in Japan.

Joint ventures

Joint ventures have been the traditional route into the Japanese market, particularly for manufacturing companies. It eases usage of appropriate sites and facilities (for it is not uncommon to find manufacturing taking place on an existing site of the Japanese joint venture partner); secures access to complex and multi-layered distribution and sales networks; helps with employment of suitable personnel; and enables European companies to learn from Japanese production methods. A 1987 study among British companies then operating in Japan found positive support for the joint venture route.[12]

> ✎ **CASE STUDY**
> **United Biscuits**
> United Biscuits is one example of a British company that has found the joint venture experience rewarding. When the company started testing out the Japanese market in the early 1970s, it realised that it had neither the knowledge nor the financial strength to break into it. So it spent two to three years looking for a suitable partner, which turned out to be Meiji Seika, a large food and pharmaceutical company. The resultant Meiji McVitie is still going strong and is a good profitable business. Robert Clarke, United Biscuits' Chairman, admits that without Meiji's know-how, particularly on sales and packaging, they probably would have conducted their marketing along British lines and 'come unstuck'.

However, there can be occasional problems, deriving from a lack of direct access to the customer, differing management methods, and most crucially, divergence in market strategies and long-term objectives. This can end with one side or the other taking control. Lack of commitment to joint ventures in Japan is one of the major reasons why they fail. The common reasons for joint venture failure worldwide can be applied to the Japanese market, but sometimes with a different set of details. Learning opportunities are often not understood or poorly exploited by Western partners. Added to this imbalance in the commitment of the Japanese and Western partners is the problem of cultural differences that inevitably hinder the smooth functioning of joint ventures in Japan. Although such cultural problems exist in most joint ventures, those in arrangements between Japanese and Western firms are more acute – for example, conflicts in corporate objectives. While the Japanese partner is managing the business so as to increase market share and the ratio of new products, the Western partner is looking for a high return on investment (ROI), and maximisation of the shareholders' return. There is also the problem of Western expatriates' understanding and adapting to the Japanese social and corporate environment, not to mention the local language.

> ✎ **CASE STUDY**
> Unique technology and persistence are key to success in the Japanese market. Although Birmingham-based Ultraseal International had been selling impregnation sealants to Japan for almost ten years, *Export Today* reported in 1993 that they had recently succeeded in selling equipment into the market for the first time. The contract from Nippon Rakaki Co. Ltd. (NRK) was for a complete MX Vacuum Impregnation System for sealing porosity in metal castings, worth between £150,000 and £200,000. NRK had since bought two aqueous washing machines from Ultraseal, which use the same principles as the impregnation system.
>
> Ten years before, Ultra had entered the Japanese market through a wholly owned subsidiary. Because of the differences between British culture and Japanese culture and the complexity of the Japanese market, particularly its distribution systems, they encountered enormous problems such as high operational costs and sluggish sales.

Five years later, the management came to the conclusion that a joint venture with a local Japanese partner would help the company solve these problems by taking advantage of the local partner's established position within the local distribution systems. NRK, one of Ultra's clients, was chosen to be the local partner. NRK is a manufacturer in its own right, mainly making filtration systems, and had bought the system for use in its own operations; but the system was also being demonstrated to other Japanese manufacturers such as Mitsubishi. This would undoubtedly help Ultra's future business in Japan, as NRK's customers include some big names such as Caterpillar, Komatsu, Toyota, Nissan and Mitsubishi.

Another reason for the recent success was, according to Ultra's marketing executive, Mr Paul Young, the advanced technology which was not available in Japan. The equipment was manufactured to very high specifications including the use of Japanese-specified stainless steel. Ultra was now considering the next move: whether to continue to sell equipment manufactured in the UK, or to manufacture the product in Japan. They understood that although there were advantages for the company in making it in the UK, there was a greater potential in manufacturing it in Japan, as the Japanese prefer the latter. Experience told Ultra that the Japanese customers liked to be involved in the manufacturing process right down the line, to visit weekly and have a very close relationship with their suppliers.

There was every indication, according to *Export Today*, that Ultraseal were well placed to reap the reward of being patient and persistent in the Japanese market.

Source: adapted from *Export Today*, 1993

Several case studies have revealed that failures are not the result of a conspiracy on the part of the Japanese partners. Rather the failure stems mainly from the classical problems linked to international joint ventures: commitment, communications between partners, clear sharing of roles, planning, the complexity of the project, shifting strategic imperatives and cultural differences. The key success factors observed are as follows:

- Define clearly the corporate objectives of the new firm, the scope of the business and the responsibilities of each side.
- From the start of the joint venture, the top management of both parent companies must commit themselves to the success of the joint venture, and contribute some of their best managers to get the new company going.
- Both parents should agree to start 'small', to treat the joint venture as a truly independent company, and not to interfere in its day-to-day management[13].
- Mutual understanding, trust and adequate communication between the partners are of extreme importance.

Foreign direct investment

By investing in Japan, European firms can gain an accurate understanding of how to cope with the highly competitive Japanese market. The Japanese domestic market, as explained above, is becoming more open and accessible. For example, MITI has proposed a package of measures to improve the investment climate in Japan. MITI is interested in rectifying the huge imbalance between high levels of Japanese investment abroad and low levels of foreign investment in Japan.

Investment can also provide evidence of a commitment to Japan, which is extremely important there. Being close to the customers, European firms can react to changing demand more quickly. Some investment incentives are now also available for inward foreign investment. They include preferential tax treatment for foreign affiliates, enabling them to recoup investment costs at an early stage in the life of the business. Financial programmes by government institutions such as the Japan Development Bank (JDB) are being expanded by improving foreign affiliate eligibility for low interest loans.

An increasing number of European firms – not only multinationals such as Glaxo, Shell, ICI and Guinness, but also many small and medium-sized firms – are learning the commercial advantages of setting up some form of operation in Japan. The flow of net direct European investment into Japan rose from US$500 million in 1987 to US$1.4 billion in 1991. ICI has been involved in Japan for over 70 years, but during the 1980s it began to feel that its existing range of trading, licensing and joint venture activities was not sufficient to meet its strategic needs. It felt that the only way to develop intimate customer-supplier relationships and maintain adequate control was to carry out its own technical development and manufacturing locally in Japan[14].

However, the potential problems of going it alone can more than offset the benefits of establishing a wholly-owned subsidiary in Japan. Although it may seem that a European firm will have 100% control of the firm, and therefore of its operations and strategies, in reality many European firms have to recruit local staff and managers. In the past, the greatest problems for foreign investors in Japan were high initial investment and business costs due to high land prices, difficulty in finding staff, and the complexity of doing business in Japan. Therefore, a wholly-owned subsidiary will be more suitable for experienced firms, whether multinationals or medium-sized companies. They must have experience of operating in Japan either through exporting, licensing or joint ventures or related international experiences. Before such a commitment is undertaken, careful study of the Japanese market is essential.

Acquisitions and mergers

Acquisitions and mergers (A and M) have been one of the most important strategies enabling firms to diversify, beat the competition and enter into a foreign market. However, while the Japanese have been active in recent years in taking over American and European firms as part of their globalisation strategy, foreign bidders are faced with numerous hurdles in taking over Japanese firms. As has been true for domestic combinations, extra-legal barriers such as industrial group membership, reciprocal shareholdings among Japanese companies, and the opprobrium associated with A and M activities in Japan have doubtless impeded cross-border acquisitions involving Japanese companies as targets. Acquisitions and mergers in Japan have never been popular. In this respect, Japanese-style capitalism and Anglo-Saxon capitalism diverge. The cultural and social structure is as important a determinant of the organisation of human economic activity as economic self-interest – perhaps more so.

For example, in order to maintain peace and harmony in society, 'face-saving' is one of the pre-requisites in Japan and in other Far Eastern countries. Loss of 'face' means that a person loses dignity and others' respect. Being acquired implies that the present owner of the company is incompetent and unable to manage the company successfully. This would mean a great loss of face to the owner of the company concerned. Naturally, that owner will furiously fight off any take-over attempts, particularly hostile ones. Another problem which can be encountered by the foreign acquirer is that Japanese employees treat the company as their family. A foreign take-over will obviously create doubt among the employees as to whether the future foreign owner will care for them in the same way as their Japanese owner; there will also be concern whether the foreign owner's objective in taking over is long-term-oriented, and whether it is committed to the further growth of the company.

Figures 10.8 and 10.9 suggest that while take-over activities involving Japanese firms are declining, mainly as a result of economic slow-down, the number of transactions and amount of money involved in foreign firms' A and M activity are noticeably smaller than is the case both in Japanese domestic A and M activity and in Japanese buying of foreign firms abroad.

	1989	1990	1991	1992	1993*
Foreigners buying Japanese companies	22	3	48	27	12
Japanese buying foreign companies	2,899	2,583	710	254	106
Japanese buying Japanese companies	109	176	227	269	101

* Total for the first six months

Source: Yamaichi Securities, reported in the Financial Times, 17 September 1993

Figure 10.8   A and M activity in Japan (¥ billion)

	1985	1986	1987	1988	1989	1990*
Japanese buyer/Japanese seller	163	226	219	223	210	199
Japanese buyer/overseas seller	100	204	228	315	405	292
Overseas buyer/Japanese seller	26	21	22	17	15	12

* First eight months

Source: Yamaichi Securities, reported in the Financial Times, 18 October 1990

Figure 10.9   Japanese acquisitions and mergers: number of transactions

Nevertheless, A and M can be an effective method of entering the Japanese market. Greenfield operations in Japan have problems such as recruiting local labour. Skilled workers are reluctant to take up posts in foreign firms, as there is a fear that the lifetime employment and care of employees which are common in Japanese firms may not be readily available in a foreign company; A and M can readily solve this problem. The complex distribution system in Japan is well-known, as mentioned above, and taking over an existing firm can provide the foreign firm with existing distribution channels.

Hostile A and Ms have been virtually non-existent in Japan.[15] As Japanese firms do not like hostile take-overs, European firms intending to use this method should be extremely cautious in approaching the firms concerned. Usually, mutual understanding and trust should be established.

It has been found that three categories of Japanese firms were easier targets. The first is those which are finding difficulty in continuing independent operation, or which simply have bad management. The second is those with a desire to overcome growth constraints; the firm has been doing well, but lacks the managerial resources needed to grow further, and thus opts to sell itself. The third is those affected by restructuring policy on the part of a former parent company.

In order to avoid the potential problem of unifying the different labour practices of acquired Japanese firms and their foreign acquirers, loose combinations of acquisition and capital participation are encouraged. European firms which can provide international distribution networks and superior technology are more likely to succeed in a friendly take-over bid for a Japanese firm in one of the three categories above.

CASE STUDY
The BOC Group

The BOC Group had been active in a number of ventures in Japan for over a decade without ever making a profit, until in the early 1980s they decided to expand the range of their business by acquiring a Japanese company. Three candidate companies failed to be attracted, but BOC succeeded with the fourth, Osaka Sanso, in which BOC now has a 49 per cent stake. It took three years of careful negotiation with the Japanese company's management and the regulatory authorities. Initial operations faltered, mainly because of poor inter-company communication, but after restructuring and an enhanced investment programme, the new company has had – according to Sir Richard Giordano, former Chairman of the BOC Group – a 'dramatic improvement' in its performance.

Although Japanese practitioners of mergers and acquisitions may still be unwelcome, they are definitely becoming part of Japan's business activities. The number and value of inbound A and M deals appear set to increase further, as Japanese firms increasingly find themselves facing the same sort of competitive free-for-all at home that foreign rivals have grappled with for years in other leading markets.

The decision on entry mode choice should be based on the trade-offs between the advantages and disadvantages each mode provides, plus the entry firms' own strategy. Of course, the specific characteristics of the Japanese market are the key factor to be taken into account.

Summary

With its unique management systems and distribution systems, Japan has been regarded as a tough market to crack. However, there are increasing number of European firms which have adapted quite successfully to the Japanese market. Many of them are reaping handsome profits.

The Japanese market itself is changing all the time. European firms need to be patient and persistent in entering it. It is extremely important to appreciate local culture and customs. The correct selection of entry mode must depend on a balance between what companies want and what local market conditions permit.

Case study
Eurotech in Japan

Eurotech, a multinational company with its headquarters based in the EU, selected a new managing director for its Japanese subsidiary to replace the existing MD who was about to retire in a couple of months' time. Having operated in Japan for the past 10 years, Eurotech is well established in that market. Eurotech's main line of business in Japan is the personal computer market, which has seen increasing competition both from American competitors such as IBM, Compaq and Dell and from Japanese producers such as Fujitsu.

After fierce discussion and debate, the company finally reached a decision that Maurice Donnelley, an Oxford graduate in Political Economy and an MBA from an esteemed European management school, would take up the position in Japan. Those who favoured the choice of Mr Donnelley thought that he was young, energetic, quick-thinking, experienced in international assignments and with sound academic qualifications. Those who were against his selection pointed out that though he was experienced, Mr Donnelley's previous assignments were mainly within Europe.

No sooner had he arrived than he went to see his predecessor. During their talk, the old man specifically told Mr Donnelley to be sensitive to Japanese culture and its management styles. This advice later proved not to have been taken seriously by Mr Donnelley, who was busy designing his own grandiose plan to achieve success in Japan as he had always done back in Europe.

Before long, he found himself in an isolated position. It had become obvious that his plan for effective competition with Eurotech's rivals could not be fully implemented; he had not taken into account the fact that the competitiveness of the firm depended on its relationship with its suppliers and buyers in Japan. Some of the old suppliers and buyers had been neglected, because a new selection method based on competition was introduced. His Japanese deputy and some middle managers, who were older than him, did not take him too seriously in the first place. They felt that he had been arrogant and inconsiderate to his subordinates, and did not want to listen to their advice.

Eurotech's PC market share has started to shrink dramatically, thanks to its competitors' successful advertising campaign and public relations efforts. Meanwhile, headquarters has been flooded with complaints from Japan about Mr Donnelley. When Mr Donnelley heard the news, he was determined to get rid of those who had complained. This action has worsened the already troubled relationship between Mr Donnelley and his Japanese colleagues.

Now it is time for headquarters to decide what actions it should take in order to solve this problem and regain the lost market share in Japan.

Questions for discussion

1 What is likely to be the solution? Why?
2 Should Eurotech have chosen Maurice Donnelley in the first place?
3 What have been the major problems which caused the decline of Eurotech's sales in Japan?
4 Why did Maurice Donnelley, highly qualified and internationally experienced, have trouble in Japan?
5 What are the main lessons we can learn from this case?

Further reading

The following are particularly useful:

Michael R. Czinkota and Jon Woronoff, *Unlocking Japan's Markets*, Probus Publishing Company, 1991.

William Duncan, *Doing Business with Japanese*, Gower Press, 1976.

Boye De Mente, *Japanese Etiquette and Ethics in Business*, NTC Business Books, 1990.

Boye De Mente, *How to Do Business with the Japanese*, NTC Business Books, 1991.

Carl W. Kester, *Japanese Takeovers*, Harvard Business School Press, 1991.

David Kilburn, 'The Sun Sets on Japan's Lifers', *Management Today*, September 1993.

Nick Oliver and Barry Wilkinson, *The Japanisation of British Industry*, Blackwell, 1992.

Naoto Sasaki, *Management and Industrial Structure in Japan*, Pergamon Press, 1990.

L. Tsoukalis and M. White (eds.), *Japan and Western Europe*, Frances Pinter (Publishers), 1982.

Yoshi Tsurumi, *The Japanese Are Coming*, Ballinger Publishing Company, 1976.

Arthur M. Whitehall, *Japanese Management: Tradition and Transition*, Routledge, 1991.

Mark Zimmerman, *How to Do Business with Japanese*, Random House, 1985.

Other helpful books and articles include:

Vernon R. Alden, 'Who Says You Can't Crack Japanese Markets?', *Harvard Business Review*, January-February 1987.

DTI, *Hints to Exporters to Japan*, August 1990.

Economist, Survey of Japan, 5 December 1987.

Economist, Survey of Japanese Technology, 2 December 1989.

Economist, Survey of Japanese Economy, 6 March 1993.

EIU, *Country Profile: Japan 1992-1993*, October 1992.

EIU, *Country Profile: Japan 1993-1994*, October 1993.

'Long Road to the Japanese Consumer', *Export Today*, May/June 1992.

'High Technology Market is not Impregnable', *Export Today*, May/June 1993.

Financial Times, Survey of Japan and the European Community, 13 November 1992.

Financial Times, Survey of International Mergers and Acquisitions, 17 September 1993.

Financial Times, Survey of Japanese Industry, 3 December 1993.

Friedrich Fürstenber, *Why the Japanese Have Been So Successful in Business*, Leviathan House, 1974.

Paul A. Herbig and Frederick Palumbo, 'Serving the Aftermarket in Japan and the United States', *Industrial Marketing Management*, 22, 1993.

Carl W. Kester, *Japanese Takeovers*, Harvard Business School Press, 1991.

Emily Thornton, 'Retailing Revolution in Japan', *Fortune*, 7 February 1994.

Wilton Woods, 'The World's Top Automakers Change Lanes', *Fortune*, 4 October 1993.

Notes

1   *Fortune*, 4 October 1993.

2   George Sansom, *A History of Japan, Vol. 2: 1344-1615*, The Cresset Press, 1961.

3   L. Tsoukalis and M. White (eds.), *Japan and Western Europe*, Frances Pinter (Publishers), 1982.

4   Carla Rapoport, 'You Can Make Money in Japan', *Fortune*, 12 February 1990.

5   Michio, Morishima, 'Why Has Japan "Succeeded"?' *Western Technology and The Japanese Ethos*, Cambridge Press, 1982.

6   Hiroyuki Odagiri, *Growth Through Competition, Competition Through Growth*, Clarendon Press, 1992.

7   Arthur M. Whitehill, *Japanese Management: Tradition and Transition*, Routledge, 1991.

8   Brenton R. Schlender, 'Japan's White Collar Blues', *Fortune*, 21 March 1994.

9   David Kilburn, 'The Sun Sets on Japan's Lifers', *Management Today*, September 1993.

10   Yoshihiro Tajima, 'Japan's Distribution System – Myth and Truth', *The Anglo-Japanese Economic Journal*, Vol.1 No.3, 1987.

11   Charles Leadbeater, 'US Survey Sheds Light on Japan's Barriers', *Financial Times*, 21 November 1991.

12   Peter Buckley, Hafiz Mirza and John Sparkes, *Japan: An Investor's Chronicle*, University of Bradford Management Centre, 1987.

13   Dominique Turpin, 'Strategic Alliances with Japanese Firms: Myths and Realities', *Long Range Planning*, Vol. 26 No. 4, 1993.

14   Brian Bridges, 'Investing in Japan: From a Trickle to a Flow', *Anglo-Japanese Journal*, Vol. 6 No. 2, 1992.

15   Hiroyuki Odagiri (see note 6 above).

Index